Basic Grammar in use

Self-study reference and practice for students of North American English

한국어판

with answers

Raymond Murphy
with William R. Smalzer
권진아

CAMBRIDGE
UNIVERSITY PRESS

CAMBRIDGE
UNIVERSITY PRESS

University Printing House, Cambridge CB2 8BS, United Kingdom

One Liberty Plaza, 20th Floor, New York, NY 10006, USA

477 Williamstown Road, Port Melbourne, VIC 3207, Australia

314–321, 3rd Floor, Plot 3, Splendor Forum, Jasola District Centre, New Delhi – 110025, India

79 Anson Road, #06–04/06, Singapore 079906

Cambridge University Press is part of the University of Cambridge.

It furthers the University's mission by disseminating knowledge in the pursuit of
education, learning and research at the highest international levels of excellence.

www.cambridge.org

This Korea bilingual edition is based on *Basic Grammar in Use* Student's Book with Answers,
Third edition ISBN 978-0-521-13334-0 first published by Cambridge University Press in 2011.

© Cambridge University Press 2011

First published 2011
Korea bilingual edition 2011
20 19 18

Printed in Malaysia by Vivar Printing

ISBN 978-0-521-26959-9 paperback Korea bilingual edition

Book design and layout: Adventure House, NYC

Illustration credits: Carlos Castellanos, Richard Deverell, Travis Foster, Peter Hoey, Randy Jones,
Gillian Martin, Sandy Nichols, Roger Penwill, Lisa Smith, Ian West, Simon Williams, and Tracy Wood

Cambridge University Press thanks Heshim Song (송희심) for her translation work on
Basic Grammar in Use with Answers Second edition (Korea bilingual edition published in 2005).

차례

어느 단원을 공부해야 할지 잘 모를 경우에는 **263쪽**의 학습가이드를 활용하십시오.

옮긴이의 말

케임브리지 대학출판부의 'Grammar in Use' 시리즈는 오래 전부터 한국에 소개되어 영어 학습서로의 입지를 탄탄히 구축하고 있습니다. 'Grammar in Use' 시리즈 중에서도 가장 큰 인기를 모아온 *Basic Grammar in Use*는 초급 학습자를 대상으로 한 문법 학습서로, 문법 학습뿐만 아니라 학습한 문법을 활용할 수 있도록 도모하고 있습니다. 초급 학습자에게 다소 부담스럽고 딱딱하게 느껴질 수 있는 문법을 간단명료한 설명과 실용적인 예문, 다채로운 삽화 등을 통해 가르치고 있어, 문법에 대한 기본적이고도 전반적인 이해를 돕습니다. *Basic Grammar in Use*는 자가학습용은 물론 강의용 교재로 사용하실 수 있습니다.

'Grammar in Use' 시리즈만의 특징으로 세분화된 단원 구성을 들 수 있습니다. 일목요연하게 정리된 문법은 학습자의 수준에 맞게끔 쉬우면서도 초급 학습자가 꼭 알아야 할 주요 문법사항들을 담고 있으며, 다양한 연습문제들은 학습자가 스스로 응용 및 심화학습을 할 수 있도록 구성되어 있습니다. 특히, 이 책에 실린 예문은 실생활에서 자주 사용되는 표현들을 주로 다루고 있어서 학습자의 이해를 도울 뿐 아니라 교재의 예문을 반복 학습할 경우 의사소통 능력 향상에도 많은 도움이 될 것입니다.

Basic Grammar in Use 한국어판은 기본적으로 영어판을 충실히 따랐지만 학습자의 이해를 돕기 위하여 문법 설명과 연습문제의 지시문을 한국어로 번역하였습니다. 그리고 주요 예문의 한국어 번역을 추가하여, 원서에 부담을 느끼는 사람이라도 큰 불편 없이 혼자서 공부할 수 있게끔 하였습니다. 교재의 뒷부분에는 문법 용어를 쉽고 빠르게 찾아볼 수 있도록 한글 색인을 추가했습니다.

Basic Grammar in Use 한국어판이 여러분의 영어 학습에 많은 도움이 되기를 바라며, 마지막으로 출간에 도움을 주신 분들께 감사를 전합니다. 우선, 한국어판 출간을 총괄한 Richard Walker씨와 Katherine Wong씨에게 고마움을 전합니다. 특히, 편집을 맡아 작업과정 내내 조언과 조력을 아끼지 않은 김준섭씨와 박진희씨에게 깊은 감사를 전합니다.

권진아
Basic Grammar in Use 한국어판 어댑터

학생들에게

이 책은 초급영어 학습자를 위한 문법책입니다. 이 책은 총 116단원(units)으로 구성되어 있으며, 각 단원별로 주요 문법사항을 다루고 있습니다. 전체 단원의 목록은 책의 앞쪽에 있는 차례에 실려 있습니다.

효과적인 공부를 위해서는 처음부터 끝까지 순서대로 보기보다는 자신에게 필요한 단원을 골라서 보는 것이 더 좋습니다. 예를 들어, 현재완료(*I have been, he has done* 등)를 잘 모른다면, 16~21단원을 공부하십시오.

공부하고자 하는 단원을 찾을 때는 차례 또는 책의 뒤쪽에 있는 색인을 참조하십시오.

어느 단원을 공부해야 할지 잘 모를 경우, 책의 뒤쪽에 있는 학습가이드를 활용하십시오.

학습가이드 (263~275쪽)

각 단원은 두 면으로
이루어져 있으며,
문법사항은 왼쪽 면에,
연습문제는 오른쪽 면에
제시되어 있습니다.

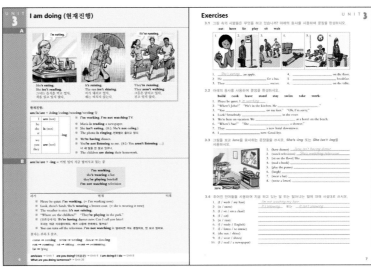

문법사항   **연습문제**

왼쪽 면의 문법사항을 공부한 다음 오른쪽 면의
연습문제를 푸십시오.

정답은 276–302쪽에 있는 해답지에서 확인하십시오.
정답을 확인한 후, 필요하면 왼쪽 면의 문법사항을
복습하십시오.

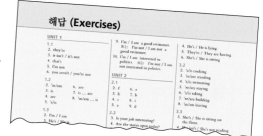

235–243쪽에 실린
7개의 부록도 잊지
마시기 바랍니다. 각각의
부록에는 능동태와 수동태,
불규칙동사, 축약형, 철자,
동사구에 대한 설명이
정리되어 있습니다.

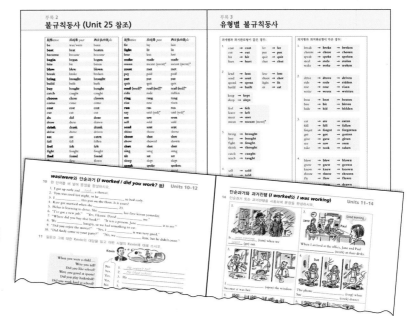

244–262쪽에는
추가연습문제가 실려
있습니다. 이에 대한
연습문제 목록은 244쪽에서
확인하실 수 있습니다.

CD-ROM

게임과 퀴즈 등을 통해 재미있게 공부할 수 있는
CD-ROM에는 단원별 연습문제가 추가로 들어
있으며, 600개 이상의 실전문제들도 포함되어
있습니다.

CD-ROM이 들어 있는 책은 별도로 판매되고
있습니다.

선생님들에게

이 책의 주요 특징은 다음과 같습니다.

■ 이 책은 문법책입니다. 따라서 문법 이외의 요소는 다루지 않습니다.
  이 책은 초급영어 학습자들을 위한 책입니다. 따라서 초급 단계에서 일반적으로
  가르치고 있는 문법사항들을 다루고 있으며, 중급이나 그 이상 단계의 수업에서
  다루는 문법사항들은 포함하고 있지 않습니다.
  이 책은 단원별로 문법사항과 연습문제를 담고 있습니다. 순차적으로 수업하도록
  구성되어 있는 코스북과 달리, 이 책은 교재 안의 어떤 단원부터 수업을 시작해도
  상관없도록 구성되어 있습니다.
  이 책은 자습서나 부교재로도 사용이 가능합니다.

이 책의 구성

이 책은 총 116단원으로 이루어져 있으며, 각 단원은 특정 문법사항을 중점적으로 다루고
있습니다. 이 책은 시제, 의문문, 관사 등 문법 항목별로 구성되어 있습니다. 각 단원들은
난이도 순서대로 배열된 것이 아니므로, 필요한 단원을 선택하여 학습자들에게 적합한 순서로
사용하는 것이 좋습니다. 첫 단원부터 순서대로 공부할 필요는 없습니다. 각 단원의 내용은
차례에 소개되어 있으며, 책의 뒤쪽에 있는 색인에서도 상세한 내용을 확인하실 수 있습니다.

각 단원은 두 면으로 이루어져 있습니다. 왼쪽 면에는 문법사항과 그에 대한 설명이, 오른쪽
면에는 해당 문법에 대한 연습문제가 실려 있습니다. 능동태와 수동태, 불규칙동사, 축약형,
철자, 동사구에 대한 설명이 담긴 부록도 7개(235-243쪽) 실려 있습니다. 학생들이 부록을
잘 활용할 수 있도록 지도해 주시기 바랍니다.

책의 뒤쪽에는 추가연습문제(244-262쪽)와 학습가이드(263-275쪽)가 수록되어 있습니다.
추가연습문제는 여러 단원(특히 동사 형식)에서 다루어진 문법사항들이 '섞여' 있어서, 문법을
응용하고 심화 학습을 할 수 있는 기회를 제공합니다. 여기에는 총 35개의 연습문제가
포함되어 있으며, 문제의 목록은 244쪽에서 찾아볼 수 있습니다.

학습가이드는 학생들이 어느 단원을 공부해야 할지 결정할 수 있도록 도와줍니다.

마지막으로, 단원별 연습문제의 정답을 확인할 수 있는 해답(276-302쪽)이 수록되어
있습니다.

수준

이 책은 영어의 기초가 약한 초급 학습자를 대상으로 하고 있습니다. 하지만 다른 영역에 비해
문법이 약하거나 일부 기초문법에 자신감이 부족한 중급 수준의 학습자에게도 적합합니다.

문법 설명은 초급 학습자에게 맞춰져 있으며, 가능한 한 쉽고 간결하게 제시되어 있습니다.
예문과 연습문제에 사용된 어휘 또한 초급 학습자의 수준에 맞춰져 있습니다.

활용

이 책은 초급 문법 학습을 위한 자습용('학생들에게' 참조) 또는 수업 보충자료로 사용할 수
있습니다.

수업자료로 쓸 경우, 문법정리나 복습, 보충용으로 사용할 수 있습니다. 학급 전체 또는
별도의 보충학습이 필요한 학생들이 사용할 수 있습니다.

몇몇 단원의 경우 왼쪽 면에 제시된 문법사항 설명을 수업시간에 그대로 사용할 수도
있겠지만, 이 문법설명들은 자습과 참고용으로 쓰여진 것들입니다. 대부분의 경우,
선생님들께서 각자의 방식대로 문법사항을 설명하고, 연습문제는 숙제로 주는 것이 더 좋을
것입니다. 학생들은 나중에 왼쪽 면의 문법설명을 참고하며 공부할 수 있습니다.

이 책을 복습이나 보충용으로 사용하고자 하는 선생님들께서는 학생들이 자습 또는 복습해야
할 단원들을 알려주시면 됩니다.

CD-ROM

CD-ROM에는 단원별로 연습문제가 추가로 들어 있으며, 600개 이상의 실전문제들도
포함되어 있습니다. 선생님들께서는 실전문제들 중 일부를 뽑아 시험지를 만드실 수도
있습니다. CD-ROM이 들어 있는 책은 별도로 판매되고 있습니다.

Basic Grammar in Use 한국어판

이 책은 *Basic Grammar in Use* 한국어판입니다. 한국어판은 기본적으로 영어판(*Basic Grammar in Use*,
Third edition)을 충실하게 따르면서, 한국 학습자들의 이해를 돕기 위하여 다음과 같이 수정하거나
보충하였습니다.

- 문법 설명과 연습문제의 지시문을 한국어로 번역하였습니다.

  주요 예문에 대한 한국어 번역을 추가하였습니다.

  학습자에게 익숙하지 않은 지명과 인명을 수정하였습니다.

  필요한 경우, 문법 설명을 보충하였습니다.

  해당 문법사항을 쉽고 빠르게 찾아볼 수 있도록 한글 색인을 추가하였습니다.

Basic Grammar
in use

am/is/are

A

My name **is** Lisa. 1

I'm 22. 5

I'm **not** married. 6

I'm American. I'm from Chicago. 2

My favorite color **is** blue. 7

I'm a student. 3

Lisa

My favorite sports **are** tennis and swimming. 8

My father **is** a doctor, and my mother **is** a journalist. 4

I'm interested in art. 9

1. 제 이름은 리사입니다.
2. 미국인이고 시카고 출신이에요.
3. 저는 학생입니다.
4. 저희 아버지는 의사이고, 어머니는 언론인이세요.
5. 나이는 스물두 살이에요.
6. 결혼은 안 했어요.
7. 가장 좋아하는 색깔은 파란색이에요.
8. 가장 좋아하는 운동은 테니스와 수영이에요.
9. 저는 예술에 관심이 있어요.

B

긍정		
I	**am**	(**I'm**)
he she it	**is**	(he**'s**) (she**'s**) (it**'s**)
we you they	**are**	(we**'re**) (you**'re**) (they**'re**)

축약형

부정				
I	**am not**	(**I'm not**)		
he she it	**is not**	(he**'s not** (she**'s not** (it**'s not**	또는 또는 또는	he **isn't**) she **isn't**) it **isn't**)
we you they	**are not**	(we**'re not** (you**'re not** (they**'re not**	또는 또는 또는	we **aren't**) you **aren't**) they **aren't**)

축약형

- **I'm** cold. Can you close the window, please?
  추워요. 창문 좀 닫아 주실래요?
- **I'm** 32 years old. My sister **is** 29.
- Steve **is** sick. He**'s** in bed.
- My brother **is** afraid of dogs. 우리 형은 개를 무서워해요.
- It**'s** 10:00. You**'re** late again.
- Ann and I **are** good friends.
- Your keys **are** on the table. 당신 열쇠는 탁자 위에 있어요.

- **I'm** tired, but **I'm not** hungry.
- Tom **isn't** interested in politics. He**'s** interested in music.
  탐은 정치에 관심이 없다. 그는 음악에 관심이 있다.
- Jane **isn't** a teacher. She**'s** a student.
- Those people **aren't** Canadian. They**'re** Australian.
- It**'s** sunny today, but it **isn't** warm.

I'm afraid of dogs.

C

that**'s** = that **is**   there**'s** = there **is**   here**'s** = here **is**

- Thank you. That**'s** very nice of you.
  고맙습니다. 참 친절하시군요.
- Look! There**'s** Chris. 저기 봐! 크리스가 있어.
- "Here**'s** your key." 여기 열쇠가 있습니다.
  "Thank you." 고맙습니다.

Here's your key.

Thank you.

am/is/are (의문문) → Unit 2   **there is/are** → Unit 38   **a/an** → Unit 66   축약형 → 부록 4

Exercises

1.1 축약형을 쓰시오(*she's* / *we aren't* 등).

1. she is ___*she's*___
2. they are _____
3. it is not _____
4. that is _____
5. I am not _____
6. you are not _____

1.2 빈칸에 *am/is/are*를 써 넣으시오.

1. The weather __*is*__ nice today.
2. I _____ not rich.
3. This bag _____ heavy.
4. These bags _____ heavy.
5. Look! There _____ Carol.
6. My brother and I _____ good tennis players.
7. Amy _____ at home. Her children _____ at school.
8. I _____ a taxi driver. My sister _____ a nurse.

1.3 문장을 완성하시오.

1. Steve is sick. ___*He's*___ in bed.
2. I'm not hungry, but _____ thirsty.
3. Mr. Thomas is a very old man. _____ 98.
4. These chairs aren't beautiful, but _____ comfortable.
5. The weather is nice today. _____ warm and sunny.
6. "_____ late." "No, I'm not. I'm early!"
7. Catherine isn't at home. _____ at work.
8. "_____ your coat." "Oh, thank you very much."

1.4 1A에 나온 Lisa의 자기소개를 읽고 자신에 대해 쓰시오.

1. (name?)   My _____
2. (from?)   I _____
3. (age?)   I _____
4. (job?)   I _____
5. (favorite color or colors?)
   My _____
6. (interested in … ?)
   I _____

1.5 아래의 단어를 사용하여 그림에 맞는 문장을 쓰시오.

afraid   angry   cold   hot   hungry   ~~thirsty~~

1. ___*She's thirsty.*___
2. They _____
3. He _____
4. _____
5. _____
6. _____

1.6 *is/isn't* 또는 *are/aren't*를 사용하여 사실에 맞게 긍정문 또는 부정문을 쓰시오.

1. (it / hot today)   ___*It isn't hot today.*___ 또는 ___*It's hot today.*___
2. (it / windy today)   It _____
3. (my hands / cold)   My _____
4. (Brazil / a very big country)   _____
5. (diamonds / cheap)   _____
6. (Toronto / in the United States)   _____

이번에는 *I'm / I'm not*을 사용하여 문장을 쓰시오.

7. (tired)   ___*I'm tired.*___ 또는 ___*I'm not tired.*___
8. (hungry)   I _____
9. (a good swimmer)   _____
10. (interested in politics)   _____

→ 추가연습문제 1 (244쪽)

3

am/is/are (의문문)

A

평서문	
I	**am**
he she it	**is**
we you they	**are**

의문문	
am	I?
is	he? she? it?
are	we? you? they?

What's your name?

David.

Are you married?

No, I'm single.

How old **are you**?

25.

Are you a student?

Yes, I am.

- ■ "**Am I** late?" "No, **you're** on time." 아뇨, 제시간에 오셨어요.
- ■ "**Is your mother** at home?" "No, **she's** out." 아뇨, 외출하셨어요.
- ■ "**Are your parents** at home?" "No, **they're** out."
- ■ "**Is it** cold in your room?" "Yes, a little."
- ■ **Your shoes are** nice. **Are they** new? 신발이 멋지네요. 새 신발인가요?

주의:
- ■ **Is she** at home? / **Is your mother** at home? (Is at home your mother?는 틀림)
- ■ **Are they** new? / **Are your shoes** new? (Are new your shoes?는 틀림)

B 의문사가 있는 경우: 의문사 (**Where/What/Who/How/Why**) + **is/are** … ?

- ■ **Where is** your mother? Is she at home?
- ■ "**Where are** you from?" "Canada."
- ■ "**What color is** your car?" "It's red."
- ■ "**How old is** Joe?" 조는 몇 살인가요? "He's 24."
- ■ "**How are** your parents?" "They're fine."
- ■ These postcards are nice. **How much are** they? 이 엽서 예쁘군요. 얼마예요?
- ■ This hotel isn't very good. **Why is** it so expensive?
  이 호텔은 아주 좋지도 않아. 왜 그리 비싼 거야?

축약형: what's = what **is** who's = who **is** how's = how **is** where's = where **is**

- ■ **What's** your phone number?
- ■ **Who's** that man?
- ■ **Where's** Lucy?
- ■ **How's** your father?

C 짧게 답하기

Yes,	I	**am**.
	he she it	**is**.
	we you they	**are**.

No,	I'm	
	he's she's it's	**not**.
	we're you're they're	

또는

No,	he she it	**isn't**.
	we you they	**aren't**.

That's my seat.

No, it **isn't**.

- ■ "**Are you** tired?" "**Yes, I am.**"
- ■ "**Are you** hungry?" "**No, I'm not**, but I'm thirsty."
- ■ "**Is your friend** Japanese?" "**Yes, he is.**"
- ■ "**Are** these **your keys**?" "**Yes, they are.**"
- ■ "**That's** my seat." "**No, it isn't.**"

Exercises

2.1 각 질문에 알맞은 대답을 고르시오.

1.	Where's the camera?	a)	Toronto.	1. _g_
2.	Is your car blue?	b)	No, I'm not.	2. ___
3.	Is Linda from London?	c)	Yes, you are.	3. ___
4.	Am I late?	d)	My sister.	4. ___
5.	Where's Ann from?	e)	Black.	5. ___
6.	What color is your bag?	f)	No, it's black.	6. ___
7.	Are you hungry?	g)	In your bag.	7. ___
8.	How is George?	h)	No, she's American.	8. ___
9.	Who's that woman?	i)	Fine.	9. ___

2.2 주어진 단어들을 사용하여 의문문을 만드시오.

1. (is / at home / your mother) _Is your mother at home_ _____ ?
2. (your parents / are / how) _How are your parents_ _____ ?
3. (interesting / is / your job) _____ ?
4. (the stores / are / open today) _____ ?
5. (from / where / you / are) _____ ?
6. (interested in sports / you / are) _____ ?
7. (is / near here / the post office) _____ ?
8. (at school / are / your children) _____ ?
9. (you / are / late / why) _____ ?

2.3 *What ... / Who ... / Where ... / How ...* 를 사용하여 질문을 완성하시오.

1. _____ _How are_ your children? — They're fine.
2. _____ the bus stop? — At the end of the block.
3. _____ your children? — Five, six, and ten.
4. _____ these oranges? — $1.50 a pound.
5. _____ your favorite sport? — Skiing.
6. _____ the man in this photograph? — That's my father.
7. _____ your new shoes? — Black.

2.4 각 대답에 맞는 질문을 쓰시오.

Paul

1. (name?) _What's your name?_ _____ — Paul.
2. (Australian?) _____ — No, I'm Canadian.
3. (how old?) _____ — I'm 30.
4. (a teacher?) _____ — No, I'm a lawyer.
5. (married?) _____ — Yes, I am.
6. (wife a lawyer?) _____ — No, she's a teacher.
7. (from?) _____ — She's from Mexico.
8. (her name?) _____ — Ana.
9. (how old?) _____ — She's 27.

2.5 질문에 짧게 답하시오(*Yes, I am. / No, he isn't.* 등).

1. Are you married? _No, I'm not._ _____
2. Are you thirsty? _____
3. Is it cold today? _____
4. Are your hands cold? _____
5. Is it dark now? _____
6. Are you a teacher? _____

→ 추가연습문제 1–2 (244–245쪽)

I am doing (현재진행)

I'm eating.

We're running.

She**'s eating**.
She **isn't reading**.
그녀는 음식을 먹고 있다.
책을 읽고 있지 않다.

It**'s raining**.
The sun **isn't shining**.
비가 내리고 있다.
해는 비치지 않는다.

They**'re running**.
They **aren't walking**.
그들은 달리고 있다.
걷고 있지 않다.

현재진행:

am/is/are + do**ing**/eat**ing**/runn**ing**/writ**ing** 등

I	**am** (not)	
he she it	**is** (not)	**-ing**
we you they	**are** (not)	

- I**'m working**. I**'m not watching** TV.

- Maria **is reading** a newspaper.
- She **isn't eating**. (또는 She**'s not eating**.)
- The phone **is ringing**. 전화벨이 울리고 있다.

- We**'re having** dinner.
- You**'re not listening** to me. (또는 You **aren't listening** ...)
  너 내 말을 안 듣고 있구나.
- The children **are doing** their homework.

B

am/is/are + **-ing** = 어떤 일이 지금 벌어지고 있는 중

> I**'m working**
> she**'s wearing** a hat
> they**'re playing** baseball
> I**'m not watching** television

과거   현재   미래

- Please be quiet. I**'m working**. (= I'm working now)
- Look, there's Sarah. She**'s wearing** a brown coat. (= she is wearing it now)
- The weather is nice. It**'s not raining**.
- "Where are the children?" "They**'re playing** in the park."
- (전화상에서) We**'re having** dinner now. Can I call you later?
  우리는 지금 식사중이에요. 제가 나중에 전화해도 될까요?
- You can turn off the television. I**'m not watching** it. 텔레비전 꺼도 괜찮아요. 안 보고 있어요.

철자는 부록 5 참조.

come → com**ing**   write → writ**ing**   dance → danc**ing**
run → runn**ing**   sit → sitt**ing**   swim → swimm**ing**
lie → lying

am/is/are → Unit 1   **are you doing?** (의문문) → Unit 4   **I am doing**과 **I do** → Unit 8
What are you doing tomorrow? → Unit 26

Exercises

3.1 그림 속의 사람들은 무엇을 하고 있습니까? 아래의 동사를 사용하여 문장을 완성하시오.

~~eat~~   have   lie   play   sit   wait

1. _She's eating_ an apple.
2. He _____ for a bus.
3. They _____ soccer.
4. _____ on the floor.
5. _____ breakfast.
6. _____ on the table.

3.2 아래의 동사를 사용하여 문장을 완성하시오.

build   cook   leave   stand   stay   swim   take   ~~work~~

1. Please be quiet. I _'m working_ .
2. "Where's John?"   "He's in the kitchen. He _____."
3. "You _____ on my foot."   "Oh, I'm sorry."
4. Look! Somebody _____ in the river.
5. We're here on vacation. We _____ at a hotel on the beach.
6. "Where's Sue?"   "She _____ a shower."
7. They _____ a new hotel downtown.
8. I _____ now. Goodbye.

3.3 그림을 보고 Jane을 묘사하는 문장들을 쓰시오. *She's + -ing* 또는 *She isn't + -ing*를 사용하시오.

Jane

1. (have dinner) _Jane isn't having dinner._
2. (watch television) _She's watching television._
3. (sit on the floor) She _____
4. (read a book) _____
5. (play the piano) _____
6. (laugh) _____
7. (wear a hat) _____
8. (write a letter) _____

3.4 주어진 단어들을 사용하여 지금 하고 있는 일 또는 일어나는 일에 대해 사실대로 쓰시오.

1. (I / wash / my hair) _I'm not washing my hair._
2. (it / snow) _It's snowing._ 또는 _It isn't snowing._
3. (I / sit / on a chair) _____
4. (I / eat) _____
5. (it / rain) _____
6. (I / study / English) _____
7. (I / listen / to music) _____
8. (the sun / shine) _____
9. (I / wear / shoes) _____
10. (I / read / a newspaper) _____

7

are you doing? (현재진행 의문문)

A

평서문		
I	**am**	**doing** **working** **going** **staying** 등
he she it	**is**	
we you they	**are**	

의문문		
am	I	**doing?** **working?** **going?** **staying?** 등
is	he she it	
are	we you they	

What **are** you **doing**?

뭘 하고 있는 거니?

- ■ "**Are** you **feeling** OK?" "Yes, I'm fine, thanks."
- ■ "**Is** it **raining**?" 지금 비 오니? "Yes, take an umbrella." 응, 우산 가져가.
- ■ Why **are** you **wearing** a coat? It's not cold.
- ■ "What**'s** Paul **doing**?" "He**'s reading** the newspaper."
- ■ "What **are** the children **doing**?" "They**'re watching** television."
- ■ Look, there's Emily! Where**'s** she **going**? 저기 봐, 에밀리야! 어딜 가고 있는 거지?
- ■ Who **are** you **waiting** for? **Are** you **waiting** for Sue?
  누구를 기다리고 있니? 수를 기다리고 있어?

B

어순:

	is/are	+ 주어	+ -ing
	Is	he	**working** today?
	Is	Paul	**working** today? (Is working Paul today?는 틀림)
Where	**are**	they	**going**?
Where	**are**	those people	**going**? (Where are going those people?은 틀림)

C

짧게 답하기

Yes,	I	**am.**
	he she it	**is.**
	we you they	**are.**

No,	I'm	**not.**	또는
	he**'s** she**'s** it**'s**		
	we**'re** you**'re** they**'re**		

No,	he she it	**isn't.**
	we you they	**aren't.**

- ■ "**Are** you **leaving** now?" "**Yes, I am.**"
- ■ "**Is** Paul **working** today?" "**Yes, he is.**"
- ■ "**Is** it **raining**?" "**No, it isn't.**"
- ■ "**Are** your friends **staying** at a hotel?" 네 친구들은 호텔에 머물고 있니?
  "**No, they aren't.** They're staying with me." 아니. 친구들은 우리 집에 있어.

Exercises

4.1 그림의 상황에 맞게 질문을 만드시오.

1. (you / watch / it?)
Are you watching it?
No, you can turn it off.

2. (you / leave / now?) _____
Yes, see you tomorrow.

3. (it / rain?) _____
No, not right now.

4. (you / enjoy / the movie?) ____
Yes, it's very funny.

5. (that clock / work?) _____
No, it's broken.

6. (you / wait / for a bus?) ____
No, for a taxi.

4.2 그림을 보고 아래의 단어를 사용하여 질문을 완성하시오.

cry   eat   go   laugh   look at   ~~read~~

1. What _are you reading_ ?

2. Where _____ she ?

3. What _____ ?

4. Why _____ ?

5. What _____ ?

6. Why _____ ?

4.3 주어진 단어들을 올바른 어순으로 배열하여 의문문을 만드시오.

1. (is / working / Paul / today) _Is Paul working today_ ?
2. (what / the children / are / doing) _What are the children doing_ ?
3. (you / are / listening / to me) _____ ?
4. (where / your friends / are / going) _____ ?
5. (are / watching / your parents / television) _____ ?
6. (what / Jessica / is / cooking) _____ ?
7. (why / you / are / looking / at me) _____ ?
8. (is / coming / the bus) _____ ?

4.4 질문에 짧게 답하시오(***Yes, I am. / No, he isn't.*** 등).

1. Are you watching TV? _No, I'm not._
2. Are you wearing a watch? _____
3. Are you eating something? _____
4. Is it raining? _____
5. Are you sitting on the floor? _____
6. Are you feeling all right? _____

I do/work/like 등 (단순현재)

We **read** a lot.

I **like** ice cream.

They're looking at their books.
They **read** a lot.
그들은 책을 바라보고 있다.
그들은 독서를 많이 한다.

He's eating an ice cream cone.
He **likes** ice cream.
그는 아이스크림 콘을 먹고 있다.
그는 아이스크림을 좋아한다.

They **read** / he **likes** / I **work** 등 = 단순현재:

I/we/you/they	**read**	**like**	**work**	**live**	**watch**	**do**	**have**
he/she/it	**reads**	**likes**	**works**	**lives**	**watches**	**does**	**has**

3인칭 단수가 주어인 경우:
he works / **she** lives / **it** rains 등
- **I work** in an office. **My brother works** in a bank. (My brother work는 틀림)
- **Lucy lives** in Houston. **Her parents live** in Chicago.
- **It rains** a lot in the winter.

I **have** → he/she/it **has**:
- **John has** lunch at home every day.

철자는 부록 5 참조.

-s / -sh / -ch 뒤에는 -es:	pass → pass**es**	finish → finish**es**	watch → watch**es**
-y → -ies:	study → stud**ies**	try → tr**ies**	
또한:	do → do**es**	go → go**es**	

단순현재는 일반적인 사실 또는 항상/때때로 일어나는 일에 대해 사용한다.
- I **like** big cities.
- Your English is good. You **speak** very well.
- Tim **works** very hard. He **starts** at 7:30 and **finishes** at 8:00 at night.
- The earth **goes** around the sun. 지구는 태양 주위를 돈다.
- We **do** a lot of different things in our free time. 우리는 자유시간에 여러 가지 다양한 것들을 한다.
- It **costs** a lot of money to build a hospital. 병원을 짓는 데는 돈이 많이 든다.

always/never/often/usually/sometimes + 단순현재
- Sue **always gets** to work early. (Sue gets always는 틀림)
- I **never eat** breakfast. (I eat never는 틀림)
- We **often sleep** late on weekends. 우리는 주말에 곧잘 늦잠을 잔다.
- Mark **usually plays** tennis on Sundays.
- I **sometimes walk** to work, but not very often.
  나는 때로는 걸어서 직장에 가지만 자주 그러지는 않는다.

I don't ... (부정문) → Unit 6   Do you ... ? (의문문) → Unit 7   I am doing과 I do → Unit 8
always/usually/often 등 (어순) → Unit 95

Exercises

5.1 괄호 안의 동사에 **-s** 또는 **-es**를 붙여 쓰시오.

1. (read) she _reads_
2. (think) he _____
3. (fly) it _____
4. (dance) he _____
5. (have) she _____
6. (finish) it _____

5.2 아래의 동사를 사용하여 그림 속의 사람들에 대한 문장을 완성하시오.

eat   go   live   ~~play~~   play   sleep

1. My piano.
2. Our house.
3.
4. Tennis is my favorite sport.
5. We love movies.
6. Seven hours a night

1. _He plays_ the piano.
2. They _____ in a very big house.
3. _____ a lot of fruit.
4. _____ tennis.
5. _____ to the movies a lot.
6. _____ seven hours a night.

5.3 아래의 동사를 넣어 문장을 완성하시오.

boil   close   cost   cost   like   like   meet   open   ~~speak~~   teach   wash

1. Maria _speaks_ four languages.
2. Banks usually _____ at 9:00 in the morning.
3. The art museum _____ at 5:00 in the afternoon.
4. Tina is a teacher. She _____ math to young children.
5. My job is very interesting. I _____ a lot of people.
6. Peter's car is always dirty. He never _____ it.
7. Food is expensive. It _____ a lot of money.
8. Shoes are expensive. They _____ a lot of money.
9. Water _____ at 100 degrees Celsius.
10. Julia and I are good friends. I _____ her, and she _____ me.

5.4 주어진 단어들을 적절한 어순으로 배열하여 문장을 만드시오. 동사를 알맞은 형태로 쓰시오 (**arrive** 또는 **arrives**).

1. (always / early / Sue / arrive) _Sue always arrives early._
2. (to the movies / never / I / go) _____
3. (work / Martina / hard / always) _____
4. (like / chocolate / children / usually) _____
5. (Julia / parties / enjoy / always) _____
6. (often / people's names / I / forget) _____
7. (television / Tim / watch / never) _____
8. (usually / dinner / we / have / at 6:30) _____
9. (Jenny / always / nice clothes / wear) _____

5.5 **always/never/often/usually/sometimes**를 사용하여 자신에 대한 문장을 쓰시오.

1. (watch TV in the evening) _I usually watch TV in the evening._
2. (read in bed) I _____
3. (get up before 7:00) _____
4. (go to work/school by bus) _____
5. (drink coffee in the morning) _____

UNIT 6

I don't ... (단순현재 부정문)

A

단순현재 부정문은 **don't/doesn't** + 동사이다.

She **doesn't drink** coffee.
그녀는 커피를 마시지 않는다.

He **doesn't like** his job.
그는 자신의 일을 좋아하지 않는다.

긍정		부정		
I we you they	**work** **like** **do** **have**	I we you they	**don't** (**do not**)	**work** **like** **do** **have**
he she it	**works** **likes** **does** **has**	he she it	**doesn't** (**does not**)	

- I **drink** coffee, but I **don't drink** tea.
- Sue **drinks** tea, but she **doesn't drink** coffee. 그녀는 차를 마시지만 커피는 마시지 않는다.
- You **don't work** very hard.
- We **don't watch** television very often.
- The weather is usually nice. It **doesn't rain** very often. 날씨는 보통 좋다. 비는 자주 내리지 않는다.
- Gary and Nicole **don't know** many people.

B

주어가 3인칭 단수(**he/she/it/Fred/car** 등)인 경우 주의하자.

I/we/you/they	**don't** ...
he/she/it	**doesn't** ...

- **I don't** like football.
- **He doesn't** like football.

- **I don't** like Fred, and **Fred doesn't** like me. (Fred don't like는 틀림)
- **My car doesn't** use much gas. 내 차는 기름을 많이 쓰지 않는다.
- Sometimes he is late, but **it doesn't** happen very often. (it don't happen은 틀림)

C

don't/doesn't 다음에는 동사원형을 쓴다(don't **like** / doesn't **speak** / doesn't **do** 등).

- I **don't like** to wash the car. I **don't do** it very often.
- Sarah **speaks** Spanish, but she **doesn't speak** Italian. (doesn't speaks는 틀림)
- Bill **doesn't do** his job very well. (Bill doesn't his job은 틀림)
- Paula **doesn't** usually **have** breakfast. (doesn't ... has는 틀림)

Exercises

6.1 부정문으로 바꾸시오.

1. I play the piano very well.   _I don't play the piano very well._
2. Jane plays the piano very well.   Jane _____
3. They know my phone number.   They _____
4. We work very hard.   _____
5. Mike has a car.   _____
6. You do the same thing every day.   _____

6.2 아래의 정보를 잘 읽어본 다음, *like*를 사용하여 문장을 만드시오.

Do you like ... ?

	Bill and Rose	Carol	You
1. classical music?	yes	no	?
2. boxing?	no	yes	?
3. horror movies?	yes	no	?

1. _Bill and Rose like classical music._
    Carol _____
    I _____ classical music.

2. Bill and Rose _____
    Carol _____
    I _____

3. _____
    _____
    _____

6.3 주어진 단어들과 *I never ... / I ... a lot / I don't ... very often*을 사용하여 자신에 대해 쓰시오.

1. (watch TV)   _I never watch TV._ 또는 _I watch TV a lot._ 또는
   I don't watch TV very often.
2. (go to the theater) _____
3. (ride a bicycle)   _____
4. (eat in restaurants) _____
5. (travel by train)   _____

6.4 아래의 동사를 부정형(*don't/doesn't* + 동사)으로 써 넣어 문장을 완성하시오.

cost   go   know   ~~read~~   see   use   wear

1. I buy a newspaper every day, but sometimes I _don't read_ it.
2. Paul has a car, but he _____ it very often.
3. Paul and his friends like movies, but they _____ to the movie theater very often.
4. Amanda is married, but she _____ a ring.
5. I _____ much about politics. I'm not interested in it.
6. The Regent Hotel isn't expensive. It _____ much to stay there.
7. Brian lives near us, but we _____ him very often.

6.5 괄호 안의 동사를 문맥에 맞게 긍정 또는 부정형으로 써 넣으시오.

1. Margaret _speaks_ four languages – English, Japanese, Arabic, and Spanish. (speak)
2. I _don't like_ my job. It's very boring. (like)
3. "Where's Martin?" "I'm sorry. I _____ ." (know)
4. Sue is a very quiet person. She _____ very much. (talk)
5. Andy _____ a lot of coffee. It's his favorite drink. (drink)
6. It's not true! I _____ it! (believe)
7. That's a very beautiful picture. I _____ it a lot. (like)
8. Mark is a vegetarian. He _____ meat. (eat)

13

Do you ... ? (단순현재 의문문)

A

단순현재 의문문에서는 **do/does**를 사용한다.

Do you **play** the guitar?

평서문			의문문		
I we you they	work like do have		**do**	I we you they	work? like? do? have?
he she it	works likes does has		**does**	he she it	

기타를 치세요?

B

어순:

	do/does	+ 주어 +	동사원형	
	Do	you	**work**	on Sundays?
	Do	your friends	**live**	near here?
	Does	Chris	**play**	tennis?
Where	**do**	your parents	**live?**	
How often	**do**	you	**wash**	your hair?
What	**does**	this word	**mean?**	
How much	**does**	it	**cost**	to fly to Tokyo?

의문문에서 **always/usually/ever**의 위치:

	Do	you	**always**	**have**	breakfast?
	Does	Chris	**ever**	**call**	you?
What	**do**	you	**usually**	**do**	on weekends?

What do you **do**? = What's your job?

■ "**What do** you **do**?" 무슨 일 하세요? (직업이 뭐예요?) "I work in a bank." 은행에서 일합니다.

C

주어가 3인칭 단수인 경우는 does를 쓴다.

do	I/we/you/they ...
does	he/she/it ...

■ **Do they** like music?
■ **Does he** like music?

D

짧게 답하기

Yes,	I/we/you/they **do**.
	he/she/it **does**.

No,	I/we/you/they **don't**.
	he/she/it **doesn't**.

■ "**Do you** play tennis?" "**No, I don't.**"
■ "**Do your parents** speak English?" 당신 부모님께선 영어를 하세요?
  "**Yes, they do.**" 예, 하십니다.
■ "**Does Gary** work hard?" "**Yes, he does.**"
■ "**Does your sister** live in Vancouver?" 언니가 밴쿠버에 사세요?
  "**No, she doesn't.**" 아뇨, 안 살아요.

Exercises

7.1 *Do ... ?* 또는 *Does ... ?* 를 사용하여 의문문을 만드시오.

1. I like chocolate. How about you? _Do you like chocolate_ ?
2. I play tennis. How about you? _____ you _____ ?
3. You live near here. How about Lucy? _____ Lucy _____ ?
4. Tom plays tennis. How about his friends? _____ ?
5. You speak English. How about your brother? _____ ?
6. I do yoga every morning. How about you? _____ ?
7. Sue often travels on business. How about Paul? _____ ?
8. I want to be famous. How about you? _____ ?
9. You work hard. How about Anna? _____ ?

7.2 주어진 단어들과 *do/does*를 사용하여 의문문을 만드시오. 단어들을 올바른 어순으로 쓰시오.

1. (where / live / your parents) _Where do your parents live_ ?
2. (you / early / always / get up) _Do you always get up early_ ?
3. (how often / TV / you / watch) _____ ?
4. (you / want / what / for dinner) _____ ?
5. (like / you / football) _____ ?
6. (your brother / like / football) _____ ?
7. (what / you / do / in your free time) _____ ?
8. (your sister / work / where) _____ ?
9. (to the movies / ever / you / go) _____ ?
10. (what / mean / this word) _____ ?
11. (often / snow / it / here) _____ ?
12. (go / usually / to bed / what time / you)
    _____ ?
13. (how much / to call Mexico / it / cost)
    _____ ?
14. (you / for breakfast / have / usually / what)
    _____ ?

7.3 아래의 동사를 사용하여 질문을 완성하시오.

~~do~~   do   enjoy   get   like   start   teach   work

1. What _do you do_ ? — I work in a bookstore.
2. _____ it? — It's OK.
3. What time _____ in the morning? — At 9:00.
4. _____ on Saturdays? — Sometimes.
5. How _____ to work? — Usually by bus.
6. And your husband. What _____ ? — He's a teacher.
7. What _____ ? — Science.
8. _____ his job? — Yes, he loves it.

7.4 질문에 짧게 답하시오(*Yes, he does.* / *No, I don't.* 등).

1. Do you watch TV a lot? _No, I don't._   또는 _Yes, I do._
2. Do you live in a big city? _____
3. Do you ever ride a bicycle? _____
4. Does it rain a lot where you live? _____
5. Do you play the piano? _____

→ 추가연습문제 4–7 (245–246쪽)

I am doing과 I do
(현재진행과 단순현재)

A

Jack is watching television.
He is *not* playing the guitar.

But Jack has a guitar.
He plays it a lot, and he plays very well.

Jack **plays** the guitar,
but he **is not playing** the guitar now.
잭은 기타를 치지만, 지금은 기타를 치고 있지 않다.

Is he playing the guitar?	**No, he isn't.**	(현재진행)
Does he play the guitar?	**Yes, he does.**	(단순현재)

B

현재진행 (**I am doing**) = 말하는 시점인 지금:

I'm doing

과거	현재	미래

- Please be quiet. **I'm** work**ing**. (I work는 틀림)
- Tom **is** tak**ing** a shower at the moment. (Tom takes는 틀림)
- Take an umbrella with you. It**'s** rain**ing**. 우산 가져가. 비가 오고 있어.
- You can turn off the television. **I'm** not watch**ing** it.
- Why **are** you under the table? What **are** you do**ing**?
  왜 탁자 밑에 들어가 있니? 뭘 하고 있는 거니?

C

단순현재 (**I do**) = 일반적으로, 항상 또는 때때로:

I do

과거	현재	미래

- I **work** every day from 9:00 to 5:30.
- Tom **takes** a shower every morning. 탐은 매일 아침 샤워를 한다.
- It **rains** a lot in the winter. 겨울에는 비가 많이 내린다.
- I **don't watch** television very often.
- What **do** you usually **do** on weekends? 주말에는 주로 뭘 하니?

D

아래의 동사들은 현재진행(**I am -ing**)으로 쓰지 않는다.

like	love	want	know	understand	remember	depend
prefer	hate	need	mean	believe	forget	

위의 동사들은 단순현재로만 쓴다(**I want** / **do you like?** 등).

- I'm tired. I **want** to go home. (I'm wanting은 틀림)
- "**Do** you **know** that girl?" "Yes, but I **don't remember** her name."
- I **don't understand**. What **do** you **mean**? 난 이해가 안 돼. 무슨 뜻이야?

현재진행 → Units 3–4 단순현재 → Units 5–7 미래의 의미를 가지는 현재 → Unit 26

Exercises

8.1 그림을 보고 질문에 답하시오.

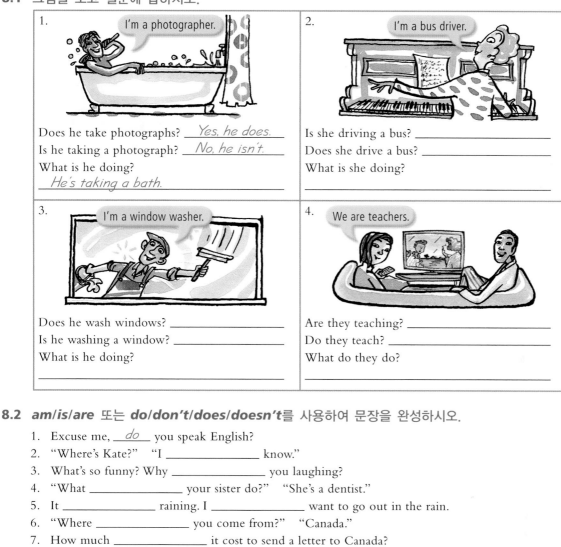

1. *I'm a photographer.*

Does he take photographs? _Yes, he does._
Is he taking a photograph? _No, he isn't._
What is he doing?
He's taking a bath.

2. *I'm a bus driver.*

Is she driving a bus? _____
Does she drive a bus? _____
What is she doing?
_____

3. *I'm a window washer.*

Does he wash windows? _____
Is he washing a window? _____
What is he doing?
_____

4. *We are teachers.*

Are they teaching? _____
Do they teach? _____
What do they do?
_____

8.2 *am/is/are* 또는 *do/don't/does/doesn't*를 사용하여 문장을 완성하시오.

1. Excuse me, __do__ you speak English?
2. "Where's Kate?"   "I _____ know."
3. What's so funny? Why _____ you laughing?
4. "What _____ your sister do?"   "She's a dentist."
5. It _____ raining. I _____ want to go out in the rain.
6. "Where _____ you come from?"   "Canada."
7. How much _____ it cost to send a letter to Canada?
8. Steve is a good tennis player, but he _____ play very often.

8.3 현재진행(*I am doing*) 또는 단순현재(*I do*)를 사용하여 문장을 완성하시오.

1. Excuse me, _do you speak_ (you / speak) English?
2. "Where's Tom?"   _"He's taking_ (he / take) a shower."
3. _I don't watch_ (I / not / watch) television very often.
4. Listen! Somebody _____ (sing).
5. Sandra is tired. _____ (she / want) to go home now.
6. How often _____ (you / read) a newspaper?
7. "Excuse me, but _____ (you / sit) in my seat."   "Oh, I'm sorry."
8. I'm sorry, _____ (I / not / understand). Can you speak more slowly?
9. It's late. _____ (I / go) home now. _____ (you / come) with me?
10. What time _____ (your father / finish) work every day?
11. You can turn off the radio. _____ (I / not / listen) to it.
12. "Where's Paul?"   "In the kitchen. _____ (he / cook) something."
13. Martin _____ (not / usually / drive) to work. He _____ (usually / walk).
14. Sue _____ (not / like) coffee. _____ (she / prefer) tea.

I have ... 와 I've got ...

A

I **have**, he **has**라고 말할 수도 있고 I've **got**, he's **got**이라고 말할 수도 있다.

I we you they	**have**	또는
he she it	**has**	또는

I we you they	**have got**	(I've got) (we've got) (you've got) (they've got)
he she it	**has got**	(he's got) (she's got) (it's got)

축약형

I've **got** a headache.

머리가 아파.

- I **have** blue eyes.   또는   I've **got** blue eyes.
- Tim **has** two sisters.   또는   Tim **has got** two sisters.
- Our car **has** four doors.   또는   Our car **has got** four doors.
- Sarah isn't feeling well. She **has** a headache.   또는   She's **got** a headache.
  사라는 기분이 좋지 않다. 두통이 있다.
- They like animals. They **have** a horse, three dogs, and six cats.   또는   They've **got** a horse ...

B

I **don't have** / I **haven't got** 등 (부정문)

다음과 같이 말할 수 있다.

I/we/you/they	**don't**	**have**	또는
he/she/it	**doesn't**		

I/we/you/they	**haven't**	**got**
he/she/it	**hasn't**	

- I **have** a bike, but I **don't have** a car.   또는   I've **got** a bike, but I **haven't got** a car.
- Mr. and Mrs. Harris **don't have** any children.   또는   ... **haven't got** any children.
- It's a nice house, but it **doesn't have** a garage.   또는   ... it **hasn't got** a garage.
  집은 좋지만 차고가 없다.
- Mariko **doesn't have** a job.   또는   Mariko **hasn't got** a job.

C

Do you **have** ... ? / **Have** you **got** ... ? 등 (의문문)

다음과 같이 말할 수 있다.

do	I/we/you/they	**have?**	또는
does	he/she/it		

have	I/we/you/they	**got?**
has	he/she/it	

- **Do** you **have** a camera?   또는   **Have** you **got** a camera?
- **Does** Helen **have** a car?   또는   **Has** Helen **got** a car?
- What kind of car **does** she **have**?   또는   What kind of car **has** she **got**?
- What **do** you **have** in your bag?   또는   What **have** you **got** in your bag?
  가방 안에 뭐가 있니?

D

짧게 답하기

- "**Do** you have a camera?"   "Yes, I **do**." / "No, I **don't**."   또는
  "**Have** you got a camera?"   "Yes, I **have**." / "No, I **haven't**."
- "**Does** Anne have a car?"   "Yes, she **does**." / "No, she **doesn't**."   또는
  "**Has** Anne got a car?"   "Yes, she **has**." / "No, she **hasn't**."

Exercises

9.1 축약형을 쓰시오(*we've got / he hasn't got* 등).

1. we have got __we've got__
2. he has got _____
3. they have got _____
4. she has not got _____
5. it has got _____
6. I have not got _____

9.2 질문과 대답을 읽고 Mark에 대해 쓰시오.

1.	Have you got a car?	No.	1. __He hasn't got a car.__
2.	Have you got a computer?	Yes.	2. He _____
3.	Have you got a dog?	No.	3. _____
4.	Have you got a cell phone?	No.	4. _____
5.	Have you got a watch?	Yes.	5. _____
6.	Have you got any brothers or sisters?	Yes, two brothers and a sister.	6. _____

Mark

당신은 어떻습니까? *I've got* 또는 *I haven't got*을 사용하여 자신에 대해 쓰시오.

7. (a computer) _____
8. (a dog) _____
9. (a bike) _____
10. (brothers / sisters) _____

9.3 have/has 또는 *don't have / doesn't have*를 사용하여 문장을 다시 쓰시오. 문장의 의미는 같아야 합니다.

1. They have got two children.   __They have two children.__
2. She hasn't got a key.   __She doesn't have a key.__
3. He has got a new job.   _____
4. They haven't got much money.   _____
5. Have you got an umbrella?   _____
6. We have got a lot of work to do.   _____
7. I haven't got your phone number.   _____
8. Has your father got a car?   _____
9. How much money have we got?   _____

9.4 do, doesn't, don't, got, has 또는 *have*를 써 넣으시오.

1. Sarah hasn't __got__ a car. She goes everywhere by bicycle.
2. They like animals. They __have__ three dogs and two cats.
3. Charles isn't happy. He _____ got a lot of problems.
4. They don't read much. They _____ have many books.
5. "What's wrong?" "I've _____ something in my eye."
6. "Where's my pen?" "I don't know. I don't _____ it."
7. Julia wants to go to the concert, but she _____ have a ticket.

9.5 have/has 또는 *don't have / doesn't have*를 사용하여 문장을 완성하시오. 아래 표현 중 하나를 사용하시오.

a lot of friends	four wheels	a headache	six legs
a big yard	much time	a key	

1. I'm not feeling well. I __have a headache.__
2. It's a nice house, but it __doesn't have a big yard.__
3. Most cars _____
4. Everybody likes Tom. He _____
5. I can't open the door. I _____
6. An insect _____
7. Hurry! We _____

→ 추가연습문제 5–7 (246쪽)

was/were

A

어젯밤   지금

Now Robert **is** at work.
지금 로버트는 직장에 있다.

At midnight last night,
he **wasn't** at work.
어젯밤 자정에 그는 직장에
있지 않았다.

He **was** in bed.
그는 침대에 있었다.
He **was** asleep.
그는 잠들어 있었다.

am/is (현재) → **was** (과거):

- I **am** tired. (지금)   I **was** tired **last night**.
- Where **is** Kate? (지금)   Where **was** Kate **yesterday**?
- The weather **is** nice today.   The weather **was** nice **last week**.

are (현재) → **were** (과거):

- You **are** late. (지금)   You **were** late **yesterday**.
- They **aren't** here. (지금)   They **weren't** here **last Sunday**.

B

긍정문	
I he she it	**was**
we you they	**were**

부정문	
I he she it	**was not** (**wasn't**)
we you they	**were not** (**weren't**)

의문문	
was	I? he? she? it?
were	we? you? they?

- Last year Rachel **was** 22, so she **is** 23 now.
- When I **was** a child, I **was** afraid of dogs.
- We **were** hungry after the trip, but we **weren't** tired. 여행을 마친 후 배는 고팠지만 피곤하지는 않았다.
- The hotel **was** comfortable, but it **wasn't** expensive. 그 호텔은 편안했지만 비싸지는 않았다.

- **Was** the weather nice when you **were** on vacation? 휴가 중에 날씨가 좋았니?
- Your shoes are nice. **Were** they expensive?
- Why **were** you late this morning? 오늘 아침에는 왜 늦었니?

C

짧게 답하기

Yes,	I/he/she/it **was**.
	we/you/they **were**.

No,	I/he/she/it **wasn't**.
	we/you/they **weren't**.

- "**Were you** late?" "**No, I wasn't.**"
- "**Was Ted** at work yesterday?" "**Yes, he was.**"
- "**Were Sue and Steve** at the party?" 수와 스티브는 파티에 있었니?
  "**No, they weren't.**" 아니, 없었어.

   am/is/are → Units 1–2   **I was doing** → Unit 13

Exercises

10.1 어제 오후 **3**시에 이 사람들이 어디 있었는지 쓰시오.

1. Gary   2. Jack Kate   3. Sue   4. Mr. and Mrs. Hall   5. Ben

1. _Gary was in bed._
2. Jack and Kate _____
3. Sue _____
4. _____
5. _____
6. And you? I _____

10.2 *am*/*is*/*are* (현재) 또는 *was*/*were* (과거)를 써 넣으시오.

1. Last year she __was__ 22, so she __is__ 23 now.
2. Today the weather _____ nice, but yesterday it _____ very cold.
3. I _____ hungry. Can I have something to eat?
4. I feel fine this morning, but I _____ very tired last night.
5. Where _____ you at 11:00 last Friday morning?
6. Don't buy those shoes. They _____ very expensive.
7. I like your new jacket. _____ it expensive?
8. This time last year I _____ in Paris.
9. "Where _____ the children?" "I don't know. They _____ here a few minutes ago."

10.3 *was*/*were* 또는 *wasn't*/*weren't*를 써 넣으시오.

1. We weren't happy with the hotel. Our room __was__ very small, and it __wasn't__ clean.
2. Mark _____ at work last week because he _____ sick. He's better now.
3. Yesterday _____ a holiday, so the banks _____ closed. They're open today.
4. "_____ Kate and Bill at the party?" "Kate _____ there, but Bill _____ ."
5. "Where are my keys?" "I don't know. They _____ on the table, but they're not there now."
6. You _____ at home last night. Where _____ you?

10.4 주어진 단어들과 *was*/*were*를 사용하여 질문을 쓰시오. 단어들을 올바른 어순으로 배열하시오.

1. (late / you / this morning / why?)
   Why were you late this morning? → The traffic was bad.
2. (difficult / your exam?)
   _____ → No, it was easy.
3. (last week / where / Sue and Chris?)
   _____ → They were on vacation.
4. (your new camera / how much?)
   _____ → One hundred and twenty dollars.
5. (angry / you / yesterday / why?)
   _____ → Because you were late.
6. (nice / the weather / last week?)
   _____ → Yes, it was beautiful.

worked/got/went 등 (단순과거)

A

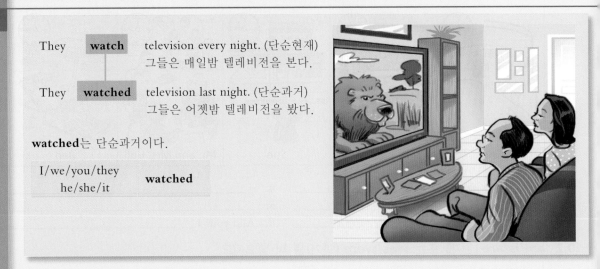

They **watch** television every night. (단순현재)
그들은 매일밤 텔레비전을 본다.

They **watched** television last night. (단순과거)
그들은 어젯밤 텔레비전을 봤다.

watched는 단순과거이다.

I/we/you/they he/she/it	**watched**

B

동사의 단순과거는 보통 **-ed**를 붙인다(규칙동사). 예를 들어,

work → **worked**	dance → **danced**
clean → **cleaned**	stay → **stayed**
start → **started**	need → **needed**

- I brush my teeth every morning. This morning I **brushed** my teeth.
  나는 매일 아침 이를 닦는다. 오늘 아침 나는 이를 닦았다.
- Terry **worked** in a bank from 1996 to 2003.
- Yesterday it **rained** all morning. It **stopped** at lunchtime.
  어제는 아침 내내 비가 내렸다. 비는 점심 때 멈췄다.
- We **enjoyed** the party last night. We **danced** a lot and **talked** to a lot of people. The party **ended** at midnight.

철자는 부록 5 참조.

try → **tried**	study → stud**ied**	copy → cop**ied**
sto**p** → sto**pped**	plan → plan**ned**	

C

일부 동사들은 단순과거에 **-ed**를 붙이지 않는 불규칙동사들이다. 다음은 주요 불규칙동사들의 예이다(더 많은 예는 부록 2-3 참조).

begin → **began**	fall → **fell**	leave → **left**	sell → **sold**
break **broke**	find **found**	lose **lost**	sit **sat**
bring **brought**	fly **flew**	make **made**	sleep **slept**
build **built**	forget **forgot**	meet **met**	speak **spoke**
buy **bought**	get **got**	pay **paid**	stand **stood**
catch **caught**	give **gave**	put **put**	take **took**
come **came**	go **went**	read **read***	tell **told**
do **did**	have **had**	ring **rang**	think **thought**
drink **drank**	hear **heard**	say **said**	win **won**
eat **ate**	know **knew**	see **saw**	write **wrote**

*발음은 "red"

- I usually get up early, but this morning I **got** up at 9:30.
- We **did** a lot of work yesterday. 우리는 어제 일을 많이 했다.
- Caroline **went** to the movies three times last week. 캐롤라인은 지난주에 영화를 보러 극장에 세 번 갔다.
- James **came** into the room, **took** off his coat, and **sat** down. 제임스는 방에 들어와서 코트를 벗고 앉았다.

Exercises

11.1 아래의 동사를 사용하여 문장을 완성하시오.

~~brush~~	die	end	enjoy	happen	open	rain	start	stay	want

1. I _brushed_ my teeth three times yesterday.
2. It was hot in the room, so I _____ the window.
3. The movie was very long. It _____ at 7:15 and _____ at 10:00.
4. When I was a child, I _____ to be a doctor.
5. The accident _____ last Sunday afternoon.
6. It's a nice day today, but yesterday it _____ all day.
7. We _____ our vacation last year. We _____ at a very nice place.
8. Anna's grandfather _____ when he was 90 years old.

11.2 다음 동사의 단순과거를 쓰시오.

1. get _got_
2. see _____
3. play _____
4. pay _____
5. visit _____
6. buy _____
7. go _____
8. think _____
9. copy _____
10. know _____
11. put _____
12. speak _____

11.3 Lisa의 멕시코 여행 이야기를 읽고 주어진 동사를 올바른 형태로 써 넣으시오.

Last Tuesday, Lisa (1) _flew_ from Los Angeles to Mexico City. She
(2) _____ up at 6:00 in the morning and (3) _____ a cup
of coffee. At 7:15 she (4) _____ home and (5) _____ to
the airport. When she (6) _____ there, she (7) _____ the
car, (8) _____ to the terminal, and (9) _____ in. Then she
(10) _____ breakfast at an airport café and (11) _____ for
her flight. The plane (12) _____ on time and (13) _____
in Mexico City four hours later. Finally she (14) _____ a taxi from the
airport to her hotel downtown.

fly
get, have
leave, drive
get, park
walk, check
have, wait
depart, arrive
take

11.4 과거(*yesterday* / *last week* 등)에 대한 문장을 쓰시오.

1. James always goes to work by car. Yesterday _he went to work by car._
2. Rachel often loses her keys. She _____ last week.
3. Kate meets her friends every night. She _____ last night.
4. I usually buy two newspapers every day. Yesterday I _____
5. We often go to the movies on weekends. Last Sunday we _____
6. I eat an orange every day. Yesterday I _____
7. Tom always takes a shower in the morning. This morning he _____
8. Our friends often come to see us. They _____ last Friday.

11.5 당신이 어제 한 일에 대해 쓰시오.

1. _I went to the theater._
2. _____
3. _____
4. _____
5. _____
6. _____

I didn't ... Did you ... ?
(단순과거 부정문과 의문문)

A 단순과거 부정문과 의문문에는 **did**를 쓴다.

원형
play
start
watch
have
see
do
go

긍정문	
I	**played**
we	**started**
you	**watched**
they	**had**
he	**saw**
she	**did**
it	**went**

부정문		
I		play
we		start
you		watch
they	**did not**	have
he	**(didn't)**	see
she		do
it		go

의문문		
	I	play?
	we	start?
	you	watch?
did	they	have?
	he	see?
	she	do?
	it	go?

B **do/does** (현재) → **did** (과거):

- I **don't** watch television very often.
  I **didn't** watch television **yesterday**.
- **Does** she go out often? 그녀는 자주 외출합니까?
  Did she go out **last night**? 그녀는 어젯밤에 외출했습니까?

C **did/didn't** 다음에는 원형(**watch/play/go** 등)이 온다.

I **watched**	그러나	I **didn't watch**	(I didn't watched는 틀림)
they **went**		**did** they **go**?	(did they went?는 틀림)
he **had**		he **didn't have**	
you **did**		**did** you **do**?	

- I **played** tennis yesterday, but I **didn't win**.
- "**Did** you **do** your homework?" "No, I **didn't have** time."
- We **went** to the movies, but we **didn't enjoy** the film.
  우리는 영화를 보러 갔지만, 영화는 재미없었다.

D 의문문의 어순:

	did +	주어 +	원형	
	Did	your sister	**call**	you?
What	**did**	you	**do**	last night?
How	**did**	the accident	**happen**?	
Where	**did**	your parents	**go**	for vacation?

E 짧게 답하기

Yes,	I/we/you/they he/she/it	**did.**

No,	I/we/you/they he/she/it	**didn't.**

- "**Did you** see Joe yesterday?" "**No, I didn't.**"
- "**Did it** rain on Sunday?" "**Yes, it did.**"
- "**Did Helen** come to the party?" "**No, she didn't.**"
- "**Did your parents** have a good trip?" 부모님께서는 여행 잘 하셨니?
  "**Yes, they did.**" 응, 잘 하셨어.

Exercises

12.1 동사의 부정형을 써 넣어 문장을 완성하시오.

1. I saw Barbara, but I ___didn't see___ Jane.
2. They worked on Monday, but they _____ on Tuesday.
3. We went to the post office, but we _____ to the bank.
4. She had a pen, but she _____ any paper.
5. Jack did some work in the yard, but he _____ any work in the house.

12.2 *Did ... ?*로 시작하는 의문문을 쓰시오.

1. I watched TV last night. How about you? ___Did you watch TV last night___ ?
2. I enjoyed the party. How about you? _____ ?
3. I had a nice vacation. How about you? _____ ?
4. I finished work early. How about you? _____ ?
5. I slept well last night. How about you? _____ ?

12.3 당신은 어제 무엇을 했습니까? 긍정문 또는 부정문을 쓰시오.

1. (watch TV) ___I watched TV.___ 또는 ___I didn't watch TV.___
2. (get up before 7:00) I _____
3. (take a shower) _____
4. (buy a magazine) _____
5. (eat meat) _____
6. (go to bed before 10:30) _____

12.4 아래의 단어들을 사용하여 B의 질문을 쓰시오.

cost   get to work   go   go to bed late   happen   have a nice time   ~~stay~~   win

1. *A:* We went to Chicago last month. *B:* Where ___did you stay___ ? *A:* With some friends.	5. *A:* We came home by taxi. *B:* How much _____ ? *A:* Twenty dollars.
2. *A:* I was late for the meeting. *B:* What time _____ ? *A:* Half past nine.	6. *A:* I'm tired this morning. *B:* _____ ? *A:* No, but I didn't sleep very well.
3. *A:* I played tennis this afternoon. *B:* _____ ? *A:* No, I lost.	7. *A:* We went to the beach yesterday. *B:* _____ ? *A:* Yes, it was great.
4. *A:* I had a nice vacation. *B:* Good. Where _____ ? *A:* To the mountains.	8. *A:* The window is broken. *B:* How _____ ? *A:* I don't know.

12.5 괄호 안의 동사를 긍정이나 부정, 의문형으로 알맞게 써 넣으시오.

1. We went to the movies, but the film wasn't very good. We ___didn't enjoy___ it. (enjoy)
2. Tim _____ some new clothes yesterday – two shirts, a jacket, and a sweater. (buy)
3. "_____ yesterday?" "No, it was a nice day." (rain)
4. We were tired, so we _____ long at the party. (stay)
5. It was very warm in the room, so I _____ a window. (open)
6. "Did you call Chris this morning?" "No, I _____ time." (have)
7. "I cut my hand this morning." "How _____ that?" (do)
8. "Why weren't you at the meeting yesterday?" "I _____ about it." (know)

→ 추가연습문제 10–13 (248쪽)

I was doing (과거진행)

A

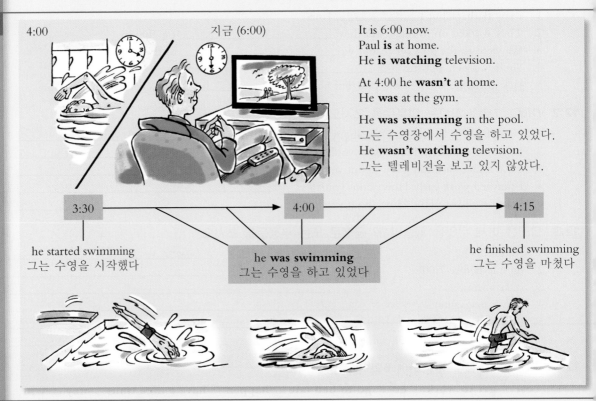

It is 6:00 now.
Paul **is** at home.
He **is watching** television.

At 4:00 he **wasn't** at home.
He **was** at the gym.

He **was swimming** in the pool.
그는 수영장에서 수영을 하고 있었다.
He **wasn't watching** television.
그는 텔레비전을 보고 있지 않았다.

4:00　　　　　　　　　지금 (6:00)

3:30　　　　　　　4:00　　　　　　　4:15

he started swimming
그는 수영을 시작했다

he **was swimming**
그는 수영을 하고 있었다

he finished swimming
그는 수영을 마쳤다

B

was/were + **-ing**는 과거진행이다.

긍정문		
I he she it	**was**	doing watching playing swimming living 등
we you they	**were**	

부정문		
I he she it	**was not (wasn't)**	doing watching playing swimming living 등
we you they	**were not (weren't)**	

의문문		
was	I he she it	doing? watching? playing? swimming? living? 등
were	we you they	

- What **were** you **doing** at 11:30 yesterday? **Were** you **working**?
- "What did he say?" 그가 뭐라고 말했니?
  "I don't know. I **wasn't listening**." 몰라. 안 듣고 있었어.
- It **was raining**, so we didn't go out.
- In 2001 we **were living** in Japan.
- Today she's wearing a skirt, but yesterday she **was wearing** pants.
  그녀는 오늘은 치마를 입고 있지만, 어제는 바지를 입고 있었다.
- I woke up early yesterday. It was a beautiful morning. The sun **was shining**, and the birds **were singing**.

주의할 철자 (live → living / run → running / lie → lying 등) → 부록 5

C

am/is/are + **-ing** (현재) → **was/were** + **-ing** (과거):

현재	과거
- **I'm working** (now).	- **I was working** at 10:30 last night.
- It **isn't raining** (now).	- It **wasn't raining** when we went out.
- What **are** you **doing** (now)?	- What **were** you **doing** at 3:00?

Exercises

13.1 다음 그림은 어제 오후 **3**시의 상황입니다. 사람들이 어디에 있었는지, 그리고 무엇을 하고 있었는지를 두 문장으로 쓰시오.

1. Rachel	2. Kate Jack	3. Tim	4. Tracey	5. Mr. and Mrs. Hall
at home	at the supermarket	in his car	at the station	in the park
watch TV	buy food	drive	wait for a train	walk

1. _Rachel was at home. She was watching TV._
2. Jack and Kate _____ . They _____
3. Tim _____
4. _____
5. _____
6. 당신은? I _____

13.2 Sarah는 어제 많은 일을 했습니다. 그림을 보고 문장을 완성하시오.

7:10–7:25	7:30–8:10	8:30–9:00
9:20–10:00	10:15–11:45	12:00–12:45

1. At 8:45 _she was washing her car._
2. At 10:45 she _____
   _____
3. At 8:00 _____
   _____
4. At 12:10 _____
   _____
5. At 7:15 _____
   _____
6. At 9:30 _____

13.3 *was/were -ing*를 사용하여 문장을 완성하시오. 필요한 경우 *what/where/why*를 쓰시오.

1. (you / live) _Where were you living_ _____ in 1999? — In Brazil.
2. (you / do) _____ at 2:00? — I was asleep.
3. (it / rain) _____ when you got up? — No, it was sunny.
4. (Sue / drive) _____ so fast? — Because she was late.
5. (Tim / wear) _____ a suit yesterday? — No, a T-shirt and jeans.

13.4 당신은 어제 오후 길에서 **Joe**를 만났습니다. 그가 무엇을 하고 있었는지 괄호 안의 단어들을 사용하여 긍정문 또는 부정문을 쓰시오.

Hi. I'm going shopping.

Joe

1. (wear / a jacket) _He wasn't wearing a jacket._
2. (carry / a bag) _____
3. (go / to the dentist) _____
4. (eat / an ice cream cone) _____
5. (carry / an umbrella) _____
6. (go / home) _____
7. (wear / a hat) _____
8. (ride / a bicycle) _____

I was doing과 I did
(과거진행와 단순과거)

Jack **was reading**
a book.
잭은 책을 읽고 있었다.

The phone **rang**.
전화가 울렸다.

He **stopped** reading.
그는 책 읽기를
멈췄다.

He **answered** the
phone.
그는 전화를 받았다.

What **happened**? The phone **rang**. (단순과거)
What **was** Jack **doing** when the phone rang?　　　} (과거진행)
　　He **was reading** a book.

What **did** he **do** when the phone rang?　　　} (단순과거)
　　He **stopped** reading and **answered** the phone.

Jack began reading *before* the phone rang. So *when* the phone rang, he **was reading**.
잭은 전화가 울리기 '전에' 책을 읽기 시작했다. 그래서 전화가 울렸을 '때' 그는 책을 읽고 있었다.

| he began reading | | the phone rang | he stopped reading | he answered the phone |

he was reading

단순과거

■ A: What **did** you **do** yesterday morning?
　 B: We **played** tennis. (from 10:00 to 11:30)

시작　　　　　　　　　　　　　끝
10:00　　　　　　　　　　*11:30*

we **played**
완료된 행동

과거진행

■ A: What **were** you **doing** at 10:30?
　 B: We **were playing** tennis.

시작
10:00

we **were playing**
끝나지 않은 행동

■ Jack **read** a book yesterday.
　(= 처음부터 끝까지)
■ **Did** you **watch** the basketball game on
　television last night?
　어젯밤에 텔레비전에서 야구경기 봤니?
■ It **didn't rain** while we were on vacation.
　휴가 중에는 비가 내리지 않았다.

■ Jack **was reading** a book when the
　phone rang.
■ **Were** you **watching** television when I
　called you?
　내가 전화했을 때 텔레비전 보고 있었니?
■ It **wasn't raining** when I got up.
　내가 일어났을 때 비는 내리고 있지 않았다.

■ I **started** work at 9:00 and **finished** at 4:30. At 2:30 **I was working**.
■ It **was raining** when we **went** out. (= it started raining *before* we went out)
■ I **saw** Lucy and Steve this morning. They **were waiting** at the bus stop.
■ Kelly **fell** asleep while she **was reading**. 케이트는 책을 읽다가 잠이 들었다.

Exercises

14.1 그림에 맞게 동사를 과거진행 또는 단순과거로 써 넣으시오.

1.

Lucy ___broke___ (break) her arm last week.
It _____ (happen) when
she _____ (paint) her
room. She _____ (fall)
off the ladder.

2.

The train _____ (arrive)
at the station, and Paula _____
(get) off. Two friends of hers, Jon and Rachel,
_____ (wait) to
meet her.

3.

Yesterday Sue _____ (walk)
down the street when she _____ (meet)
James. He _____ (go)
to the station to catch a train, and he
_____ (carry) a
bag. They _____ (stop)
to talk for a few minutes.

14.2 동사를 과거진행 또는 단순과거로 써 넣으시오.

1. *A:* What ___were you doing___ (you / do) when the phone ___rang___ (ring)?
   B: I ___was watching___ (watch) television.
2. *A:* Was Jane busy when you went to see her?
   B: Yes, she _____ (study).
3. *A:* What time _____ (the mail / arrive) this morning?
   B: It _____ (come) while I _____ (have) breakfast.
4. *A:* Was Tracey at work today?
   B: No, she _____ (not / go) to work. She was sick.
5. *A:* How fast _____ (you / drive) when the police
   _____ (stop) you?
   B: I'm not sure, but I _____ (not / drive) very fast.
6. *A:* _____ (your team / win) the baseball game yesterday?
   B: No, the weather was very bad, so we _____ (not / play).
7. *A:* How _____ (you / break) the window?
   B: We _____ (play) baseball. I _____ (hit) the ball
   and it _____ (break) the window.
8. *A:* _____ (you / see) Jenny last night?
   B: Yes, she _____ (wear) a very nice jacket.
9. *A:* What _____ (you / do) at 2:00 this morning?
   B: I was asleep.
10. *A:* I _____ (lose) my key last night.
    B: How _____ (you / get) into your apartment?
    A: I _____ (climb) in through a window.

→ 추가연습문제 14–15 (249–250쪽)

I used to …

A

몇 년 전의 데이브   현재의 데이브

> I work in a factory.

> I work in a supermarket.
> I **used to work** in a factory.

Dave

Dave **used to work** in a factory. Now he **works** in a supermarket.
데이브는 전에 공장에서 일했다. 이제 그는 슈퍼마켓에서 일한다.

Dave **used to work** in a factory. = 그는 전에 공장에서 일했지만 이제는 거기서 일하지 않는다.

←——— he **used to** work ———→	←——— he works ———→
과거	현재

B

used to는 '…하곤 했다'라는 뜻으로 **I used to work** … / **she used to have** … / **they used to be** …와 같이 쓴다.

I/you/we/they he/she/it	used to	**be** **work** **have** **play** 등

- When I was a child, I **used to like** chocolate.
- I **used to read** a lot of books, but I don't read much these days.
- Liz has short hair now, but it **used to be** very long.
- They **used to live** on the same street as us, so we **used to see** them a lot. But we don't see them very often these days.
  전에 그들은 우리와 같은 거리에 살아서 우리는 그들을 자주 봤다. 하지만 요즘은 자주 못 본다.
- Helen **used to have** a piano, but she sold it a few years ago.
  헬렌은 전에는 피아노를 가지고 있었지만 몇 년 전에 팔아치웠다.

> I **used to have** very long hair.

부정문은 **I didn't use to** …이다.

- When I was a child, I **didn't use to like** tomatoes.

의문문은 **did you use to** … **?**이다.

- Where **did** you **use to live** before you came here?

C

used to …는 과거의 일에 대해서만 쓴다. 현재형으로 'I use to …'라고 쓸 수 없다.

- I **used to play** tennis. These days I **play** golf. (I use to play golf는 틀림)
- We usually **get** up early. (We use to get up early는 틀림)

Exercises

15.1 그림을 보고 *used to* ...를 사용하여 문장을 완성하시오.

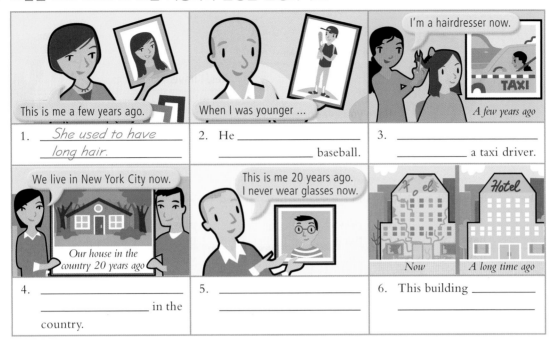

1. *She used to have long hair.*

2. He _____ baseball.

3. _____ a taxi driver.

4. _____ in the country.

5. _____

6. This building _____

15.2 Karen은 열심히 일하느라 요즘 여가시간이 거의 없지만, 몇 년 전에는 그렇지 않았습니다.

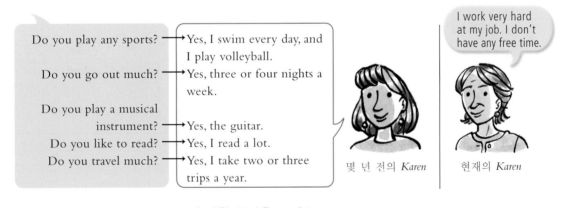

Do you play any sports? → Yes, I swim every day, and I play volleyball.

Do you go out much? → Yes, three or four nights a week.

Do you play a musical instrument? → Yes, the guitar.

Do you like to read? → Yes, I read a lot.

Do you travel much? → Yes, I take two or three trips a year.

I work very hard at my job. I don't have any free time.

몇 년 전의 Karen

현재의 Karen

used to ...를 사용하여 Karen에 대한 문장을 쓰시오.

1. *She used to swim every day.*
2. She _____ volleyball.
3. _____
4. _____
5. _____
6. _____

15.3 *used to* 또는 단순현재(*I play* / *he lives* 등)를 사용하여 문장을 완성하시오.

1. I _used to play_ tennis. I stopped playing a few years ago.
2. "Do you play any sports?" "Yes, I _play_ basketball."
3. "Do you have a car?" "No, I _____ one, but I sold it."
4. George _____ a waiter. Now he's the manager of a hotel.
5. "Do you go to work by car?" "Sometimes, but most days I _____ by train."
6. When I was a child, I never _____ meat, but I eat it now.
7. Mary loves to watch TV. She _____ TV every night.
8. We _____ near the airport, but we moved downtown a few years ago.
9. Normally I start work at 7:00, so I _____ up very early.
10. What games _____ you _____ when you were a child?

31

Have you ever ... ?

멕시코시티에 가본 적 있어요?

Have you been to Mexico City?

네, 여러 번 가봤어요.

Yes, I have. Many times.

Have you ever been to Japan?

일본에는 가본 적 있어요?

No, **I've never been** to Japan.

아니요, 일본에는 한번도 가본 적 없어요.

have + 과거분사(**have been** / **have driven** / **have played** 등)는 현재완료이다.

I we you they	**have** (**'ve**) **have not** (**haven't**)	**played** **lived** **visited** **read**
he she it	**has** (**'s**) **has not** (**hasn't**)	**lost** **been** **flown**

have	I we you they	**played**? **lived**? **visited**? **read**?
has	he she it	**lost**? **been**? **flown**?

규칙동사

불규칙동사

규칙동사 과거분사형은 **-ed**이다(과거형과 같음):

play → I have play**ed**   live → I have liv**ed**   visit → she has visit**ed**

불규칙동사 과거분사형은 **-ed**가 아니다.
때로는 과거분사형과 과거형이 같다:

buy → I **bought** / I have **bought**   have → he **had** / he has **had**

때로는 과거분사형은 다르다(부록 2–3 참조).

break → I **broke** / I have **broken**   see → you **saw** / you have **seen**

현재완료는 과거부터 현재까지의 시간, 예를 들어 지금까지 살아오면서 있었던 일에 대해 이야기할
때 사용한다.

Have you ever been to Japan?

──────── 과거부터 현재까지의 시간 ────────

과거   현재

- "**Have** you **been** to France?"   "No, I **haven't**."
- We**'ve been** to Canada, but we **haven't been** to Alaska.
- Mary is an interesting person. She **has had** many different jobs and **has lived**
  in many places. 메리는 재미있는 사람이다. 그녀는 여러 가지 직업을 가져봤고 여러 곳에서 살아봤다.
- I**'ve seen** that woman before, but I can't remember where.
- How many times **has** Brazil **won** the World Cup? 브라질이 월드컵에서 몇 번이나 우승했니?
- "**Have** you **read** this book?"   "Yes, I**'ve read** it twice." (**twice** = two times)

현재완료 + **ever** (의문문에서)와 **never**:

- "**Has** Ann **ever been** to Australia?"   "Yes, once." (**once** = one time)
- "**Have** you **ever played** golf?" 골프를 쳐보신 적이 있나요?   "Yes, I play a lot." 예, 많습니다.
- My sister **has never traveled** by plane. 내 누이는 비행기를 타고 여행한 적이 한번도 없다.
- I**'ve never ridden** a horse. 나는 한번도 말을 타본 적이 없다.
- "Who is that man?"   "I don't know. I**'ve never seen him** before."

Exercises

16.1 Helen에게 ***Have you ever** ... ?*로 시작하는 질문을 하고 있습니다.
괄호 안의 단어들을 사용하여 질문을 만드시오.

Helen

1. (Montreal?)   *Have you ever been to Montreal?*   No, never.
2. (play / golf?)   *Have you ever played golf?*   Yes, many times.
3. (South Korea?)   Have _____   Yes, once.
4. (lose / your passport?) _____   No, never.
5. (fly / in a helicopter?) _____   Yes, a few times.
6. (win / a race?)   _____   No, never.
7. (Peru?)   _____   Yes, twice.
8. (drive / a bus?)   _____   No, never.
9. (break / your leg?) _____   Yes, once.

16.2 위의 대답들을 참고하여 Helen에 대한 문장을 쓰시오.

1. (Peru) _She's been to Peru twice._
2. (South Korea) She _____
3. (win / a race) _____
4. (fly / in a helicopter) _____

이번에는 당신에 대해 쓰시오. 당신은 아래의 일들을 얼마나 해보았습니까?

5. (New York) I _____
6. (play / tennis) _____
7. (drive / a truck) _____
8. (be / late for work or school) _____

16.3 65세의 Mary는 흥미진진한 삶을 살아 왔습니다. 상자 속의 단어들과 현재완료를 사용하여
그녀의 경험에 대해 쓰시오.

Mary

~~have~~	be	all over the world	a lot of interesting things
do	write	~~many different jobs~~	a lot of interesting people
travel	meet	10 books	married three times

1. _She has had many different jobs._
2. She _____
3. _____
4. _____
5. _____
6. _____

16.4 동사를 현재완료로 써 넣으시오.

1. ___I've seen___ (I / see) that woman before, but I can't remember her name.
2. "___Have you ever played___ (you / ever / play) golf?"   "Yes, I play golf a lot."
3. "_____ (you / ever / write) a poem?"   "Yes, in high school."
4. "Does Emma know Sam?"   "No, _____ (she / never / meet) him."
5. Ann and Eli have lots of books, and _____ (they / read) all of them.
6. _____ (I / never / be) to Australia, but _____ (my brother / be) there twice.
7. Joy's favorite movie is *Howard and Belinda*. _____ (she / see) it five times, but _____ (I / never / see) it.
8. _____ (I / travel) by plane, bus, and train. Someday, I want to take a trip by boat.

→ 추가연습문제 16–18 (250–251쪽)   33

How long have you ...?

A

Jane is on vacation in Brazil.
She is there now.

She arrived in Brazil on Monday.
Today is Thursday.

How long **has she been** in Brazil?
제인은 브라질에 얼마나 있었는가?

She **has been** in Brazil { **since Monday.**
{ **for three days.**

그녀는 {월요일부터 / 사흘 동안} 브라질에
있었다.

How long **have you been** in Brazil?

Since Monday.

is와 **has been**의 비교:

She is in Brazil **now**.

is = 현재

She **has been** in Brazil { **since Monday.**
{ **for three days.**

has been = 현재완료

Monday

now
Thursday

B

비교:

단순현재	현재완료 (**have been** / **have lived** / **have known** 등)
Dan and Kate **are** married.	They **have been** married **for five years**. (They are married for five years는 틀림)
Are you married? 결혼하셨어요?	**How long have** you **been** married? 결혼하신 지 얼마나 되셨어요? (How long are you married?는 틀림)
Do you **know** Lisa?	**How long have** you **known** her? (How long do you know her?는 틀림)
I **know** Lisa.	**I've known** her **for a long time**. (I know her for ...는 틀림)
Vera **lives** in Brasília.	**How long has** she **lived** in Brasília? She **has lived** there **all her life**.
I **have** a car. 나는 차가 있습니다.	**How long have** you **had** your car? 차를 가진 지 얼마나 됐습니까? **I've had** it **since April**. 4월부터 가지고 있었습니다.

현재진행	현재완료 진행 (**have been** + **-ing**)
I'm studying German. 나는 독어를 공부하고 있습니다.	**How long have** you **been studying** German? 독어를 공부한 지 얼마나 됐습니까? (How long are you studying German?은 틀림) **I've been studying** German **for two years**. 2년째 공부하고 있습니다.
David **is watching** TV.	**How long has** he **been watching** TV? He**'s been** (= He **has been**) **watching** TV **since 5:00**.
It**'s raining**.	It**'s been** (= It **has been**) **raining all day**.

Exercises

17.1 다음 문장을 완성하시오.

1. Jane is in Brazil. She _has been_____ there since Monday.
2. I know Lisa. I _have known_____ her for a long time.
3. Sarah and Andy are married. They _____ married since 1999.
4. Brian is sick. He _____ sick for the last few days.
5. We live on Main Street. We _____ there for a long time.
6. Catherine works in a bank. She _____ in a bank for five years.
7. Alan has a headache. He _____ a headache since he got up this morning.
8. I'm studying English. I _____ English for six months.

17.2 다음 정보를 읽고 **How long ... ?**으로 시작하는 질문을 만드시오.

1. Jane is on vacation. _How long has she been on vacation_____ ?
2. Scott and Judy are in Brazil. How long _____ ?
3. I know Amy. How long _____ you _____ ?
4. Diana is studying Italian. _____ ?
5. My brother lives in Seattle. _____ ?
6. I'm a teacher. _____ ?
7. It is raining. _____ ?

17.3

1. We're married.
2. I live in South Korea.
3. We're on vacation.
4. The sun is shining.
5. I'm waiting.
6. I have a beard.

그림을 보고 아래의 단어들을 사용하여 문장을 완성하시오.

for 10 minutes	all day	all her life
~~for 10 years~~	since he was 20	since Sunday

1. _They have been married for 10 years._
2. She _____
3. They _____
4. The sun _____
5. She _____
6. He _____

17.4 맞는 것을 고르시오.

1. Mark ~~lives~~ / has lived in Canada since April. (*has lived*가 맞음)
2. Jane and I are friends. I know / I've known her very well.
3. Jane and I are friends. I know / I've known her for a long time.
4. *A:* Sorry I'm late. How long are you waiting / have you been waiting?
   B: Not long. Only five minutes.
5. Martin works / has worked in a hotel now. He likes his job a lot.
6. Ruth is reading the newspaper. She is reading / She has been reading it for two hours.
7. "How long do you live / have you lived in this house?" "About 10 years."
8. "Is that a new coat?" "No, I have / I've had this coat for a long time."
9. Tom is / has been in Seattle right now. He is / He has been there for the last three days.

→ 추가연습문제 16–18 (250–251쪽)

UNIT
18

for since ago

for와 since

기간(how long)에 대해 말할 때 **for**와 **since**를 사용한다.

- Jane **is** in Brazil. She **has been** there { **for three days.**
  since Monday.

for + 기간 (**three days / two years** 등):

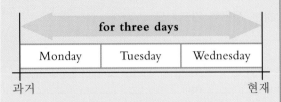

for	
three days	10 minutes
an hour	two hours
a week	four weeks
a month	six months
five years	a long time

- Richard has been in Canada **for six months.** (since six months는 틀림)
- We've been waiting **for two hours.** (since two hours는 틀림)
- I've lived in Chicago **for a long time.** 나는 오랫동안 시카고에서 살았다.

since + 시작점 (**Monday / 9:00** 등):

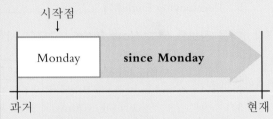

since	
Monday	Wednesday
9:00	12:30
July 4th	my birthday
January	I was 10 years old
1995	we arrived

- Richard has been in Canada **since January.** (= 1월부터 지금까지)
- We've been waiting **since 9:00.** (= 9시부터 지금까지)
- I've lived in Chicago **since I was 10 years old.** 나는 10살 때부터 시카고에서 살았다.

ago

ago: 이전에 (= before now)

- Susan started her new job **three weeks ago.** (= three weeks before now)
- "When did Tom leave?" "**Ten minutes ago.**" (= ten minutes before now)
- I had dinner **an hour ago.**
- Life was very different **a hundred years ago.**

ago는 과거와 함께 쓴다(**started/did/had/was** 등).

ago와 **for**의 비교:

- **When did** Jane **arrive** in Brazil? 제인은 브라질에 언제 도착했나요?
  She **arrived** in Brazil **three days ago.** 그녀는 사흘 전에 브라질에 도착했습니다.
- **How long has** she **been** in Brazil? 그녀는 브라질에 얼마 동안 있었나요?
  She **has been** in Brazil **for three days.** 그녀는 사흘 동안 브라질에 있었습니다.

Exercises

18.1 *for* 또는 *since*를 써 넣으시오.

1. Jane has been in Brazil _*since*_ Monday.
2. Jane has been in Brazil _*for*_ three days.
3. My aunt has lived in Australia _____ 15 years.
4. Jennifer is in her office. She has been there _____ 7:00.
5. Mexico has been an independent country _____ 1821.
6. The bus is late. We've been waiting _____ 20 minutes.
7. Nobody lives in those houses. They have been empty _____ many years.
8. Michael has been sick _____ a long time. He has been in the hospital _____ October.

18.2 *ago*를 사용하여 질문에 답하시오.

1. When was the last time you ate? _Three hours ago._ _____
2. When was the last time you were sick? _____
3. When was the last time you went to the movies? _____
4. When was the last time you were in a car? _____
5. When was the last time you went on vacation? _____

18.3 *for* 또는 *ago*를 괄호 안의 단어와 함께 사용하여 문장을 완성하시오.

1. Jane arrived in Brazil _three days ago._ _____ (three days)
2. Jane has been in Brazil _for three days._ _____ (three days)
3. Lynn and Mark have been married _____ (20 years)
4. Lynn and Mark got married _____ (20 years)
5. Dan arrived _____ (an hour)
6. I bought these shoes _____ (a few days)
7. Silvia has been studying English _____ (six months)
8. Have you known Lisa _____ ? (a long time)

18.4 *for* 또는 *since*를 사용하여 문장을 완성하시오.

1. (Jane is in Brazil – she arrived there three days ago)
   Jane has been in Brazil for three days. _____
2. (Jack is here – he arrived on Tuesday)
   Jack has _____
3. (It's raining – it started an hour ago)
   It's been _____
4. (I know Sue – I met her in 2002)
   I've _____
5. (Claire and Matthew are married – they got married six months ago)
   Claire and Matthew have _____
6. (Liz is studying medicine at the university – she started three years ago)
   Liz has _____
7. (David plays the piano – he started when he was seven years old)
   David has _____

18.5 아래의 구문들을 사용하여 자신에 대해 쓰시오.

I've lived …   I've been …   I've been studying …   I've known …   I've had …

1. _I've lived in this town for three years._ _____
2. _____
3. _____
4. _____
5. _____

I have done과 I did
(현재완료와 단순과거 1)

His car is dirty.
그의 차는 지저분하다.

He is washing his car.
그는 차를 닦고 있다.

He **has washed** his car. (= his car is clean *now*) 그는 세차를 마쳤다.

They are at home.
그들은 집에 있다.

They are going out.
그들은 외출하고 있다.

They **have gone** out. (= they are not at home *now*) 그들은 외출했다.

B

현재완료는 현재까지 영향을 미치는 과거의 행동에 대해 사용한다.

- **I've lost** my passport. 여권을 잃어버렸어. (= I can't find my passport *now*)
- "Where's Rebecca?" "She**'s gone** to bed." 자러 갔어. (= she is in bed *now*)
- We**'ve bought** a new car. (= we have a new car *now*)
- It's Rachel's birthday tomorrow, and I **haven't bought** her a present.
  내일이 레이첼 생일인데 아직 선물을 못 샀어. (= I don't have a present for her *now*)
- "Bob is away on vacation." "Oh, where **has** he **gone**?" (= where is he *now*?)
- **Have** you **met** my brother, or should I introduce you?
- I was a very slow typist in college, but I**'ve gotten** faster.
  나는 대학 다닐 때는 타자가 무척 느렸는데 지금은 빨라졌다.

이러한 상황에서는 보통 다음과 같이 단순과거(he **washed** / I **lost** 등)를 쓸 수도 있다.

- "Where's your key?" "I**'ve lost** it." 또는 "I **lost** it."
- "Is Peter here?" "No, he**'s gone** home." 또는 "He **went** home."
- We**'ve bought** a new car. 또는 We **bought** a new car.

C

종결된 시간(**yesterday**, **last week** 등)에 대해서는 현재완료가 아니라 단순과거를 사용한다.

- I **lost** my key **yesterday**. (I have lost my key yesterday는 틀림)
- We **bought** a new car **last week**. (We have bought a new car last week는 틀림)

Exercises

19.1 아래의 단어들과 현재완료를 사용하여 그림의 상황을 설명하는 문장을 쓰시오.

go to bed   ~~wash her car~~   stop raining   close the door   fall down   take a shower

이전   →   지금

1. _She has washed her car._

2. He _____ .

3. They _____ .

4. It _____ .

5. He _____ .

6. The _____ .

19.2 밑줄 친 동사가 있는 문장을 현재완료로 다시 쓰시오.

1. Lee Ming isn't here. He <u>went</u> home. _He has gone home._
2. I don't need to call them. I <u>wrote</u> them a letter. _____
3. Karen's not coming to the party. She <u>broke</u> her arm. _____
4. My brother and his wife don't live here any more. They <u>moved</u> to Seattle.

   _____
5. I <u>made</u> a big mistake. _____
6. I <u>lost</u> my wallet. _____
   <u>Did</u> you <u>see</u> it anywhere? _____
7. <u>Did</u> you <u>hear</u>? _____
   Mark <u>got</u> married. _____

이제 다음의 현재완료 문장을 단순과거로 다시 쓰시오.

8. I've <u>done</u> the shopping. _I did the shopping._
9. Brian <u>has taken</u> my bike again without asking. _____
10. <u>Have</u> you <u>told</u> your friends the good news? _____
11. We <u>haven't paid</u> the electric bill. _____

UNIT 20
just, already와 yet
(현재완료와 단순과거 2)

A

just = 조금 전

just는 현재완료 또는 단순과거와 사용한다.

- A: Are Diane and Paul here?
  B: Yes, they**'ve just arrived**.　또는
  Yes, **they just** arrived.
- A: Are you hungry?
  B: No, I**'ve just had** dinner.　또는
  I **just had** dinner.
- A: Is Tom here?
  B: No, sorry, he**'s just left**.　또는
  He **just left**.

Hi! Come in.

They **have just arrived**.
그들은 막 도착했다.

B

already = 벌써 (예상보다 먼저)

already는 현재완료 또는 단순과거와 사용한다.

- A: What time are Diane and Paul coming?
  B: They**'ve already arrived**.　또는
  They **already arrived**.
- It's only 9:00 and Anna **has already gone** to bed.
  또는　… Anna **already went** to bed.
  (= before I expected)
- A: Jon, this is Emma.
  B: Yes, I know. We**'ve already met**.　또는
  We **already met**.

Jon, this is Emma.

Yes, I know. We**'ve already met**.

C

yet = 아직

yet은 현재완료 또는 단순과거와 사용한다. **yet**은 부정문과 의문문에 사용하며, 주로 문장의 끝에 위치한다.

부정문의 **yet**

- A: Are Diane and Paul here?
  B: No, they **haven't arrived yet**.　또는
  … they **didn't arrive yet**.
  (B는 다이안과 폴이 곧 도착할 거라고 예상하고 있음)
- A: Does James know that you're going away?
  B: No, I **haven't told** him **yet**.　또는
  … I **didn't tell** him **yet**.
  (B는 제임스에게 곧 말하려고 함)
- Silvia has bought a new dress, but she **hasn't worn** it **yet**.　또는　… she **didn't wear** it **yet**.

The film **hasn't started yet**.
영화는 아직 시작하지 않았다.

의문문의 **yet**

- A: **Have** Diane and Paul **arrived yet**?　또는
  Did Diane and Paul **arrive yet**?
- B: No, not yet. We're still waiting for them.
- A: **Has** Nicole **started** her new job **yet**?　또는
  Did Nicole **start** her new job **yet**?
- B: No, she's starting next week.
- A: This is my new dress.
  B: Oh, it's nice. **Have** you **worn** it **yet**?　또는
  Did you **wear** it **yet**?

This is my new dress.

Oh, it's nice. **Have** you **worn** it **yet**?

Exercises

20.1 *just*를 사용하여 각 그림에 맞는 문장을 쓰시오.

1. _They've just arrived._   3. They _____
2. He _____   4. The race _____

20.2 *already*와 현재완료를 사용하여 문장을 완성하시오.

1.   What time is Paul arriving?   _He's already arrived._
2.   Do your friends want to see the movie?   No, they _____ it.
3.   Don't forget to call Tom.   I _____
4.   When is Martin going to work?   He _____
5.   Do you want to read the newspaper?   I _____
6.   When does Sarah start her new job?   She _____

20.3 현재완료를 사용하여 문장을 다시 쓰시오.

1. <u>Did Sarah start</u> her new job yet? _Has Sarah started her new job yet?_
2. <u>Did you tell</u> your father about the accident yet? _____
3. <u>I just ate</u> a big dinner, so I'm not hungry. _____
4. Jenny can watch TV because <u>she already did</u> her homework. _____
5. You can't go to bed – <u>you didn't brush</u> your teeth yet. _____
6. You can't talk to Pete because <u>he just went</u> home. _____
7. <u>Nicole just got out</u> of the hospital, so she can't go to work. _____

이제 아래의 문장을 단순과거로 다시 쓰시오.

8. <u>Have you given</u> the post office our new address yet?
   Did you give the post office our new address yet?
9. <u>The mail carrier hasn't come</u> yet. _____
10. <u>I've just spoken</u> to your sister. _____
11. <u>Has Mario bought</u> a new computer yet? _____
12. <u>Ted and Alice haven't told</u> anyone they're getting married yet.
   _____
13. <u>We've already done</u> our packing for our trip. _____
14. <u>I've just swum</u> a mile. I feel great! _____

20.4 현재완료와 *yet*을 사용하여 질문을 쓰시오.

1. Your friend has a new job. Perhaps she has started it. You ask her:
   Have you started your new job yet?
2. Your friend has some new neighbors. Maybe he has met them. You ask him:
   _____ you _____ ?
3. Your friend has to pay her phone bill. Perhaps she has paid it. You ask her:
   _____ ?
4. Tom was trying to sell his car. Maybe he has sold it. You ask a friend about Tom.
   _____ ?

I've lost my key. I lost my key last week.
(현재완료와 단순과거 3)

A

때로는 현재완료(I **have lost** / he **has gone** 등)와 단순과거(I **lost** / he **went** 등)를
모두 쓸 수 있다.

- "Is Peter here?" "No, he**'s gone** home." 또는 "No, he **went** home."

하지만 종결된 시간(**yesterday** / **last week** 등)과 함께 쓸 때는 단순과거만 가능하다(현재완료는
불가능).

단순과거 + 종결된 시간

We **arrived**	yesterday. last week. at 3:00. in 2002. six months ago.

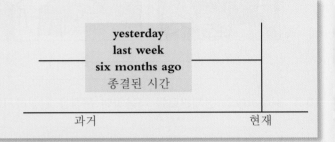

현재완료(**have arrived** / **have done** / **have been** 등)는 종결된 시간과 함께 쓰지 않는다.

- I **saw** Paula **yesterday**. (I have seen Paula yesterday는 틀림)
- Where **were** you **on Sunday afternoon**? (Where have you been on Sunday … ?는 틀림)
- We **didn't take** a vacation **last year**. 우리는 작년에 휴가를 가지 않았다.
- "What **did** you **do last night**?" "I **stayed** at home."
- William Shakespeare **lived from 1564 to 1616**. He **was** a writer. He **wrote** many plays and poems.
  윌리엄 셰익스피어는 1564년부터 1616년까지 살았다. 그는 작가였다. 그는 많은 희곡과 시를 썼다.

When … ? 또는 **What time … ?**은 단순과거와 함께 쓴다.

- **When did** you **buy** your computer? (When have you bought?는 틀림)
- **What time did** Andy **go** out? 앤디는 언제 나갔니?

B

비교:

현재완료 또는 단순과거를 모두 쓸 수 있는 경우

- I **have lost** my key. 또는 I **lost** my key. (= I can't find it *now*)
- Ben **has gone** home. 또는 Ben **went** home. (= he isn't here *now*)
- **Have** you **had** lunch? 또는 **Did** you **have** lunch?
- The letter **hasn't arrived** yet. 또는 The letter **didn't arrive** yet.

현재완료만 쓰는 경우	단순과거만 쓰는 경우
지금까지의 시간 → 과거 ————— 현재	종결된 시간 ——— 과거 ————— 현재
■ **Have** you **ever been** to Spain? (= 일생 동안, 지금까지)	■ **Did** you **go** to Spain **last year**?
■ My friend is a writer. He **has written** many books.	■ William Shakespeare (1564–1616) **wrote** many plays and poems.
■ The letter **hasn't arrived** yet.	■ The letter **didn't arrive** yesterday.
■ We**'ve lived** in Boston for six years. (= 지금 거기서 살고 있음)	■ We **lived** in Chicago for six years, but now we live in Boston. 우리는 시카고에서 6년간 살았지만 지금은 보스턴에서 산다.

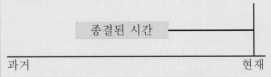

Exercises

21.1 질문에 대한 답을 완성하시오.

1.	Have you had lunch?
2.	Have you started your new job?
3.	Have your friends arrived?
4.	Has Sarah gone out?
5.	Have you worn your new suit?

Yes, _I had it_ _____ an hour ago.
Yes, I _____ last week.
Yes, they _____ on Friday.
Yes, _____ at 5:00.
Yes, _____ yesterday.

21.2 밑줄 친 동사 중 틀린 것을 고치시오. 맞으면 **OK**라고 쓰시오.

1. <u>I've lost</u> my key. I can't find it.   _OK_
2. <u>Have you seen</u> Kate yesterday?   _Did you see_
3. <u>I've finished</u> my work at 2:00.   _____
4. I'm ready now. <u>I've finished</u> my work.   _____
5. What time <u>have you finished</u> your work?   _____
6. Sue isn't here. <u>She's gone</u> out.   _____
7. Steve's grandmother <u>has died</u> two years ago.   _____
8. Where <u>have you been</u> last night?   _____

21.3 괄호 안의 동사를 현재완료 또는 단순과거로 쓰시오.

1. My friend is a writer. He _has written_ (write) many books.
2. We _didn't take_ (not / take) a vacation last year.
3. I _____ (play) tennis yesterday afternoon.
4. What time _____ (you / go) to bed last night?
5. _____ (you / ever / meet) a famous person?
6. The weather _____ (not / be) very good yesterday.
7. Kathy travels a lot. She _____ (visit) many countries.
8. I _____ (turn) off the light before leaving this morning.
9. I live in New York now, but I _____ (live) in Mexico for many years.
10. "What's Peru like? Is it beautiful?" "I don't know. I _____ (not / be) there."

21.4 동사를 현재완료 또는 단순과거로 써 넣으시오.

1. *A:* _Have you ever been_ (you / ever / be) to Florida?
   B: Yes, we _went_ (go) there on vacation two years ago.
   A: _____ (you / have) a good time?
   B: Yes, it _____ (be) great.

2. *A:* What does your friend do?
   B: She's a painter. She _____ (win) many prizes for her paintings.
   A: _____ (you / see) any of her paintings?
   B: Yes, I _____ (see) some of her work last week.

3. Rose works in a factory, but she _____ (have) a lot of different jobs.
   Five years ago she _____ (be) a waitress in a restaurant. After that, she
   _____ (work) on a ranch, but she _____
   (not / enjoy) it very much.

4. *A:* Do you know Martin's sister?
   B: I _____ (see) her a few times, but I _____
   (never / speak) to her. _____ (you / ever / speak) to her?
   A: Yes. I _____ (meet) her at a party last week. She's very nice.

is done   was done (수동태 1)

A

The office is **cleaned** every day.
사무실은 매일 청소된다.

The office was **cleaned** yesterday.
사무실은 어제 청소됐다.

능동태와 수동태의 비교:
Somebody **cleans** the office every day.　(능동)

The office **is cleaned** every day.　(수동)

Somebody **cleaned** the office yesterday.　(능동)

The office **was cleaned** yesterday.　(수동)

B

수동태:

				과거분사	
단순현재	**am/is/are**	(not)	+	cleaned	done
단순과거	**was/were**			invented	built
				injured	taken 등

규칙동사의 과거분사는 **-ed**이다(cleaned/damaged 등).

불규칙동사의 과거분사(**done/built/taken** 등) 목록은 부록 2–3 참조.

- Butter **is made** from milk.
- Oranges **are imported** into Korea. 오렌지는 한국으로 수입된다.
- How often **are** these rooms **cleaned**?
- I **am** never **invited** to parties. 나는 파티에 초대되는 법이 없다.

- This house **was built** 100 years ago.
- These houses **were built** 100 years ago.
- When **was** the telephone **invented**? 전화는 언제 발명되었습니까?
- We **weren't invited** to the party last week.
- "**Was** anybody **injured** in the accident?" 그 사고로 부상당한 사람이 있었습니까?
  "Yes, two people **were taken** to the hospital." 네, 두 사람이 병원으로 실려 갔어요.

C

was/were born
- I **was born** in Colombia in 1989. (I am born은 틀림)
- "Where **were** you **born**?"   "In Cairo."

D

수동태 + **by**: …에 의하여
- The telephone was invented **by Alexander Graham Bell** in 1876.
  (= Alexander Graham Bell invented it)
- I was bitten **by a dog** a few days ago. 며칠 전 나는 개한테 물렸다.
- Do you like these paintings? They were painted **by a friend of mine**.

---

is being done / has been done → Unit 23 불규칙동사 → Unit 25, 부록 2–3 **by** → Unit 112

능동태와 수동태 → 부록 1

Exercises

22.1 주어진 단어들을 사용하여 평서문 또는 의문문을 만드시오.
1-7번 문장은 현재시제입니다.

1. (the office / clean / every day) _The office is cleaned every day._
2. (these rooms / clean / every day?) _Are these rooms cleaned every day?_
3. (glass / make / from sand) Glass _____
4. (stamps / sell / in a post office) _____
5. (this word / not / use / very often) _____
6. (we / allow / to park here?) _____
7. (how / this word / pronounce?) _____

8-15번 문장은 과거시제입니다.

8. (the office / clean / yesterday) _The office was cleaned yesterday._
9. (the house / paint / last month) The house _____
10. (my phone / steal / a few days ago) _____
11. (three people / injure / in the accident) _____
12. (when / this bridge / build?) _____
13. (I / not / wake up / by the noise) _____
14. (how / these windows / break?) _____
15. (you / invite / to Jon's party last week?) _____
    _____

22.2 다음 문장에서 틀린 곳을 고쳐 쓰시오.
1. (This house built) 100 years ago. _This house was built 100 years ago._
2. Soccer plays in most countries of the world. _____
3. Why did the letter send to the wrong address? _____
4. A garage is a place where cars repair. _____
5. Where are you born? _____
6. How many languages are speaking in Switzerland? _____
7. Somebody broke into our house, but nothing stolen. _____
8. When was invented the bicycle? _____

22.3 아래 동사의 수동태(현재 또는 과거)를 사용하여 문장을 완성하시오.

~~clean~~   damage   find   give   invite   make   make   show   steal   ~~take~~

1. The room _is cleaned_ every day.
2. I saw an accident yesterday. Two people _were taken_ to the hospital.
3. Paper _____ from wood.
4. There was a fire at the hotel last week. Two of the rooms _____ .
5. "Where did you get this picture?" "It _____ to me by a friend of mine."
6. Many British programs _____ on American television.
7. "Did Jim and Sue go to the wedding?" "No. They _____ , but they didn't go."
8. "How old is this movie?" "It _____ in 1965."
9. My car _____ last week, but the next day it _____ by the police.

22.4 다음 사람들이 어디서 태어났는지 문장으로 쓰시오.
1. (Makoto / Tokyo) _Makoto was born in Tokyo._
2. (Isabel / São Paulo) Isabel _____
3. (her parents / Rio de Janeiro) Her _____
4. (you / ???) I _____
5. (your mother / ???) _____

is being done   has been done (수동태 2)

A   is/are being ... (현재진행 수동태)

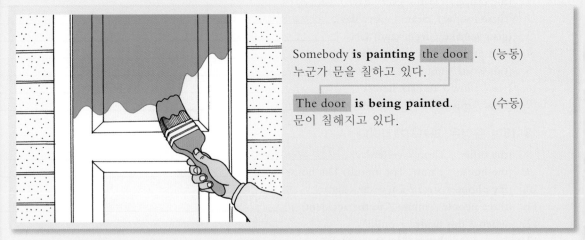

Somebody **is painting** the door . (능동)
누군가 문을 칠하고 있다.

The door **is being painted**. (수동)
문이 칠해지고 있다.

- My car is at the garage. It **is being repaired**. (= somebody is repairing it)
- Some new houses **are being built** across from the park. (= somebody is building them)

현재진형 수동태와 단순현재 수동태의 비교:
- The office **is being cleaned** right now. (현재진행 수동태)
  The office **is cleaned** every day. (단순현재 수동태)
- In the United States, football games **are** usually **played** on weekends, but no big games **are being played** next weekend.

현재진행과 단순현재에 대한 일반적인 설명은 Units 8, 26 참조.

B   has/have been ... (현재완료 수동태)

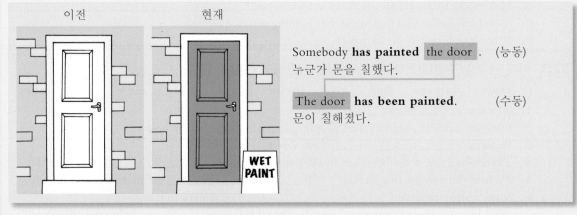

이전   현재

WET PAINT

Somebody **has painted** the door . (능동)
누군가 문을 칠했다.

The door **has been painted**. (수동)
문이 칠해졌다.

- My key **has been stolen**. (= somebody has stolen it)
- My keys **have been stolen**. (= somebody has stolen them)
- I'm not going to the party. I **haven't been invited**. (= nobody has invited me)
  난 파티에 안 가. 초대를 안 받았어.
- **Has** this shirt **been washed**? (= has somebody washed it?) 이 셔츠는 빨래가 된 거니?

현재완료와 단순과거의 비교:
- The room isn't dirty any more. It **has been cleaned**. (현재완료 수동태)
  The room **was cleaned** yesterday. (단순과거 수동태)
- I can't find my keys. I think they**'ve been stolen**. (현재완료 수동태)
  My keys **were stolen** last week. (단순과거 수동태)

현재완료와 단순과거는 Units 19–21 참조.

Exercises

23.1 무슨 일이 일어나고 있는지 쓰시오.

1. The car _is being repaired._
2. A bridge _____
3. The windows _____
4. The grass _____

23.2 현재진행(*is/are being* ...) 또는 현재완료(*has/have been* ...)를 사용하여 그림에 맞게 문장을 쓰시오.

1. (the office / clean) _The office is being cleaned._
2. (the shirts / iron) _The shirts have been ironed._
3. (the window / break) The window _____
4. (the roof / repair) The roof _____
5. (the car / damage) _____
6. (the houses / tear / down) _____
7. (the trees / cut / down) _____
8. (they / invite / to a party) _____

23.3 문장을 완성하시오(문제를 풀기 전에 **Unit 22**를 학습하시오).

1. I can't use my office right now. _It is being painted_ (paint).
2. We didn't go to the party. We _weren't invited_ (not / invite).
3. The washing machine was broken, but it's OK now. It _____ (repair).
4. The washing machine _____ (repair) yesterday afternoon.
5. A factory is a place where things _____ (make).
6. How old are these houses? When _____ (they / build)?
7. *A:* _____ (the computer / use) at the moment?
   B: Yes, Steve is using it.
8. I've never seen these flowers before. What _____ (they / call)?
9. My sunglasses _____ (steal) at the beach yesterday.
10. The bridge is closed. It _____ (damage) last week, and it
    _____ (not / repair) yet.

→ 추가연습문제 24–27 (255–256쪽)

현재시제와 과거시제에서 be/have/do

A

be (= am/is/are/was/were) + -ing (cleaning/working 등)

am/is/are + -ing (현재진행) → Units 3-4, 26

- Please be quiet. **I'm working**.
  제발 조용히 좀 해. 나 지금 공부하고 있어.
- It **isn't raining** right now.
- What **are** you **doing** tonight?

was/were + -ing (과거진행) → Unit 13

- I **was working** when she arrived.
- It **wasn't raining**, so we didn't need an umbrella.
  비가 오고 있지 않았기 때문에 우리는 우산이 필요 없었다.
- What **were** you **doing** at 3:00?

B

be + 과거분사 (cleaned/made/eaten 등)

am/is/are + 과거분사 (단순현재 수동태) → Unit 22

- I'm never **invited** to parties.
- Butter **is made** from milk.
  버터는 우유로 만들어진다.
- These offices **aren't cleaned** every day.

was/were + 과거분사 (단순과거 수동태) → Unit 22

- The office **was cleaned** yesterday.
- These houses **were built** 100 years ago.
- How **was** the window **broken**?
  유리창이 어떻게 깨졌니?
- Where **were** you **born**?

C

have/has + 과거분사 (cleaned/lost/eaten/been 등)

have/has + 과거분사 (현재완료) → Units 16-17, 19-21

- **I've lived** in this house for 10 years.
- Tom **has never ridden** a horse.
  탐은 한번도 말을 타 본 적이 없다.
- Kate **hasn't been** to South America.
- Where **have** Paul and Nicole **gone**?

D

do/does/did + 원형 (clean/like/eat/go 등)

do/does + 원형 (단순현재 부정문과 의문문) → Units 6-7

- I like coffee, but I **don't like** tea.
- Chris **doesn't go** out very often.
  크리스는 그다지 자주 외출하지 않는다.
- What **do** you usually **do** on weekends?
- **Does** Silvia **live** alone?

did + 원형 (단순과거 부정문과 의문문) → Unit 12

- I **didn't watch** TV yesterday.
  나는 어제 텔레비전을 보지 않았다.
- It **didn't rain** last week.
- What time **did** Paul and Nicole **go** out?

Exercises

24.1 *is/are* 또는 *do/does*를 써 넣으시오.

1. __*Do*__ you work at night?
2. Where __*are*__ they going?
3. Why _____ you looking at me?
4. _____ Bill live near you?
5. _____ you like to cook?
6. _____ the sun shining?
7. What time _____ the stores close?
8. _____ Maria working today?
9. What _____ this word mean?
10. _____ you feeling all right?

24.2 *am not/isn't/aren't* 또는 *don't/doesn't*를 써 넣으시오. 모든 문장은 부정문입니다.

1. Tom __*doesn't*__ work at night.
2. I'm very tired. I _____ want to go out tonight.
3. I'm very tired. I _____ going out tonight.
4. Gary _____ working this week. He's on vacation.
5. My parents are usually at home. They _____ go out very often.
6. Nicole has traveled a lot, but she _____ speak any foreign languages.
7. You can turn off the television. I _____ watching it.
8. Liz has invited us to her party next week, but we _____ going.

24.3 *was/were/did/have/has*를 써 넣으시오.

1. Where __*were*__ your shoes made?
2. _____ you go out last night?
3. What _____ you doing at 10:30?
4. Where _____ your mother born?
5. _____ Barbara gone home?
6. What time _____ she go?
7. When _____ these houses built?
8. _____ Steve arrived yet?
9. Why _____ you go home early?
10. How long _____ they been married?

24.4 *is/are/was/were/have/has*를 써 넣으시오.

1. Joe __*has*__ lost his passport.
2. This bridge _____ built 10 years ago.
3. _____ you finished your work yet?
4. This town is always clean. The streets _____ cleaned every day.
5. Where _____ you born?
6. I _____ just made some coffee. Would you like some?
7. Glass _____ made from sand.
8. This is a very old photograph. It _____ taken a long time ago.
9. David _____ bought a new car.

24.5 아래의 동사를 올바른 형태로 사용하여 문장을 완성하시오.

| damage | ~~rain~~ | enjoy | ~~go~~ | pronounce | eat |
| listen | use | open | go | understand | |

1. I'm going to take an umbrella with me. It's __*raining*__ .
2. Why are you so tired? Did you __*go*__ to bed late last night?
3. Where are the chocolates? Have you _____ all of them?
4. How is your new job? Are you _____ it?
5. My car was badly _____ in the accident, but I was OK.
6. Chris has a car, but she doesn't _____ it very often.
7. Mary isn't at home. She has _____ away for a few days.
8. I don't _____ the problem. Can you explain it again?
9. Martin is in his room. He's _____ to music.
10. I don't know how to say this word. How is it _____ ?
11. How do you _____ this window? Can you show me?

규칙동사와 불규칙동사

Exercises

A 규칙동사

규칙동사의 단순과거와 과거분사는 **-ed**로 끝난다:

clean → clean**ed**   live → liv**ed**   paint → paint**ed**   study → stud**ied**

단순과거 (→ Unit 11)

- I **cleaned** my room yesterday.
- Charlie **studied** engineering in college. 찰리는 대학에서 공학을 공부했다.

과거분사

have/has + 과거분사 (현재완료 → Units 16–17, 19–21):

- I **have cleaned** my room.
- Tina **has lived** in Miami for 10 years.

be (**is/are/were/has been** 등) + 과거분사 (수동태 → Units 22–23):

- These rooms **are cleaned** every day.
- My car **has been repaired**.

B 불규칙동사

불규칙동사의 단순과거와 과거분사는 **-ed**로 끝나지 않는다.

	make	break	cut
단순과거	**made**	**broke**	**cut**
과거분사	**made**	**broken**	**cut**

단순과거와 과거분사가 같은 경우도 있다. 예를 들어,

	make	find	buy	cut
단순과거 } 과거분사 }	**made**	**found**	**bought**	**cut**

- I **made** a cake yesterday. (단순과거)
- I **have made** some coffee. (과거분사 – 현재완료)
- Butter **is made** from milk. (과거분사 – 현재 수동태)

단순과거와 과거분사가 다른 경우도 있다. 예를 들어,

	break	know	begin	go
단순과거	**broke**	**knew**	**began**	**went**
과거분사	**broken**	**known**	**begun**	**gone**

- Somebody **broke** this window last night. (단순과거)
- Somebody **has broken** this window. (과거분사 – 현재완료)
- This window **was broken** last night. (과거분사 – 과거 수동태)

불규칙동사 → 부록 2–3   철자 (불규칙동사) → 부록 5

Exercises

25.1 아래의 동사들은 단순과거와 과거분사가 같습니다. 각 동사의 단순과거/과거분사를 쓰시오.

1. make   *made*
2. cut   *cut*
3. say   _____
4. bring   _____
5. pay   _____
6. enjoy   _____
7. buy   _____
8. sit   _____
9. leave   _____
10. happen _____
11. hear   _____
12. put   _____
13. catch _____
14. watch _____
15. understand _____

25.2 아래 동사의 단순과거와 과거분사를 쓰시오.

1. break *broke*   *broken*
2. begin _____   _____
3. eat   _____   _____
4. drink _____   _____
5. drive _____   _____
6. speak _____   _____
7. write _____   _____
8. come   _____   _____
9. know   _____   _____
10. take _____   _____
11. go   _____   _____
12. give _____   _____
13. throw _____   _____
14. get   _____   _____

25.3 괄호 안의 동사를 알맞은 형태로 써 넣으시오.

1. I _washed_ my hands because they were dirty. (wash)
2. Somebody has _broken_ this window. (break)
3. I feel good. I _____ very well last night. (sleep)
4. We _____ a really good movie yesterday. (see)
5. It _____ a lot while we were on vacation. (rain)
6. I've _____ my bag. (lose) Have you _____ it? (see)
7. Rosa's bicycle was _____ last week. (steal)
8. I _____ to bed early because I was tired. (go)
9. Have you _____ your work yet? (finish)
10. The shopping mall was _____ about 20 years ago. (build)
11. Anna _____ to drive when she was 16. (learn)
12. I've never _____ a horse. (ride)
13. Julia is a good friend of mine. I've _____ her for a long time. (know)
14. Yesterday I _____ and _____ my leg. (fall / hurt)
15. My brother _____ in the Boston Marathon last year. Have you ever _____ in a marathon? (run / run)

25.4 아래의 동사를 알맞은 형태로 사용하여 문장을 완성하시오.

cost	drive	fly	~~make~~	meet	sell
speak	swim	tell	think	wake up	win

1. I have _made_ some coffee. Would you like some?
2. Have you _____ John about your new job?
3. We played basketball on Sunday. We didn't play very well, but we _____ the game.
4. I know Gary, but I've never _____ his wife.
5. We were _____ by loud music in the middle of the night.
6. Stephanie jumped into the river and _____ to the other side.
7. "Did you like the movie?" "Yes, I _____ it was very good."
8. Many different languages are _____ in the Philippines.
9. Our vacation _____ a lot of money because we stayed in an expensive hotel.
10. Have you ever _____ a very fast car?
11. All the tickets for the concert were _____ very quickly.
12. A bird _____ in through the open window while we were having our dinner.

UNIT
26

What are you doing tomorrow?

A

오늘은 일요일이다.

I'm playing tennis tomorrow.

They **are playing** tennis (**now**).
그들은 (지금) 테니스를 치고 있다.

He **is playing** tennis **tomorrow**.
그는 내일 테니스를 친다.

am/is/are + -ing (현재진행)는 지금 일어나고 있는 일에 대해 말할 때 사용한다.
- "Where are Sue and Amanda?" "They**'re playing** tennis in the park."
- Please be quiet. I**'m working**.

am/is/are + -ing는 미래(tomorrow / next week 등)에 대해 말할 때도 사용한다.
- Andrew **is playing** tennis tomorrow.
- I**'m** not **working** next week. 나는 다음주에 일하지 않는다.

B

I am doing something tomorrow = 이미 예정해놓거나 계획한 일

I'm going to a concert tomorrow.

- Sophie **is going** to the dentist on Friday.
  (= 치과에 예약을 해놓음)
- We**'re having** a party next weekend.
- **Are** you **meeting** your friends tonight?
  오늘밤에 친구들 만나니?
- What **are** you **doing** tomorrow night?
- I**'m** not **going** out tonight. I**'m staying** at home.

"**I am going** to do something"도 같은 의미이다(→ Unit 27).

C

개인적으로 계획해놓은 일에 대해 말할 때는 단순현재(**I stay / do you go** 등)를 쓰지 않는다.
- I**'m staying** at home this evening. (I stay는 틀림)
- **Are** you **going** out tonight? (Do you go는 틀림)
- Lisa **isn't coming** to the party next week. 리사는 다음주 파티에 오지 않는다.

하지만 버스 운행, 영화 상영, 수업 시간과 같은 스케줄에 대해서는 단순현재를 쓴다.
- The plane **arrives** in New York at 7:30 tomorrow morning.
- What time **does** the movie **end** tonight? 오늘밤 영화가 몇 시에 끝나니?

비교:

현재진행 (사람들에 대해)	단순현재 (스케줄에 대해)
■ I**'m going** to a concert tomorrow.	■ The concert **starts** at 7:30.
■ What time **are** you **leaving**? 너는 몇 시에 떠나니?	■ What time **does** your plane **leave**? 네 비행기는 몇 시에 떠나니?

현재진행 → **Units 3–4**   단순현재 → **Units 5–7**   **I'm going to ...** → **Unit 27**

Exercises

26.1 그림을 보고 이들이 다음주 금요일에 무엇을 하는지 쓰시오.

| 1. Andrew | 2. Richard | 3. Rachel | 4. Karen | 5. Tom and Sue |

1. _Andrew is playing tennis on Friday._
2. Richard _____ to the movies.
3. Rachel _____
4. _____ lunch with Ken.
5. _____

26.2 괄호 안의 단어들로 의문문을 만드시오. 모든 문장은 미래입니다.

1. (you / go / out / tonight?) _Are you going out tonight?_
2. (you / work / next week?) _____
3. (what / you / do / tomorrow night?) _____
4. (what time / your friends / come?) _____
5. (when / Liz / go / on vacation?) _____

26.3 당신이 앞으로 며칠 안에 할 일에 대해 쓰시오.

1. _I'm staying at home tonight._
2. _I'm going to the theater on Monday._
3. _____
4. _____
5. _____
6. _____

26.4 현재진행(*he is leaving* 등) 또는 단순현재(*the train leaves* 등)를 사용하여 문장을 완성하시오.

1. "_Are you going_ (you / go) out tonight?" "No, I'm too tired."
2. _We're going_ (we / go) to a concert tonight. _It starts_ (it / start) at 7:30.
3. Listen to this! _____ (Karen / get) married next month!
4. *A:* My parents _____ (go) on vacation next week.
   B: Oh, that's nice. Where _____ (they / go)?
5. Silvia is taking an English course this semester. The course _____ (end) on Friday.
6. There's a party tomorrow night, but _____ (I / not / go).
7. _____ (I / go) out with some friends tonight. Why don't you come, too? _____ (we / meet) at John's house at 8:00.
8. *A:* How _____ (you / get) home after the party tomorrow? By taxi?
   B: No, I can go by bus. The last bus _____ (leave) at midnight.
9. *A:* Do you want to go to the movies tonight?
   B: Yes, what time _____ (the movie / begin)?
10. *A:* What _____ (you / do) tomorrow afternoon?
    B: _____ (I / work).

I'm going to …

A

I'm going to do something: …할 것이다, …할 계획이다

I'm going to watch TV tonight.

아침   오늘밤

She **is going to watch** TV tonight.   그녀는 오늘밤 텔레비전을 볼 것이다.

am/is/are going to …는 앞으로 할 일에 대해 쓴다.

I **am** he/she/it **is** we/you/they **are**	(not) **going to**	do … drink … watch …

am I **is** he/she/it **are** we/you/they	**going to**	buy … ? eat … ? wear … ?

B

I am going to do something = 나는 …하기로 결정했다, 나는 …할 작정이다

I decided to do it ⟶ **I'm going to do it** ⟶

과거   현재   미래

- **I'm going to buy** some books tomorrow.
- Sarah **is going to sell** her car.
- **I'm not going to have** breakfast this morning. I'm not hungry.
  오늘 아침엔 아침을 안 먹을 거야. 배가 안 고파.
- What **are** you **going to wear** to the wedding next week? 다음주 결혼식 때 뭘 입을 거니?
- "Your hands are dirty." "Yes, I know. **I'm going to wash** them."
- **Are** you **going to invite** Martin to your party? 파티에 마틴을 초대할 작정이니?

미래에 대해, 특히 주로 예정해놓은 일에 대해 말할 때 현재진행(**I am doing**)을
쓰기도 한다(→ Unit 26).

- I **am playing** tennis with Julia tomorrow. 나는 내일 줄리아와 테니스를 친다.

C

Something **is going to happen** = 현재 상황으로
보아 어떤 일이 일어날 것이 분명하다

- Look at the sky! It**'s going to rain**.
  (현재 검은 구름이 끼었음 → 비)
- Oh, no! It's 9:00, and I'm not ready.
  I'm going to be late.
  (현재 9시이고 준비가 되어 있지 않음 → 지각)

It's **going to rain**.

Exercises

27.1 그림을 보고 **be going to ...**를 사용하여 이들이 할 말을 적으시오.

27.2 **going to** + 아래의 동사를 사용하여 문장을 완성하시오.

> do   eat   give   lie down   stay   walk   ~~wash~~   watch   ~~wear~~

1. My hands are dirty. _I'm going to wash_ them.
2. What _are you going to wear_ to the party tonight?
3. It's a nice day. I don't want to take the bus. I _____ .
4. Steve is going to San Diego next week. He _____ with some friends.
5. I'm hungry. I _____ this sandwich.
6. It's Sharon's birthday next week. We _____ her a present.
7. Sue says she's feeling very tired. She _____ for an hour.
8. The president's speech is on television tonight. _____ you _____ it?
9. What _____ Rachel _____ when she finishes school?

27.3 그림을 보고 앞으로 무슨 일이 벌어질 것인지 쓰시오.

1. _It's going to rain._ _____
2. The shelf _____
3. The car _____
4. He _____

27.4 오늘이나 내일 당신이 하려고 하는 일을 **going to ...**를 사용하여 쓰시오.

1. I'm _____
2. _____
3. _____

will   1

A

Sarah goes to work every day. She is always there from 8:30 until 4:30.
사라는 매일 직장에 간다. 그녀는 8시 30분 부터 4시 30분까지 항상 직장에 있다.

It is 11:00 now. Sarah **is** at work.
지금은 11시이다. 사라는 직장에 있다.

At 11:00 yesterday, she **was** at work.
어제 11시에 그녀는 직장에 있었다.

At 11:00 tomorrow, she **will be** at work.
내일 11시에 그녀는 직장에 있을 것이다.

Sarah

will + 원형 (will be / will win / will come 등):

I/we/you/they he/she/it	**will ('ll)** **will not (won't)**	**be** **win** **eat** **come** 등

will	I/we/you/they he/she/it	**be?** **win?** **eat?** **come?** 등

'll = will: I**'ll** (I will) / you**'ll** / she**'ll** 등

won't = will not: I **won't** (= I will not) / you **won't** / she **won't** 등

B

will은 미래(tomorrow / next week 등)에 대해 말할 때 쓴다.
■ Sue travels a lot. Today she is in Los Angeles. Tomorrow she**'ll be** in Mexico City.
Next week she**'ll be** in New York.
■ You can call me tonight. I**'ll be** at home. 오늘밤 나한테 전화해도 돼. 나는 집에 있을 거야.
■ Leave the old bread in the yard. The birds **will eat** it.
오래된 빵은 마당에 둬라. 새들이 먹을 거야.
■ We**'ll** probably **go** out tonight.
■ **Will** you **be** at home tonight?

■ I **won't be** here tomorrow. 난 내일 여기 없을 거야. (= I will not be here)
■ Don't drink coffee before you go to bed. You **won't sleep**.

I think ... will ...이라는 표현을 많이 쓴다.
■ **I think** Kelly **will pass** her driver's test. 나는 켈리가 운전면허 시험에 합격할 것이라고 생각해.
■ **I don't think** it **will rain** this afternoon. 오늘 오후에 비가 올 것 같지가 않아.
■ **Do you think** the test **will be** difficult? 시험이 어려울 것 같니?

C

이미 예정되어 있거나 결정한 일에 대해서는 **will**을 쓰지 않는다(→ Units 26–27).
■ We**'re going** to the movies on Saturday. Do you want to come with us?
(We will go는 틀림) 우린 토요일에 영화 보러 갈 거야. 너도 같이 갈래?
■ I**'m** not **working** tomorrow. (I won't work는 틀림)
■ **Are** you **going to take** your driver's test tomorrow? (Will you take는 틀림)
내일 운전면허 시험 볼 거니?

Exercises

28.1 Helen은 남아메리카를 여행하고 있습니다. *she was /*
*she's / she'll be*를 사용하여 문장을 완성하시오.

1. Yesterday ___she was___ in Rio de Janeiro.
2. Tomorrow _____ in Bogotá.
3. Last week _____ in Santiago.
4. Next week _____ in Caracas.
5. Right now _____ in Lima.
6. Three days ago _____ in Buenos Aires.
7. At the end of her trip _____ very tired.

Helen

28.2 아래의 구문을 사용하여 다음 시각에 당신이 어디 있을지 쓰시오.
I'll be ... 또는 *I'll probably be ...* 또는 *I don't know where I'll be.*

1. (내일 10시) ___I'll be at work.___ 또는 ___I'll probably be at the beach.___
2. (지금부터 한 시간 뒤) _____
3. (오늘밤 자정) _____
4. (내일 오후 3시) _____
5. (지금부터 2년 뒤) _____

28.3 *will ('ll)* 또는 *won't*를 써 넣으시오.

1. Don't drink coffee before you go to bed. You ___won't___ sleep.
2. "Are you ready yet?" "Not yet. I _____ be ready in five minutes."
3. I'm going away for a few days. I'm leaving tonight, so I _____ be at home tomorrow.
4. It _____ rain, so you don't need to take an umbrella.
5. *A:* I don't feel very well tonight.
   B: Well, go to bed early, and you _____ feel better in the morning.
6. It's Bill's birthday next Monday. He _____ be 25.
7. I'm sorry I was late this morning. It _____ happen again.

28.4 *I think ...* 또는 *I don't think ...*를 사용하여 문장을 쓰시오.

1. (Kelly will pass the driver's test) ___I think Kelly will pass the driver's test.___
2. (Kelly won't pass the driver's test) ___I don't think Kelly will pass the driver's test.___
3. (we'll win the game) I _____
4. (I won't be here tomorrow) _____
5. (Sue will like her present) _____
6. (they won't get married) _____
7. (you won't like the movie) _____

28.5 맞는 것을 고르시오(문제를 풀기 전에 **Unit 26**을 학습하시오).

1. ~~We'll go~~ / We're going to the theater tonight. We've got tickets. (*We're going*이 맞음)
2. "What <u>will you do</u> / <u>are you doing</u> tomorrow night?" "Nothing. I'm free."
3. <u>They'll leave</u> / <u>They're leaving</u> tomorrow morning. Their train is at 8:40.
4. I'm sure your aunt <u>will lend</u> / <u>is lending</u> us some money. She's very rich.
5. "Why are you putting on your coat?" "<u>I'll go</u> / <u>I'm going</u> out."
6. Do you think Claire <u>will call</u> / <u>is calling</u> us tonight?
7. Steve can't meet us on Saturday. <u>He'll work</u> / <u>He's working</u>.
8. Let's fly to Miami instead of driving. It <u>won't take</u> / <u>isn't taking</u> as long.
9. *A:* What are your plans for the weekend?
   B: Some friends <u>will come</u> / <u>are coming</u> to stay with us.

A

> **I'll carry** it for you.

> Bye, **I'll call** you tomorrow, OK?

I'll ... (I will)은 무언가를 해주겠다고 제안하거나 어떤 것을 하겠다고 결심할 때 사용한다.
- "My suitcase is very heavy." "**I'll carry** it for you." 제가 들어드릴게요.
- "**I'll call** you tomorrow, OK?" 내일 전화할게. "OK, bye."

어떤 일을 하기로 결심할 때 **I think I'll ... / I don't think I'll ...**이라는 표현을 잘 쓴다.
- I'm tired. **I think I'll go** to bed early tonight. 피곤해. 오늘밤은 일찍 자야겠어.
- It's a nice day. **I think I'll sit** outside. 날씨가 좋네. 바깥에 앉을래.
- It's raining. **I don't think I'll go** out.

이러한 문장에서는 단순현재(**I go / I call** 등)를 쓰지 않는다.
- **I'll call** you tomorrow, OK? (I call you는 틀림)
- I think **I'll go** to bed early. (I go to bed는 틀림)

B

이미 결심한 일에 대해서는 **I'll ...**을 쓰지 않는다(→ Units 26-27).
- **I'm working** tomorrow. (I'll work는 틀림)
- There's a good program on TV tonight. **I'm going to watch** it.
  오늘밤 텔레비전에서 좋은 프로그램을 해. 나는 그걸 볼까 해.
- What **are** you **doing** this weekend? 이번 주말에 뭐 하니?

C

Shall I ... ? Shall we ... ?

> **Shall I** answer the phone?

> No, that's OK. I'll answer it.

Shall I / Shall we ... ? = ···해도 될까요/괜찮을까요? (상대방의 의견을 물어보는 표현)
- It's very warm in this room. **Shall I open** the window? 창문을 열어도 될까요?
- "**Shall I call** you tonight?" "OK."
- It's a nice day. **Shall we go** for a walk? 날씨가 좋군요. 같이 산책할까요?
- What **shall we have** for dinner? 저녁으로 뭘 먹을까요?

should도 같은 의미로 쓰인다.
- "**Should I call** you tonight?" 오늘밤에 전화해도 될까요? "OK."
- It's a nice day. **Should we go** for a walk?
- What **should we have** for dinner?

Exercises

29.1 *I'll (I will)* + 아래의 동사를 사용하여 문장을 완성하시오.

~~carry~~   do   eat   send   show   sit   stay

1. My suitcase is very heavy.   _I'll carry_ _____ it for you.
2. Enjoy your vacation.   Thank you. _____ you a postcard.
3. I don't want this banana.   Well, I'm hungry. _____ it.
4. Do you want a chair?   No, it's OK. _____ on the floor.
5. Did you call Jenny?   Oh no, I forgot. _____ it now.
6. Are you coming with me?   No, I don't think so. _____ here.
7. How do you use this camera?   Give it to me and _____ you.

29.2 *I think I'll ...* 또는 *I don't think I'll ...* + 아래의 동사를 사용하여 문장을 완성하시오.

buy   **buy**   ~~go~~   **have**   **play**

1. It's cold today. _I don't think I'll go_ _____ out.
2. I'm hungry. I _____ something to eat.
3. I feel very tired. _____ tennis.
4. I like this hat. _____ it.
5. This camera is too expensive. _____ it.

29.3 맞는 것을 고르시오.

1. ~~I call~~ / I'll call you tomorrow, OK? (*I'll call*이 맞음)
2. I haven't done the shopping yet. I do / I'll do it later.
3. I like sports. I watch / I'll watch a lot of sports on TV.
4. I need some exercise. I think I go / I'll go for a walk.
5. Gerry is going to buy / will buy a new car. He told me last week.
6. "This letter is for Rose."   "OK. I give / I'll give / I'm going to give it to her."
7. *A:* Are you doing / Will you do anything this evening?
   B: Yes, I'm going / I'll go out with some friends.
8. I can't go out with you tomorrow night. I work / I'm working / I'll work.
9. I like this hat. I think I buy / I'll buy it.

29.4 Anne이 Kathy에게 뭐라고 말합니까? 알맞은 대답을 고르시오.

Kathy   Anne

1. It's very warm in this room.   _d_   a) If you want. Where should we go?
2. This TV program isn't very good.   ___   b) Yes, who shall we invite?
3. Should we have a party?   ___   c) No, shall I go and get some?
4. It's dark in this room.   ___   d) Shall I open the window?
5. Should I go to the store?   ___   e) Should I turn on the light?
6. Shall we go out?   ___   f) OK, how many shall we buy?
7. Shall I wait here?   ___   g) Should I turn it off?
8. Do we have any bread?   ___   h) No, come with me.
9. Should we get some lottery tickets? ___   i) No, it's OK. I'll go.

→ 추가연습문제 28–31 (256–259쪽)   59

might

Where are you going for your vacation?

I'm not sure. I **might go** to Costa Rica.

It **might rain**.

He **might go** to Costa Rica.
그는 코스타리카에 갈지도 모른다.
(= it is possible that he will go to Costa Rica)

It **might rain**.
비가 올지도 모른다.
(= it is possible that it will rain)

might + 원형 (**might go** / **might be** / **might rain** 등):

I/we/you/they he/she/it	**might** (not)	**be** **go** **play** **come** 등

I might = ···할지도 모른다

- I **might go** to the movies tonight, but I'm not sure. (= it is possible that I will go)
- *A:* When is Rebecca going to call you?
  B: I don't know. She **might call** this afternoon.
- Take an umbrella with you. It **might rain**.
- Buy a lottery ticket. You **might be** lucky. 복권을 사. 운이 좋을지도 몰라.
- "Are you going out tonight?" "**I might**." (= I might go out)

차이점을 살펴보자.

- **I'm playing** tennis tomorrow. 난 내일 테니스 쳐. (확신)
  I **might play** tennis tomorrow. 난 내일 테니스 칠지도 몰라. (가능)
- Rebecca **is going to call** later. 레베카가 나중에 전화할 거야. (확신)
  Rebecca **might call** later. 레베카가 나중에 전화할지도 몰라. (가능)

I might not = ··· 안 할지도 모른다 / ··· 아닐지도 모른다

- I **might not go** to work tomorrow. 내일 회사에 안 갈지도 모른다.
- Sue **might not come** to the party. 수는 파티에 안 올지도 모른다.

may

may는 **might**와 의미가 같다.

- I **may go** to the movies tonight. (= I might go)
- Sue **may not come** to the party. (= Sue might not come)

May I ... ? = Is it OK to ... ? / Can I ... ? (···해도 될까요?)

- **May I** ask a question? (= is it OK to ask / can I ask?)
- "**May I** sit here?" 여기 앉아도 될까요? "Sure." 물론이에요.

Exercises

30.1 *might*를 사용하여 문장을 쓰시오.

1. (it's possible that I'll go to the movies) _I might go to the movies._
2. (it's possible that I'll see you tomorrow) I _____
3. (it's possible that Sarah will forget to call) _____
4. (it's possible that it will snow today) _____
5. (it's possible that I'll be late tonight) _____

*might not*을 사용하여 문장을 쓰시오.

6. (it's possible that Mark will not be here next week) _____
7. (it's possible that I won't have time to go out) _____

30.2 누군가 당신의 계획을 묻고 있지만 당신은 아직 확실한 계획이 없는 상태입니다.
아래의 단어와 *I might*를 사용하여 질문에 답하시오.

fish   ~~**Italy**~~   **Monday**   **a new car**   **take a trip**   **take a taxi**

1.	Where are you going for your vacation?	I'm not sure. _I might go to Italy._
2.	What are you doing this weekend?	I don't know. I _____
3.	When will you see Kate again?	I'm not sure. _____
4.	What are you going to have for dinner?	I don't know. _____
5.	How are you going to get home tonight?	I'm not sure. _____
6.	I hear you won some money. What are you going to do with it?	I haven't decided yet. _____

30.3 내일 **Bill**의 계획에 대한 아래의 질문과 대답을 읽으시오.

1.	Are you playing tennis tomorrow?	Yes, in the afternoon.
2.	Are you going out tomorrow evening?	Possibly.
3.	Are you going to get up early?	Maybe.
4.	Are you working tomorrow?	No, I'm not.
5.	Will you be at home tomorrow morning?	Maybe.
6.	Are you going to watch television?	I might.
7.	Are you going out in the afternoon?	Yes, I am.
8.	Are you going shopping?	Perhaps. I'm not sure.

Bill

이제 **Bill**에 대한 문장을 쓰시오. 필요한 경우 *might*를 사용하시오.

1. _He's playing tennis tomorrow afternoon._
2. _He might go out tomorrow evening._
3. He _____
4. _____
5. _____
6. _____
7. _____
8. _____

30.4 *might*를 사용하여 당신이 내일 할지도 모르는 일을 세 가지 쓰시오.

1. _____
2. _____
3. _____

can과 could

A

I **can play** the piano.

He **can play** the piano.
그는 피아노를 칠 수 있다.

Could you **open** the door, please?

"문 좀 열어 주시겠어요?"

can + 원형 (**can do** / **can play** / **can come** 등):

I/we/you/they he/she/it	**can** **can't (cannot)**	**do** **play** **see** **come** 등		**can**	I/we/you/they he/she/it	**do**? **play**? **see**? **come**? 등

B

I can do something = …을 할 줄 안다, …이 가능하다

■ I **can play** the piano. My brother **can play** the piano, too.
■ Sarah **can speak** Italian, but she **can't speak** Spanish.
■ "**Can** you **swim**?" "Yes, but I'm not a very good swimmer."
■ "**Can** you **change** a twenty-dollar bill?" 20달러짜리 지폐를 잔돈으로 바꿔줄 수 있어요?
"I'm sorry, I **can't**." 미안하지만 안 되겠는데요.
■ I'm having a party next week, but Paul and Rachel **can't come**.

C

과거의 일(**yesterday** / **last week** 등)에 대해서는 **could/couldn't**를 사용한다.

■ When I was young, I **could run** very fast.
■ Before Maria came to the United States, she **couldn't understand** much English.
Now she **can understand** everything.
■ I was tired last night, but I **couldn't sleep**.
■ I had a party last week, but Paul and Rachel **couldn't come**.

D

Can you … ? Could you … ? Can I … ? Could I … ?

Can you … ? / Could you … ?: 무엇을 해달라고 요청할 때

■ **Can you** open the door, please? 또는 **Could you** open the door, please?
■ **Can you** wait a minute, please? 또는 **Could you** wait … ?

Can I have … ? / Could I have … ?: 무엇을 달라고 요청할 때

■ (가게에서) **Can I have** change for a dollar, please? 또는 **Could I have** … ?

Can I … ? / Could I … ?: …해도 될까요? (= Is it OK to do something?)

■ Tom, **can I** borrow your umbrella? 또는 Tom, **could I** borrow your umbrella?
■ (전화상에서) Hello, **can I** speak to Gary, please? 또는 … **could I** speak … ?

May I … ? → Unit 30

Exercises

31.1 Steve에게 다음의 일들을 할 수 있는지 질문하시오.

1. 2. 3.

chess

4. 5. 6.

10 kilometers

You   Steve

1. ___Can you swim?___
2. _____
3. _____
4. _____
5. _____
6. _____

당신은 어떻습니까? **I can** 또는 **I can't**를 사용하여 자신에 대해 쓰시오.

7. I _____   10. _____
8. _____   11. _____
9. _____   12. _____

31.2 **can** 또는 **can't** + 아래의 동사를 사용하여 문장을 완성하시오.

~~come~~   find   hear   see   speak

1. I'm sorry, but we ___can't come___ to your party next Saturday.
2. I like this hotel room. You _____ the mountains from the window.
3. You are speaking very quietly. I _____ you.
4. Have you seen my suitcase? I _____ it.
5. Catherine got the job because she _____ five languages.

31.3 **can't** 또는 **couldn't** + 아래의 동사를 사용하여 문장을 완성하시오.

decide   eat   find   go   go   ~~sleep~~

1. I was tired, but I ___couldn't sleep___ .
2. I wasn't hungry yesterday. I _____ my dinner.
3. Kate doesn't know what to do. She _____ .
4. I wanted to speak to Martin yesterday, but I _____ him.
5. James _____ to the concert next Saturday. He has to work.
6. Paula _____ to the meeting last week. She was sick.

31.4 다음 상황에서 그림 속의 사람이 할 말을 쓰시오. **can** 또는 **could**를 사용하시오.

63

must

A

Tracey's not at work today.

She **must be** sick.

트레이시가 오늘 회사에 안 나왔군요.

그녀가 아픈 게 틀림없어요.

She **must be** sick = I am sure she is sick; it is clear that she is sick.

must + 원형 (**must be** / **must know** 등):

		be
I/we/you/they he/she/it	**must (not)**	know
		have
		live 등

must: …임에 틀림없다

- You worked 10 hours today. You **must be** tired.
- My brother has worked at your company for years. You **must know** him.
- My friends have the same zip code as you. They **must live** near you.
  내 친구들은 너랑 우편번호가 같아. 너희 집 근처에 살고 있는 게 틀림없어.
- (전화상에서) This isn't the Smiths'? I'm sorry. I **must have** the wrong number.

must not: …가 아닌 게 틀림없다

- The phone rang eight times and Karen didn't answer. She **must not be** at home.
  전화가 8번 울렸는데도 캐런이 받지 않았어. 집에 없는 게 분명해.
- Carlos takes the bus everywhere. He **must not have** a car.
- The Silvas are always home on Fridays. They **must not work** then.

B

You **must do** something: …해야 한다

- You **must be** careful with this knife. It's very sharp.
  이 칼은 조심해야 해. 무척 날카로워.
- Workers **must wear** safety glasses at this machine.
- In the United States, you **must be** 18 to vote.

과거의 일에 대해서는 **had to**를 사용한다 (must는 쓸 수 없음).

- They were in a dangerous situation. They **had to be** careful.
  (They must be careful은 틀림)
- We **had to wear** safety glasses when we visited the factory last week.
  지난주 공장을 방문했을 때 우리는 보안경을 써야 했다.

You **must not do** something = …하지 않아야 한다, …해서는 안 된다

- Bicyclists **must not ride** on the sidewalk.
  보도에서 자전거를 타서는 안 된다.
  (= they must ride in the street)
- You **must not be** late for school again!

Workers Must Wear Safety Glasses!

Bicyclists Must Not Ride on the Sidewalk

Exercises

32.1 *must be* + 아래의 단어를 사용하여 문장을 완성하시오.

> **for you**   **good**   **hungry**   **in the kitchen**   ~~**tired**~~   **very happy**

1. Silvia worked 10 hours today. She _must be tired_ .
2. It's evening, and you haven't eaten anything all day. You _____ .
3. It's the most popular restaurant in town, so the food _____ .
4. "I got the job." "You did? You _____ ."
5. The phone's ringing. I know it's not for me. It _____ .
6. My keys aren't in the living room, so they _____ .

32.2 *must* + 아래의 동사를 사용하여 문장을 완성하시오.

> **drink**   **have**   ~~**know**~~   **like**   **work**

1. My brother has worked at your company for years. You _must know_ him.
2. Marilyn wears something blue every day. She _____ the color blue.
3. The Hills have six children and three dogs. They _____ a big house.
4. Mrs. Lee bought three gallons of milk at the store. Her children _____ a lot of milk.
5. I know Mrs. Romo has a job, but she's always home during the day. She _____ at night.

32.3 *must* 또는 *must not*을 써 넣으시오.

1. (전화상에서) This isn't the Smiths'? I _must_ have the wrong number.
2. Carlos takes the bus everywhere. He _must not_ have a car.
3. Brandon is very thin. He _____ eat very much.
4. I never see my neighbor in the morning. He _____ leave for work very early.
5. I always have to repeat things when I talk to Kelly. She _____ hear very well.
6. Jim wears the same clothes every day. He _____ have many clothes.
7. You have a cold and a fever? Poor thing! You _____ feel awful.

32.4 *must* + 아래의 동사를 사용하여 문장을 완성하시오.

> ~~**be**~~   **be**   **get**   **know**   **take**   **wear**

1. In most of the United States, you _must be_ at least 16 to get a driver's license.
2. For this job, you _____ both Spanish and German.
3. People in the front seat of a car _____ a seat belt.
4. High school students who want to go to college _____ good grades.
5. This highway is closed. Drivers _____ another road.
6. A tennis player _____ very good to play professionally.

32.5 빈칸에 *must, mustn't* 또는 *had to*를 써 넣으시오.

1. We _mustn't_ forget to send Sam a birthday card.
2. We _had to_ wear safety glasses when we visited the factory.
3. I _____ hurry or I'll be late.
4. "Why were you so late?" "I _____ wait half an hour for the bus."
5. Keep these papers in a safe place. You _____ lose them.
6. Bicyclists _____ follow the same traffic rules as drivers.
7. We _____ forget to turn off the lights when we leave.
8. I don't usually work on Saturdays, but last Saturday I _____ work.

should

A

You **shouldn't watch** TV so much.   텔레비전을 그렇게 많이 봐서는 안 돼.

should + 원형 (should do / should watch 등):

		do
I/we/you/they	**should**	stop
he/she/it	**shouldn't**	go
		watch 등

B

You **should do** something = ···해야 한다 (좋고 옳은 일이기 때문에 해야 한다는 의미)

- Tom doesn't study enough. He **should study** harder.
  탐은 공부를 충분히 하지 않는다. 그는 더 열심히 공부해야 한다.
- It's a good movie. You **should go** and see it.
- When you play tennis, you **should** always **watch** the ball.
  테니스를 칠 때는 항상 공을 잘 봐야 한다.

Should I/we **do** something? = ···하는 게 좋을까? / ···해야 하나?

- **Should** I **invite** Karen to dinner? 캐런을 저녁식사에 초대하는 게 좋을까요?
- **Should** we **make** something special for dinner?

C

You **shouldn't do** something = ···하지 않는 게 좋다 (**shouldn't** = should not)

- Tom **shouldn't go** to bed so late.
- You watch TV all the time. You **shouldn't watch** TV so much.

D

I think ... **should** ... = ···하는 게 좋겠다

- **I think** Lisa **should buy** some new clothes.
  리사는 새 옷을 좀 사는 게 좋겠어.
  (= I think it is a good idea.)
- It's late. **I think** I **should go** home now.
- *A:* Shall I buy this coat?
  B: Yes, **I think** you **should**.

Do you think I **should
buy** this hat?

I **don't think** ... **should** ... = ···하지 않는 게 좋겠다

- **I don't think** you **should work** so hard.
  (= I don't think it is a good idea.)
- **I don't think** we **should go** yet. It's too early.

Do you think ... **should** ... ? = ···하는 게 좋을까?

- **Do you think** I **should buy** this hat?
- What time **do you think** we **should go** home?
  몇 시에 집에 가는 게 좋을까?

E

should는 **have to**와 다르다.

- I **should** study tonight, but I think I'll go to the movies.
  오늘밤에는 공부하는 게 마땅하지만 난 영화 보러 가야겠어.
- I **have to** study tonight. I can't go to the movies.
  난 오늘밤 공부를 해야 해. 극장에 갈 수가 없어.

F

should 대신 **ought to**를 사용할 수 있다.

- I **ought to study** tonight, but I think I'll go to the movies. (= I should study)
- I think Lisa **ought to buy** some new clothes. (= Lisa should buy)

    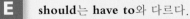 **shall/should** → Unit 29   **must** → Unit 32   **have to** → Unit 34

Exercises

33.1 *you should* + 아래의 동사를 사용하여 문장을 완성하시오.

> eat   go   read   visit   ~~watch~~   wear

1. When you play tennis, __*you should watch*__ the ball.
2. It's late, and you're very tired. _____ to bed.
3. _____ plenty of fruit and vegetables.
4. If you have time, _____ the Science Museum. It's very interesting.
5. When you're driving, _____ a seat belt.
6. It's a very good book. _____ it.

33.2 *He/She shouldn't ... so ...*를 사용하여 그림 속 사람들에 대해 쓰시오.

1. ____*She shouldn't watch TV so much.*_____   3. _____ hard.
2. He _____   4. _____

33.3 당신은 결정을 못 내리고 친구의 의견을 묻고 있습니다. *Do you think I should ... ?*를 사용하여 질문을 쓰시오.

1. You are in a store. You are trying on a jacket. (buy?)
   You ask your friend: __*Do you think I should buy this jacket?*_____
2. You can't drive. (learn?)
   You ask your friend: Do you think _____
3. You don't like your job. (get another job?)
   You ask your friend: _____
4. You are going to have a party. (invite Gary?)
   You ask your friend: _____

33.4 *I think ... should ...* 또는 *I don't think ... should ...*를 사용하여 문장을 쓰시오.

1. We have to get up early tomorrow. (go home now) __*I think we should go home now.*__
2. That coat is too big for you. (buy it) __*I don't think you should buy it.*__
3. You don't need your car. (sell it) _____
4. Karen needs a change. (take a trip) _____
5. Sally and Dan are too young. (get married) _____
6. You're still sick. (go to work) _____
7. James isn't feeling well today. (go to the doctor) _____
8. The hotel is too expensive for us. (stay there) _____

33.5 *should*를 사용하여 당신의 의견을 쓰시오.

1. I think __*everybody should learn another language.*__
2. I think everybody _____
3. I think _____
4. I don't think _____
5. I think I _____

I have to ...

A

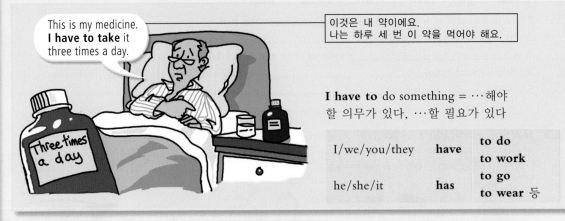

This is my medicine. **I have to take** it three times a day.

Three times a day

이것은 내 약이에요.
나는 하루 세 번 이 약을 먹어야 해요.

I have to do something = ···해야 할 의무가 있다, ···할 필요가 있다

| I/we/you/they | **have** | **to do**
to work |
| he/she/it | **has** | **to go**
to wear 등 |

- I'll be late for work tomorrow. I **have to go** to the dentist.
  내일 직장에 좀 늦을 거예요. 치과에 가야 하거든요.
- Jane starts work at 7:00, so she **has to get up** at 6:00.
- You **have to pass** a test before you can get a driver's license.
  운전면허를 따려면 그 전에 시험에 합격해야 한다.

B

과거(**yesterday** / **last week** 등)는 **had to** ...를 사용한다.

- I was late for work yesterday. I **had to go** to the dentist.
- We **had to walk** home last night. There were no buses.

C

의문문과 부정문에서는 **do/does** (현재)와 **did** (과거)를 사용한다.

현재

| **do** | I/we/you/they | **have to** ... ? |
| **does** | he/she/it | |

| I/we/you/they | **don't** | **have to** ... |
| he/she/it | **doesn't** | |

과거

| **did** | I/we/you/they
he/she/it | **have to** ... ? |

| I/we/you/they
he/she/it | **didn't have to** ... |

- What time **do you have to go** to the dentist tomorrow? 내일 치과에 몇 시에 가야 하니?
- **Does** Jane **have to work** on Saturdays?
- Why **did** they **have to leave** the party early? 왜 그렇게 일찍 파티장을 떠나야 했니?

I don't have to (do something) = ···할 필요가 없다

- I'm not working tomorrow, so I **don't have to get** up early.
- Mike **doesn't have to work** very hard. He's got an easy job.
  마이크는 별로 열심히 일해야 할 필요가 없다. 그가 하는 일은 쉽다.
- We didn't **have to wait** very long for the bus – it came in a few minutes.
  우리는 버스를 오랫동안 기다릴 필요가 없었다. 버스는 몇 분 만에 왔다.

D

must

'···해야 할 필요가 있다'라는 의미로 또한 **must**를 사용할 수 있다.

- You **must** pass a test before you can get a driver's license.
- In many countries, men **must** do military service.
  많은 나라에서 남자들은 군복무를 해야 한다.

일상회화에서는 **must**보다 **have to**를 더 많이 사용한다.

Exercises

34.1 *have to* 또는 *has to* + 아래의 동사를 사용하여 문장을 완성하시오.

hit   read   speak   take   travel   ~~wear~~

1. My eyes are not very good. I _*have to wear*_ glasses.
2. At the end of the course all the students _____ a test.
3. Sarah is studying literature. She _____ a lot of books.
4. Alberto doesn't understand much English. You _____ very slowly to him.
5. Kate is not at home much. She _____ a lot for her job.
6. In tennis you _____ the ball over the net.

34.2 *have to* 또는 *had to* + 아래의 동사를 사용하여 문장을 완성하시오.

answer   buy   change   go   take   wake   ~~walk~~

1. We _*had to walk*_ home last night. There were no buses.
2. It's late. I _____ now. I'll see you tomorrow.
3. I went to the store after work yesterday. I _____ some food.
4. This train doesn't go all the way downtown. You _____ at First Avenue.
5. We took a test yesterday. We _____ six questions out of ten.
6. I'm going to bed. I _____ up early tomorrow.
7. Amy and her cousin can't go out with us tonight. They _____ care of Amy's little brother.

34.3 질문을 완성하시오. 일부는 현재이고 일부는 과거입니다.

1.	I have to get up early tomorrow.	What time _*do you have to get up*_ ?
2.	George had to wait a long time.	How long _____ ?
3.	Liz has to go somewhere.	Where _____ ?
4.	We had to pay a lot of money.	How much _____ ?
5.	I have to do some work.	What exactly _____ ?
6.	They had to leave early.	Why _____ ?
7.	Paul has to go to Moscow.	When _____ ?

34.4 *don't/doesn't/didn't have to* ...를 사용하여 문장을 쓰시오.

1. Why are you going out? You _*don't have to go*_ out.
2. Why is Sue waiting? She _____ .
3. Why did you get up early? You _____ .
4. Why is Paul working so hard? He _____ .
5. Why do you want to leave now? We _____ .
6. Why did they tell me something I already know? They _____ .

34.5 당신(또는 친구나 가족)이 해야 하는 일 또는 해야 했던 일을 *have to / had to*를 사용하여 쓰시오.

1. (every day) _*I have to drive 50 miles to work every day.*_
2. (every day) _____
3. (yesterday) _____
4. (tomorrow) _____
5. (last week) _____
6. (when I was younger) _____

Would you like … ?   I'd like …

A

Would you like … ? = …하시겠어요?
(Do you want … ?)

Would you like … ?는 뭔가를 권할 때 사용한다.

- *A:* **Would you like** some coffee?
  커피 드시겠어요?
  B: No, thank you. 아니요, 괜찮습니다.
- *A:* **Would you like** a piece of candy?
  사탕 드시겠어요?
  B: Yes, thanks. 네, 고마워요.
- *A:* Which **would you like**, tea or coffee?
  B: Tea, please.

Would you like to … ?는 뭔가를 하자고 청할 때 사용한다.

- **Would you like to go** for a walk? 산책하실래요?
- *A:* **Would you like to have** dinner with us on Sunday?
  B: Yes, **I'd love to**. (= I would love to have dinner with you)
- What **would you like to do** tonight?

B

I'd like … 는 'I want'보다 공손한 표현이다. (**I'd** like = **I would** like)

- I'm thirsty. **I'd like** a drink.
- (관광 안내소에서) **I'd like** some information about hotels, please.
  호텔에 대한 정보를 알고 싶습니다.
- I'm feeling tired. **I'd like to stay** home tonight.

C

Would you like … ?와 **Do you like … ?**

Would you like … ? / I'd like …

Would you like some coffee? = 커피 좀
드시겠어요?

- *A:* **Would you like** to go to the movies
  tonight?
  (= do you want to go *tonight*?)
  B: Yes, I'd love to.

- **I'd like** an orange, please.
  (= can I have an orange?)

- What **would you like** to do next
  weekend? 다음 주말에 뭘 하고 싶으세요?

Do you like … ? / I like …

Do you like coffee? = 커피 좋아하세요?

- *A:* **Do you like** to go to the movies?
  (일반적으로)
  B: Yes, I go to the movies a lot.

- **I like** oranges. (일반적으로)

- What **do you like** to do on weekends?
  주말에 뭘 하는 걸 좋아해요?

like to do와 **like -ing** → Unit 53   **I would do** something **if** … → Unit 101

Exercises

35.1 그림 속의 사람들이 할 말을 *Would you like ... ?*를 사용하여 쓰시오.

1. Would you like a piece of candy?
2.
3.
4.
5.
6.

35.2 다음 상황에서 Sue에게 할 질문을 *Would you like to ... ?*를 사용하여 만드시오.

1. You want to go to the movies tonight. Perhaps Sue will go with you. (go)
   You ask: _Would you like to go to the movies tonight?_
2. You want to play tennis tomorrow. Perhaps Sue will play, too. (play)
   You ask: _____
3. You have an extra ticket for a concert next week. Perhaps Sue will come. (come)
   You ask: _____
4. It's raining and Sue is going out. She doesn't have an umbrella, but you have one. (borrow)
   You ask: _____

35.3 맞는 것을 고르시오.

1. "~~Do you like~~ / Would you like a piece of candy?"   "Yes, thanks." (*Would you like*가 맞음)
2. "Do you like / Would you like bananas?"   "Yes, I love them."
3. "Do you like / Would you like some ice cream?"   "No, thank you."
4. "What do you like / would you like to drink?"   "A glass of water, please."
5. "Do you like / Would you like to go out for a walk?"   "Not now. Maybe later."
6. I like / I'd like tomatoes, but I don't eat them very often.
7. What time do you like / would you like to have dinner tonight?
8. "Do you like / Would you like something to eat?"   "No, thanks. I'm not hungry."
9. "Do you like / Would you like your new job?"   "Yes, I'm enjoying it."
10. I'm tired. I like / I'd like to go to bed now.
11. "I like / I'd like a sandwich, please."   "Sure. What kind of sandwich?"
12. "What kind of music do you like / would you like?"   "All kinds."

I'd rather ...

A

Would you like to sit here?

여기 앉을래요?

No, thanks. **I'd rather** sit on the floor.

아뇨, 괜찮아요.
전 그냥 바닥에 앉을래요.

Ann은 바닥에 앉는 걸 좋아한다. 그녀는 의자에 앉고 싶어하지 않는다. 그래서 그녀는 다음과 같이 말한다.

I'd rather sit on the floor. (= I would prefer to sit on the floor.)

I'd rather ... = I **would** rather ...

I **would rather** do something = 나는 …하는 게 더 좋다 (I would prefer to do something)

긍정문		부정문		의문문	
I'd rather (I **would rather**)	do stay have be	**I'd rather not** (I **would rather not**)	do stay have be	**would** you **rather**	do … ? stay … ? have … ? be … ?

- I don't really want to go out. **I'd rather stay** home. (= I'd prefer to stay home)
- "Should we go now?"   "No, not yet. **I'd rather wait** until later."
- I'd like to go now, but Tom **would rather wait** until later.
  난 지금 가고 싶지만, 탐은 나중까지 기다리길 원한다.
- I don't like to be late. **I'd rather be** early.

- I'm feeling tired. **I'd rather not go out** tonight. (= I'd prefer not to go out)
- Sue is feeling tired. She**'d rather not go out** tonight.
- We're not hungry. We**'d rather not eat** yet.
- "Would you like to go out tonight?"   "**I'd rather not**." (= I'd rather not go out)

- "**Would** you **rather have** milk or juice?"   "Juice, please."
- Which **would** you **rather do** – go to the movies or watch a DVD at home?
  영화관에 가는 것과 집에서 DVD 보는 것, 둘 중에 어느 걸 더 하고 싶니?

B

I **would rather** + 동사원형:
- **I'd rather sit** on the floor. (I'd rather to sit는 틀림)
- Sue **would rather** not **go** out. (would rather not to go는 틀림)

I **would prefer** + to 부정사:
- **I'd prefer to sit** on the floor.
- Sue **would prefer** not **to go** out.

C

I'd rather ... than ... = …보다 …하는 게 더 좋다
- **I'd rather** go out **than** stay home. 집에 있기보다는 밖에 나갔으면 좋겠어.
- **I'd rather** have a dog **than** a cat.
- We**'d rather** go to the movies **than** watch a DVD at home.
- **I'd rather** be at home right now **than** here.

Exercises

36.1 그림을 보고 *I'd rather* ...를 사용하여 B의 문장을 완성하시오.

A   B

1. Would you like to sit here? → No, thanks. *I'd rather sit* _____ on the floor.

2. Don't you want to watch TV? → No, I _____ my book.

3. Would you like some tea? → Well, _____ coffee if you have some.

4. Should we go out now? → _____ until it stops raining.

36.2 *would you rather* ...를 사용하여 질문을 완성하시오.

1. Do you want to go out, or _would you rather stay_ home?
2. Should we have dinner now, or _____ later?
3. Would you like a glass of juice, or _____ water?
4. Do you want to go to the movies, or _____ TV?
5. Should we call your brother tonight, or _____ tomorrow morning?

36.3 동사를 써 넣어 문장을 완성하시오. *to*를 넣어야 하는 경우도 있습니다.

1. I'd rather _stay_ home tonight. I'd prefer not _to go_ out.
2. Should we walk home, or would you rather _____ a taxi?
3. Do you want me to come with you, or would you prefer _____ alone?
4. Mary doesn't want to go to college. She'd rather _____ a job.
5. "Can I help you with your suitcase?"   "No, thank you. I'd rather _____ it myself."
6. I'd rather not _____ him. I'd prefer _____ him a letter.

36.4 자신의 생각대로 질문에 답하시오. *I'd rather ... than* ...을 사용하시오.

1. Which would you prefer to be – a bus driver or an airplane pilot?
   I'd rather be a bus driver than an airplane pilot.

2. Which would you prefer to be – a journalist or a school teacher?
   _____

3. Where would you prefer to live – in a big city or a small town?
   _____

4. Which would you prefer to have – a small house or a big one?
   _____

5. Which would you prefer to study – electronics or philosophy?
   _____

6. Which would you prefer to watch – a soccer game or a movie?
   _____

Do this!   Don't do that!   Let's do this!

명령문은 **come**, **look**, **go**, **wait**, **do**, **be** 등 동사원형을 사용한다.

■ "**Come** here and **look** at this." 이리 와서 이것 좀 봐.   "What is it?"
■ I don't want to talk to you. **Go** away! 당신과 얘기하고 싶지 않아요. 가세요!
■ I'm not ready yet. Please **wait** for me.
■ Please **be** quiet. I'm working.

일반동사 **have**의 명령문:

■ Bye! **Have** a good trip! / **Have** a nice time! / **Have** a good flight! / **Have** fun!
  (= I hope you have a good trip. 등)
■ "**Have** some candy."   "Oh, thanks."
  (= would you like some candy?)

B

부정명령문은 **don't** ...를 사용한다.

■ Be careful! **Don't fall**. 조심해. 떨어지지 마.
■ Please **don't go**. Stay here with me.
■ Be here on time. **Don't be** late. 여기에 정시에 와. 늦지 마.

C

사람들에게 어떤 것을 같이 하자는 뜻으로 **Let's** ...를 사용할 수 있다. (**let's** = let us)

■ It's a nice day. **Let's go** out.
■ Come on! **Let's dance**.
■ Are you ready? **Let's go**.

■ **Let's have** fish for dinner tonight.
  오늘 저녁에는 생선을 먹자.
■ *A:* Should we go out tonight?
  B: No, I'm tired. **Let's stay** home.

부정형은 **Let's not** ...이다.

■ It's cold. **Let's not** go out. Let's stay home.
  날씨가 춥구나. 나가지 말자. 집에 있자.
■ **Let's not** have fish for dinner tonight. Let's have chicken.
■ I'm tired of arguing. **Let's not** do it anymore.
  말다툼하는 것에 지쳤어. 더 이상 말다툼을 하지 말자.

Exercises

37.1 그림 속의 사람들이 할 말을 아래의 동사를 사용하여 쓰시오. 일부는 긍정문(***buy/come*** 등) 이고 일부는 부정문(***don't buy / don't come*** 등)입니다.

be   buy   ~~come~~   ~~drink~~   drop   forget   have   sit   sleep   smile

1. _Come_ in!

2. _Don't drink_ the water.

3. It's too expensive. _____ it.

4. OK, are you ready? _____ !

5. _____ on the cat!

6. Bye! _____ a nice time.

7. _____ to call me.
   Don't worry. I won't.

8. I'm going to bed now.
   OK. _____ well.

9. _____ careful with that vase. _____ it!

37.2 ***let's***와 아래의 표현을 사용하여 문장을 완성하시오.

~~go for a swim~~   go to a restaurant   take the bus   wait a little   watch TV

1. Would you like to play tennis?   No, _let's go for a swim_ .
2. Do you want to walk home?   No, _____ .
3. Shall I put a CD on?   No, _____ .
4. Should we have dinner at home?   No, _____ .
5. Would you like to go now?   No, _____ .

37.3 ***No, don't*** ... 또는 ***No, let's not*** ...을 사용하여 답하시오.

1. Shall I wait for you?   _No, don't wait for me._
2. Should we go home now?   _No, let's not go home yet._
3. Shall we go out?   _____
4. Do you want me to close the window? _____
5. Should I call you tonight?   _____
6. Do you think we should wait for Andy? _____
7. Do you want me to turn on the light? _____
8. Should we take a taxi?   _____

there is   there are

There's a man on the roof.
지붕 위에 한 남자가 있다.

There's a train at 10:30.
10시 30분에 기차가 있다.

There are seven days in a week.
1주일은 7일이다.

단수

there is ...	(there's)
is there ... ?	
there is not ...	(there isn't
	또는 **there's not**)

- **There's** a big tree in the yard.
- **There's** nothing on TV tonight.
  오늘밤에는 TV에 볼 것이 없다.
- *A:* Do you have any money?
  B: Yes, **there's** some in my wallet.
- *A:* Excuse me, **is there** a hotel near here?
  B: Yes, **there is**. / No, **there isn't**.
- We can't go skiing. **There isn't** any snow.

복수

there are ...	
are there ... ?	
there are not ...	(there aren't)

- **There are** some big trees in the yard.
- **There are** a lot of accidents on this road.
- *A:* **Are there** any restaurants near here?
  B: Yes, **there are**. / No, **there aren't**.
- This restaurant is very quiet. **There aren't** many people here.
- How many players **are there** on a soccer team?
  축구팀에는 선수가 몇 명 있는가?
- **There are** 11 players on a soccer team.

there is와 **it is**

there is

it is

There's a book on the table.
탁자 위에 책이 있다.
(It's a book on the table은 틀림)

I like this book . **It's** interesting.
나는 이 책을 좋아한다. 그것은 재미있다.
(**it** = this book)

비교:

- "What's **that noise**?"   "**It's** a train." (It = that noise)
  There's a train at 10:30. **It's** a fast train. (It = the 10:30 train)
  10시 30분에 기차가 있다. 급행열차이다.

- **There's** a lot of salt in this soup. 이 수프에는 소금이 많이 들어가 있다.
  I don't like **this soup**. **It's** too salty. (It = this soup)

there was / were / has been 등 → Unit 39   **it**과 **there** → Unit 40   **some**과 **any** → Unit 77

Exercises

38.1 Springfield라는 마을에 관한 다음 정보를 보고 *There is/are* 또는 *There isn't/aren't*를 사용하여 문장을 쓰시오.

1.	a golf course?	No
2.	any restaurants?	Yes (a lot)
3.	a hospital?	Yes
4.	a swimming pool?	No
5.	any movie theaters?	Yes (two)
6.	a university?	No
7.	any big hotels?	No

1. _There isn't a golf course._
2. _There are a lot of restaurants._
3. _____
4. _____
5. _____
6. _____
7. _____

38.2 당신이 사는 동네(또는 아는 동네)에 대해 쓰시오. *There is/are* 또는 *There isn't/aren't*를 사용하시오.

1. _There are a few restaurants._
2. _There's a big park._
3. _____
4. _____
5. _____
6. _____

38.3 빈칸에 *there is / there isn't / is there* 또는 *there are / there aren't / are there*를 써 넣으시오.

1. Springfield isn't an old town. _There aren't_ any old buildings.
2. Look! _____ a photograph of your brother in the newspaper!
3. "Excuse me, _____ a bank near here?"   "Yes, at the end of the block."
4. _____ five people in my family: my parents, my two sisters, and me.
5. "How many students _____ in the class?"   "Twenty."
6. The road is usually very quiet. _____ much traffic.
7. "_____ a bus from downtown to the airport?"   "Yes, every 20 minutes."
8. "_____ any problems?"   "No, everything is OK."
9. _____ nowhere to sit down. _____ any chairs.

38.4 아래의 단어들을 사용하여 *There are* ...로 시작하는 문장을 쓰시오.

five	twenty-six	letters	~~days~~	September	the solar system
~~seven~~	thirty	players	days	the United States	~~a week~~
eight	fifty	planets	states	a basketball team	the English alphabet

1. _There are seven days in a week._
2. _____
3. _____
4. _____
5. _____
6. _____

38.5 *there's / is there* 또는 *it's / is it*을 써 넣으시오.

1. "_There's_ a flight at 10:30."   "_Is it_ a nonstop flight?"
2. I'm not going to buy this shirt. _____ too expensive.
3. "What's wrong?"   "_____ something in my eye."
4. _____ a red car outside your house. _____ yours?
5. "_____ anything good on TV tonight?"   "Yes, _____ a movie at 8:00."
6. "What's that building?"   "_____ a school."
7. "_____ a restaurant in this hotel?"   "No, I'm afraid not."

there was/were   there has/have been
there will be

A
there was / there were (과거)

There is a train every hour.
기차는 매 시간 있다.

The time now is 11:15.
지금 시각은 11시 15분이다.
There was a train at 11:00.
기차는 11시에 있었다.

비교:

there is/are (현재)
- **There is** a good nature program on TV tonight.
- We are staying at a very big hotel. **There are** 1,250 rooms.
- **Are there** any phone messages for me this morning?
- I'm hungry, but **there isn't** anything to eat.

there was/were (과거)
- **There was** a good nature program on TV last night.
- We stayed at a very big hotel. **There were** 1,250 rooms.
- **Were there** any phone messages for me yesterday?
- I was hungry when I got home, but **there wasn't** anything to eat.

B
there has been / there have been (현재완료)

There's been an accident.

- Look! **There's been** an accident.
  (**there's been** = there **has** been)
- This road is very dangerous. **There have been** many accidents on it.
  이 길은 굉장히 위험해. 여기서 사고가 많이 일어났었어.

there was (과거)와의 비교:
- **There was** an accident **last night**.
  어젯밤 사고가 일어났어.
  (There has been an accident last night는 틀림)

단순과거와 현재완료의 비교는 Units 19–21 참조.

C
there will be (미래)

There will be rain tomorrow afternoon.

- Do you think **there will be** a lot of people at the party on Saturday?
  토요일 파티에 사람들이 많이 올 거라고 생각하니?
- The manager of the company is leaving, so **there will be** a new manager soon.
- I'm going out of town tomorrow. I'm packing my things today because **there won't be** time tomorrow. 내일은 시간이 없을 테니까 오늘 짐을 싸.
  (**there won't be** = there **will not** be)

was/were → Unit 10   has/have been → Units 16–17   will → Unit 28   there is/are → Unit 38
there와 it → Units 38, 40   some과 any → Unit 77

Exercises

39.1 다음 두 그림을 보시오. 지금은 방이 비어 있지만 일주일 전에는 그렇지 않았습니다. 아래 단어와 *There was/were* 구문을 사용하여 일주일 전 방의 모습을 설명하시오.

an armchair	a carpet	some flowers	a sofa
some books	~~a clock~~	three pictures	a small table

지난주   지금

1. _There was a clock_ _____ on the wall near the window.
2. _____ on the floor.
3. _____ on the wall near the door.
4. _____ in the middle of the room.
5. _____ on the table.
6. _____ on the shelves.
7. _____ in the corner near the door.
8. _____ opposite the armchair.

39.2 *there was / there wasn't / was there* 또는 *there were / there weren't / were there*를 써 넣으시오.

1. I was hungry, but _there wasn't_ anything to eat.
2. _Were there_ any phone messages for me yesterday?
3. I opened the envelope, but it was empty. _____ nothing in it.
4. "We stayed at a very nice hotel."   "Really? _____ a swimming pool?"
5. "Did you buy any cherries?"   "No, _____ any at the store."
6. The wallet was empty. _____ any money in it.
7. "_____ many people at the meeting?"   "No, very few."
8. We didn't visit the museum. _____ enough time.
9. I'm sorry I'm late. _____ a lot of traffic.
10. Twenty years ago _____ many tourists here. Now there are a lot.

39.3 *there + is / are / was / were / has been / have been / will be*를 써 넣으시오.

1. _There was_ a good program on TV last night.
2. _____ 24 hours in a day.
3. _____ a party at work last Friday, but I didn't go.
4. "Where can I buy a newspaper?"   "_____ a drugstore at the end of the block."
5. "Why are the police outside the bank?"   "_____ a robbery."
6. When we got to the theater, _____ a long line outside.
7. When you arrive tomorrow, _____ somebody at the airport to meet you.
8. Ten years ago _____ 500 children in the school. Now _____ more than a thousand.
9. Last week I went back to the town where I was born. It's very different now. _____ a lot of changes.
10. I think everything will be OK. I don't think _____ any problems.

It ...

A

시각, 요일, 날짜, 거리, 날씨 등에 대해 말할 때 **it**을 사용한다.

시각

- What time is **it**?
- **It**'s half past 10. 10시 반이다.
- **It**'s late.
- **It**'s time to go home. 집에 갈 시간이다.

날짜/
요일

- What day is **it**?
- **It**'s Thursday.
- **It**'s March 16th.
- **It** was my birthday yesterday.

거리

- **It**'s two miles from our house to downtown.
- How far is **it** from New York to Los Angeles?
- **It**'s a long way from here to the airport.
- We can walk home. **It** isn't far.

far는 의문문(**is it far?**)과 부정문(**it isn't far**)에 사용한다.
긍정문에는 **a long way** (**it's a long way**)를 사용한다.

날씨

- **It**'s raining.   **It** isn't raining.   **Is** it snowing?
- **It** rains a lot here.   **It** didn't rain yesterday.
  Does **it** snow very often? 눈이 아주 자주 옵니까?
- **It**'s warm/hot/cold/nice/cloudy/windy/sunny/clear/dry/
  humid/foggy/dark (등).
- **It**'s a nice day today.

it과 **there**의 비교:
- **It rains** a lot in the winter.
  It's very **rainy** in the winter.
  There is **a lot of rain** in the winter.
- **It** was very **windy** yesterday.
  There was **a strong wind** yesterday.

B

It's nice to ... 등

It's	easy / difficult / impossible / dangerous / safe expensive / interesting / nice / wonderful / terrible 등	**to ...**

- **It**'s nice **to see you again**.
- **It**'s impossible **to understand her**. 그녀를 이해하기란 불가능하다.
- **It** wasn't easy **to find your house**.

이런 문장들에서 it은 의미가 없으므로 해석하지 않는다.

C

it은 특별한 의미가 없지만 생략해서는 안 된다.
- **It**'s raining again. (Is raining again은 틀림)
- Is **it** true that you're moving to Dallas? 댈러스로 이사 간다는 거 정말이야?

Exercises

40.1 *It's ...*를 사용하여 그림 속의 날씨를 설명하시오.

1. ___It's raining.___
2. _____
3. _____
4. _____
5. _____
6. _____

40.2 *it is* (*it's*) 또는 *is it*을 써 넣으시오.

1. What time ___is it___ ?
2. We have to go now. _____ very late.
3. _____ true that Bill can fly a helicopter?
4. "What day _____ today? Tuesday?"   "No, _____ Wednesday."
5. _____ 10 kilometers from downtown to the airport.
6. _____ OK to call you at the office?
7. "Do you want to walk to the hotel?"   "I don't know. How far _____ ?"
8. _____ Lisa's birthday today. She's 27.
9. I don't believe it! _____ impossible.

40.3 *How far ...* ?로 시작하는 의문문을 쓰시오.

1. (here / the station)   ___How far is it from here to the station?___
2. (the hotel / the beach)   ___How___
3. (New York / Washington)   _____
4. (your house / the airport)   _____

40.4 *it* 또는 *there*를 써 넣으시오.

1. The weather isn't so nice today. ___It___'s cloudy.
2. ___There___ was a strong wind yesterday.
3. _____ 's hot in this room. Open a window.
4. _____ was a nice day yesterday. _____ was warm and sunny.
5. _____ was a storm last night. Did you hear it?
6. I was afraid because _____ was very dark.
7. _____ 's often cold here, but _____ isn't much rain.
8. _____ 's a long way from here to the nearest gas station.

40.5 아래에서 적절한 표현을 골라 문장을 완성하시오.

it's	easy ~~difficult~~ impossible	dangerous nice interesting	to	work in this office visit different places see you again	~~get up early~~ go out alone make friends

1. If you go to bed late, ___it's difficult to get up early___ in the morning.
2. Hello, Jane. _____ . How are you?
3. _____ . There is too much noise.
4. Everybody is very nice at work. _____ .
5. I like traveling. _____ .
6. Some cities are not safe. _____ at night.

I am, I don't 등

> I'm not tired.
>
> I am.
>
> Do you like tea?
>
> No, **I don't**.
>
> Yes, I do.

She isn't tired, but **he is**.
그녀는 피곤하지 않지만 그는 피곤하다.
(**he is** = he is tired)

He likes tea, but **she doesn't**.
그는 차를 좋아하지만 그녀는 좋아하지 않는다.
(**she doesn't** = she doesn't like tea)

위의 문장에서는 같은 단어를 반복("he is *tired*," "she doesn't *like tea*")하여 쓸 필요가 없다.

다음 동사들은 뒤에 반복되는 단어가 올 때 생략할 수 있다.

am/is/are
was/were
have/has
do/does/did
can
will
might
should

- I haven't seen the movie, but my sister **has**. (= my sister has seen the movie)
- *A:* Please help me.
  B: I'm sorry. I **can't**. (= I can't help you)
- *A:* Are you tired?
  B: I **was**, but **I'm not** now. (= I was tired, but I'm not tired now)
- *A:* Do you think Jane will call tonight?
  B: She **might**. (= she might call)
- *A:* Are you going to study tonight?
  B: I **should**, but I probably **won't**. (= I should study, but
  I probably won't study)

이렇게 뒤의 단어를 생략할 때는 축약형('**m**/'**s**/'**ve** 등)을 쓸 수 없다. **am/is/have** 등으로 써야 한다.
- She isn't tired, but he **is**. (... but he's는 틀림)

하지만 **isn't/haven't/won't** 등(부정 축약형)은 쓸 수 있다.
- My sister has seen the movie, but I **haven't**.
- "Are you and Jane working tomorrow?" "I am, but Jane **isn't**."

반복되는 말은 생략하고 **Yes, I am / No, I'm not** 등으로 질문에 짧게 답할 수 있다.
- "Are you tired?" "Yes, I **am**. / No, **I'm not**."
- "Will Bill be here tomorrow?" "Yes, he **will**. / No, he **won't**."
- "Is there a bus to the airport?" 공항으로 가는 버스가 있습니까?
  "Yes, there **is**. / No, there **isn't**." 네, 있습니다. / 아니오, 없습니다.

일반동사가 쓰인 경우, 단순현재에서는 **do/does**를 사용한다(Units 6–7 참조).
- I don't like hot weather, but Sue **does**. (= Sue likes hot weather)
  난 더운 날씨를 싫어하지만 수는 좋아한다.
- Sue works hard, but I **don't**. (= I don't work hard)
- "Do you enjoy your work?" "Yes, I **do**."

단순과거에는 **did**를 사용한다(Unit 12 참조).
- *A:* Did you and Chris like the movie?
- *B:* I **did**, but Chris **didn't**. (= I liked it, but Chris didn't like it)
- "I had a good time." "I **did**, too." (= I had a good time, too)
- "Did it rain yesterday?" "No, it **didn't**."

You have? / Have you? 등 → Unit 42   **so am I / neither do I** 등 → Unit 43

Exercises

41.1 빈칸에 동사(is/have/can 등)를 하나만 써 넣어 문장을 완성하시오.

1. Kate wasn't hungry, but we __were__ .
2. I'm not married, but my brother _____ .
3. Bill can't help you, but I _____ .
4. I haven't read the book, but Tom _____ .
5. Karen won't be here, but Chris _____ .
6. You weren't late, but I _____ .

41.2 동사의 부정형(isn't/haven't/can't 등)을 사용하여 문장을 완성하시오.

1. My sister can play the piano, but I __can't__ .
2. Sam is working today, but I _____ .
3. I was working, but my friends _____ .
4. Mark has been to China, but I _____ .
5. I'm ready to go, but Tom _____ .
6. I've seen the movie, but Kim _____ .

41.3 do/does/did 또는 don't/doesn't/didn't를 사용하여 문장을 완성하시오.

1. I don't like hot weather, but Sue __does__ .
2. Sue likes hot weather, but I __don't__ .
3. My mother wears glasses, but my father _____ .
4. You don't know Paul very well, but I _____ .
5. I didn't enjoy the party, but my friends _____ .
6. I don't watch TV much, but Peter _____ .
7. Kate lives in Canada, but her parents _____ .
8. You had breakfast this morning, but I _____ .

41.4 아래 예처럼 문장을 완성하시오. 당신과 다른 사람들에 대해 쓰시오.

1. I didn't __go out last night, but my friends did.__
2. I like _____ , but _____
3. I don't _____ , but _____
4. I'm _____
5. I haven't _____

41.5 동사를 긍정 또는 부정형으로 써 넣으시오.

1. "Are you tired?" "I __was__ earlier, but I'm not now."
2. Steve is happy today, but he _____ yesterday.
3. The stores aren't open yet, but the post office _____ .
4. I don't have a telescope, but I know somebody who _____ .
5. I would like to help you, but I'm sorry I _____ .
6. I don't usually drive to work, but I _____ yesterday.
7. A: Have you ever been to Costa Rica?
   B: No, but Sandra _____ . She went there on vacation last year.
8. "Do you and Luke watch TV a lot?" "I _____ , but Luke doesn't."
9. I've been invited to Sam's wedding, but Kate _____ .
10. "Do you think Sarah will pass her driving test?" "Yes, I'm sure she _____ ."
11. "Are you going out tonight?" "I _____ . I don't know for sure."

41.6 질문에 사실대로 답하시오. Yes, I have. / No, I'm not. 등의 구문을 사용하시오.

1. Are you Brazilian? __No, I'm not.__
2. Do you have a car? _____
3. Do you feel OK? _____
4. Is it snowing? _____
5. Are you hungry? _____
6. Do you like classical music? _____
7. Will you be in Boston tomorrow? _____
8. Have you ever broken your arm? _____
9. Did you buy anything yesterday? _____
10. Were you asleep at 3:00 a.m.? _____

You have? / Have you? / You are? / Are you? 등

상대방의 말에 가벼운 놀람이나 흥미를 표할 때 **you have?** / **it is?** / **he can't?** 등으로 말한다.

- "**You're** late." 늦으셨네요.   "**I am?** I'm sorry." 그런가요? 미안합니다.
- "**I was** sick last week."   "**You were?** I didn't know that."
- "**It's** raining again."   "**It is?** It was sunny 10 minutes ago."
- "**There's** a letter for you." 너한테 온 편지가 있어.
  "**There is?** Where is it?" 그래? 어디 있는데?
- "**Bill can't** drive."   "**He can't?** I didn't know that."
- "**I'm not** hungry." 난 배고프지 않아.   "**You aren't?** I am." 그래? 난 배고픈데.
- "**Sue isn't** at work today."   "**She isn't?** Is she sick?"

단순현재에는 **do/does**를, 단순과거에는 **did**를 사용한다.

- "**I speak** four languages."   "**You do?** Which ones?"
- "**Tim doesn't** eat meat." 팀은 고기를 안 먹어.   "**He doesn't?** Does he eat fish?" 그래? 생선은 먹어?
- "**Nicole got** married last week."   "**She did?** Really?"

부가의문문

문장 뒤에 **have you?** / **is it?** / **can't she?** 등을
사용할 수 있다.
이러한 짧은 의문문을 **부가의문문**이라고 한다.

긍정문 → 부정의 부가의문문

It's a nice day,	**isn't it?**	Yes, it's perfect.
Sally lives in Portland,	**doesn't she?**	Yes, that's right.
You closed the window,	**didn't you?**	Yes, I think so.
Those shoes are nice,	**aren't they?**	Yes, very nice.
Tom will be here soon,	**won't he?**	Yes, probably.

부정문 → 긍정의 부가의문문

That isn't your car,	**is it?**	No, it's my mother's.
You haven't met my mother,	**have you?**	No, I haven't.
Sally doesn't go out much,	**does she?**	No, she doesn't.
You won't be late,	**will you?**	No, I'm never late.

Exercises

42.1 *You do? / She doesn't? / They did?* 등으로 답하시오.

1. I speak four languages.   _You do_ ? Which ones?
2. I work in a bank.   _____ ? I work in a bank, too.
3. I didn't go to work yesterday.   _____ ? Were you sick?
4. Jane doesn't like me.   _____ ? Why not?
5. You look tired.   _____ ? I feel fine.
6. Kate called me last night.   _____ ? What did she say?

42.2 *You have? / You haven't? / She did? / She didn't* 등으로 답하시오.

1. I've bought a new car.   _You have_ ? What kind is it?
2. Tim doesn't eat meat.   _He doesn't_ ? Does he eat fish?
3. I've lost my key.   _____ ? When did you have it last?
4. Sue can't drive.   _____ ? She should learn.
5. I was born in Italy.   _____ ? I didn't know that.
6. I didn't sleep well last night.   _____ ? Was the bed uncomfortable?
7. There's a football game on TV tonight.   _____ ? Are you going to watch it?
8. I'm not happy.   _____ ? Why not?
9. I saw Paula last week.   _____ ? How is she?
10. Maria works in a factory.   _____ ? What kind of factory?
11. I won't be here next week.   _____ ? Where will you be?
12. The clock isn't working.   _____ ? It was working yesterday.

42.3 부가의문문(*isn't it? / haven't you?* 등)을 사용하여 문장을 완성하시오.

1. It's a nice day, _isn't it_ ? Yes, it's beautiful.
2. These flowers are nice, _____ ? Yes, what kind are they?
3. Jane was at the party, _____ ? Yes, but I didn't speak to her.
4. You've been to Chile, _____ ? Yes, many times.
5. You speak Thai, _____ ? Yes, but not very well.
6. Bill looks tired, _____ ? Yes, he works very hard.
7. You'll help me, _____ ? Yes, of course I will.

42.4 긍정의 부가의문문(*is it? / do you?* 등) 또는 부정의 부가의문문(*isn't it? / don't you?* 등)을 사용하여 문장을 완성하시오.

1. You haven't eaten yet, _have you_ ? No, I'm not hungry.
2. You aren't tired, _____ ? No, I feel fine.
3. Lisa is a very nice person, _____ ? Yes, everybody likes her.
4. You can play the piano, _____ ? Yes, but I'm not very good.
5. You don't know Mike's sister, _____ ? No, I've never met her.
6. Sarah went to college, _____ ? Yes, she studied psychology.
7. The movie wasn't very good, _____ ? No, it was terrible.
8. Anna lives near you, _____ ? Yes, just a few blocks away.
9. You won't tell anybody what I said, _____ ? No, of course not.

too/either so am I / neither do I 등

A too와 either

> I'm happy.
> I'm happy, **too**.
> I'm not happy.
> I'm **not** happy, **either**.

too와 **either**는 상대방에게 동의를 표하는 말로 문장 맨 뒤에 위치한다.

too는 문장의 동사가 긍정일 때 쓴다.	**either**는 문장의 동사가 부정일 때 쓴다.
■ *A:* I'm happy. 　*B:* I'm happy, **too**. ■ *A:* I liked the movie. 　*B:* I **liked** it, **too**. ■ Jane is a doctor. Her husband **is** 　a doctor, **too**. 　제인은 의사이다. 그녀의 남편도 의사이다.	■ *A:* I'm not happy. 　*B:* I'm **not** happy, **either**. 　　(I'm not …, too는 틀림) ■ *A:* I can't cook. 　*B:* I **can't**, **either**. (I can't, too는 틀림) ■ Bill doesn't watch TV. He **doesn't** read 　newspapers, **either**. 　빌은 TV를 보지 않는다. 그는 신문도 읽지 　않는다.

B so am I / neither do I 등

> I'm happy.
> So am I.
> I'm not happy.
> Neither am I.

so	am/is/are … was/were … do/does … did … have/has … can … will … should …
neither	

so am I = I am, too **so have I** = I have, too: ■ *A:* **I'm** working. 　*B:* **So am I.** (= I'm working, too) ■ *A:* **I was** late for work today. 　*B:* **So was Sam.** (= Sam was late, too) ■ *A:* **I work** in a bank. 　*B:* **So do I.** ■ *A:* **We went** to the movies last night. 　우린 어젯밤에 영화 보러 갔어. 　*B:* You did? **So did we.** 　그랬어? 우리도 갔어. ■ *A:* **I'd like** to go to Australia. 　*B:* **So would I.**	**neither am I** = I'm not, either **neither can I** = I can't, either: ■ *A:* **I haven't** been to China. 　난 중국에 가본 적 없어. 　*B:* **Neither have I.** (= I haven't, either) 　나도 가본 적 없어. ■ *A:* **Kate can't** cook. 　*B:* **Neither can Tom.** 　　(= Tom can't, either) ■ *A:* **I won't** (= will not) be here 　tomorrow. 　*B:* **Neither will I.** ■ *A:* **I never go** to the movies. 　*B:* **Neither do I.**

주어와 동사가 도치된다는 점에 유의하자: So **am** I. (So I am은 틀림), Neither **have** I. (Neither I have는 틀림)

Exercises

43.1 *too* 또는 *either*를 써 넣으시오.

1. I'm happy.   I'm happy, _too_ .
2. I'm not hungry.   I'm not hungry, _____ .
3. I'm going out.   I'm going out, _____ .
4. It rained on Saturday.   It rained on Sunday, _____ .
5. Jenny can't drive a car.   She can't ride a bicycle, _____ .
6. I don't like to go shopping.   I don't like to go shopping, _____ .
7. Linda's mother is a teacher.   Her father is a teacher, _____ .

43.2 *So ... I* (*So am I* / *So do I* / *So can't I* 등) 구문을 사용하여 답하시오.

1. I went to bed late last night.   _So did I._
2. I'm thirsty.   _____
3. I've already read this book.   _____
4. I need a vacation.   _____
5. I'll be late tomorrow.   _____
6. I was very tired this morning.   _____

Neither ... I 구문을 사용하여 답하시오.

7. I can't go to the party.   _____
8. I didn't call Alex last night.   _____
9. I haven't eaten lunch yet.   _____
10. I'm not going out tonight.   _____
11. I don't know what to do.   _____

43.3 당신은 Maria와 대화를 나누고 있습니다. *So ... I* / *Neither ... I* / *I am* / *I'm not* / *I do* / *I don't* 등을 사용하여 자신에 대해 사실대로 답하시오.

I'm tired today.   대답: _So am I._   또는   _I'm not._

I don't work hard.   대답: _Neither do I._   또는   _I do._

Maria   You

1. I'm studying English.   _____
2. I can ride a bicycle.   _____
3. I'm not American.   _____
4. I like to cook.   _____
5. I don't like cold weather.   _____
6. I slept well last night.   _____
7. I've never been to India.   _____
8. I don't use my phone much.   _____
9. I'm going out tomorrow night.   _____
10. I wasn't sick last week.   _____
11. I didn't watch TV last night.   _____
12. I go to the movies a lot.   _____

isn't, haven't, don't 등 (부정문)

A

부정문에 **not (n't)**을 사용한다.

긍정 → 부정

am	**am not ('m not)**
is	**is not (isn't** 또는 **'s not)**
are	**are not (aren't** 또는 **'re not)**
was	**was not (wasn't)**
were	**were not (weren't)**
have	**have not (haven't)**
has	**has not (hasn't)**
will	**will not (won't)**
can	**cannot (can't)**
could	**could not (couldn't)**
should	**should not (shouldn't)**
would	**would not (wouldn't)**
must	**must not**

- I**'m not** tired.
- It **isn't** (또는 It**'s not**) raining.
- They **aren't** (또는 They**'re not**) here.
- Brian **wasn't** hungry.
- The stores **weren't** open.
- I **haven't** finished my work.
- Sue **hasn't** been to Mexico.
  수는 멕시코에 간 적이 없다.
- We **won't** be here tomorrow.
  우리는 내일 여기에 없을 것이다.
- George **can't** drive.
- I **couldn't** sleep last night.
- You **shouldn't** work so hard.
- I **wouldn't** like to be an actor.
  나는 배우가 되고 싶지 않다.
- They **must not** have a car.
  그 사람들에게 차가 있을 리 없다.

B

don't / doesn't / didn't

단순현재 부정문	I/we/you/they	**do not (don't)**	
	he/she/it	**does not (doesn't)**	**work/live/go** 등
단순과거 부정문	I/they/he/she 등	**did not (didn't)**	

긍정 → 부정

I **want** to go out.	→	I **don't want** to go out.
They **work** hard.	→	They **don't work** hard.
Liz **plays** the guitar.	→	Liz **doesn't play** the guitar.
My father **likes** his job.	→	My father **doesn't like** his job.
I **got** up early this morning.	→	I **didn't get** up early this morning.
They **worked** hard yesterday.	→	They **didn't work** hard yesterday.
We **played** tennis.	→	We **didn't play** tennis.
Diane **had** dinner with us.	→	Diane **didn't have** dinner with us.

명령문의 부정: **Don't** ...

Look!	→	**Don't look!**
Wait for me.	→	**Don't wait** for me.

때로는 **do**가 본동사로 쓰인다(**don't do / doesn't do / didn't do**).

Do something!	→	**Don't do** anything!
Sue **does** a lot on weekends.	→	Sue **doesn't do** much on weekends.
수는 주말에 많은 것을 한다.		수는 주말에 별로 하는 것이 없다.
I **did** what you said.	→	I **didn't do** what you said.

단순현재 부정문 → Unit 6   단순과거 부정문 → Unit 12   **don't look / don't wait** 등 → Unit 37
Why isn't/don't ... ? → Unit 45

Exercises

44.1 다음 문장을 부정문으로 만드시오.

1. He's gone out. _He hasn't gone out._
2. They're married. _____
3. I've had dinner. _____
4. It's cold today. _____
5. We'll be late. _____
6. You should go. _____

44.2 **don't/doesn't/didn't**를 사용하여 다음 문장을 부정문으로 만드시오.

1. She saw me. _She didn't see me._
2. I like cheese. _____
3. They understood. _____
4. He lives here. _____
5. Go away! _____
6. I did the dishes. _____

44.3 다음 문장을 부정문으로 만드시오.

1. She can swim. _She can't swim._
2. They've arrived. _____
3. I went to the bank. _____
4. He speaks Japanese. _____
5. We were angry. _____
6. He'll be happy. _____
7. Call me tonight. _____
8. It rained yesterday. _____
9. I could hear them. _____
10. I believe you. _____

44.4 동사의 부정형(**isn't/haven't/don't** 등)을 써 넣어 문장을 완성하시오.

1. They aren't rich. They _don't_ have much money.
2. "Would you like something to eat?" "No, thank you. I _____ hungry."
3. I _____ find my glasses. Have you seen them?
4. Steve _____ use e-mail much. He'd rather talk on the phone.
5. We can walk to the station from here. It _____ very far.
6. "Where's Jane?" "I _____ know. I _____ seen her today."
7. Be careful! _____ fall!
8. We went to the movies last night. I _____ like the movie very much.
9. I've been to Japan many times, but I _____ been to South Korea.
10. Julia _____ be here tomorrow. She'll be out of town.
11. "Who broke that window?" "Not me. I _____ do it."
12. We didn't see what happened. We _____ looking at the time.
13. Lisa bought a new coat a few days ago, but she _____ worn it yet.
14. You _____ drive so fast. It's dangerous.

44.5 당신의 질문에 대한 **Gary**의 대답(**Yes** 또는 **No**)을 보고 **Gary**에 대한 문장을 쓰시오. 긍정 또는 부정으로 쓰시오.

You	Gary	
Are you married?	No.	1. _He isn't married._
Do you live in Los Angeles?	Yes.	2. _He lives in Los Angeles._
Were you born in Los Angeles?	No.	3. _____
Do you like Los Angeles?	No.	4. _____
Would you like to live someplace else?	Yes.	5. _____
Can you drive?	Yes.	6. _____
Have you traveled abroad?	No.	7. _____
Do you read the newspaper?	No.	8. _____
Are you interested in politics?	No.	9. _____
Do you usually watch TV at night?	Yes.	10. _____
Did you watch TV last night?	No.	11. _____
Did you go out last night?	Yes.	12. _____

is it … ? have you … ? do they … ? 등
(의문문 1)

A

| 평서문 | you | are | **You are** eating. |

| 의문문 | are | you | **Are you** eating? | What **are you** eating? |

의문문에서는 첫번째 동사(**is/are/have** 등)가 주어 앞에 위치한다.

평서문		의문문	
주어 + 동사		동사 + 주어	
I	**am** late.	→	**Am** I late?
That seat	**is** free.	→	**Is** that seat free? 저 자리는 비어 있나요?
She	**was** angry.	→	Why **was** she angry?
David	**has** gone.	→	Where **has** David gone?
You	**have** been to Japan.	→	**Have** you been to Japan? 일본에 가보신 적 있어요?
They	**will** be here soon.	→	When **will** they be here? 그들은 여기에 언제 오나요?
Paula	**can** swim.	→	**Can** Paula swim?

주어는 첫번째 동사의 뒤에 위치한다는 점에 유의하자.

- Where **has David** gone? (Where has gone David?는 틀림)
- **Are those people** waiting for something? (Are waiting … ?은 틀림)
- When **was the telephone** invented? (When was invented … ?는 틀림)

B

do … ? / **does** … ? / **did** … ?

단순현재 의문문	**do**	I/we/you/they	
	does	he/she/it	**work/live/go** 등 … ?
단순과거 의문문	**did**	I/they/he/she 등	

평서문		의문문
They **work** hard.	→	**Do** they **work** hard?
You **watch** television.	→	How often **do** you **watch** television?
Chris **has** a car.	→	**Does** Chris **have** a car?
She **gets up** early.	→	What time **does** she **get** up?
They **worked** hard.	→	**Did** they **work** hard?
You **had** dinner.	→	What **did** you **have** for dinner?
She **got** up early.	→	What time **did** she **get** up?

때로는 **do**가 본동사로 쓰인다(do you **do** / did he **do** 등).

- What **do** you usually **do** on weekends?
- "What **does** your brother **do**?" "He works in a bank."
- "I broke my finger last week." 지난주에 손가락을 부러트렸어.
  "How **did** you **do** that?" 어쩌다가 그랬니? (How did you that?은 틀림)

C

Why isn't … ? / **Why don't** … ? 등 (**Why** + 부정형)

- Where's John? **Why isn't** he here? (Why he isn't here?는 틀림)
- **Why can't Paula** come to the meeting tomorrow? 폴라는 왜 내일 모임에 못 나오니?
  (Why Paula can't … ?는 틀림)
- **Why didn't you** call me last night? 왜 어젯밤에 전화 안 했니?

단순현재 의문문 → Unit 7   단순과거 의문문 → Unit 12   의문문 2–3 → Units 46–47
what/which/how → Units 48–49

Exercises

45.1 제시된 주어를 사용하여 의문문을 만드시오.

1. I can swim. (and you?) _Can you swim?_
2. I work hard. (and Jack?) _Does Jack work hard?_
3. I was late this morning. (and you?) _____
4. I've seen that movie. (and Kate?) _____
5. I'll be here tomorrow. (and you?) _____
6. I'm going out tonight. (and Paul?) _____
7. I like my job. (and you?) _____
8. I live near here. (and Nicole?) _____
9. I enjoyed the movie. (and you?) _____
10. I had a good vacation. (and you?) _____

45.2 당신은 친구와 운전에 대하여 이야기하고 있습니다.
주어진 단어를 사용하여 질문을 만드시오.

You

1. (have / a car?) _Do you have a car?_ _____ Yes, I do.
2. (use / a lot?) _____ it _____ Yes, almost every day.
3. (use / yesterday?) _____ Yes, to go to work.
4. (enjoy driving?) _____ Not very much.
5. (a good driver?) _____ I think I am.
6. (ever / have / an accident?) _____ No, never.

45.3 괄호 안의 단어들을 올바른 순서로 배열하여 의문문을 만드시오.

1. (has / gone / where / David?) _Where has David gone?_
2. (working / Rachel / is / today?) _Is Rachel working today?_
3. (the children / what / are / doing?) What _____
4. (made / is / how / cheese?) _____
5. (to the party / coming / is / your sister?) _____
6. (you / the truth / tell / don't / why?) _____
7. (your guests / have / yet / arrived?) _____
8. (leave / what time / your plane / does?) _____
9. (to work / Jenny / why / go / didn't?) _____
10. (your car / in the accident / was / damaged?) _____

45.4 질문을 완성하시오.

1. I want to go out. | Where _do you want to go?_
2. Kate and Paul aren't going to the party. | Why _aren't they going?_
3. I'm reading. | What _____
4. Sue went to bed early. | What time _____
5. My parents are going on vacation. | When _____
6. I saw Tom a few days ago. | Where _____
7. I can't come to the party. | Why _____
8. Tina has moved. | Where _____
9. I need some money. | How much _____
10. Angela doesn't like me. | Why _____
11. It rains sometimes. | How often _____
12. I did the shopping. | When _____

Who saw you? Who did you see?
(의문문 2)

A

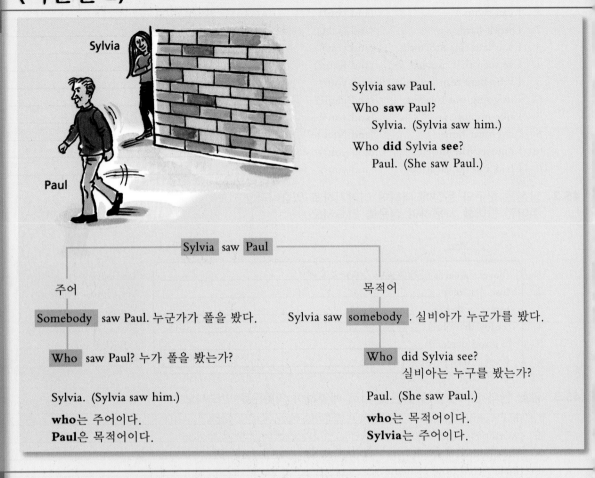

Sylvia

Paul

Sylvia saw Paul.

Who **saw** Paul?
  Sylvia. (Sylvia saw him.)

Who **did** Sylvia **see**?
  Paul. (She saw Paul.)

Sylvia saw Paul

주어

Somebody saw Paul. 누군가가 폴을 봤다.

Who saw Paul? 누가 폴을 봤는가?

Sylvia. (Sylvia saw him.)

who는 주어이다.
Paul은 목적어이다.

목적어

Sylvia saw somebody. 실비아가 누군가를 봤다.

Who did Sylvia see?
  실비아는 누구를 봤는가?

Paul. (She saw Paul.)

who는 목적어이다.
Sylvia는 주어이다.

B

다음 의문문에서 **who/what**은 주어이다.

- **Who lives** in this house? (= somebody lives in it – who?)
  (Who does live?는 틀림)
- **What happened**? (= something happened – what?)
  (What did happen?은 틀림)
- **What's happening**? (What's = What **is**)
- **Who's got** my keys? (Who's = Who **has**)

다음 의문문에서 **who/what**은 목적어이다.

- **Who** did **you** meet yesterday? (= you met somebody – who?)
- **What** did **Paul** say? (= Paul said something – what?)
- **Who** are **you** calling? 넌 누구에게 전화를 하고 있니?
- **What** was **Sylvia** wearing?

비교:

- George likes oranges. → **Who likes** oranges? – George.
                            What does George like? – Oranges.
- Jane won a new car. → **Who won** a new car? 누가 새 차를 탔나? – Jane.
  제인은 새 차를 탔다(획득했다).   **What** did Jane win? 제인이 탄 것은 무엇인가? – A new car.

C

who는 사람, **what**은 사물에 대해 쓴다.

- **Who** is your favorite **singer**?
- **What** is your favorite **song**?

Exercises

46.1 *who* 또는 *what*을 사용하여 의문문을 만드시오. 여기서 *who/what*은 주어입니다.

1.	Somebody broke the window.	*Who broke the window?*
2.	Something fell off the shelf.	What _____
3.	Somebody wants to see you.	_____ me?
4.	Somebody took my umbrella.	_____
5.	Something made me sick.	_____
6.	Somebody is coming.	_____

46.2 *who* 또는 *what*을 주어나 목적어로 사용하여 의문문을 만드시오.

1.	I bought something.	*What did you buy?*
2.	Somebody lives in this house.	*Who lives in this house?*
3.	I called somebody.	_____
4.	Something happened last night.	_____
5.	Somebody knows the answer.	_____
6.	Somebody did the dishes.	_____
7.	Jane did something.	_____
8.	Something woke me up.	_____
9.	Somebody saw the accident.	_____
10.	I saw somebody.	_____
11.	Somebody has my pen.	_____
12.	This word means something.	_____

46.3 문장 중 빠져 있는 정보(**XXXXX**)를 알아내고자 합니다. *who* 또는 *what*을 사용하여 의문문을 만드시오.

1. I lost **XXXXX** yesterday, but fortunately **XXXXX** found it and gave it back to me.

   What did you lose?
   Who found it?

2. **XXXXX** called me last night. She wanted **XXXXX**.

   Who _____
   What _____

3. I needed some advice, so I asked **XXXXX**. He said **XXXXX**.

4. I hear that **XXXXX** got married last week. **XXXXX** told me.

5. I met **XXXXX** on my way home tonight. She told me **XXXXX**.

6. Steve and I played tennis yesterday. **XXXXX** won. After the game, we **XXXXX**.

7. It was my birthday last week, and I got some presents. **XXXXX** gave me a book, and Catherine gave me **XXXXX**.

Who is she talking to?   What is it like?
(의문문 3)

A

Julia

Julia is talking to somebody.
줄리아가 누군가와 이야기하고 있다.

Who is she talking to?
그녀는 누구와 이야기하고 있는가?

Who … ? / **What** … ? / **Where** … ? / **Which** … ?로 시작하는 의문문에서 전치사(**to/from/with** 등)는 주로 문장의 맨 뒤에 쓴다.

- "**Where** are you **from**?" "I'm from Thailand."
- "Jack was afraid." 잭은 무서워해요. "**What** was he afraid **of**?" 뭘 무서워해요?
- "**Who** do these books belong **to**?" 이 책은 누구 소유입니까?
  "They're mine." 제 것입니다.
- "Tom's father is in the hospital." 탐의 아버지가 입원하셨어요.
  "**Which hospital** is he **in**?" 어느 병원에 계세요?
- "Kate is going on vacation." "**Who with**?" / "**Who** is she going **with**?"
- "Can we talk?" "Sure. **What** do you want to talk **about**?"

B

What's it like? / What are they like? 등

What's your new house like?

It's very big.

What**'s** it like? = What **is** it like?

What's it like? = 어때요? (좋은지, 나쁜지, 큰지, 작은지, 오래된 것인지 새 것인지 등의 의견을 묻는 표현)

What is it like?에서 **like**는 전치사이다. 동사가 아니다. (비교: **Do** you **like** your new house?)

- *A:* There's a new restaurant near my house. 집 근처에 새 레스토랑이 생겼어.
  B: **What's** it **like**? Is it good? 어때? 좋아?
  A: I don't know. I haven't eaten there yet. 몰라. 아직 거기서 먹어본 적 없어.

- *A:* **What's** your new teacher **like**?
  B: She's very good. We learn a lot.

- *A:* I met Nicole's parents yesterday. 어제 니콜의 부모님을 만났어.
  B: You did? **What** are they **like**? 그랬니? 어떤 분이시니?
  A: They're very nice. 아주 좋은 분이셔.

- *A:* Did you have a good vacation? **What** was the weather **like**?
  B: It was great. It was sunny every day.

의문문 → Units 45–46   **what/which/how** → Unit 48   전치사 → Units 104–114

Exercises

47.1 문장 중 빠져 있는 정보(XXXXX)를 알아내고자 합니다. *who* 또는 *what*을 사용하여
의문문을 만드시오.

1.	The letter is from **XXXXX**.
2.	I'm looking for a **XXXXX**.
3.	I went to the movies with **XXXXX**.
4.	The movie was about **XXXXX**.
5.	I gave the money to **XXXXX**.
6.	The book was written by **XXXXX**.

1. _Who is the letter from?_
2. What _____ you _____
3. _____
4. _____
5. _____
6. _____

47.2 그림 속의 사람들에 대해 묻는 의문문을 쓰시오. 아래의 동사 + 전치사를 사용하시오.

go   listen   look   ~~talk~~   talk   wait

1. 1. _Who is she talking to?_
2. What _____
3. Which restaurant _____
4. 4. What _____
5. 5. What _____
6. 6. Which bus _____

47.3 *Which ... ?* 를 사용하여 의문문을 쓰시오.

1.	Tom's father is in the hospital.
2.	We stayed at a hotel.
3.	Jack plays for a football team.
4.	I went to school in this town.

1. _Which hospital is he in?_
2. _____ you _____
3. _____
4. _____

47.4 당신은 외국을 다녀온 친구에게 다음 사항들에 대한 정보를 얻고자 합니다.
What is/are ... like? 구문을 사용하여 질문을 만드시오.

1. (the roads) _What are the roads like?_
2. (the food) _____
3. (the people) _____
4. (the weather) _____

47.5 *What was/were ... like?* 구문을 사용하여 각 상황에 맞는 질문을 하시오.

1. Your friend has just come back from a trip. Ask about the weather.
   What was the weather like?
2. Your friend has just come back from the movies. Ask about the movie.
   _____
3. Your friend has just finished a computer course. Ask about the classes.
   _____
4. Your friend has just come back from a business trip. Ask about the hotel.
   _____

What … ? Which … ? How … ?
(의문문 4)

A

What + 명사 (What color … ? / What kind … ? 등): 무슨 … ?

- **What color** is your car?
- **What color** are your eyes? 당신의 눈은 무슨 색입니까?
- **What size** is this shirt?
- **What nationality** is she? 그녀의 국적은 어디입니까?
- **What time** is it?
- **What day** is it today? 오늘은 무슨 요일입니까?
- **What kind** of job do you want? (또는 **What type** of job … ? / **What sort** of job … ?)

명사 없이 **What**만 사용한 경우:

- **What's** your favorite color?
- **What** do you want to do tonight?

B

Which + 명사 (사물 또는 사람): 어느 … ?

- **Which train** did you catch – the 9:50 or the 10:30?
- **Which doctor** did you see – Doctor Lopez, Doctor Gray, or Doctor Hill?

사물을 지칭할 때는 명사 없이 **which**만 쓸 수 있다. (사람은 안 됨)

- **Which** is bigger – Canada or Australia?

사람을 지칭할 때는 (명사 없이) **who**를 쓴다.

- **Who** is taller – Joe or Gary? (Which is taller?는 틀림)

C

what 또는 which

선택의 폭이 좁을 때(2–4개 정도)는 **which**를 사용한다.

- We can go this way or that way.
  Which way should we go?
  이 길이나 저 길로 갈 수 있어.
  어느 길로 갈까?
- There are four umbrellas here.
  Which is yours?

? 또는 **?** 또는 **?** 또는 **?**
WHICH?

what은 좀 더 포괄적이다.

- **What's** the capital of Argentina? (아르헨티아에 있는 모든 도시들 중에서) 아르헨티나의 수도는 어디니?
- **What kind** of music do you like? (모든 종류의 음악 중에서) 어떤 음악을 좋아하니?

비교:

- **What color** are his eyes? (Which color?는 틀림)
  Which color do you prefer, **pink or yellow**?
- **What** is the longest river in the world? 세계에서 가장 긴 강은 무엇입니까?
  Which is the longest river – **the Mississippi, the Amazon, or the Nile**?
  어느 강이 가장 깁니까 – 미시시피강, 아마존강, 나일강?

D

How … ?

- "**How** was the party last night?" "It was great."
- "**How** do you get to work?" "By bus."

How + 형용사/부사 (How tall / How old / How often 등): 얼마나 …?

"**How**	**tall** are you?" "I'm five feet 10." (5 feet 10 inches 또는 1.78 meters)	
	big is the house?" 집이 얼마나 큰가요? "Not very big." 아주 크지는 않아요.	
	old is your mother?" "She's 45."	
	far is it from here to the airport?" "Ten miles." (약 16 kilometers)	
	often do you use your car?" "Every day."	
	long have they been married?" 그들은 결혼한 지 얼마나 되었나요? "Ten years."	
	much was the taxi?" "Ten dollars."	

의문문 → Units 45–47   How long does it take … ? → Unit 49   which one(s) → Unit 76

Exercises

48.1 *What ... ?*으로 시작하는 의문문을 쓰시오.

1. This shirt is nice.   (size?)   *What size is it?*
2. I want a job.   (kind?)   *What kind of job do you want?*
3. I have a new sweater.   (color?)   What _____
4. I got up early this morning.   (time?)   _____ get up?
5. I like music.   (type?)   _____
6. I want to buy a car.   (kind?)   _____

48.2 *Which ... ?*를 사용하여 질문을 완성하시오.

1. *Which way* should we go?
   Kendall Sq. Cambridge Storrow Dr.
2. _____ is yours?
3. _____ do you want to see?
4. _____ goes downtown?

48.3 *What/Which/Who*를 써 넣으시오.

1. ___*What*___ is that man's name?
2. ___*Which*___ way should we go? Left or right?
3. You can have tea or coffee. _____ do you prefer?
4. "_____ day is it today?" "Friday."
5. _____ is your favorite sport?
6. This is a nice office. _____ desk is yours?
7. _____ is more expensive, meat or fish?
8. _____ is older, Liz or Steve?
9. _____ kind of camera do you have?
10. *A:* I've got three cameras.
    B: _____ camera do you use most?

48.4 *How* + 형용사/부사(*high*/*long* 등)를 사용하여 질문을 완성하시오.

1. ___*How high*___ is Mount Everest?   Over 29,000 feet.
2. _____ is it to the station?   Almost two miles.
3. _____ is Helen?   She's 26.
4. _____ do the buses run?   Every 10 minutes.
5. _____ is the water in the pool?   Seven feet.
6. _____ have you lived here?   Almost three years.

48.5 *How ... ?*로 시작하는 의문문을 쓰시오.

1. Are you five feet nine? Five feet 10? Five feet 11?   *How tall are you?*
2. Is this box one kilogram? Two? Three?   _____
3. Are you 20 years old? 22? 25?   _____
4. Did you spend $20? $30? $50?   _____
5. Do you watch TV every day? Once a week? Never?

   _____
6. Is it 2,000 miles from New York to Los Angeles? 2,500? 3,000?

   _____

How long does it take … ?

A

How long does it take to get from … to … ?: …에서 …까지 가는 데 시간이 얼마나 걸립니까?

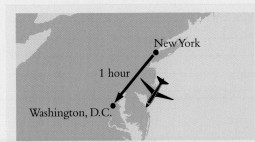

New York

1 hour

Washington, D.C.

How long **does it take to get** from New York to Washington, D.C., by plane?
뉴욕에서 워싱턴 DC까지 비행기로 가는 데 시간이 얼마나 걸립니까?

It takes an hour. 한 시간 걸립니다.

- How long **does it take to get from** Los Angeles to New York by train?
- **It takes** several days **to get from** Los Angeles to New York by train.
- How long **does it take to get from** your house to the airport by car?
- **It takes** ten minutes **to get from** my house to the airport by car.

B

How long does it take to do something?: …하는 데 시간이 얼마나 걸립니까?

How long	does did will	it take to … ?

It	takes took will take	a week a long time three hours	to …
	doesn't didn't won't	take	long	

- How long **does it take to cross** the Atlantic by ship?
  배로 대서양을 건너는 데 시간이 얼마나 걸립니까?
- "I came by train."   "You did? How long **did it take** (**to get** here)?"
- How long **will it take to get** from here to the hotel?

- **It takes** a long time **to learn** a language.
- **It doesn't take** long **to make** an omelet.
- **It won't take** long **to fix** the computer.

C

How long does it take you to do something?: 당신이 …하는 데 시간이 얼마나 걸립니까?

Day 1   *Day 2*   *Day 3*

How long	does did will	it take	you Tom them	to … ?

It	takes took will take	me Tom them	a week a long time three hours	to …

I started reading the book on Monday. 나는 월요일에 책을 읽기 시작했다.
I finished it on Wednesday evening. 나는 수요일 저녁에 책을 다 읽었다.

It **took me** three days **to read** it. 내가 책을 읽는 데는 사흘이 걸렸다.

- How long **will it take me to learn** to drive? 운전을 배우는 데 시간이 얼마나 걸릴까요?
- **It takes Tom** 20 minutes **to get** to work in the morning.
- **It took us** an hour **to do** the shopping.
- **Did it take you** a long time **to find** a job?
- **It will take me** an hour **to cook** dinner.

Exercises

49.1 그림을 보고 *How long ... ?*을 사용하여 의문문을 쓰시오.

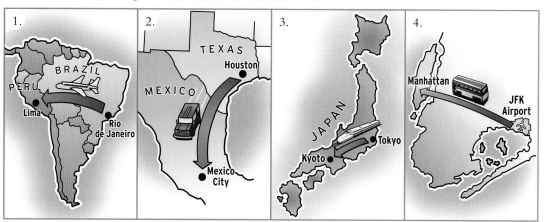

1. _How long does it take to get from Rio de Janeiro to Lima by plane?_
2. _____
3. _____
4. _____

49.2 아래의 일을 하는 데는 시간이 얼마나 걸립니까? 완전한 문장으로 쓰시오.

1. fly from your city/country to Los Angeles
   It takes about 11 hours to fly from Seoul to Los Angeles.
2. fly from your city/country to Australia
   _____
3. become a doctor in your country
   _____
4. walk from your home to the nearest supermarket
   _____
5. get from your house to the nearest airport
   _____

49.3 *How long did it take ... ?*를 사용하여 의문문을 쓰시오.

1. (Jane found a job.) _How long did it take her to find a job?_
2. (I walked to the station.) _____ you _____
3. (Tom painted the bathroom.) _____
4. (I learned to ski.) _____
5. (They repaired the computer.) _____

49.4 아래의 상황을 읽고 *It took ...*를 사용하여 문장을 쓰시오.

1. I read a book last week. I started reading it on Monday. I finished it three days later.
   It took me three days to read the book.
2. We walked home last night. We left at 10:00, and we got home at 10:20.
   _____
3. I learned to drive last year. I had my first driving lesson in January. I passed my driving test six months later.
   _____
4. Mark drove to Houston yesterday. He left home at 7:00 and got to Houston at 10:00.
   _____
5. Lisa began looking for a job a long time ago. She got a job last week.
   _____
6. 자신에 대해 쓰시오.
   _____

Do you know where ... ?
I don't know what ... 등

> **Do you know where** Paula **is**?
>
> 폴라가 어디에 있는지 아세요?

두 문장의 어순을 비교해 보자: Where **is** Paula? (동사 + 주어)

Do you know where Paula **is**? (주어 + 동사)

(Do you know where is Paula?는 틀림)

다음 문장들도 '주어 + 동사'의 어순인 점에 유의한다:

I know
I don't know } where **Paula is**.

Can you tell me where **Paula is**?

비교:

동사 + 주어		주어 + 동사	
Who **are those people**?	**Do you know**	who **those people are**	?
How old **is Nicole**?	**Can you tell me**	how old **Nicole is**	
What time **is it**?		what time **it is**	
Where **can I** go?		where I **can** go	
How much **is this camera**?	**I know**	how much **this camera is**	.
When **are you** leaving town?	**I don't know**	when **you're** leaving town	
Where **have they** gone?	**I don't remember**	where **they have** gone	
What **was Jenny** wearing?		what **Jenny was** wearing	

do/does/did가 들어가는 의문문 (단순현재와 단순과거)

Where **does he live**?

Do you know where **he lives**? (Do you know where does he live?는 틀림)

비교:

동사 + 주어	주어 + 동사	
How **do airplanes** fly?	**Do you know**	how **airplanes fly**	?
What **does Jane** want?	**I don't know**	what **Jane wants**	
Why **did she** go home?	**I don't remember**	why **she went** home	.
Where **did I** put the key?	**I know**	where **I put** the key	
내가 열쇠를 어디다 뒀지?			

Is ... ? / Do ... ? / Can ... ? 등으로 시작하는 의문문 (yes/no 의문문)

비교:

동사 + 주어			주어 + 동사	
Is Jack at home?	Do you know	if	**Jack is** at home	?
Have they got a car?			**they've got** a car	
Can Brian swim?		또는	**Brian can** swim	
Do they live near here?	I don't know	whether	**they live** near here	.
Did anybody see you?			**anybody saw** you	

Do you know if/whether ... ?: 너는 ···인지 아닌지 아니?

- Do you know **if** they've got a car?   또는   Do you know **whether** they've got a car?
  그들에게 차가 있는지 없는지 아니?
- I don't know **if** anybody saw me.   또는   I don't know **whether** anybody saw me.

Exercises

50.1 다음 질문에 *I don't know where/when/why ...* 등의 구문을 사용하여 답하시오.

1.	Have your friends gone home?	(where) _I don't know where they've gone._
2.	Is Sue in her office?	(where) I don't know _____
3.	Is the building very old?	(how old) _____
4.	Will Paul be here soon?	(when) _____
5.	Was he angry because I was late?	(why) _____
6.	Has Donna lived here a long time?	(how long) _____

50.2 다음 문장을 완성하시오.

1. (How do airplanes fly?)   Do you know _how airplanes fly_ ?
2. (Where does Susan work?)   I don't know _____ .
3. (What did Peter say?)   Do you remember _____ ?
4. (Why did he go home early?)   I don't know _____ .
5. (What time does the meeting begin?)   Do you know _____ ?
6. (How did the accident happen?)   I don't remember _____ .

50.3 맞는 것을 고르시오.

1. Do you know what time ~~is it~~ / it is?   (*it is*가 맞음)
2. Why <u>are you / you are</u> leaving?
3. I don't know where <u>are they / they are</u> going.
4. Can you tell me where <u>is the museum / the museum is</u>?
5. Where <u>do you want / you want</u> to go for vacation?
6. Do you know what <u>do elephants eat / elephants eat</u>?
7. I don't know how far <u>is it / it is</u> from the hotel to the station.

50.4 *Do you know if/whether... ?*를 사용하여 의문문을 쓰시오.

1. (Do they have a car?)   _Do you know if/whether they have a car?_
2. (Are they married?)   Do you know _____
3. (Does Sue know Bill?)   _____
4. (Will Gary be here tomorrow?)   _____
5. (Did he pass his exam?)   _____

50.5 *Do you know ... ?*로 시작하는 의문문을 쓰시오.

1. (What does Laura want?)   _Do you know what Laura wants?_
2. (Where is Paula?)   Do _____
3. (Is she working today?)   _____
4. (What time does she start work?)   _____
5. (Are the banks open tomorrow?)   _____
6. (Where do Sarah and Tim live?)   _____
7. (Did they go to Jane's party?)   _____

50.6 자신의 생각대로 아래의 문장을 완성하시오.

1. Do you know why _the bus was late_ ?
2. Do you know what time _____ ?
3. Excuse me, can you tell me where _____ ?
4. I don't know what _____ .
5. Do you know if _____ ?
6. Do you know how much _____ ?

She said that . . .   He told me that . . .

A

지난주 당신은 파티에 갔습니다. 다음은 거기서 만난 친구들이 당신에게 한 말입니다.

오늘 당신은 폴을 만나 파티 이야기를 했습니다. 당신은 폴에게 친구들의 말을 전했습니다.

현재　　과거

> **I'm** enjoying my new job.
> **My father isn't** very happy.

Diane

am
is　}→　was

- Diane said that **she was** enjoying her new job.
  다이앤은 새 일이 즐겁다고 말했다.
- She said that **her father wasn't** very happy.

> **We're** going to buy a house.

Sarah　Tim

are　→　were

- Sarah and Tim said that **they were** going to buy a house.

> **I have** to leave early.
> **My sister has** gone to Australia.

Peter

have
has　}→　had

- Peter said that **he had** to leave early.
  피터는 일찍 가야 한다고 말했다.
- He said that **his sister had** gone to Australia.

> **I can't** find a job.

Kate

can　→　could

- Kate said that **she couldn't** find a job.

> **I'll** call you.

Steve

will　→　would

- Steve said that **he would** call me.
  스티브는 나에게 전화하겠다고 말했다.

> **I don't** like my job.
> **My son doesn't** like school.

Rachel

do
does　}→　did

- Rachel said that **she didn't** like her job.
- She said that **her son didn't** like school.

> **You look** tired.
> **I feel** fine.

Mike　You

look
feel
등　}→
looked
felt
등

- Mike said that **I looked** tired.
  마이크는 내가 피곤해 보인다고 말했다.
- I said that **I felt** fine.
  나는 괜찮다고 말했다.

B　say와 tell

say (→ said)	tell (→ told)
■ He **said** that he was tired.	■ He **told me** that he was tired.
(He said me는 틀림)	(He told that은 틀림)
■ What did she **say to** you?	■ What did she **tell you**?
(say you는 틀림)	(tell to you는 틀림)
주의: **He said to me, I said to Ann**	주의: **He told me, I told Ann**
(he said me, I said Ann은 틀림)	(He told to me, I told to Ann은 틀림)

C　that은 생략할 수 있다.

- He said **that** he was tired.　또는　He said he was tired.
- Kate told me **that** she couldn't find a job.　또는　Kate told me she couldn't find a job.

　I told you to ... → Unit 54

Exercises

51.1 다음 사람들이 하는 말을 읽고 **He/She/They said (that)** ...를 사용하여 문장을 쓰시오.

1. I've lost my watch.

   He said he had lost his watch.

2. I'm very busy.

   _____

3. I can't go to the party.

   _____

4. I have to go out.

   _____

5. I'm learning Russian.

   _____

6. I don't feel very well.

   _____

7. We'll be home late.

   _____

8. I've just gotten back from vacation.

   _____

9. I'm going to buy a new computer.

   _____

10. We don't have a key.

    _____

51.2 그림을 보고 문장을 완성하시오.

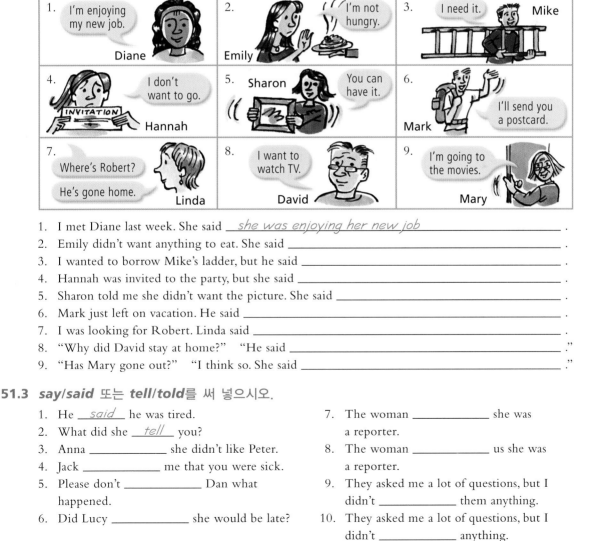

1. I met Diane last week. She said __she was enjoying her new job__ .
2. Emily didn't want anything to eat. She said _____ .
3. I wanted to borrow Mike's ladder, but he said _____ .
4. Hannah was invited to the party, but she said _____ .
5. Sharon told me she didn't want the picture. She said _____ .
6. Mark just left on vacation. He said _____ .
7. I was looking for Robert. Linda said _____ .
8. "Why did David stay at home?" "He said _____ ."
9. "Has Mary gone out?" "I think so. She said _____ ."

51.3 **say/said** 또는 **tell/told**를 써 넣으시오.

1. He __said__ he was tired.
2. What did she __tell__ you?
3. Anna _____ she didn't like Peter.
4. Jack _____ me that you were sick.
5. Please don't _____ Dan what happened.
6. Did Lucy _____ she would be late?
7. The woman _____ she was a reporter.
8. The woman _____ us she was a reporter.
9. They asked me a lot of questions, but I didn't _____ them anything.
10. They asked me a lot of questions, but I didn't _____ anything.

103

work/working go/going do/doing

A

동사원형: **work/go/be** 등

will/can/must 등과 같은 조동사 뒤에는 동사원형을 쓴다.

will shall might may can could must should would	■ Anna **will be** here soon. ■ **Shall** I **open** the window?	} → Units 28–29
	■ I **might call** you later. ■ **May** I **sit** here?	} → Unit 30
	■ I **can't meet** you tomorrow. ■ **Could** you **pass** the salt, please?	} → Unit 31
	■ It's late. You **must be** tired. 늦었어. 너 정말 피곤하겠다.	→ Unit 32
	■ You **shouldn't work** so hard.	→ Unit 33
	■ **Would** you **like** some coffee? 커피 좀 드시겠어요?	→ Unit 35

do/does/did 뒤에도 동사원형이 온다.

| do/does
(단순현재) | ■ **Do** you **work**?
■ They **don't work** very hard.
■ Helen **doesn't know** many people.
 헬렌은 사람들을 많이 알지 못한다.
■ How much **does** it **cost**? 그건 값이 얼마니? | → Units 6–7 |
| did
(단순과거) | ■ What time **did** the train **leave**?
■ We **didn't sleep** well. | → Unit 12 |

B

to 부정사: **to work** / **to go** / **to be** 등

(I'm) **going to** ...	■ I'm **going to play** tennis tomorrow. ■ What **are** you **going to do**?	→ Unit 27
(I) **have to** ...	■ I **have to go** now. ■ Everybody **has to eat**.	→ Unit 34
(I) **want to** ...	■ Do you **want to go** out? ■ They don't **want to come** with us.	→ Unit 53
(I) **would like to** ...	■ I'd **like to talk** to you. ■ **Would** you **like to go** out?	→ Unit 35
(I) **used to** ...	■ Dave **used to work** in a factory. 데이브는 예전에 공장에서 일했다.	→ Unit 15

C

현재분사: **working/going/playing** 등

| am/is/are + -ing
(현재진행) | ■ Please be quiet. I'm **working**.
■ Tom **isn't working** today.
■ What time **are** you **going** out? | → Units 3–4, 8, 26 |
| was/were + -ing
(과거진행) | ■ It **was raining**, so we didn't go out.
■ What **were** you **doing** when the phone rang?
 전화가 왔을 때 넌 뭘 하고 있었니? | → Units 13–14 |

Exercises

52.1 *call Paul* 또는 *to call Paul*을 넣어 문장을 완성하시오.

1. I'll _call Paul_ .
2. I'm going _to call Paul_ .
3. Can you _____ Paul?
4. Shall I _____ ?
5. I'd like _____ .
6. Do you have _____ ?
7. You should _____ .
8. I want _____ .
9. I might _____ .
10. Could you _____ ?

52.2 아래에서 알맞은 동사를 골라 원형(*work/go* 등) 또는 *-ing* (*working/going* 등)
형태로 써 넣어 문장을 완성하시오.

do/doing	eat/eating	fly/flying	get/getting
go/going	listen/listening	~~sleep/sleeping~~	stay/staying
wait/waiting	watch/watching	wear/wearing	~~work/working~~

1. Please be quiet. I'm _working_ .
2. I feel tired today. I didn't _sleep_ very well last night.
3. What time do you usually _____ up in the morning?
4. "Where are you _____ ?" "To the bank."
5. Did you _____ television last night?
6. Look at that plane! It's _____ very low.
7. You can turn off the radio. I'm not _____ to it.
8. They didn't _____ anything because they weren't hungry.
9. My friends were _____ for me when I arrived.
10. "Does Susan always _____ glasses?" "No, only for reading."
11. "What are you _____ tonight?" "I'm _____ home."

52.3 괄호 안의 동사를 다음 중 한 형태로 써 넣으시오.

원형 (*work/go* 등)
to 부정사 (*to work / to go* 등)
-ing (*working/going* 등)

1. Should I _open_ the window? (open)
2. It's late. I have _to go_ now. (go)
3. Amanda isn't _working_ this week. She's on vacation. (work)
4. I'm tired. I don't want _____ out. (go)
5. It might _____ , so take an umbrella with you. (rain)
6. What time do you have _____ tomorrow morning? (leave)
7. I'm sorry I can't _____ you. (help)
8. My brother is a student. He's _____ physics. (study)
9. Would you like _____ on a trip around the world? (go)
10. When you saw Maria, what was she _____ ? (wear)
11. When you go to London, where are you going _____ ? (stay)
12. "Where's Gary?" "He's _____ a bath." (take)
13. I used _____ a car, but I sold it last year. (have)
14. He spoke very quietly. I couldn't _____ him. (hear)
15. You don't look well. I don't think you should _____ to work today. (go)
16. I don't know what he said. I wasn't _____ to him. (listen)
17. I'm sorry I'm late. I had _____ a phone call. (make)
18. I want _____ a doctor. (be) Medical students must _____ courses in
    biology and chemistry. (take)
19. May I please _____ your phone? (use)

UNIT 53

to ... (I want to do)와 -ing (I enjoy doing)

A

동사 + to ... (I want to do)

want	plan	decide	try
hope	expect	offer	forget
need	promise	refuse	learn

+ to ... (to do / to work / to be 등)

- What do you **want to do** tonight?
- It's not very late. We don't **need to go** home yet.
- Tina has **decided to sell** her car.
- You **forgot to turn** off the light when you went out. 당신은 나갈 때 불 끄는 걸 잊었어요.
- My brother is **learning to drive**.
- I **tried to read** my book, but I was too tired. 나는 책을 읽으려고 했지만 너무 피곤했다.

B

동사 + -ing (I enjoy doing)

enjoy	stop	
mind	finish	suggest

+ -ing (doing/working/being 등)

- I **enjoy dancing**. (enjoy to dance는 틀림)
- I don't **mind getting** up early.
  난 일찍 일어나는 것도 괜찮아요.
- Has it **stopped raining**?
- Sonia **suggested going** to the movies.
  소냐는 영화관에 가자고 제안했다.

I enjoy dancing.

C

동사 + -ing 또는 to ...

like	love	start
prefer	hate	begin

continue + -ing (doing 등) 또는 to ... (to do 등)

- Do you **like getting** up early? 또는 Do you **like to get** up early?
- I **prefer traveling** by car. 또는 I **prefer to travel** by car.
  나는 차로 여행하는 것을 더 좋아한다.
- Anna **loves dancing**. 또는 Anna **loves to dance**.
- I **hate being** late. 또는 I **hate to be** late. 나는 늦는 것을 싫어한다.
- It **started raining**. 또는 It **started to rain**.

D

would like to ... 등

would like	**would** love
would prefer	**would** hate

+ to ... (to do / to work / to be 등)

- Julia **would like to meet** you.
- **I'd love to go** to Australia. (I'd = I would)
- "**Would** you **like to sit** down?" 앉으시겠어요?
  "No, **I'd prefer to stand**, thank you." 아니요, 전 서 있는 게 더 좋아요. 감사합니다.
- I like this city very much. I **wouldn't like to move**.
- **I'd hate to lose** my cell phone.

would like → Unit 35   I want you to ... → Unit 54   go + -ing → Unit 56   전치사 + -ing → Unit 113

Exercises

53.1 괄호 안의 동사를 **to ...** 또는 **-ing** 형태로 써 넣으시오.

1. I enjoy _dancing_ . (dance)
2. What do you want _to do_ tonight? (do)
3. Goodbye! I hope _____ you again soon. (see)
4. I learned _____ when I was five years old. (swim)
5. Have you finished _____ the kitchen? (clean)
6. Where's Anna? I need _____ her something. (ask)
7. Do you enjoy _____ other countries? (visit)
8. The weather was nice, so I suggested _____ for a walk by the river. (go)
9. Where's Bill? He promised _____ here on time. (be)
10. I'm not in a hurry. I don't mind _____ . (wait)
11. What have you decided _____ ? (do)
12. Gary was very angry and refused _____ to me. (speak)
13. I'm tired. I want _____ to bed. (go)
14. I was very upset and started _____ . (cry)
15. I'm trying _____ . (work) Please stop _____ . (talk)

53.2 아래의 동사를 **to ...** 또는 **-ing** 형태로 넣어 문장을 완성하시오.

~~go~~   go   help   lose   rain   read   see   send   wait   watch

1. "Have you ever been to Australia?" "No, but I'd love _to go_ ."
2. Jane had a lot to do, so I offered _____ her.
3. I'm surprised that you're here. I didn't expect _____ you.
4. Nicole has a lot of books. She enjoys _____ .
5. This ring was my grandmother's. I'd hate _____ it.
6. Don't forget _____ us a postcard when you're on vacation.
7. I'm not going out until it stops _____ .
8. What should we do this afternoon? Would you like _____ to the beach?
9. When I'm tired in the evening, I like _____ television.
10. "Do you want to go now?" "No, I'd prefer _____ a few minutes."

53.3 질문에 대한 답을 완성하시오.

1. Do you usually get up early?
2. Do you ever go to museums?
3. Would you like to go to a museum now?
4. Do you write e-mails often?
5. Have you ever been to Rome?
6. Do you ever travel by train?
7. Do you want to walk home or take a taxi?

Yes, I like _to get up early_ .
Yes, I love _____ .
No, I'm hungry. I'd prefer _____ to a restaurant.
No, I don't like _____ .
No, but I'd love _____ one day.
Yes, I enjoy _____ .
I don't mind _____ , but a taxi would be quicker.

53.4 **to ...** 또는 **-ing**를 사용하여 자신의 생각대로 문장을 완성하시오.

1. I enjoy _____
2. I don't like _____
3. If it's a nice day tomorrow, I'd like _____
4. When I'm on vacation, I like _____
5. I don't mind _____ , but _____
6. I wouldn't like _____

→ 추가연습문제 32 (260쪽)

I want you to ... I told you to ...

A   **I want you to**

The woman **wants to leave**.
여자는 떠나려고 한다.
The man **doesn't want** the woman to leave.
남자는 여자가 떠나기를 원치 않는다.
He **wants** her **to stay**.
그는 여자가 있기를 원한다.

want + 사람 + **to** ...: ···가 ···하기를 원하다

I want	you somebody Sarah	**to do** something

- I **want you to be** happy. (I want that you are happy는 틀림)
- They didn't **want anybody to know** their secret.
  그들은 자신들의 비밀이 알려지는 것을 원치 않았다.
- Do you **want me to lend** you some money? 내가 돈을 좀 빌려줬으면 좋겠니?

would like도 같은 형식으로 사용된다.
- **Would** you **like me to lend** you some money?

B   동사 + 사람 + **to** ... 구문을 쓰는 동사들:

	동사 +	사람 +	to ...	
ask	Sue **asked**	a friend	**to lend**	her some money.
tell	I **told**	you	**to be**	careful.
advise	What do you **advise**	me	**to do**?	
expect	I didn't **expect**	them	**to be**	here.
persuade	We **persuaded**	Gary	**to come**	with us.
teach	I **am teaching**	my brother	**to swim**.	

C   **I told** you to ... / **I told** you **not to** ...

Wait for me.

Jane   Me

→ Jane **told** me **to wait** for her.
제인은 내게 자기를 기다리라고 말했다.

Don't wait for me.

Paul   Sue

→ Paul **told** Sue **not to wait** for him.
폴은 수에게 자기를 기다리지 말라고 말했다.

D   **make**와 **let**

make와 **let** 뒤에는 **to**를 쓰지 않는다.
- He's very funny. He **makes** me **laugh**. (makes me to laugh는 틀림)
- At school our teacher **made us work** very hard.
- Sue **let** me **use** her computer because mine wasn't working. (let me to use는 틀림)
  내 컴퓨터가 고장났기 때문에 수는 자기 컴퓨터를 쓰게 해줬다.

Let's ... (= **Let us**)는 사람들에게 무엇을 함께 하자고 청할 때 쓴다.
- Come on! **Let's dance**.
- "Do you want to go out tonight?" "No, I'm tired. **Let's stay** home."

Exercises

54.1 *I want you ... / I don't want you ... / Do you want me ... ?*로 시작하는 문장을 쓰시오.

1. (you have to come with me) ___*I want you to come with me.*___
2. (listen carefully) I want _____
3. (please don't be angry) I don't _____
4. (should I wait for you?) Do you _____
5. (don't call me tonight) _____
6. (you should meet Sarah) _____

54.2 그림을 보고 문장을 완성하시오.

1. Dan persuaded ___*me to go to the movies.*___
2. I wanted to get to the station. A woman told _____
3. Brian was sick. I advised _____
4. Linda had a lot of luggage. She asked _____
5. I was too busy to talk to Tom. I told _____
6. I wanted to make a phone call. Paul let _____
7. Sue is going to call me later. I told _____
8. Ann's mother taught _____

54.3 아래의 동사를 to ... (*to go / to wait* 등) 또는 원형(*go/wait* 등)으로 사용하여 문장을 완성하시오.

       arrive   borrow   get   go   ~~leave~~   make   repeat   tell   think   wait

1. Please stay here. I don't want you ___*to leave*___ yet.
2. I didn't hear what she said, so I asked her _____ it.
3. "Should we begin?"   "No, let's _____ a few minutes."
4. Are they already here? I expected them _____ much later.
5. Kevin's parents didn't want him _____ married.
6. I want to stay here. You can't make me _____ with you.
7. "Is that your bicycle?"   "No, it's John's. He let me _____ it."
8. Rachel can't come to the party. She told me _____ you.
9. Would you like something to drink? Would you like me _____ some coffee?
10. "Kate doesn't like me."   "What makes you _____ that?"

I went to the store to ...

A

Paula wanted some fruit, so she went to the store.

Why did she go to the store?
To get some fruit.

She went to the store **to get** some fruit.
그녀는 과일을 사러 가게에 갔다.

to ... (**to get** / **to see** 등)는 어떤 행동의 목적을 말할 때 사용한다.

- "Why are you going out?" "**To get** some bread."
- Amy went to the station **to meet** her friend.
- Sue turned on the television **to watch** the news. 그녀는 뉴스를 보기 위해 텔레비전을 켰다.
- I'd like to go to Mexico **to learn** Spanish. 나는 스페인어를 배우러 멕시코에 가고 싶다.

money/time to (do something): ···할 돈/시간

- We need some **money to buy** food. 우리는 음식을 살 돈이 필요하다.
- I don't have **time to watch** television.

B

to ...와 **for ...**

to + 동사 (**to get** / **to see** 등)	**for** + 명사 (**for food** / **for a newspaper** 등)
■ I went to the store **to get** some fruit. (for get은 틀림)	■ I went to the store **for some fruit**.
■ They're going to Brazil **to see** their friends.	■ They're going to Brazil **for a vacation**.
■ We need some money **to buy** food.	■ We need some money **for food**.

C

wait for ...: ···를 기다리다

- Please **wait for** me.
- Are you **waiting for** the bus?

wait to (do something): ···하려고 기다리다

- I'm **waiting to talk** to the manager.
  저는 매니저와 이야기하려고 기다리고 있습니다.
- Are you **waiting to see** the doctor?

wait for (somebody/something) **to ...**:
···가 ···하기를 기다리다

- I can't leave yet. I'm **waiting for John to call**.
  아직 떠날 수가 없어요. 존에게서 전화가 오기를 기다리고 있어요.
- Are you **waiting for the mail to come**?
  편지가 오기를 기다리고 있니?

I can't leave yet. I'm **waiting for** John to call.

go to ...와 **go for ...** → Unit 56 **something to eat / nothing to do** 등 → Unit 80
enough + to/for ... → Unit 92 **too + to/for ...** → Unit 93

Exercises

55.1 아래의 표현을 사용하여 *I went to ...*로 시작하는 문장을 쓰시오.

a coffee shop	the drugstore		buy some food	get some medicine
~~the post office~~	the supermarket	+	~~get some stamps~~	meet a friend

1. ___I went to the post office to get some stamps.___
2. I went _____
3. _____
4. _____

55.2 아래의 표현을 사용하여 문장을 완성하시오.

to get some fresh air	to open this door	to read the newspaper
to see who it was	to wake him up	~~to watch the news~~

1. I turned on the television ___to watch the news___ .
2. Alice sat down in an armchair _____ .
3. Do I need a key _____ ?
4. I went for a walk by the river _____ .
5. I knocked on the door of David's room _____ .
6. The doorbell rang, so I looked out of the window _____ .

55.3 *to ...*를 사용하여 자신의 생각대로 문장을 완성하시오.

1. I went to the store ___to get some fruit___
2. I'm very busy. I don't have time _____ .
3. I called Ann _____ .
4. I'm going out _____ .
5. I borrowed some money _____ .

55.4 *to* 또는 *for*를 써 넣으시오.

1. I went to the store ___to___ get some bread.
2. We went to a restaurant _____ have dinner.
3. Robert wants to go to college _____ study economics.
4. I'm going to Boston _____ an interview next week.
5. I'm going to Toronto _____ visit some friends of mine.
6. Do you have time _____ a cup of coffee?
7. I got up late this morning. I didn't have time _____ comb my hair.
8. Everybody needs money _____ live.
9. We didn't have any money _____ a taxi, so we walked home.
10. The office is very small. There's only enough room _____ a desk and chair.
11. *A:* Excuse me, are you waiting _____ use the phone?
    B: No, I'm waiting _____ somebody.

55.5 아래의 단어를 사용하여 문장을 완성하시오.

~~John / call~~   it / to arrive   you / tell me   the movie / begin

1. I can't go out yet. I'm waiting ___for John to call___
2. I sat down in the movie theater and waited _____ .
3. We called an ambulance and waited _____ .
4. "Do you know what to do?" "No, I'm waiting _____ ."

go to ...   go on ...   go for ...   go + -ing

A

go to ... (**go to work** / **go to San Francisco** / **go to a concert** 등): ···에 가다

- What time do you usually **go to work**?
  보통 몇 시에 출근합니까?
- I'm **going to China** next week.
- Jean didn't want to **go to the concert**.
- What time did you **go to bed** last night?
  어제 몇 시에 잤어요?
- I **went to the dentist** yesterday.

go to sleep: 잠들다 (= start to sleep)
- I was very tired and **went to sleep** quickly.

go home (**to**를 안 씀)
- I'm **going home** now. (going to home은 틀림)

go to ⟶

B

go on ...: (여행 등을) 가다, (파업을) 하다

go on	vacation a trip a tour an excursion a cruise strike

- We're **going on vacation** next week.
- Children often **go on school trips**.
- When we were in Egypt, we **went on a tour** of the Pyramids.
  이집트에 있을 때 우리는 피라미드 투어를 갔다.
- Workers at the airport have **gone on strike**.
  공항 근무자들은 파업 중이다.

C

go for ...: ···하러 가다

go (somewhere) **for**	a walk a run a swim lunch dinner 등

- "Where's Joan?"   "She **went for a walk**."
- Do you **go for a run** every morning?
- The water looks nice. I'm **going for a swim**.
- Should we **go** out **for dinner**? I know a good restaurant.
  나가서 저녁 먹을까? 내가 좋은 레스토랑을 알아.

D

go + -ing: ···하러 가다

go는 흔히 운동(**swimming/skiing** 등)이나 **shopping** 등의 표현과 함께 쓰인다.

I **go** he is **going** we **went** they have **gone** she wants to **go**	shopping swimming fishing sailing skiing jogging running 등

I'm **going skiing**.

- Are you **going shopping** this afternoon?
- It's a nice day. Let's **go swimming**.
  (또는 Let's **go for a** swim.)
- Richard has a small boat, and he often **goes sailing**.
- I **went jogging** before breakfast this morning.
  나는 오늘 아침 식사 전에 조깅하러 갔다.

Exercises

56.1 필요한 곳에 *to/on/for*를 써 넣으시오.

1. I'm going ___to___ China next week.
2. Richard often goes ___−___ sailing. (전치사가 필요없음)
3. Sue went _____ Mexico last year.
4. Would you like to go _____ the movies tonight?
5. Jack goes _____ jogging every morning.
6. I'm going out _____ a walk. Do you want to come?
7. I'm tired because I went _____ bed very late last night.
8. Jim is going _____ a trip _____ Turkey next week.
9. The weather was warm, and the river was clean, so we went _____ a swim.
10. The taxi drivers went _____ strike when I was in New York.
11. I need some stamps, so I'm going _____ the post office.
12. It's late. I have to go _____ home now.
13. Would you like to go _____ a tour of the city?
14. Do you want to go out _____ dinner this evening?
15. My parents are going _____ a cruise this summer.

56.2 그림을 보고 *go/goes/going/went* + *-ing*를 사용하여 문장을 완성하시오.

1. often	2. last Saturday	3. every day	4. next winter	5. later	6. yesterday
Richard	Diane	Gary	Nicole	Peter	Sarah

1. Richard has a boat. He often ___goes sailing___ .
2. Last Saturday Diane _____ .
3. Gary _____ every day.
4. Nicole is going to Colorado next winter. She is _____ .
5. Peter is going out later. He has to _____ .
6. Sarah _____ after work yesterday.

56.3 아래의 단어를 사용하여 문장을 완성하시오. 필요한 경우 *to/on/for*를 넣으시오.

~~a swim~~	vacation	Hawaii	shopping	bed
a walk	home	riding	skiing	college

1. The water looks nice. Let's go ___for a swim___ .
2. After finishing high school, Tina went _____ , where she studied psychology.
3. I'm going _____ now. I have to buy a few things.
4. I was very tired last night. I went _____ early.
5. I wasn't enjoying the party, so I went _____ early.
6. We live near the mountains. In winter we go _____ almost every weekend.
7. Richard has a horse. He goes _____ a lot.
8. It's a beautiful day! Would you like to go _____ in the park?
9. *A:* Are you going _____ soon?
   B: Yes, next month. We're going _____ . We've never been there before.

get

A

get + 명사 (**get a letter** / **get a job** 등): …를 받다/사다/찾다

you **don't have** something → you **get** it → you **have** it

- "Did you **get** my postcard?" "Yes, I **got** it yesterday." (= 받다, receive)
- I like your sweater. Where did you **get** it? (= 사다, buy)
- Is it difficult to **get** a job at the moment? (= 찾다, find) 지금 당장은 일자리를 구하기가 힘듭니까?
- (전화상으로) "Hello, can I speak to Lisa, please?" "Sure. I'll **get** her."

B

get + 형용사 (**get hungry** / **get cold** / **get tired** 등): …되다, …지다

you**'re not hungry** → you **get hungry** → you **are hungry**

- If you don't eat, you **get hungry**.
- Drink your coffee. It**'s getting cold**. 커피 마셔요. 커피가 식고 있어요.
- I'm sorry your mother is sick. I hope she **gets better** soon.
- It was raining very hard. We didn't have an umbrella, so we **got** very **wet**.

또한
get married
get dressed (= 옷을 입다, put your clothes on)
get lost (= 길을 잃다, lose your way)

- Nicole and Frank are **getting married** soon.
- I got up and **got dressed** quickly.
- We didn't have a map, so we **got lost**. 우리는 지도가 없어서 길을 잃었다.

C

get to a place: 도착하다 (= arrive)

- I usually **get to work** before 8:30. (= arrive at work)
- We left Boston at 10:15 and **got to Ottawa** at 11:45.

get to

get here/there (**to**를 안 씀):

- How did you **get here**? By bus?

get home (**to**를 안 씀):

- What time did you **get home** last night?

D

get in/out/on/off

get in (a car): (차에) 타다

get out (of a car): (차에서) 내리다

get on (a bus/a train/ a plane): (버스/기차/ 비행기에) 타다

get off: (버스/기차/ 비행기에서) 내리다

- Kate **got in the car** and drove away. (= Kate got **into** the car and …)
- A car stopped and a man **got out**. (비교: A man got out of the car.) 차 한 대가 멈추더니 한 남자가 내렸다.
- We **got on the bus** outside the hotel and **got off** at Church Street.

Exercises

57.1 *get/gets*와 아래의 단어를 사용하여 문장을 완성하시오.

another one	a doctor	a lot of rain	~~my postcard~~	the job
a good salary	a new computer	a ticket	some milk	your jacket

1. Did you _get my postcard_ ? I sent it a week ago.
2. Where did you _____ ? It's very nice.
3. Quick! This man is sick. We have to _____ .
4. I want to return this phone. It doesn't work. Can I _____ , please?
5. Tom has an interview tomorrow. I hope he _____ .
6. When you go out, can you _____ ?
7. "Are you going to the concert?"   "Yes, if I can _____ ."
8. Margaret has a well-paid job. She _____ .
9. The weather is horrible here in winter. We _____ .
10. I'm going to _____ . The one I have is too slow.

57.2 *getting* + 아래의 단어를 사용하여 문장을 완성하시오.

~~cold~~   dark   late   married   ready

1. Drink your coffee. It's _getting cold_ .
2. Turn on the light. It's _____ .
3. "I'm _____ next week."   "Really? Congratulations!"
4. "Where's Karen?"   "She's _____ to go out."
5. It's _____ . It's time to go home.

57.3 *get/gets/got* + 아래의 단어를 사용하여 문장을 완성하시오.

angry   better   ~~hungry~~   lost   married   old   wet

1. If you don't eat, you _get hungry_ .
2. Don't go out in the rain. You'll _____ .
3. My brother _____ last year. His wife's name is Sarah.
4. Dan is always very calm. He never _____ .
5. We tried to find the hotel, but we _____ .
6. Everybody wants to stay young, but we all _____ .
7. Yesterday the weather wasn't so good at first, but it _____ during the day.

57.4 *I left ... and got to ...* 를 사용하여 문장을 쓰시오.

1. home / 7:30 → work / 8:15
   I left home at 7:30 and got to work at 8:15.
2. Toronto / 10:15 → New York / 12:00
   I left Toronto at 10:15 and _____
3. the party / 11:15 → home / midnight
   _____
4. 자신에 대한 문장을 쓰시오.
   I left _____

57.5 *got in / got out of / got on / got off*를 써 넣으시오.

1. Kate _got in_ the car and drove away.
2. I _____ the bus and walked to my house from the bus stop.
3. Lisa _____ the car, locked the doors, and went into a store.
4. I made a stupid mistake. I _____ the wrong train.

do와 make

A

do는 행위를 포괄적으로 지칭하는 단어이다.

- What are you **doing** tonight? (What are you making?은 틀림)
- "Shall I open the window?" "No, it's OK. I'll **do** it."
- Linda's job is very boring. She **does** the same thing every day.
- I **did** a lot of things yesterday.

What do you do?: 직업이 무엇입니까? (= What's your job?)

- "What do you **do**?" "I work in a bank."

B

make: 만들다 (= produce/create)

She's **making** coffee.
그녀는 커피를 만들고
있다.

He has **made** a cake.
그는 케익을 만들었다.

They **make** toys.
그들은 장난감을
만든다.

It was **made** in China.
그것은 중국에서
만들어졌다.

do와 **make**의 비교:

- I **did** a lot yesterday. I **cleaned** my room, I **wrote** some letters, and I **made** a cake.
- *A:* What do you **do** in your free time? Read? Play sports?
  B: I **make** clothes. I **make** dresses and jackets. I also **make** toys for my children.

C

do를 사용하는 표현들

do	homework housework (somebody) a favor an exercise (your) best the laundry the dishes

- Have the children **done their homework**?
- I hate **doing housework**, especially cleaning.
- Barbara, could you **do me a favor**?
- I have to **do four exercises** for homework tonight.
- I **did my best**, but I didn't win the race.
- Tim usually **does the laundry** on Saturdays.
  팀은 주로 토요일에 빨래를 한다.
- I cooked, so you should **do the dishes**.
  내가 요리를 했으니 너는 설거지를 해야 해.

D

make를 사용하는 표현들

make	a mistake an appointment a phone call a list (a) noise a bed

- I'm sorry, I **made a mistake**.
- I need to **make an appointment** to see the doctor.
- Excuse me, I have to **make a phone call**.
- Have you **made a shopping list**?
- It's late. Don't **make any noise**.
- Sometimes I forget to **make my bed** in the morning.
  가끔 나는 아침에 침대 정리하는 것을 잊어버린다.

make a movie는 '영화를 만들다', **take a picture**는 '사진을 찍다'라는 뜻이다.

- When was **this movie made**? 그러나 When was **this picture taken**?

58.1 **make/making/made** 또는 **do/doing/did/done**을 써 넣으시오.

1. "Shall I open the window?" "No, that's OK. I'll __do__ it."
2. What did you _____ last weekend? Did you leave town?
3. Do you know how to _____ bread?
4. Paper is _____ from wood.
5. Richard didn't help me. He sat in an armchair and _____ nothing.
6. "What do you _____ ?" "I'm a doctor."
7. I asked you to clean the bathroom. Have you _____ it?
8. "What do they _____ in that factory?" "Shoes."
9. I'm _____ some coffee. Would you like some?
10. Why are you angry with me? I didn't _____ anything wrong.
11. "What are you _____ tomorrow afternoon?" "I'm working."

58.2 그림 속의 사람들이 무엇을 하고 있는지 쓰시오.

1. ___He's making a cake.___
2. They _____
3. He _____
4. _____
5. _____
6. _____
7. _____
8. _____
9. _____
10. _____

58.3 **make** 또는 **do**를 올바른 형태로 써 넣으시오.

1. I hate __doing__ housework, especially cleaning.
2. Why do you always _____ the same mistake?
3. "Can you _____ me a favor?" "It depends what it is."
4. "Have you _____ your homework?" "Not yet."
5. I need to see the dentist, but I haven't _____ an appointment.
6. Joe _____ his best, but he didn't pass his driver's test.
7. I painted the door, but I didn't _____ it very well.
8. How many phone calls did you _____ yesterday?
9. When you've finished Exercise 1, you can _____ Exercise 2.
10. There's something wrong with the car. The engine is _____ a strange noise.
11. It was a bad mistake. It was the worst mistake I've ever _____ .
12. Let's _____ a list of all the things we have to _____ today.

have

A

have와 **have got**

I have (something) 또는 **I've got** (something): 나는 …를 가지고 있다

- I **have** a new car.   또는   **I've got** a new car.
- Sue **has** long hair.   또는   Sue **has got** long hair.
- **Do** they **have** any children?   또는   **Have** they **got** any children?
- Tim **doesn't have** a job.   또는   Tim **hasn't got** a job.
- How much time **do** you **have**?   또는   How much time **have** you **got**?

have/**'ve got** + 병, 증상:

I **have**	a headache / a toothache / a pain (in my leg 등)
	두통 / 치통 / (다리 등의) 통증
I **'ve got**	a cold / a cough / a sore throat / a fever / the flu 등
	감기 / 기침 / 인후통 / 열 / 독감 등

- I **have** a headache.   또는   **I've got** a headache.
- **Do** you **have** a cold?   또는   **Have** you **got** a cold?

과거형은 **I had** (got 없이) / **I didn't have** / **Did you have**? 등으로 나타낸다.

- When I first met Sue, she **had** short hair.
- He **didn't have** any money because he **didn't have** a job.
- **Did** you **have** enough time to do everything you wanted?

B

have breakfast / **have a good time** 등

다음 표현에서 **have**의 의미는 '먹다/마시다(**eat/drink**)'이다. 이러한 의미로 쓰이는 have는 have got으로 바꿔 쓸 수 없다.

have	breakfast / lunch / dinner
	a meal / a sandwich / (a) pizza 등
	a cup of coffee / a glass of milk 등
	something to eat/drink

- "Where's Liz?"   "She**'s having** lunch."
- I **don't** usually **have** breakfast.
- I **had** three cups of coffee this morning.
- "**Have** a cookie."   "Oh, thank you."

다음 표현에도 **have**를 사용한다(have got은 쓸 수 없음).

have	a party / a meeting
	a nice time / a good trip / fun 등
	a (nice) day / a (nice) weekend /
	a (great) vacation
	a (good) flight / a safe trip
	a dream / an accident
	an argument / a discussion
	a baby

- We**'re having** a party next week. Please come.
- Enjoy your vacation. **Have** a good trip!
- I**'m having** a bad day. Everything is going wrong. I hope I **have** a better day tomorrow.
- We **have** a 12-hour flight to Lima tomorrow.
- Mark **had** an accident on his first day in Rome.
- Boss, can we **have** a discussion about my pay?
- Sandra **has** just **had** a baby. It's a boy.
  산드라는 방금 아기를 낳았다. 사내아이이다.

C

비교:

have got 또는 **have**
- **I've got** / I **have** three cups of coffee
  for this office.

have (**have got**은 쓸 수 없음)
- I **have** coffee with my breakfast every morning.
  (I've got coffee every morning은 틀림)
- *A*: Where's Paul?
  B: He's on break. He**'s having** a cup of coffee.
   (= he's drinking it now)

I**'ve got** three
cups of coffee
for this office.

I'm on break.
I**'m having** a
cup of coffee.

Exercises

59.1 *have* 또는 *have got*의 올바른 형태를 쓰시오.

1. *I didn't have* time to do the shopping yesterday.   (I / not / have)
2. " *Does Lisa have (또는 Has Lisa got)* a car?"   (Lisa / have?)
   "No, she can't drive."
3. He can't open the door. _____ a key.   (he / not / have)
4. _____ a cold last week. He's better now.   (Gary / have)
5. What's wrong? _____ a headache?   (you / have?)
6. We wanted to go by taxi, but _____ enough money.   (we / not / have)
7. Liz is very busy. _____ much free time.   (she / not / have)
8. _____ any problems when you were on vacation?   (you / have?)

59.2 아래의 단어를 사용하여 그림 속의 사람들이 무엇을 하고 있는지 한 문장으로 쓰시오.

an argument   **breakfast**   **a cup of tea**   **dinner**   **fun**   ~~**a party**~~

1. _They're having a party._   4. They _____
2. She _____   5. _____
3. He _____   6. _____

59.3 다음 상황에서 할 말을 *have*를 사용하여 쓰시오.

1. Barbara is going on vacation. What do you say to her before she goes?
   Have a nice vacation!
2. You meet Claire at the airport. She has just gotten off her plane. Ask her about the flight.
   Did you have a good flight?
3. Tim is going on a long trip. What do you say to him before he leaves?
   _____
4. It's Monday morning. You are at work. Ask Paula about her weekend.
   _____
5. Paul has just come back from vacation. Ask him about his vacation.
   _____
6. Rachel is going out tonight. What do you say to her before she goes?
   _____
7. Sue's little boy will be one year old next week. Is there going to be a birthday party? Ask her.
   _____

59.4 *have/had*와 아래의 단어들을 사용하여 문장을 완성하시오.

an accident   **a glass of water**   **a baby**
a bad dream   ~~**a party**~~   **something to eat**

1. We _had a party_ a few weeks ago. We invited 50 people.
2. "Should we _____ ?"   "No, I'm not hungry."
3. I was thirsty, so I _____ .
4. I _____ last night. It woke me up.
5. Tina is a very good driver. She has never _____ .
6. Rachel is going to _____ . It will be her first child.

I/me he/him they/them 등

A 사람

주격	I	we	you	he	she	they
목적격	me	us	you	him	her	them

주격		목적격	
I	**I** know Tom.	Tom knows **me**.	me
we	**We** know Tom.	Tom knows **us**.	us
you	**You** know Tom.	Tom knows **you**.	you
he	**He** knows Tom.	Tom knows **him**.	him
she	**She** knows Tom.	Tom knows **her**.	her
they	**They** know Tom.	Tom knows **them**.	them

B 사물

It's nice. I like it.

They're nice. I like them.

주격	it	they
목적격	it	them

- I don't want **this book**. You can have **it**.
- I don't want **these books**. You can have **them**.
- Diane never drinks **milk**. She doesn't like **it**.
- I never go to **parties**. I don't like **them**.

C

전치사(**for/to/with** 등) 뒤에는 **me/her/them** 등(목적격)을 사용한다.

- This letter isn't **for me**. It's **for you**. 이 편지는 나한테 온 게 아니야. 너한테 온 거지.
- Who is that woman? Why are you looking **at her**?
- We're going to the movies. Do you want to come **with us**?
- Sue and Kevin are going to the movies. Do you want to go **with them**?
- "Where's the newspaper?" 신문은 어디 있지? "You're sitting **on it**." 네가 깔고 앉아 있잖아.

give it/them to ... :

- I want that book. Please give **it to me**. (give me it은 틀림)
- Robert needs these books. Can you give **them to him**, please?

Exercises

60.1 *him/her/them*을 넣어 문장을 완성하시오.

1. I don't know those girls. Do you know ___them___ ?
2. I don't know that man. Do you know _____ ?
3. I don't know those people. Do you know _____ ?
4. I don't know David's wife. Do you know _____ ?
5. I don't know Mr. Stevens. Do you know _____ ?
6. I don't know Sarah's parents. Do you know _____ ?
7. I don't know the woman in the black coat. Do you know _____ ?

60.2 *I/me/you/she/her* 등을 넣어 문장을 완성하시오.

1. **I** want to see **her**, but ___she___ doesn't want to see ___me___ .
2. **They** want to see **me**, but _____ don't want to see _____ .
3. **She** wants to see **him**, but _____ doesn't want to see _____ .
4. **We** want to see **them**, but _____ don't want to see _____ .
5. **He** wants to see **us**, but _____ don't want to see _____ .
6. **They** want to see **her**, but _____ doesn't want to see _____ .
7. **I** want to see **them**, but _____ don't want to see _____ .
8. **You** want to see **her**, but _____ doesn't want to see _____ .

60.3 *I like ... , I don't like ...* 또는 *Do you like ... ?*로 시작하는 문장을 쓰시오.

1. I don't eat tomatoes. ___I don't like them___ .
2. George is a very nice man. I like _____ .
3. This jacket isn't very nice. I don't _____ .
4. This is my new car. Do _____ ?
5. Mrs. Clark is not very friendly. I _____ .
6. These are my new shoes. _____ ?

60.4 *I/me/he/him* 등을 넣어 문장을 완성하시오.

1. Who is that woman? Why are you looking at ___her___ ?
2. "Do you know that man?"   "Yes, I work with _____ ."
3. Where are the tickets? I can't find _____ .
4. I can't find my keys. Where are _____ ?
5. We're going out. You can come with _____ .
6. I have a new computer. Do you want to see _____ ?
7. Maria likes music. _____ plays the piano.
8. I don't like dogs. I'm afraid of _____ .
9. I'm talking to you. Please listen to _____ .
10. Where is Anna? I want to talk to _____ .
11. You can have these DVDs. I don't want _____ .
12. My brother has a new job, but _____ doesn't like _____ very much.

60.5 문장을 완성하시오.

1. I need that book. Can you ___give it to me___ ?
2. He wants the key. Can you give _____ ?
3. She wants the keys. Can you _____ ?
4. I want that letter. Can you _____ ?
5. They want the money. Can you _____ ?
6. We want the photos. Can you _____ ?

my/his/their 등

A

| my umbrella | our umbrella | your umbrella | his umbrella | her umbrella | their umbrella |

I	→	my
we	→	our
you	→	your
he	→	his
she	→	her
they	→	their

I	like	**my**	house.
We	like	**our**	house.
You	like	**your**	house.
He	likes	**his**	house.
She	likes	**her**	house.
They	like	**their**	house.

it	→	**its**

Hawaii (= **it**) is famous for **its** beaches.

my/your/his 등 + 명사:

my hands	**his** new **car**	**her parents**
our clothes	**your** best **friend**	**their room**

B his/her/their

Donna

her car
(= Donna's car)

her husband
(= Donna's
husband)

her children
(= Donna's
children)

Andy

his bicycle

his sister

his parents

Mr. and
Mrs. Lee

their son

their daughter

their children

C its와 it's

its	Hawaii is famous for **its** beaches. 하와이는 해변으로 유명하다.
it's (= it **is**)	I like Hawaii. **It's** a beautiful place. (= It **is** a beautiful place.) 나는 하와이가 좋다. 그곳은 아름다운 곳이다.

mine/yours 등 → Unit 62   I/me/my/mine → Unit 63

Exercises

61.1 보기와 같이 문장을 완성하시오.

1. I'm going to wash ___my hands___ .
2. She's going to wash _____ hands.
3. We're going to wash _____ .
4. He's going to wash _____ .
5. They're going to wash _____ .
6. Are you going to wash _____ ?

61.2 보기와 같이 문장을 완성하시오.

1. He ___lives with his parents___ .
2. They live with _____ parents.
3. We _____ parents.
4. Jane lives _____ .
5. I _____ parents.
6. John _____ .
7. Do you live _____ ?
8. Most children _____ .

61.3 아래의 가계도를 보고 *his/her/their*를 넣어 문장을 완성하시오.

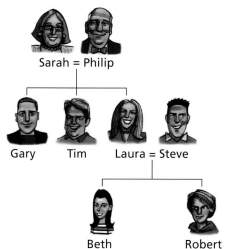

Sarah = Philip

Gary   Tim   Laura = Steve

Beth   Robert

1. I saw Sarah with ___her___ husband, Philip.
2. I saw Laura and Steve with _____ children.
3. I saw Steve with _____ wife, Laura.
4. I saw Gary with _____ brother, Tim.
5. I saw Laura with _____ brother, Tim.
6. I saw Sarah and Philip with _____ son, Tim.
7. I saw Laura with _____ parents.
8. I saw Beth and Robert with _____ parents.

61.4 *my/our/your/his/her/their/its*를 써 넣으시오.

1. Do you like ___your___ job?
2. I know Mr. Watson, but I don't know _____ wife.
3. Alice and Tom live in San Francisco. _____ son lives in Mexico.
4. We're going to have a party. We're going to invite all _____ friends.
5. Anna is going out with _____ friends tonight.
6. I like tennis. It's _____ favorite sport.
7. "Is that _____ car?" "No, I don't have a car."
8. I want to call Maria. Do you know _____ phone number?
9. Do you think most people are happy with _____ jobs?
10. I'm going to wash _____ hair before I go out.
11. This is a beautiful tree. _____ leaves are a beautiful color.
12. John has a brother and a sister. _____ brother is 25, and _____ sister is 21.

61.5 *my/his/their* 등과 아래의 단어를 사용하여 문장을 완성하시오.

    coat   homework   house   husband   ~~job~~   key   name

1. Jim doesn't like ___his job___ . It's not very interesting.
2. I can't get in. I don't have _____ .
3. Sally is married. _____ works in a bank.
4. Please take off _____ and sit down.
5. "What are the children doing?" "They're doing _____ ."
6. "Do you know that man?" "Yes, but I don't know _____ ."
7. We live on Main Street. _____ is on the corner of Main and First.

Whose is this?   It's **mine/yours/hers** 등

A

I	→	**my**	→	**mine**
we	→	**our**	→	**ours**
you	→	**your**	→	**yours**
he	→	**his**	→	**his**
she	→	**her**	→	**hers**
they	→	**their**	→	**theirs**

It's **my** money.	It's **mine**.
It's **our** money.	It's **ours**.
It's **your** money.	It's **yours**.
It's **his** money.	It's **his**.
It's **her** money.	It's **hers**.
It's **their** money.	It's **theirs**.

B

my/your 등의 뒤에는 명사를 쓴다(**my hands / your book** 등).

- ■ **My hands** are cold.
- ■ Is this **your book**?
- ■ Helen gave me **her umbrella**.
- ■ It's **their problem**, not **our problem**.

mine/yours 등은 뒤에 명사를 쓰지 않는다.

- ■ Is this book **mine** or **yours**? (= my book or your book)
  이 책이 내 것이니 네 것이니?
- ■ I didn't have an umbrella, so Helen gave me **hers**. (= her umbrella)
- ■ It's their problem, not **ours**. (= not our problem)
- ■ We went in our car, and they went in **theirs**. (= their car)
  우리는 우리 차를 타고 갔고, 그들은 그들의 차를 타고 갔다.

his는 명사와 함께 쓸 수도 있고 명사 없이 쓸 수도 있다.

- ■ "Is this **his camera** or **hers**?"   "It's **his**."

C

A friend **of mine** / a friend **of his** / some friends **of yours** 등

- ■ I went to the movies with a friend **of mine**. (a friend of me는 틀림)
- ■ Tom was in the restaurant with a friend **of his**. (a friend of him은 틀림)
- ■ Are those people friends **of yours**? (friends of you는 틀림)

D

Whose ... ?

- ■ **Whose book** is this?
  (= Is it your book? his book? my book? 등)

whose는 명사와 함께 쓸 수도 있고 명사 없이 쓸 수도 있다.

- ■ **Whose money** is this?
  Whose is this? } It's mine.
- ■ **Whose shoes** are these?
  Whose are these? } They're John's.

Whose book
is this?

Exercises

62.1 *mine/yours* 등을 넣어 문장을 완성하시오.

1. It's your money. It's __yours__ .
2. It's my bag. It's _____ .
3. It's our car. It's _____ .
4. They're her shoes. They're _____ .
5. It's their house. It's _____ .
6. They're your books. They're _____ .
7. They're my glasses. They're _____ .
8. It's his coat. It's _____ .

62.2 맞는 것을 고르시오.

1. It's their/~~theirs~~ problem, not ~~our~~/ours. (*their*와 *ours*가 맞음)
2. This is a nice camera. Is it your/yours?
3. That's not my/mine umbrella. My/Mine is black.
4. Whose books are these? Your/Yours or my/mine?
5. Catherine is going out with her/hers friends tonight.
6. My/Mine room is bigger than her/hers.
7. They've got two children, but I don't know their/theirs names.
8. Can we use your washing machine? Our/Ours isn't working.

62.3 *friend(s) of mine/yours* 등을 넣어 문장을 완성하시오.

1. I went to the movies with a __friend of mine__ .
2. They went on vacation with some __friends of theirs__ .
3. She's going out with a _____ .
4. We had dinner with some _____ .
5. I played tennis with a _____ .
6. Tom is going to meet a _____ .
7. Do you know those people? Are they _____ ?

62.4 그림 속 사람들이 할 말을 써 넣으시오.

A

I/me/my/mine

I can see him, but he can't see **me**.

You give **me** your phone number, and I'll give you **mine**.

나는 그를 볼 수 있지만, 그는 나를 볼 수 없어.　　　당신 전화번호를 주면, 저도 제 번호를 줄게요.

	I 등 (→ Unit 60)	**me** 등 (→ Unit 60)	**my** 등 (→ Unit 61)	**mine** 등 (→ Unit 62)
	I know Tom.	Tom knows **me**.	It's **my** car.	It's **mine**.
	We know Tom.	Tom knows **us**.	It's **our** car.	It's **ours**.
	You know Tom.	Tom knows **you**.	It's **your** car.	It's **yours**.
	He knows Tom.	Tom knows **him**.	It's **his** car.	It's **his**.
	She knows Tom.	Tom knows **her**.	It's **her** car.	It's **hers**.
	They know Tom.	Tom knows **them**.	It's **their** car.	It's **theirs**.

B

다음 예문을 보자.

- "Do **you** know that man?"　"Yes, **I** know **him**, but **I** can't remember **his name**."
- **She** was very happy because **we** invited **her** to stay with **us** at **our house**.
  우리가 우리 집에 머무르라고 초대했더니 그녀는 매우 기뻐했다.
- *A:* Where are the children? Have **you** seen them?
  B: Yes, **they** are playing with **their friends** in the park.
- That's **my pen**. Can you give it to **me**, please?
- "Is this **your hat**?"　"No, it's **yours**."
- **He** didn't have an umbrella, so **she** gave **him hers**. (= she gave her umbrella to him)
  그는 우산이 없어서 그녀는 자기 우산을 그에게 주었다.
- **I**'m going out with a friend of **mine** tonight. (a friend of me는 틀림)

Exercises

63.1 보기와 같이 질문에 답하시오.

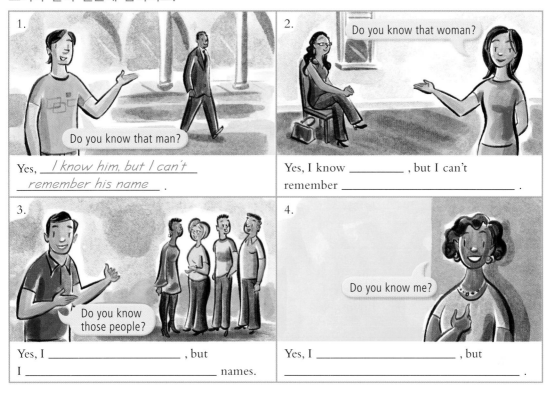

1. Do you know that man?

   Yes, _I know him, but I can't remember his name_ .

2. Do you know that woman?

   Yes, I know _____ , but I can't remember _____ .

3. Do you know those people?

   Yes, I _____ , but I _____ names.

4. Do you know me?

   Yes, I _____ , but _____ .

63.2 보기와 같이 문장을 완성하시오.

1. We invited her _to stay with us at our house_ .
2. He invited us to stay with _____ at his house.
3. They invited me to stay with _____ house.
4. I invited them to stay _____ house.
5. She invited us to stay _____ house.
6. Did you invite him _____ house?

63.3 보기와 같이 문장을 완성하시오.

1. I gave him _my_ address, and _he gave me his_ .
2. I gave her _my_ address, and she gave me _____ .
3. He gave me _his_ address, and I gave _____ .
4. We gave them _____ address, and they gave _____ .
5. She gave him _____ address, and he gave _____ .
6. You gave us _____ address, and we gave _____ .
7. They gave you _____ address, and you gave _____ .

63.4 *him/her/yours* 등을 써 넣으시오.

1. Where's Amanda? Have you seen _her_ ?
2. Where are my keys? Where did I put _____ ?
3. This letter is for Bill. Can you give it to _____ ?
4. We don't see _____ neighbors much. They're not at home very often.
5. "I can't find my pen. Can I use _____ ?" "Sure."
6. We're going to the movies. Why don't you come with _____ ?
7. Did your sister pass _____ driver's test?
8. Some people talk about _____ jobs all the time.
9. Last night I went out for dinner with a friend of _____ .

myself/yourself/themselves 등

He's looking at **himself**.
그는 자신의 모습을 보고 있다.

Help **yourself**!

(직접 담아서) 많이 드세요!

They're enjoying **themselves**.
그들은 즐거운 시간을 보내고 있다.

I	→	me	→	myself
he	→	him	→	himself
she	→	her	→	herself
you	→	you	→	{ yourself / yourselves
we	→	us	→	ourselves
they	→	them	→	themselves

- **I** looked at **myself** in the mirror. 거울 속 내 모습을 바라봤다.
- **He** cut **himself** with a knife.
- **She** fell off her bike, but she didn't hurt **herself**.
  그녀는 자전거에서 떨어졌지만 다치지 않았다.
- Please help **yourself**. (한 사람)
- Please help **yourselves**. (두 사람이나 그 이상)
- We had a good vacation. **We** enjoyed **ourselves**.
- They had a nice time. **They** enjoyed **themselves**.

비교:

me/him/them 등

She is looking at **him**.

다른 사람

- You never talk to **me**.
  당신은 나한테 말을 전혀 안 하는군요.
- I didn't pay for **them**.
- I'm sorry. Did I hurt **you**?

myself/himself/themselves 등

He is looking at **himself**.

같은 사람

- Sometimes I talk to **myself**.
  때때로 나는 혼잣말을 한다.
- They paid for **themselves**.
- Be careful. Don't hurt **yourself**.

by myself / **by yourself** 등: 혼자 (= alone)

- I went on vacation **by myself**. (= I went alone)
- "Was she with friends?" "No, she was **by herself**."

each other: 서로

- Kate and Helen are good friends. They know **each other** well.
  (= Kate knows Helen / Helen knows Kate)
- Paul and I live near **each other**. (= he lives near me / I live near him)

each other와 **-selves**의 비교:

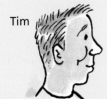

Tim   Sue

Tim   Sue

- Tim and Sue looked at **each other**.
  (= he looked at her, she looked at him)
  팀과 수는 서로를 바라보았다.

- Tim and Sue looked at **themselves**.
  (= he looked at himself, she looked
  at herself) 팀과 수는 그들 자신을 바라보았다.

me/him/them 등 → Unit 60

Exercises

64.1 *myself/yourself* 등을 넣어 문장을 완성하시오.

1. He looked at ___himself___ in the mirror.
2. I'm not angry with you. I'm angry with _____ .
3. Karen had a good time in Brazil. She enjoyed _____ .
4. My friends had a good time in Brazil. They enjoyed _____ .
5. I picked up a very hot plate and burned _____ .
6. He never thinks about other people. He only thinks about _____ .
7. I want to know more about you. Tell me about _____ . *(one person)*
8. Goodbye! Have a good trip and take care of _____ ! *(two people)*

64.2 *by myself* / *by yourself* 등을 사용하여 문장을 완성하시오.

1. I went on vacation alone.   ___I went on vacation by myself.___
2. When I saw him, he was alone.   When I saw him, he _____
3. Don't go out alone.   Don't _____
4. I went to the movies alone.   I _____
5. My sister lives alone.   My sister _____
6. Many people live alone.   Many people _____

64.3 *each other*를 사용하여 문장을 쓰시오.

1. I like her. / I like him.
___They like each other.___

2. I can't see her. / I can't see him.
They can't _____

3. I call him a lot. / I call her a lot.
They _____

4. I don't know him. / I don't know him.
_____

5. I'm sitting next to him. / I'm sitting next to her.
_____

6. I gave her a present. / I gave her a present.
_____

64.4 다음 중 하나를 사용하여 문장을 완성하시오.
each other 또는 *ourselves/yourselves/themselves* 또는 *us/you/them*

1. Paul and I live near ___each other___ .
2. Who are those people? Do you know ___them___ ?
3. You can help Tom, and Tom can help you. So you and Tom can help _____ .
4. There's food in the kitchen. If you and Chris are hungry, you can help _____ .
5. We didn't go to Linda's party. She didn't invite _____ .
6. When we go on vacation, we always enjoy _____ .
7. Mary and Jane went to school together, but they never see _____ now.
8. Diane and I are very good friends. We've known _____ for a long time.
9. "Did you see Sam and Laura at the party?" "Yes, but I didn't speak to _____ ."
10. Many people talk to _____ when they're alone.

-'s (Kate's camera / my brother's car 등)

A

Kate's camera
(**her** camera)

my brother's car
(**his** car)

the manager's office
(**his** office 또는 **her** office)

-'s는 보통 사람에 대해 쓴다.

- I stayed at **my sister's** house. (the house of my sister는 틀림)
- Have you met **Mr. Black's** wife? (the wife of Mr. Black은 틀림)
- Are you going to **James's** party?
- Paul is **a man's** name. Paula is **a woman's** name. 폴은 남자 이름이다. 폴라는 여자 이름이다.

-'s는 뒤에 명사 없이도 쓸 수 있다.

- Sophie's hair is longer than **Kate's**. (= Kate's hair)
- "Whose umbrella is this?" "It's **my mother's**." (= my mother's umbrella)
- "Where were you last night?" "I was at **Paul's**." (= Paul's house)

B

friend's와 **friends'**

my **friend's** house = 친구 한 명
(= **his** house 또는 **her** house)
's는 단수(**friend/student/mother** 등) 뒤에 쓴다.
    my mother's car (어머니 한 분)
    my father's car (아버지 한 분)

my **friends'** house = 두 명 또는 그 이상의 친구
(= **their** house)
'는 복수(friends/students/parents 등) 뒤에 쓴다.
    my parents' car (부모님 두 분)

C

of ...는 사물, 장소 등에 대해 쓴다.

- Look at the roof **of that building**. (that building's roof는 틀림)
- We didn't see the beginning **of the movie**. (the movie's beginning은 틀림)
- What's the name **of this town**?
- Do you know the cause **of the problem**? 문제의 원인이 무엇인지 아세요?
- You can sit in the back **of the car**. 차 뒷좌석에 앉아요.
- Madrid is the capital **of Spain**. 마드리드는 스페인의 수도이다.

Exercises

65.1 다음 가계도를 보고 가족 관계에 대한 문장을 완성하시오.

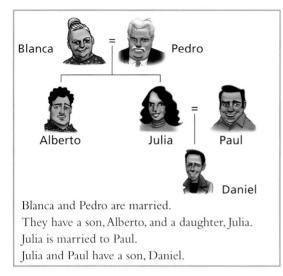

Blanca = Pedro

Alberto   Julia = Paul

Daniel

Blanca and Pedro are married.
They have a son, Alberto, and a daughter, Julia.
Julia is married to Paul.
Julia and Paul have a son, Daniel.

1. Pedro is _Blanca's_ husband.
2. Julia is Daniel's _mother_ .
3. Blanca is _____ wife.
4. Alberto is Julia's _____ .
5. Alberto is _____ uncle.
6. Julia is _____ wife.
7. Blanca is Daniel's _____ .
8. Julia is Alberto's _____ .
9. Paul is _____ husband.
10. Paul is Daniel's _____ .
11. Daniel is _____ nephew.

65.2 그림을 보고 한 단어로 질문에 답하시오.

Jane   Andy   Alice   Diane   Dave

1. Whose is this?
   Alice's

2. Whose is this?
   _____

3. And this?
   _____

4. And these?
   _____

5. And this?
   _____

6. And these?
   _____

65.3 다음 문장에서 틀린 곳이 있으면 고치시오. 맞으면 *OK*라고 쓰시오.

1. I stayed at <u>the house of my sister</u>. 　_my sister's house_
2. What is <u>the name of this village</u>? 　_OK_
3. Do you like <u>the color of this coat</u>? _____
4. Do you know <u>the phone number of Simon</u>? _____
5. <u>The job of my brother</u> is very interesting. _____
6. Write your name at <u>the top of the page</u>. _____
7. For me, morning is <u>the best part of the day</u>. _____
8. <u>The favorite color of Paula</u> is blue. _____
9. When is <u>the birthday of your mother</u>? _____
10. <u>The house of my parents</u> isn't very big. _____
11. <u>The walls of this house</u> are very thin. _____
12. The car stopped at <u>the end of the street</u>. _____
13. Are you going to <u>the party of Sylvia</u> next week? _____
14. <u>The manager of the hotel</u> is not here right now. _____

a/an

He has **a** camera.
그는 카메라를 가지고 있다.

She's waiting for **a** taxi.
그녀는 택시를 기다리고 있다.

It's **a** beautiful day.
날씨가 좋다.

a ... = 한 개 또는 한 사람
- Rachel works in **a bank**. (in bank는 틀림)
- Can I ask **a question**? (ask question은 틀림)
- I don't have **a computer**.
- There's **a woman** at the bus stop.

모음(**a/e/i/o/u**) 앞에는 **an**을 쓴다.
- Do you want **an a**pple or **a b**anana?
- I'm going to buy **a h**at and **an u**mbrella.
- There was **an i**nteresting program on TV last night.

또한   **an hour** (**h**는 발음되지 않는다: an hour)
하지만 **a university** (발음: *yuniversity*)
       a European country (발음: *yuropean*)

another (= **an** + **other**)는 한 단어이다.
- Can I have **another** cup of coffee? 커피 한 잔 더 마셔도 될까요?

a/an ...은 사물이나 사람을 정의하거나 설명할 때 쓴다.
- The sun is **a star**.
  태양은 항성이다.
- Football is **a game**.
- Dallas is **a city in Texas**.
  댈러스는 텍사스주에 있는 도시이다.
- A mouse is **an animal**. It's **a small animal**.
- Joe is **a very nice person**.

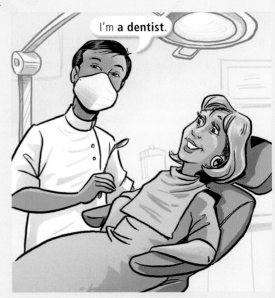

I'm **a dentist**.

a/an ...은 직업을 말할 때 쓴다.
- *A:* What do you do?
  B: I'm **a dentist**. (I'm dentist는 틀림)
- "What does Mark do?"   "He's **an engineer**."
- Would you like to be **a teacher**?
- Beethoven was **a composer**.
  베토벤은 작곡가였다.
- Picasso was **a famous painter**.
- Are you **a student**?

a bottle / some water (셀 수 있는 명사 / 셀 수 없는 명사) → Units 68–69   **a/an**과 **the** → Unit 70

Exercises

66.1 *a* 또는 *an*을 쓰시오.

1. __an__ old book
2. _____ window
3. _____ horse
4. _____ airport
5. _____ new airport
6. _____ organization
7. _____ university
8. _____ hour
9. _____ economic problem

66.2 상자 속의 단어를 사용하여 각 문제에 주어진 단어를 설명하시오.

~~bird~~	flower	fruit	game	mountain
planet	river	tool	vegetable	musical instrument

1. A duck is __a bird__ .
2. A carrot is _____ .
3. Tennis is _____ .
4. A hammer is _____ .
5. Everest is _____ .
6. Saturn is _____ .
7. A banana is _____ .
8. The Amazon is _____ .
9. A rose is _____ .
10. A trumpet is _____ .

66.3 그림 속 사람들의 직업을 아래에서 골라 문장을 완성하시오.

architect	~~dentist~~	electrician	nurse
photographer	sales clerk	taxi driver	

1. __She's a dentist.__
2. He's _____
3. She _____
4. _____
5. _____
6. _____
7. _____
8. And you? I'm _____

66.4 아래 상자 속의 문구와 단어를 사용하여 문장을 만드시오. 필요하면 *a/an*을 쓰시오.

~~I want to ask you~~	Rebecca works in		old house	artist
Tom never wears	Jane wants to learn	+	party	~~question~~
I can't ride	Mike lives in		office	foreign language
My brother is	Tonight I'm going to		hat	bicycle

1. __I want to ask you a question.__
2. _____
3. _____
4. _____
5. _____
6. _____
7. _____
8. _____

train(s)   bus(es) (단수와 복수)

A

명사의 복수형에는 주로 **-s**를 붙인다.

단수 (= 하나)	→	복수 (= 둘 이상)
a flower	→	some **flowers**
a train	→	two **trains**
one week	→	a few **weeks**
a nice place	→	some nice **places**
this student	→	these **students**

a flower   some **flowers**

철자 (부록 5 참조):

-s / -sh / -ch / -x → -es	bus → bus**es**	dish → dish**es**
	chur**ch** → chur**ches**	box → box**es**
또한	pota**to** → pota**toes**	toma**to** → toma**toes**
-y → -ies	ba**by** → ba**bies**	dictiona**ry** → dictiona**ries**
	par**ty** → par**ties**	
그러나 -ay / -ey / -oy → -ys	d**ay** → d**ays**	monk**ey** → monk**eys** b**oy** → b**oys**
-f / -fe → -ves	shel**f** → shel**ves**	kni**fe** → kni**ves** wi**fe** → wi**ves**

B

다음 단어들은 항상 복수형으로 쓴다.

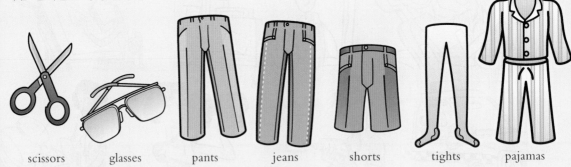

scissors   glasses   pants   jeans   shorts   tights   pajamas

- Do you wear **glasses**?
- Where **are** the **scissors**? I need **them**.

a pair of scissors / a pair of pants / a pair of pajamas처럼 **a pair of** ...를 사용할 수도 있다.
- I need **a** new **pair of jeans**.   또는   I need **some** new **jeans**. (a new jeans는 틀림)

C

어떤 명사의 복수형은 **-s**로 끝나지 않는다.

this **man** → these **men**	one **foot** → two **feet**	that **sheep** → those **sheep**
a **woman** → some **women**	a **tooth** → all my **teeth**	a **fish** → a lot of **fish**
a **child** → many **children**	a **mouse** → some **mice**	

또한 a **person** → two **people** / some **people** / a lot of **people** 등:
- **She's** a nice **person**.

그러나 - **They** are nice **people**. (nice persons는 틀림. person의 복수형은 일반적으로 **people**을 사용한다.)

D

people (사람들)은 복수이므로 **people are / people have**처럼 뒤에 동사의 복수형을 써야 한다.
- **A lot of people speak** English. (people speaks는 틀림)
- I like **the people** here. **They are** very friendly.

police는 복수이다.
- **The police want** to talk to anybody who saw the accident. (The police wants는 틀림)

Exercises

67.1 복수형을 쓰시오.

1. flower   _flowers_
2. boat   _____
3. woman   _____
4. city   _____
5. umbrella   _____
6. address   _____
7. knife   _____
8. sandwich   _____
9. family   _____
10. foot   _____
11. holiday   _____
12. potato   _____

67.2 그림을 보고 문장을 완성하시오.

1. There are a lot of ___sheep___ in the field.
2. Gary is brushing his _____ .
3. There are three _____ at the bus stop.
4. Lucy has two _____ .
5. There are a lot of _____ in the river.
6. The _____ are falling from the tree.

67.3 다음 문장에서 틀린 곳이 있으면 고치시오. 맞으면 **OK**라고 쓰시오.

1. I'm going to buy some flowers.   _OK_
2. I need a new jeans.   _I need a new pair of jeans._   또는
   I need some new jeans.
3. It's a lovely park with a lot of beautiful tree.   _____
4. There was a woman in the car with two mens.   _____
5. Sheep eat grass.   _____
6. David is married and has three childs.   _____
7. Most of my friend are student.   _____
8. He put on his pajama and went to bed.   _____
9. We went fishing, but we didn't catch many fish.   _____
10. Do you know many persons in this town?   _____
11. I like your pant. Where did you get it?   _____
12. Montreal is usually full of tourist.   _____
13. I don't like mice. I'm afraid of them.   _____
14. This scissor isn't very sharp.   _____

67.4 맞는 것을 골라 써 넣으시오.

1. It's a nice place. Many people __go__ there on vacation.   **go** 또는 **goes**?
2. Some people _____ always late.   **is** 또는 **are**?
3. The new city hall is not a very beautiful building.
   Most people _____ like it.   **don't** 또는 **doesn't**?
4. A lot of people _____ television every day.   **watch** 또는 **watches**?
5. Three people _____ injured in the accident.   **was** 또는 **were**?
6. How many people _____ in that house?   **live** 또는 **lives**?
7. _____ the police know the cause of the explosion?   **Do** 또는 **Does**?
8. The police _____ looking for the stolen car.   **is** 또는 **are**?
9. I need my glasses, but I can't find _____ .   **it** 또는 **them**?
10. I'm going to buy _____ new jeans today.   **a** 또는 **some**?

UNIT 68

a bottle / some water
(셀 수 있는 명사 / 셀 수 없는 명사 1)

A

명사에는 셀 수 있는 명사와 셀 수 없는 명사가 있다.

셀 수 있는 명사

예: (a) **car**   (a) **man**   (a) **bottle**   (a) **house**   (a) **key**   (an) **idea**   (an) **accident**

셀 수 있는 명사 앞에는 **one/two/three** 등을 붙일 수 있다:

| one **bottle** | two **bottles** | three **men** | four **houses** |

셀 수 있는 명사에는 단수(= 하나)와 복수(= 둘 이상)가 있다:

단수	a car	the car	my car 등		
복수	cars	two cars	the cars	some cars	many cars 등

- I've got **a car**.
- New **cars** are very expensive.
- There aren't **many cars** in the parking lot. 주차장에는 차들이 많지 않다.

셀 수 있는 명사의 단수형(**car/bottle/key** 등)은 홀로 쓸 수 없다. 앞에 **a/an**을 붙여야 한다.
- We can't get into the house without **a key**. (without key는 틀림)
  열쇠 없이는 집에 들어갈 수 없다.

B

셀 수 없는 명사

예: **water   air   rice   salt   plastic   money   music   tennis**

| water | salt | money | music |

셀 수 없는 명사 앞에는 **one/two/three** 등을 붙일 수 없다: ~~one water~~   ~~two music~~

셀 수 없는 명사는 한 가지 형태로만 쓰인다:

money   the **money**   my **money**   some **money**   much **money** 등

- I have **some money**. 나한테 돈이 약간 있다.
- There isn't **much money** in the box. 상자 안에는 돈이 많지 않다.
- **Money** isn't everything. 돈이 전부가 아니다.

셀 수 없는 명사 앞에는 **a/an**을 붙일 수 없다: ̶a̶**money**   ̶a̶**music**   ̶a̶**water**

하지만 **a piece of ...** / **a bottle of ...** 등 + 셀 수 없는 명사는 가능하다.

a bottle of water	a carton of milk	a bar of soap
a piece of cheese	a bottle of perfume	a piece of music
a bowl of rice	a cup of coffee	a game of tennis

Exercises

68.1 아래의 단어 중 그림에 맞는 것을 골라 써 넣으시오. 일부는 셀 수 있는 명사이고 일부는 셀 수 없는 명사입니다. 필요한 경우 **a/an**을 쓰시오.

bucket	egg	envelope	money	pitcher	~~salt~~
sand	~~spoon~~	toothbrush	toothpaste	wallet	water

1. It's _salt_ .	2. It's _a spoon_ .	3. It's _____ .	4. It's _____ .
5. It's _____ .	6. It's _____ .	7. It's _____ .	8. It's _____ .
9. It's _____ .	10. It's _____ .	11. It's _____ .	12. It's _____ .

68.2 **a/an**이 필요한 경우 써 넣으시오. 맞으면 **OK**라고 쓰시오.

1. I don't have watch. _a watch_
2. Do you like cheese? _OK_
3. I never wear hat. _____
4. Are you looking for job? _____
5. Kate doesn't eat meat. _____
6. Kate eats apple every day. _____
7. I'm going to party tonight. _____
8. Music is wonderful thing. _____
9. Jamaica is island. _____
10. I don't need key. _____
11. Everybody needs food. _____
12. I've got good idea. _____
13. Can you drive car? _____
14. Do you want cup of coffee? _____
15. I don't like coffee without milk. _____
16. Don't go out without coat. _____

68.3 **a ... of ...**를 사용하여 그림 속의 물건이 무엇인지 쓰시오. 아래 상자 속의 단어를 사용하시오.

bar	bowl	~~carton~~		bread	honey	~~milk~~
cup	glass	jar	+	paper	soap	soup
loaf	piece	piece		tea	water	wood

1. _a carton of milk_
2. _____
3. _____
4. _____
5. _____
6. _____
7. _____
8. _____
9. _____

a cake / some cake / some cakes
(셀 수 있는 명사 / 셀 수 없는 명사 2)

A

a/an과 some

a/an + 셀 수 있는 명사 (**car/apple/shoe** 등):

- I need **a** new **car**.
- Would you like **an apple**?

an apple

some + 셀 수 있는 명사 복수형 (**cars/apples/shoes** 등):

- I need **some** new **shoes**.
- Would you like **some apples**?

some apples

some + 셀 수 없는 명사 (**water/money/music** 등):

- I need **some water**.
- Would you like **some cheese**?
  (또는 Would you like a piece of cheese?)

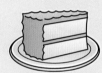
some cheese 또는
a piece of cheese

a와 **some**의 비교:

- Nicole bought **a hat**, **some shoes**, and **some perfume**.
- I read **a newspaper**, made **some phone calls**, and listened to **some music**.

B

많은 명사들은 셀 수 있는 명사와 셀 수 없는 명사 두 가지로 다 쓰인다. 예를 들어,

a cake

some cakes

some cake 또는 **a piece of cake**

a chicken

some chickens

some chicken 또는 **a piece of chicken**

a paper (= a newspaper, 신문)와 **some paper**의 비교:

- I want something to read. I'm going to buy **a paper**.
  뭔가 읽을거리가 있었으면 좋겠어. 신문을 사야겠다.

그러나 ■ I want to make a shopping list. I need **some paper** / **a piece of paper**. (a paper는 틀림)
쇼핑할 것들을 적고 싶어. 종이가 필요해.

C

주의:

advice   bread   furniture   hair   information   news   weather   work

위의 단어들은 일반적으로 셀 수 없는 명사들이다. 그러므로 **a/an**을 붙이거나(~~a bread~~, ~~an advice~~ 등)
복수형(~~advices~~, ~~furnitures~~ 등)으로 쓸 수 없다.

- Can I talk to you? I need **some advice**. (an advice는 틀림)
- I'm going to buy **some bread**. (a bread는 틀림)
- They've got **some** very nice **furniture** in their house. (furnitures는 틀림)
- Sylvia has very long **hair**. (hairs는 틀림)
- I'd like **some information** about hotels in Mexico City. (informations는 틀림)
- Listen! I've got **some** good **news**. (a good news는 틀림)
- It's nice **weather** today. (a nice weather는 틀림)
- "Do you like your job?" "Yes, but it's hard **work**." (a hard work는 틀림)

a job이라고는 말하지만 a work라고는 하지 않는다.

- I've got **a new job**. (a new work는 틀림) 난 새 일자리를 얻었어.

Exercises

69.1 그림을 보고 *I bought* ...를 사용하여 문장을 쓰시오.

1. _I bought some perfume, a hat, and some shoes._
2. I bought _____
3. _____
4. _____

69.2 *Would you like a ... ?* 또는 *Would you like some ... ?*을 사용하여 문장을 쓰시오.

1. _Would you like some cheese_ ? 4. _____ ?
2. Would you like _____ ? 5. _____ ?
3. Would _____ ? 6. _____ ?

69.3 *a/an* 또는 *some*을 써 넣으시오.

1. I read __a__ book and listened to __some__ music.
2. I need _____ money. I want to buy _____ food.
3. We met _____ interesting people at the party.
4. I'm going to open _____ window to get _____ fresh air.
5. Rachel didn't eat much for lunch – only _____ apple and _____ bread.
6. We live in _____ big house. There's _____ nice yard with _____ beautiful trees.
7. I'm going to make a table. First I need _____ wood.
8. Listen to me carefully. I'm going to give you _____ advice.
9. I want to write a letter. I need _____ paper and _____ pen.

69.4 맞는 것을 고르시오.

1. I'm going to buy some new ~~shoe~~ / shoes. (*shoes*가 맞음)
2. Mark has brown eye / eyes.
3. Paula has short black hair / hairs.
4. The tour guide gave us some information / informations about the city.
5. We're going to buy some new chair / chairs.
6. We're going to buy some new furniture / furnitures.
7. It's hard to find a work / job these days.
8. We had wonderful weather / a wonderful weather when we were on vacation.

a/an과 the

a/an

이곳에는 창문이 세 개 있다.
그래서 **a** window는 셋 중 어느 한 창문을
말한다(**a** window = 창문 1 또는 2 또는 3).

- I have **a car**.
  (많은 차들 중 내가 가진 한 대)
- Can I ask **a question**?
  (많은 질문들 중 질문 하나)
- Is there **a hotel** near here?
  (많은 호텔들 중 근처의 호텔 하나)
- Paris is **an interesting city**.
  (파리는 많은 흥미로운 도시들 중 하나)
- Lisa is **a student**.
  (리사는 많은 학생들 중 하나)

the

이곳에는 창문이 하나뿐이다. 그래서 **the**
window라고 말한다.

- I'm going to wash **the car** tomorrow.
  (= 내 차)
- Can you repeat **the question**, please?
  (= 당신이 한 질문)
- We enjoyed our vacation. **The hotel** was
  very nice. (= 우리가 묵은 호텔)
- Paris is **the capital of France**.
  (프랑스의 유일한 수도)
- Lisa is **the youngest student** in her
  class. (가장 어린 학생은 하나뿐임)

a와 **the**의 비교:

- I bought **a jacket** and **a shirt** . **The jacket** was cheap, but **the shirt** was expensive.

  (= 내가 산 재킷)　　　　　　(= 내가 산 셔츠)

B

지칭하는 대상이 분명할 때는 **the**를 사용한다. 예를 들어,

(한 방의) **the door** / **the ceiling** / **the floor** / **the carpet** / **the light** 등
(한 집의) **the roof** / **the backyard** / **the kitchen** / **the bathroom** 등
(한 도시의) **the airport** / **the police station** / **the bus station** / **the mayor's office** 등

- "Where's Tom?"　"In **the kitchen**."
  (= 그 집의 부엌)
- Turn off **the light** and close **the door**.
  (= 그 방의 전등과 문)
- Do you live far from **the airport**?
  (= 그 도시의 공항)
- I'd like to speak to **the manager**, please.
  (= 그 가게의 매니저)

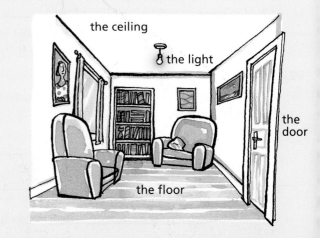

the ceiling
the light
the door
the floor

Exercises

70.1 *a/an* 또는 *the*를 써 넣으시오.

1. We enjoyed our trip. ___The___ hotel was very nice.
2. "Can I ask __a__ question?"   "Sure. What do you want to know?"
3. You look very tired. You need _____ vacation.
4. "Where's Tom?"   "He's in _____ kitchen."
5. Eve is _____ interesting person. You should meet her.
6. *A:* Excuse me, can you tell me how to get to _____ post office?
   B: Yes, go straight and then take _____ next left.
7. *A:* Let's go and see _____ movie tonight.
   B: OK, that's _____ good idea.
8. It's _____ nice morning. Let's go for _____ walk.
9. Amanda is _____ student. When she finishes school, she wants to be _____ journalist.
   She lives with two friends in _____ apartment near _____ college where she is studying.
   _____ apartment is small, but she likes it.
10. Peter and Mary have two children, _____ boy and _____ girl. _____ boy is seven years
    old, and _____ girl is three. Peter works in _____ factory. Mary doesn't have _____ job
    outside the home right now.

70.2 *a/the* + 아래의 단어를 사용하여 문장을 완성하시오.

airport   cup   dictionary   ~~door~~   floor   picture

1. Can you open ___the door___, please?
2. How far is it to _____ _____?
3. Can I have _____ of coffee, please?
4. That's _____ nice _____ – I like it.
5. Can you pass me _____ _____, please?
6. Why are you sitting on _____ _____?

70.3 틀린 곳을 고치시오. 필요한 곳에 *a/an* 또는 *the*를 써 넣으시오.

1. Don't forget to (turn off light) when you go out.   ___turn off the light___
2. Enjoy your trip, and don't forget to send me postcard.   _____
3. What is name of this town?   _____
4. Canada is very big country.   _____
5. What is largest city in Canada?   _____
6. I like this room, but I don't like color of carpet.   _____
7. "Are you OK?"   "No, I've got headache."   _____
8. We live in old house near station.   _____
9. What is name of director of movie we saw last night?   _____

the ...

A

지칭하는 대상이 분명할 경우 **the**를 쓴다.

- What is **the name** of this street? (이름은 하나뿐임)
- Who is **the best player** on your team? (최고의 선수는 하나뿐임)
- Can you tell me **the time**, please? (= 지금 시각)
- My office is on **the first floor**. (= 그 건물의 1층)
- Do you live near **the airport**? (그 도시의 공항) (near airport는 틀림)
- Excuse me, where is **the nearest bank**? (가장 가까운 은행은 하나뿐임) (where is nearest ...는 틀림)

B

the same ...: 같은 ··· (항상 **the**를 붙임)

- We live on **the same street**. (on same street는 틀림)
- "Are these two books different?" "No, they're **the same**." (they're same은 틀림)

C

항상 **the**를 붙이는 단어들

the sun / the moon / the world / the sky / the ocean / the country

- **The sky** is blue and **the sun** is shining.
- Do you live in a city or in **the country**?

(한 도시, 국가 등의) **the police / the fire department / the army**

- My brother is a soldier. He's in **the army**.
- What do you think of **the police**? Do they do a good job?
  경찰에 대해서 어떻게 생각합니까? 일을 제대로 하고 있습니까?

the top / the end / the middle / the left 등

- Write your name at **the top of** the page.
- My house is at **the end of** this block.
- The table is in **the middle of** the room.
- Do you drive on **the right** or on **the left** in your country?
  당신 나라에서는 우측으로 운전합니까, 좌측으로 운전합니까?

```
            the top

the left     the
           • middle    the right

           the bottom
```

(play) **the piano / the guitar / the trumpet** 등 (악기)

- Paula is learning to play **the piano**.

the radio

- I listen to **the radio** a lot.

the Internet

- Do you use **the Internet** much?

D

the를 붙이지 않는 단어들

television/TV

- I watch **TV** a lot.
- What's on **television** tonight?

그러나 Can you turn off **the television**? (= TV 수신기)

breakfast/lunch/dinner

- What did you have for **breakfast**? (the breakfast는 틀림)
- **Dinner** is ready!

next/last + week/month/year/summer/Monday 등

- I'm not working **next week**. (the next week는 틀림)
- Did you take a vacation **last summer**? (the last summer는 틀림)

Exercises

71.1 필요한 곳에 **the**를 써 넣으시오. 맞는 문장에는 **OK**라고 쓰시오.

1. What is name of this street?   *the name*
2. What's on television tonight?   *OK*
3. Our apartment is on second floor.   _____
4. Would you like to go to moon?   _____
5. What is best hotel in this town?   _____
6. What time is lunch?   _____
7. How far is it to football stadium?   _____
8. We're taking a trip at end of May.   _____
9. What are you doing next weekend?   _____
10. I didn't like her first time I met her.   _____
11. I'm going out after dinner.   _____
12. Internet is a good place to get information.   _____
13. My sister got married last month.   _____
14. My dictionary is on top shelf on right.   _____
15. We live in country about 10 miles from nearest town.   _____

71.2 **the same** + 아래의 단어를 사용하여 문장을 완성하시오.

     age   color   problem   ~~street~~   time

1. I live on North Street, and you live on North Street. We live on _*the same street*_ .
2. I arrived at 8:30, and you arrived at 8:30. We arrived at _____ .
3. Jim is 25, and Sue is 25. Jim and Sue are _____ .
4. My shirt is dark blue, and so is my jacket. My shirt and jacket are _____ .
5. I have no money, and you have no money. We have _____ .

71.3 그림을 보고 문장을 완성하시오. 필요한 경우 **the**를 쓰시오.

1. _*The sun*_ is shining.
2. She's playing _____ .
3. They're having _____ .
4. He's watching _____ .
5. They're swimming in _____ .
6. Tim's name is at _____ of the list.

71.4 아래의 단어를 사용하여 문장을 완성하시오. 필요한 경우 **the**를 쓰시오.

     capital   ~~dinner~~   lunch   middle   name   police   sky   television

1. We had _*dinner*_ at a restaurant last night.
2. We stayed at a very nice hotel, but I don't remember _____ .
3. _____ is very clear tonight. You can see all the stars.
4. Sometimes there are some good programs on _____ late at night.
5. _____ stopped me because I was driving too fast.
6. Tokyo is _____ of Japan.
7. "What did you have for _____ ?" "A salad."
8. I woke up in _____ of the night.

go to work   go home   go to the movies

She's **at work**.
그녀는 직장에 있다.

They're going **to school**.
그들은 학교에 가고 있다.

He's **in bed**.
그는 침대에 있다.

the를 쓰지 않는 표현

(go) **to work**, (be) **at work**, start **work**, finish **work**
- Bye! I'm **going to work** now. (to the work는 틀림)
- I **finish work** at 5:00 every day.

(go) **to school**, (be) **at school**, start **school**, finish **school** 등
- What did you learn **at school** today? (at the school은 틀림)
- Some children don't like **school**.

(go) **to college**, (be) **in college**
- Helen wants to **go to college** when she **finishes high school**.
- What did you study **in college**?

(go) **to class**, (be) **in class**
- I can't talk now. I have to **go to class**.
- I'll **be in class** until 5:00 today. I'll call you when I get out.
  오늘 5시까지는 수업을 하고 있을 거야. 나오면 전화할게.

(go) **to prison/jail**, (be) **in prison/jail**
- Why is he **in prison**? What did he do? 그 사람은 왜 감옥에 있니? 무슨 짓을 했니?

(go) **to church**, (be) **in/at church**
- David usually goes **to church** on Sundays. 데이비드는 일요일에는 보통 교회에 간다.

(go) **to bed**, (be) **in bed**
- I'm tired. I'm **going to bed**. 난 피곤해. 자야겠어. (to the bed는 틀림)
- "Where's Jane?" "She's **in bed**."

(go) **home**, (be) (**at**) **home** 등
- I'm tired. I'm **going home**. (to home은 틀림)
- Are you going out tonight, or are you **staying home**? (또는 **staying at home**)

B

the를 쓰는 표현

(go to) **the movies / the theater / the bank / the post office / the hospital /
the station / the airport**
- I never go to **the theater**, but I go to **the movies** a lot.
  나는 극장에는 전혀 안 가지만 영화관에는 많이 간다.
- "Are you going to **the bank**?" "No, to **the post office**."
- The number 5 bus goes to **the airport**; the number 8 goes to
  the train station.

(go to) **the doctor**, **the dentist**
- You're not well. Why don't you go to **the doctor**?
  너 몸 상태가 좋지 않아. 병원에 가보지 그래?
- I have to go to **the dentist** tomorrow.

Exercises

72.1 그림 속의 사람들이 어디에 있는지 문장을 완성하시오. 필요한 경우 **the**를 쓰시오.

1.	2.	3.	4.	5.	6.

1. He's in _____bed_____ .
2. They're at _____ .
3. She's in _____ .
4. She's at _____ .
5. They're at _____ .
6. He's in _____ .

72.2 아래의 단어를 사용하여 문장을 완성하시오. 필요한 경우 **the**를 쓰시오.

~~bank~~   bed   ~~church~~   home   post office   school   station

1. I need to get some money. I have to go to ___the bank___ .
2. David usually goes to ___church___ on Sundays.
3. In the United States, children start _____ at the age of five.
4. There were a lot of people at _____ waiting for the train.
5. I called you last night, but you weren't at _____ .
6. I'm going to _____ now. Good night!
7. I'm going to _____ to get some stamps.

72.3 문장을 완성하시오. 필요한 경우 **the**를 쓰시오.

1. If you want to catch a plane, you ___go to the airport_____ .
2. If you want to see a movie, you go to _____ .
3. If you are tired and you want to sleep, you _____ .
4. If you rob a bank and the police catch you, you _____ .
5. If you have a problem with your teeth, you _____ .
6. If you want to study after you finish high school, you _____ .
7. If you are badly injured in an accident, you _____ .

72.4 틀린 곳이 있으면 고치시오. 맞으면 **OK**라고 쓰시오.

1. We went (to movies) last night. ___to the movies___
2. I finish work at 5:00 every day. ___OK___
3. Lisa wasn't feeling well yesterday, so she went to doctor. _____
4. I wasn't feeling well this morning, so I stayed in bed. _____
5. Why is Angela always late for work? _____
6. "Where are your children?"   "They're at school." _____
7. We have no money in bank. _____
8. When I was younger, I went to church every Sunday. _____
9. What time do you usually get home from work? _____
10. Sorry I couldn't call you back earlier. I was in class. _____
11. "Where should we meet?"   "At station." _____
12. Kate takes her children to school every day. _____
13. Jim is sick. He's in hospital. _____
14. Would you like to go to college? _____
15. Would you like to go to theater tonight? _____

I like **music**.   I hate **exams**.

일반적인 개념이나 사물 전반을 지칭할 때는 **the**를 사용하지 않는다.

- ■ I like **music**, especially **classical music**. 나는 음악, 특히 클래식을 좋아한다.
  (the music ... the classical music은 틀림)
- ■ We don't eat **meat** very often. (the meat는 틀림)
- ■ **Life** is not possible without **water**.
  (The life ... the water는 틀림)
- ■ I hate **exams**. (the exams는 틀림)
- ■ Do you know where I can buy **foreign newspapers**?
  외국 신문을 어디서 살 수 있는지 아세요?
- ■ I'm not very good at writing **letters**.

게임이나 운동에는 **the**를 사용하지 않는다.

- ■ My favorite sports are **tennis** and **skiing**. (the tennis ... the skiing은 틀림)

언어나 학과(**history/geography/physics/biology** 등) 이름 앞에는 **the**를 사용하지 않는다.

- ■ Do you think **English** is difficult? (the English는 틀림)
- ■ Tom's brother is studying **physics** and **chemistry**.

B

flowers와 **the flowers**

비교:

- ■ **Flowers** are beautiful.
  (= 꽃들 전반)

- ■ I don't like **cold weather**.
  (= 추운 날씨 전반)

- ■ We don't eat **fish** very often.
  (= 생선 전반)

- ■ Are you interested
  in **history**?
  (= 역사 전반)

- ■ I love your garden.
  The flowers are beautiful.
  (= 당신 정원에 있는 꽃들)

- ■ **The weather** isn't very
  good today.
  (= 오늘의 날씨)

- ■ We had a great meal last
  night. **The fish** was
  excellent.
  (= 어젯밤에 먹은 생선)

- ■ Do you know much
  about **the history** of
  your country?
  (= 당신 나라의 역사)

Exercises

73.1 다음 항목들에 대해 당신은 어떻게 생각합니까?

> big cities   chocolate   computer games   dogs   exams
> housework   jazz   museums   parties   tennis

이 중 **7개**를 선택하여 아래의 구문으로 시작하는 문장을 쓰시오.

> **I like …   I don't like …   I love …   I hate …   … is/are all right**

1. ___I hate exams.___ 또는 ___I like exams.___ 또는 ___Exams are all right.___ (등) _____
2. _____
3. _____
4. _____
5. _____
6. _____
7. _____
8. _____

73.2 아래의 주제에 대해 당신은 어느 정도의 흥미를 가지고 있습니까? 다음 구문을 사용하여
문장을 쓰시오.

> **I'm (very) interested in …   I know a lot about …   I don't know much about …**
> **I'm not interested in …   I know a little about …   I don't know anything about …**

1. (history) ___I'm very interested in history.___
2. (politics) I _____
3. (sports) _____
4. (art) _____
5. (astronomy) _____
6. (economics) _____

73.3 맞는 것을 고르시오.

1. My favorite sport is <u>football</u> / ~~the football~~. (*football*이 맞음)
2. I like this hotel. ~~Rooms~~ / <u>The rooms</u> are very nice. (*The rooms*가 맞음)
3. Everybody needs <u>friends</u> / <u>the friends</u>.
4. Jane doesn't go to <u>parties</u> / <u>the parties</u> very often.
5. I went shopping at the mall this morning. <u>Stores</u> / <u>The stores</u> were very crowded.
6. "Where's <u>milk</u> / <u>the milk</u>?"   "It's in the fridge."
7. I don't like <u>milk</u> / <u>the milk</u>. I never drink it.
8. "Do you play any sports?"   "Yes, I play <u>basketball</u> / <u>the basketball</u>."
9. "What does your brother do?"   "He sells <u>computers</u> / <u>the computers</u>."
10. We went for a swim in the river. <u>Water</u> / <u>The water</u> was very cold.
11. I don't like swimming in <u>cold water</u> / <u>the cold water</u>.
12. Excuse me, can you pass <u>salt</u> / <u>the salt</u>, please?
13. I like this town. I like <u>people</u> / <u>the people</u> here.
14. <u>Vegetables</u> / <u>The vegetables</u> are good for you.
15. <u>Houses</u> / <u>The houses</u> on this street are all the same.
16. I can't sing this song. I don't know <u>words</u> / <u>the words</u>.
17. I enjoy taking <u>pictures</u> / <u>the pictures</u>. It's my hobby.
18. Do you want to see <u>pictures</u> / <u>the pictures</u> that I took when I was on vacation?
19. <u>English</u> / <u>The English</u> is used a lot in <u>international business</u> / <u>the international business</u>.
20. <u>Money</u> / <u>The money</u> doesn't always bring <u>happiness</u> / <u>the happiness</u>.

the ... (장소 이름)

A

장소 (대륙, 국가, 주, 섬, 도시 등)

일반적으로 장소 이름 앞에는 **the**를 쓰지 않는다.

- **Quebec** is a province of **Canada**.
- **Bangkok** is the capital of **Thailand**.
- **Hawaii** is an island in the Pacific.
- **Peru** is in **South America**.

그러나 **republic/states/kingdom** (공화국/주/왕국)이 들어가는 이름 앞에는 **the**를 쓴다.

the Dominican **Republic**
the Czech **Republic**
the United **States** of America (**the** USA)
the United **Kingdom** (**the** UK)

B

the -s (복수형 이름)

나라/제도(섬)/산맥 이름이 복수일 때는 **the**를 쓴다.

the Netherlands 네덜란드   **the** Hawaiian Islands 하와이 제도
the Philippines 필리핀   **the** Andes 안데스 산맥

C

바다, 강 등

대양/바다/강/운하(oceans/seas/rivers/canals) 이름에는 **the**를 쓴다.

the Atlantic (Ocean) 대서양   **the** Mediterranean (Sea) 지중해   **the** Amazon 아마존강
the Nile (River) 나일강   **the** Panama Canal 파나마 운하   **the** Black (Sea) 흑해

D

도시 내의 거리와 장소

일반적으로 거리나 광장 이름 등에는 **the**를 쓰지 않는다.

- Kevin lives on **Central Avenue**.
- Where is **Main Street**, please?
- **Times Square** is in New York.

공항, 역, 대학, 공원 이름에는 **the**를 쓰지 않는다.

O'Hare International Airport   **Harvard University**
Pennsylvania Station   **Yosemite** (National Park)

그러나 대부분의 호텔과 박물관, 극장, 기념비 이름에는 **the**를 쓴다.

the Regent Hotel   **the** National Theater
the Metropolitan (Museum) **the** Odeon (movie theater)
the Taj Mahal   **the** Lincoln Memorial

E

the ... of ...

이름 뒤에 **of** ...가 올 경우 **the**를 쓴다.

the Museum **of** Modern Art (뉴욕) 현대미술관
the Great Wall **of** China (중국) 만리장성
the University **of** California 캘리포니아 대학교
the Statue **of** Liberty 자유의 여신상

방위에는 **the**를 붙인다: **the north** / **the south** / **the east** / **the west** (of ...)

- I've been to **the north of Italy**, but not to **the south**.

Exercises

74.1 상자 속에서 알맞은 이름을 사용하여 다음 지리문제에 답하시오. 필요한 경우 *The*를 붙이시오.

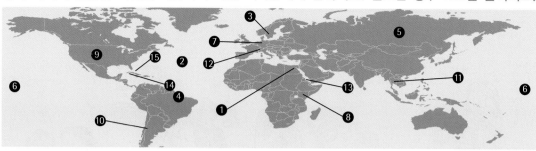

1.	_Cairo_	is the capital of Egypt.
2.	_The Atlantic_	is between Africa and America.
3.	_____	is a country in northern Europe.
4.	_____	is a river in South America.
5.	_____	is the largest continent in the world.
6.	_____	is the largest ocean.
7.	_____	is a river in Europe.
8.	_____	is a country in East Africa.
9.	_____	is between Canada and Mexico.
10.	_____	are mountains in South America.
11.	_____	is the capital of Thailand.
12.	_____	are mountains in central Europe.
13.	_____	is between Saudi Arabia and Africa.
14.	_____	is an island in the Caribbean.
15.	_____	are a group of islands near Florida.

Alps
Amazon
Andes
Asia
~~**Atlantic**~~
Bahamas
Bangkok
~~**Cairo**~~
Jamaica
Kenya
Pacific
Red Sea
Rhine
Sweden
United States

74.2 필요한 경우 *the*를 써 넣으시오. 맞는 문장에는 *OK*라고 쓰시오.

1. Kevin lives on Central Avenue. _____ OK _____
2. We went to see a play at National Theater. _____ at the National Theater _____
3. Have you ever been to China? _____
4. Have you ever been to Philippines? _____
5. Have you ever been to south of France? _____
6. Can you tell me where Washington Monument is? _____
7. Can you tell me where Hollywood Boulevard is? _____
8. Can you tell me where Museum of Art is? _____
9. Europe is bigger than Australia. _____
10. Belgium is smaller than Netherlands. _____
11. Which river is longer – Mississippi or Nile? _____
12. Did you go to National Gallery when you were in Washington? _____
13. We stayed at Park Hotel near Central Park. _____
14. How far is it from Times Square to Kennedy Airport? _____
15. Rocky Mountains are in North America. _____
16. Texas is famous for oil and cowboys. _____
17. I hope to go to United Kingdom next year. _____
18. Mary comes from west of Ireland. _____
19. Alan is a student at University of Michigan. _____
20. Panama Canal joins Atlantic Ocean and Pacific Ocean. _____

→ 추가연습문제 33–34 (261–262쪽)

this/that/these/those

A

this (단수)

Do you like **this** picture?

these (복수)

These flowers are for you.

that (단수)

Do you like **that** picture?

those (복수)

Who are **those** people?

this these

this picture
(= 여기 있는 이 그림)
these flowers
(= 여기 있는 이 꽃들)

that those

that picture
(= 저기 있는 저 그림)
those people
(= 저기 있는 저 사람들)

B

this/that/these/those는 명사와 함께(**this picture** / **those girls** 등) 또는 명사 없이 쓸 수 있다.

- **This hotel** is expensive, but it's very nice.
- "Who's **that girl**?" "I don't know."
- Do you like **these shoes**? I bought them last week.
- **Those apples** look nice. Can I have one?

명사와 함께

- **This** is a nice hotel, but it's very expensive.
- "Excuse me, is **this** your bag?" "Oh yes, thank you."
- Who's **that**? (= Who is that person?)
- Which shoes do you like better – **these** or **those**?

명사 없이

C

that = 앞서 발생한 일을 지칭:

- "I'm sorry I forgot to call you." 잊어버리고 전화 안 해서 미안해. "**That**'s all right." 괜찮아.
- **That** was a really nice meal. Thank you very much. 정말 맛있는 식사였어. 고마워.

that = 상대방이 방금 한 말을 지칭:

- "You're a teacher, aren't you?" "Yes, **that**'s right."
- "Mark has a new job." 마크가 새 일자리를 얻었어.
  "He does? I didn't know **that**." 그래? 난 몰랐어.
- "I'm going on vacation next week." "Oh, **that**'s nice."

D

전화상에서 사람을 지칭할 때는 **this is …** / **is this …** ?를 쓴다.

- Hi Sarah, **this is** David.
  (= 말하는 사람)
- **Is this** Sarah?
  (= 상대방)

사람을 소개할 때 **this is …**를 쓴다.

- A: Brian, **this is** Chris.
  브라이언, 얘는 크리스야.
  B: Hello, Chris. Nice to meet you.
  C: Hi.

Hi Sarah, **this is** David.

David

Brian, **this is** Chris.

Amanda   Brian   Chris

this one / that one → Unit 76

Exercises

75.1 *this/that/these/those* + 아래의 단어를 사용하여 문장을 완성하시오.

> birds   dishes   house   postcards   seat   ~~shoes~~

1. Do you like *these shoes* ?
2. Who lives in _____ _____ ?
3. How much are _____ _____ ?
4. Look at _____ _____ .
5. Excuse me, is _____ _____ free?
6. _____ _____ are dirty.

75.2 *Is this/that your ... ?* 또는 *Are these/those your ... ?*를 사용하여 의문문을 쓰시오.

1. *Is this your bag?*
2. _____
3. _____
4. _____
5. _____
6. _____
7. _____
8. _____
9. _____
10. _____

75.3 *this is* 또는 *that's* 또는 *that*을 넣어 문장을 완성하시오.

1. *A:* I'm sorry I'm late.
   B: *That's* all right.
2. *A:* I can't come to the party tomorrow.
   B: Oh, _____ too bad. Why not?
3. (전화상에서)
   Sue: Hello, Jane. _____ Sue.
   Jane: Oh, hi Sue. How are you?
4. *A:* You're lazy.
   B: _____ not true!
5. *A:* Beth plays the piano very well.
   B: Does she? I didn't know _____ .
6. *Mark meets Paul's sister, Helen.*
   Paul: Mark, _____ my sister, Helen.
   Mark: Hi, Helen.
7. *A:* I'm sorry I was angry yesterday.
   B: _____ OK. Forget it!
8. *A:* You're a friend of Tim's, aren't you?
   B: Yes, _____ right.

one/ones

A

one (= a ...)

These chocolates are good. Would you like **one**?

Would you like **one** ? 하나 먹을래?

= Would you like **a chocolate** ? 초콜릿 하나 먹을래?

one = **a/an** ... (a chocolate / an apple 등)

- I need **a pen**. Do you have **one**? (**one** = a pen)
- *A:* Is there **a bank** near here? 이 근처에 은행이 있나요?
  B: Yes, there's **one** on the corner. (**one** = a bank) 네, 길모퉁이에 하나 있어요.

B

one과 ones

one (단수)	**ones** (복수)

Which **one** do you want?

This **one**.

The white **ones**.

Which **ones** do you want?

Which **one**? = Which **hat**?

one = hat/car/girl 등

this one / that one
- Which **car** is yours? **This one** or **that one**? (= this car or that car)

the one ...
- *A:* Which **hotel** did you stay at?
  B: **The one** near the airport.
- I found this **key**. Is it **the one** you lost?

the ... one
- I don't like the black **coat**, but I like **the brown one**.
- Don't buy that **camera**. Buy **the other one**.

a/an ... one
- This **cup** is dirty. Can I have **a clean one**?
- That **cookie** was good. I'm going to have **another one**.

Which **ones**? = Which **flowers**?

ones = flowers/cars/girls 등

these/those (ones 없이)
- Which flowers do you want? **These** or **those**? (보통 these ones, those ones 라고는 쓰지 않음)

the ones ...
- *A:* Which **books** are yours?
  B: **The ones** on the table.
- I found these **keys**. Are they **the ones** you lost?

the ... ones
- I don't like the red **shoes**, but I like **the green ones**.
- Don't buy those **apples**. Buy **the other ones**.

some ... ones
- These **cups** are dirty. Can we have **some clean ones**?
- My **shoes** are very old. I'm going to buy **some new ones**.

which ... ? → Unit 48   another → Unit 66   this/that 등 → Unit 75

Exercises

76.1 아래의 정보를 참고하여 질문에 답하시오. *a/an* ... 대신 **one**을 사용하시오.

B doesn't need a car	B just had a cup of coffee
there's a drugstore on First Avenue	B is going to get a bike
~~B doesn't have a pen~~	B doesn't have an umbrella

1. *A:* Can you lend me a pen?   *B:* I'm sorry, _I don't have one_ .
2. *A:* Would you like to have a car?   *B:* No, I don't _____ .
3. *A:* Do you have a bike?   *B:* No, but _____ .
4. *A:* Can you lend me an umbrella? *B:* I'm sorry, but _____ .
5. *A:* Would you like a cup of coffee? *B:* No, thank you. _____ .
6. *A:* Is there a drugstore near here? *B:* Yes, _____ .

76.2 *a/an* ... **one**을 사용하여 문장을 완성하시오. 아래의 단어를 사용하시오.

better   big   ~~clean~~   different   new   old

1. This cup is dirty. Can I have _a clean one_ ?
2. I'm going to sell my car and buy _____ .
3. That's not a very good picture. This is _____ .
4. I want today's newspaper. This is _____ .
5. This box is too small. I need _____ .
6. Why do we always go to the same restaurant? Let's go to _____ .

76.3 주어진 정보에 읽고 대화를 완성하시오. *one/ones*를 사용하시오.

1. *A stayed at a hotel. It was near the airport.* *A:* We stayed at a hotel. *B:* _Which one_ ? *A:* _The one near the airport._	6. *A is looking at a picture. It's on the wall.* *A:* That's an interesting picture. *B:* _____ ? *A:* _____
2. *A sees some shoes in a store window.* *They're green.* *A:* I like those shoes. *B:* Which _____ ? *A:* The _____	7. *A sees a girl in a group of people. She's tall* *with long hair.* *A:* Do you know that girl? *B:* _____ ? *A:* _____
3. *A is looking at a house. It has a red door.* *A:* That's a nice house. *B:* _____ ? *A:* _____ with _____	8. *A is looking at some flowers in the garden.* *They're yellow.* *A:* Those flowers are beautiful. *B:* _____ ? *A:* _____
4. *A is looking at some CDs. They're on the top* *shelf.* *A:* Are those your CDs? *B:* _____ ? *A:* _____	9. *A is looking at a man in a restaurant. He has* *a mustache and glasses.* *A:* Who's that man? *B:* _____ ? *A:* _____ with _____
5. *A is looking at a jacket in a store. It's black.* *A:* Do you like that jacket? *B:* _____ ? *A:* _____	10. *A took some pictures at the party last week.* *A:* Did I show you my pictures? *B:* _____ ? *A:* _____

some과 any

A

some

I have **some** money.

나는 돈이 좀 있어요.

some은 긍정문에 쓴다.

- I'm going to buy **some** clothes.
- There's **some** ice in the fridge.
- We made **some** mistakes.

any

I **don't** have **any** money.

나는 돈이 하나도 없어요.

any는 부정문에 쓴다.

- I'm **not** going to buy **any** clothes.
- There **isn't any** milk in the fridge.
- We **didn't** make **any** mistakes.

B

의문문에서의 **any**와 **some**

대부분의 의문문에는 (**some**이 아니라) **any**를 쓴다.

- Is there **any** ice in the fridge?
- Does he have **any** friends?
- Do you need **any** help?

Do you have **any** money?

무엇인가를 권할 때는 보통 (**any**가 아니라) **some**을 쓴다(**Would you like some … ?**).

- *A:* Would you like **some** coffee? 커피 좀 드시겠어요?
  B: Yes, please. 네, 주세요.

또 무엇인가를 청할 때도 **some**을 쓴다(**Can I have some … ?** 등).

- *A:* Can I have **some** soup, please?
  B: Yes. Help yourself.
- *A:* Can you lend me **some** money? 돈 좀 빌려줄 수 있어?
  B: Sure. How much do you need? 물론. 얼마나 필요해?

Would you like **some** coffee?

C

명사 없이 쓰는 **some**과 **any**

- I didn't take any pictures, but Jane took **some**. (= some pictures)
- You can have some coffee, but I don't want **any**. (= any coffee)
- I just made some coffee. Would you like **some**? (= some coffee)
- "Where's your luggage?" 짐은 어디 있니? "I don't have **any**." (= any luggage) 아무 짐도 없어.
- "Are there any cookies?" "Yes, there are **some** in the kitchen." (= some cookies)

D

something / somebody (또는 **someone**)

- She said **something**.
- I saw **somebody** (또는 **someone**).
- Would you like **something** to eat?
- **Somebody**'s at the door.

anything / anybody (또는 **anyone**)

- She **didn't** say **anything**.
- I **didn't** see **anybody** (또는 **anyone**).
- Are you doing **anything** tonight?
- Where's Sue? Has **anybody** seen her?

Exercises

77.1 *some* 또는 *any*를 써 넣으시오.

1. I bought __*some*__ cheese, but I didn't buy __*any*__ bread.
2. I'm going to the post office. I need _____ stamps.
3. There aren't _____ gas stations in this part of town.
4. Gary and Alice don't have _____ children.
5. Do you have _____ brothers or sisters?
6. There are _____ beautiful flowers in the garden.
7. Do you know _____ good hotels in Miami?
8. "Would you like _____ tea?"   "Yes, please."
9. When we were on vacation, we visited _____ very interesting places.
10. Don't buy _____ rice. We don't need _____ .
11. I went out to buy _____ oranges, but they didn't have _____ at the store.
12. I'm thirsty. Can I have _____ water, please?

77.2 *some* 또는 *any* + 아래의 단어를 사용하여 문장을 완성하시오.

air	batteries	friends	fruit	help
languages	milk	pictures	questions	~~shampoo~~

1. I want to wash my hair. Is there __*any shampoo*__ ?
2. The police want to talk to you. They want to ask you _____ .
3. I don't have my camera, so I can't take _____ .
4. Do you speak _____ foreign _____ ?
5. Last night I went to a restaurant with _____ of mine.
6. Can I have _____ in my coffee, please?
7. This camera isn't working. There aren't _____ in it.
8. It's hot in this office. I'm going out for _____ fresh _____ .
9. *A:* Would you like _____ ?
   B: No, thank you. I've had enough to eat.
10. I can do this job alone. I don't need _____ .

77.3 주어진 단어를 *some* 또는 *any*와 함께 사용하여 문장을 완성하시오.

1. Jane didn't take any pictures, but __*I took some*__ . (I / take)
2. "Where's your luggage?"   " __*I don't have any*__ ." (I / not / have)
3. "Do you need any money?"   "No, thank you. _____ ." (I / have)
4. "Can you lend me some money?"   "I'm sorry, but _____ ." (I / not / have)
5. The tomatoes at the store didn't look very good, so _____ . (I / not / buy)
6. There were some nice oranges at the store, so _____ . (I / buy)
7. "How many phone calls did you make yesterday?"   " _____ ." (I / not / make)

77.4 *something/somebody* 또는 *anything/anybody*를 써 넣으시오.

1. A woman stopped me and said __*something*__ , but I didn't understand.
2. "What's wrong?"   "There's _____ in my eye."
3. Do you know _____ about politics?
4. I went to the store, but I didn't buy _____ .
5. _____ broke the window. I don't know who.
6. There isn't _____ in the bag. It's empty.
7. I'm looking for my keys. Has _____ seen them?
8. Would you like _____ to drink?
9. I didn't eat _____ because I wasn't hungry.
10. This is a secret. Please don't tell _____ .

not + any   no   none

The parking lot is empty. 주차장은 비어 있다.

There are**n't any** cars
There are **no** cars } in the parking lot.
주차장에 차가 없다.

How many cars are there in the parking lot?
주차장에 차가 몇 대 있는가?

None. 한 대도 없다.

not (-n't) + any: ···이 없다

- There are**n't any** cars in the parking lot.
- Tracey and Jeff do**n't** have **any** children.
- You can have some coffee, but I do**n't** want **any**.
  커피를 원하시면 커피를 드세요. 하지만 저는 마시고 싶지 않아요.

no + 명사 (**no cars / no garage** 등)

no ... = **not any** 또는 **not a**

- There are **no cars** in the parking lot. (= there are**n't any** cars)
- We have **no coffee**. (= we do**n't** have **any** coffee)
- It's a nice house, but there's **no garage**. (= there is**n't a** garage) 이 집은 좋지만 차고가 없다.

특히 **have/has**와 **there is/are** 뒤에는 **no** ...를 쓴다.

부정동사 + **any** = 긍정동사 + **no**

- They **don't** have **any** children.   또는   They **have no** children.
  (They don't have no children은 틀림)
- There **isn't any** sugar in your coffee.   또는   There**'s no** sugar in your coffee.

no와 **none**

no + 명사 (**no money / no children** 등):

- We have **no money**.
- Everything was OK. There were **no problems**.

none은 명사 없이 단독으로 사용한다.

- "How much money do you have?"   "**None**." (= no money)
- "Were there any problems?" 무슨 문제 있었습니까?
  "No, **none**." (= no problems) 아뇨, 전혀요.

none과 **no one**

none = 0 (zero)
no one = nobody

none은 **How much**? / **How many**?에 대한 대답이다(사물 또는 사람).

- "**How much** money do you have?"   "**None**." (= no money)
- "**How many** people did you meet?"   "**None**." (= no people)

No one은 **Who**?에 대한 대답이다.

- "**Who** did you meet?"   "**No one**."   또는   "**Nobody**."

Exercises

78.1 *no*를 사용하여 문장을 다시 쓰시오.

1. We don't have any money.   <u>*We have no money.*</u>
2. There aren't any stores near here.   There are _____
3. Carla doesn't have any free time.   _____
4. There isn't a light in this room.   _____

이번에는 *any*를 사용하여 다시 쓰시오.

5. We have no money.   <u>*We don't have any money.*</u>
6. There's no milk in the fridge.   _____
7. There are no buses today.   _____
8. Tom has no brothers or sisters.   _____

78.2 *no* 또는 *any*를 써 넣으시오.

1. There's <u>*no*</u> sugar in your coffee.
2. My brother is married, but he doesn't have _____ children.
3. Sue doesn't speak _____ foreign languages.
4. I'm afraid there's _____ coffee. Would you like some tea?
5. "Look at those birds!" "Birds? Where? I can't see _____ birds."
6. "Do you know where Jessica is?" "No, I have _____ idea."

no, any 또는 *none*을 써 넣으시오.

7. There aren't _____ pictures on the wall.
8. The weather was cold, but there was _____ wind.
9. I wanted to buy some oranges, but they didn't have _____ at the store.
10. Everything was correct. There were _____ mistakes.
11. "How much luggage do you have?" " _____ ."
12. "How much luggage do you have?" "I don't have _____ ."

78.3 *any* 또는 *no* + 아래의 단어를 사용하여 문장을 완성하시오.

air conditioning	answer	difference	friends	furniture
line	money	~~problems~~	questions	

1. Everything was OK. There were <u>*no problems*</u> .
2. Jack and Emily would like to take a vacation, but they have _____ .
3. I'm not going to answer _____ .
4. He's always alone. He has _____ .
5. There is _____ between these two machines. They're exactly the same.
6. There wasn't _____ in the room. It was completely empty.
7. I tried to call you yesterday, but there was _____ .
8. The house is hot because there isn't _____ .
9. There was _____ outside the movie theater, so we didn't have to wait to get our tickets.

78.4 질문에 1–2단어로 짧게 답하시오. 필요한 경우 *None*을 쓰시오.

1. How many letters did you write yesterday?   <u>*Two.*</u> 또는 <u>*A lot.*</u> 또는 <u>*None.*</u>
2. How many sisters do you have?   _____
3. How much coffee did you drink yesterday?   _____
4. How many pictures have you taken today?   _____
5. How many legs does a snake have?   _____

not + anybody/anyone/anything
nobody/no one/nothing

A

not + anybody/anyone
nobody / no one
(사람에 대해 사용)

not + anything
nothing
(사물에 대해 사용)

- There **isn't** $\left\{ \begin{array}{l} \textbf{anybody} \\ \textbf{anyone} \end{array} \right\}$ in the room.

- There **is** $\left\{ \begin{array}{l} \textbf{nobody} \\ \textbf{no one} \end{array} \right\}$ in the room.

- *A:* **Who** is in the room? 방에 누가 있니?
  B: **Nobody.** / **No one**. 아무도 없어.

-body는 -one과 같다:
any**body** = any**one**   no**body** = no **one**

- There **isn't anything** in the bag.

- There **is nothing** in the bag.

- *A:* **What's** in the bag? 가방에 뭐가 있니?
  B: **Nothing**. 아무것도 없어.

B

not + anybody/anyone
- I do**n't** know **anybody**
  (또는 **anyone**) here.

nobody = not + anybody
no one = not + anyone
- I'm lonely. I have **nobody** to talk to.
  (= I don't have **anybody**)
  나는 외로워. 얘기할 사람이 아무도 없어.
- The house is empty. There is **no one**
  in it. (= There is**n't anyone** in it.)

not + anything
- I ca**n't** remember **anything**.
  나는 아무것도 기억할 수가 없다.

nothing = not + anything
- She said **nothing**.
  (= She did**n't** say **anything**.)
  그녀는 아무 말도 하지 않았다.
- There's **nothing** to eat.
  (= There is**n't anything** to eat.)

C

nobody / **no one** / **nothing**은 문장의 맨 앞에 쓸 수 있고, 질문에 답할 때는 단독으로 쓸 수도 있다.

- The house is empty. **Nobody** lives
  there. (Anybody lives there는 틀림)
- "Who did you speak to?" **"No one."**

- **Nothing** happened.
  (Anything happened는 틀림)
- "What did you say?" **"Nothing."**

D

주의: 부정형의 동사 + **anybody** / **anyone** / **anything**
       긍정형의 동사 + **nobody** / **no one** / **nothing**

- He does**n't** know **anything**. (He doesn't know nothing은 틀림)
- Do**n't** tell **anybody**. (Don't tell nobody는 틀림)
- There **is nothing** to do in this town. (There isn't nothing은 틀림)
  이 도시에는 할 일이 하나도 없다.

Exercises

79.1 *nobody / no one* 또는 *nothing*을 사용하여 문장을 다시 쓰시오.

1. There isn't anything in the bag.   *There's nothing in the bag.*
2. There isn't anybody in the office.   There's _____
3. I don't have anything to do.   I _____
4. There isn't anything on TV.   _____
5. There wasn't anyone at home.   _____
6. We didn't find anything.   _____

79.2 *anybody/anyone* 또는 *anything*을 사용하여 문장을 다시 쓰시오.

1. There's nothing in the bag.   *There isn't anything in the bag.*
2. There was nobody on the bus.   There wasn't _____
3. I have nothing to read.   _____
4. I have no one to help me.   _____
5. She heard nothing.   _____
6. We have nothing for dinner.   _____

79.3 *nobody / no one* 또는 *nothing*을 사용하여 질문에 답하시오.

1a. What did you say? *Nothing.*   5a. Who knows the answer? _____
2a. Who saw you? *Nobody.*   6a. What did you buy? _____
3a. What do you want? _____   7a. What happened? _____
4a. Who did you meet? _____   8a. Who was late? _____

이번에는 같은 질문에 완전한 문장으로 답하시오.
nobody / no one / nothing 또는 *anybody/anyone/anything*을 사용하시오.

1b. *I didn't say anything.*
2b. *Nobody saw me.*
3b. I don't _____
4b. I _____
5b. _____ the answer.
6b. _____
7b. _____
8b. _____

79.4 *nobody / no one / nothing* 또는 *anybody/anyone/anything*을 사용하여 문장을 완성하시오.

1. That house is empty. *Nobody* lives there.
2. Jack has a bad memory. He can't remember *anything* .
3. Be quiet! Don't say _____ .
4. I didn't know about the meeting. _____ told me.
5. "What did you have to eat?"   " _____ . I wasn't hungry."
6. I didn't eat _____ . I wasn't hungry.
7. Helen was sitting alone. She wasn't with _____ .
8. I'm sorry, I can't help you. There's _____ I can do.
9. I don't know _____ about car engines.
10. The museum is free. It doesn't cost _____ to go in.
11. I heard a knock at the door, but when I opened it, there was _____ there.
12. Antonio spoke very fast. I didn't understand _____ .
13. "What are you doing tonight?"   " _____ . Why?"
14. Helen is out of town. _____ knows where she is. She didn't tell _____
    where she was going.

somebody/anything/nowhere 등

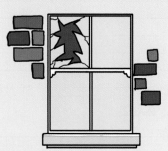

Somebody (또는 **Someone**) has broken the window.
누군가가 창문을 깼다.

She has got **something** in her mouth.
그녀는 입 안에 뭔가를 물고 있다.

● **Chicago**

Tom lives **somewhere** near Chicago.
탐은 시카고 근처 어딘가에 살고 있다.

| **somebody/someone** = 누군지 모르는 어떤 사람 | **something** = 무엇인지 모르는 어떤 것 | **somewhere** = 어딘지 모르는 어떤 곳에/곳으로 |

사람 (**-body** 또는 **-one**)

| **somebody** 또는 **someone** |
| **anybody** 또는 **anyone** |
| **nobody** 또는 **no one** |

- There is **somebody** (또는 **someone**) at the door.
- Is there **anybody** (또는 **anyone**) at the door?
- There isn't **anybody** (또는 **anyone**) at the door.
- There is **nobody** (또는 **no one**) at the door.

-body는 **-one**과 같다: **somebody = someone, nobody = no one** 등

사물 (**-thing**)

| **something** |
| **anything** |
| **nothing** |

- Lucy said **something**, but I didn't understand what she said.
  루시가 뭐라고 말했지만, 나는 무슨 말인지 이해하지 못했다.
- Are you doing **anything** this weekend?
- I was angry, but I did**n't** say **anything**.
- "What did you say?"   "**Nothing**."

장소 (**-where**)

| **somewhere** |
| **anywhere** |
| **nowhere** |

- Ruth's parents live **somewhere** in Southern California.
- Did you go **anywhere** interesting on vacation? 휴가 때 어디 재미있는 곳에 갔었니?
- I'm staying here. I'm **not** going **anywhere**. 난 여기 있어. 어디에도 안 갈 거야.
- I don't like this town. There is **nowhere** to go.

something/anybody 등 + 형용사 (**big/cheap/interesting** 등): ···한 것/사람

- Did you meet **anybody interesting** at the party?
- We always go to the same place. Let's go **somewhere different**.
  우리는 항상 똑같은 곳만 가. 어디 다른 곳 좀 가 보자.
- "What's in that letter?"   "It's **nothing important**."

something/anybody 등 + **to** ...: ···할 것/사람

- I'm hungry. I want **something to eat**. (= something that I can eat)
- Tony doesn't have **anybody to talk** to. (= anybody that he can talk to) 토니는 대화를 할 사람이 없다.
- There is **nowhere to go** in this town. (= nowhere where people can go) 이 도시에는 갈 만한 곳이 없다.

some과 **any** → Unit 77   **any**와 **no** → Unit 78   **anybody/nothing** 등 → Unit 79
everything/-body/-where → Unit 81

Exercises

80.1 *somebody* (또는 *someone*) / *something* / *somewhere*를 써 넣으시오.

1. Lucy said _*something*_ .   What did she say?
2. I lost _____ .   What did you lose?
3. Sue and Tom went _____ .   Where did they go?
4. I'm going to call _____ .   Who are you going to call?

80.2 질문에 *nobody* (또는 *no one*) / *nothing* / *nowhere*로 답하시오.

1a. What did you say?   _*Nothing.*_
2a. Where are you going?   _____
3a. What do you want?   _____
4a. Who are you looking for?   _____

이번에는 같은 질문에 완전한 문장으로 답하시오.
not + *anybody*/*anything*/*anywhere*를 사용하시오.

1b. _*I didn't say anything.*_   3b. _____
2b. I'm not _____   4b. _____

80.3 *somebody*/*anything*/*nowhere* 등을 써 넣으시오.

1. It's dark. I can't see _*anything*_ .
2. Tom lives _*somewhere*_ near San Francisco.
3. Do you know _____ about computers?
4. "Listen!" "What? I can't hear _____ ."
5. "What are you doing here?" "I'm waiting for _____ ."
6. We need to talk. There's _____ I want to tell you.
7. "Did _____ see the accident?" "No, _____ ."
8. We weren't hungry, so we didn't eat _____ .
9. "What's going to happen?" "I don't know. _____ knows."
10. "Do you know _____ in Tokyo?" "Yes, a few people."
11. "What's in that suitcase?" " _____ . It's empty."
12. I'm looking for my glasses. I can't find them _____ .
13. I don't like cold weather. I want to live _____ warm.
14. Is there _____ interesting on television tonight?
15. Have you ever met _____ famous?

80.4 아래 상자에서 각각 한 단어를 사용하여 문장을 완성하시오.

something	anything	nothing		do	drink	eat	~~go~~
something	anywhere	~~nowhere~~		park	read	sit	stay
somewhere		nowhere					

1. We don't go out very much because there's _*nowhere to go*_ .
2. There isn't any food in the house. We don't have _____ .
3. I'm bored. I have _____ .
4. "Why are you standing?" "Because there isn't _____ ."
5. "Would you like _____ ?" "Yes, please – a glass of water."
6. If you're going downtown, take the bus. Don't drive because there's
   _____ .
7. I want _____ . I'm going to buy a magazine.
8. I need _____ in Seoul. Can you recommend a hotel?

every와 all

every

Every house on the street is the same.
그 거리의 집들은 모두 똑같다.

every house on the street =
all the houses on the street

every + 단수 명사(**every house** / **every country** 등)를 쓴다.

■ Sarah has been to **every country** in Europe.
■ **Every summer** we take a vacation at the beach.
■ She looks different **every time** I see her.

every 뒤에는 단수 동사를 쓴다.

■ **Every house** on the street **is** the same. (Every house ... are the same은 틀림)
■ **Every country has** a national flag. (Every country have ...는 틀림)

every와 **all**의 비교:

■ **Every student** in the class passed the exam. ■ **Every country has** a national flag. 　모든 나라들은 국기가 있다.	■ **All the students** in the class passed the exam. ■ **All countries have** a national flag.

every day와 all day

every day = 매일:

얼마나 자주?

SUN	+	MON	+	TUE	+	WED	+	THUR	+	FRI	+	SAT

EVERY DAY

■ It rained **every day** last week.
■ Bill watches TV for about two hours **every night**. (= 매일 밤)

또한 **every morning/week/summer** 등

all day = 하루 종일:

얼마나 오래?

하루의
시작
◄————ALL DAY————►
하루의
끝

■ It rained **all day** yesterday.
■ On Monday, I watched TV **all night**. (= 밤새도록)

또한 **morning/week/summer** 등

everybody (또는 everyone) / everything / everywhere

everybody or **everyone** (사람) **everything** (사물) **everywhere** (장소)

■ **Everybody** (또는 **Everyone**) needs friends.
(= all people need friends)
■ Do you have **everything** you need?
(= all the things you need)
■ I lost my watch. I've looked **everywhere** for it.
(= I've looked in all places)

everybody/everyone/everything 다음에는 단수 동사를 쓴다.

■ **Everybody has** problems. (Everybody have는 틀림)

Exercises

81.1 *every* + 아래의 단어를 사용하여 문장을 완성하시오.

> day   room   ~~student~~   time   word

1. ___Every student___ in the class passed the exam.
2. My job is very boring. _____ is the same.
3. Kate is a very good chess player. When we play, she wins _____ .
4. _____ in the hotel has a TV.
5. "Did you understand what she said?"   "Most of it, but not _____ ."

81.2 *every day* 또는 *all day*를 넣어 문장을 완성하시오.

1. Yesterday it rained ___all day___ .
2. I buy a newspaper _____ , but sometimes I don't read it.
3. I'm not going out tomorrow. I'll be at home _____ .
4. I usually drink about four cups of coffee _____ .
5. Paula was sick yesterday, so she stayed in bed _____ .
6. I'm tired now because I've been working hard _____ .
7. Last year we went to the beach for a week, and it rained _____ .

81.3 *every* 또는 *all*을 써 넣으시오.

1. Bill watches TV for about two hours ___every___ night.
2. Julia gets up at 6:30 _____ morning.
3. The weather was nice yesterday, so we sat outside _____ afternoon.
4. I'm leaving town on Monday. I'll be away _____ week.
5. "How often do you go skiing?"   "_____ year. Usually in March."
6. *A:* Were you at home at 10 yesterday?
   B: Yes, I was at home _____ morning. I went out after lunch.
7. My sister loves new cars. She buys one _____ year.
8. I saw Sam at the party, but he didn't speak to me _____ night.
9. We take a vacation for two or three weeks _____ summer.

81.4 *everybody*/*everything*/*everywhere*를 써 넣으시오.

1. ___Everybody___ needs friends.
2. Chris knows _____ about computers.
3. I like the people here. _____ is very friendly.
4. This is a nice hotel. It's comfortable, and _____ is very clean.
5. Kevin never uses his car. He goes _____ on his motorcycle.
6. Let's have dinner. _____ is hungry.
7. Sue's house is full of books. There are books _____ .
8. You are right. _____ you say is true.

81.5 빈칸에 한 단어만 넣어 문장을 완성하시오.

1. Everybody ___has___ problems.
2. Are you ready yet? Everybody _____ waiting for you.
3. The house is empty. Everyone _____ gone out.
4. Gary is very popular. Everybody _____ him.
5. This town is completely different now. Everything _____ changed.
6. I got home very late last night. I came in quietly because everyone _____ asleep.
7. Everybody _____ mistakes!
8. *A:* _____ everything clear? _____ everybody know what to do?
   B: Yes, we all understand.

all most some any no/none

A

비교:

children/money/books 등 (일반적인 의미):	the children / the money / these books 등:
■ **Children** like to play. (= 일반적인 아이들) ■ **Money** isn't everything. (= 일반적인 돈) ■ I enjoy reading **books**. ■ Everybody needs **friends**.	■ Where are **the children**? (= 우리 아이들) ■ I want to buy a car, but I don't have **the money**. (= 차를 살 돈) ■ Have you read **these books**? ■ I often go out with **my friends**.

B

most / most of ... , some / some of ... 등

    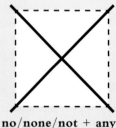

all	most	some	any	no/none/not + any

most/some 등 + 명사

all most some any no	~~of~~	cities children books money

■ **Most children** like to play.
(= 일반적인 아이들)
대부분의 아이들은 놀기 좋아한다.
■ I don't want **any money**.
■ **Some books** are better than others.
■ He has **no friends**.
■ **All cities** have the same problems.
(= 일반적인 도시들)

여기에는 **of**를 쓰지 않는다.

■ **Most people** drive too fast.
(Most of people은 틀림)
■ **Some birds** can't fly.
(Some of birds는 틀림)

most of / some of 등 + the/this/my ... 등

all	(of)	the ...
most some any none	of	this/that ... these/those ... my/your ... 등

■ **Most of the children at this school** are under 11 years old.
이 학교 아이들의 대부분은 11살 이하이다.
■ I don't want **any of this money**.
■ **Some of these books** are very old.
■ **None of my friends** live near me.

all the ... 또는 **all of the** ... 모두 쓸 수 있다.

■ **All the students in our class** passed the exam. (또는 **All of the students** ...)
우리반 학생들은 모두 시험에 합격했다.
■ Silvia has lived in Miami **all her life**.
(또는 ... **all of her life**.)

C

all of it / most of them / none of us 등

all most some any none	of	it them us you

■ You can have **some of this cake**, but not **all of it**.
이 케익을 좀 먹어도 되지만 몽땅 다 먹으면 안 돼.
■ *A:* Do you know those people? 그 사람들을 아세요?
B: **Most of them**, but not **all of them**. 대부분은 알지만 모두 알지는 못해요.
■ **Some of us** are going out tonight. Why don't you come with us?
■ I've got a lot of books, but I haven't read **any of them**.
■ "How many of these books have you read?" "**None of them**."

the ... (children / the children 등) → Unit 73   some과 any → Unit 77   no/none/any → Unit 78
all과 every → Unit 81

Exercises

82.1 괄호 안의 단어(*some/most* 등)를 사용하여 문장을 완성하시오. 때로는 *of*를 넣어야 할 수도 있습니다(*some of / most of* 등).

1. __*Most*__ children like to play. (most)
2. __*Some of*__ this money is yours. (some)
3. _____ people never stop talking. (some)
4. _____ the stores downtown close at 6:00. (most)
5. You can change money in _____ banks. (most)
6. I don't like _____ the pictures in the living room. (any)
7. He's lost _____ his money. (all)
8. _____ my friends are married. (none)
9. Do you know _____ the people in this picture? (any)
10. _____ birds can fly. (most)
11. I enjoyed _____ the movie, but I didn't like the ending. (most)
12. _____ sports are very dangerous. (some)
13. We can't find anywhere to stay. _____ the hotels are full. (all)
14. Try _____ this cheese. It's delicious. (some)
15. The weather was bad when we were on vacation. It rained _____ the time. (most)

82.2 그림을 보고 질문에 답하시오. 아래의 구문을 사용하시오.

all / most / some / none + *of them / of it*

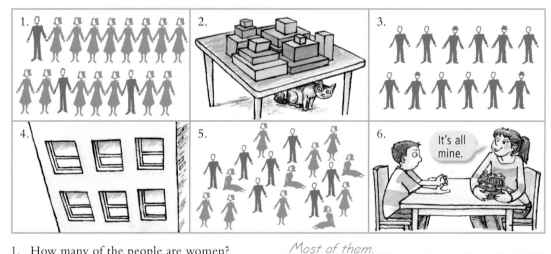

1. How many of the people are women?   __*Most of them.*__
2. How many of the boxes are on the table? _____
3. How many of the men are wearing hats? _____
4. How many of the windows are open? _____
5. How many of the people are standing? _____
6. How much of the money is Ben's? _____

82.3 틀린 문장이 있으면 고치시오. 맞는 문장에는 *OK*라고 쓰시오.

1. Most of children like to play.   __*Most children*__
2. All the students failed the test.   __*OK*__
3. Some of people work too hard. _____
4. Some of questions on the exam were very easy. _____
5. I haven't seen any of those people before. _____
6. All of insects have six legs. _____
7. Have you read all these books? _____
8. Most of students in our class are very nice. _____
9. Most of my friends are going to the party. _____
10. I'm very tired this morning – I was awake most of night. _____

both   either   neither

EXERCISES

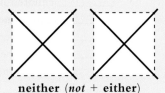

A

both/either/neither는 두 개의 사물 또는 두 명의 사람에 대해 말할 때 사용한다.

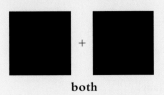

| both | either 또는 | neither (*not* + either) |

- Rebecca has two children. **Both** are married. (**both** = the two children)
- Would you like tea or coffee? You can have **either**. (**either** = tea or coffee)
  차나 커피 드시겠어요? 둘 중 아무 거나 드셔도 돼요.
- *A*: Do you want to go to the movies or the theater?
  B: **Neither**. I want to stay home. (**neither** = not the movies or the theater)

either와 neither의 비교:

- "Would you like **tea** or **coffee**?"
  - "**Either**. It doesn't matter." (= 둘 중 하나, tea or coffee)
  - "I **don't** want **either**." (I don't want neither는 틀림)
  - "**Neither**." (= 둘 다 싫음, not tea or coffee)

B

both/either/neither + 명사

| both | + 복수 |
| either / neither | + 단수 |

| both | windows/books/children 등 |
| either neither | window/book/child 등 |

- Last year I went to Miami and Seattle. I liked **both cities** very much.
- First I worked in an office and later in a store. **Neither job** was very interesting.
- There are two ways to get to the airport. You can go **either way**.
  공항 가는 길은 두 개가 있습니다. 어느 쪽으로나 갈 수 있습니다.

C

both of ... / either of ... / neither of ...

| both | (of) | the ... |
| either neither | of | these/those ... my/your/Paul's ... 등 |

I like **both of those** pictures.

- **Neither of my parents** is Canadian.
- I **haven't** read **either of these books**.

both of the/those/my ... 또는
both the/those/my ... 모두 쓸 수 있다.
- I like **both of** those pictures.   또는   I like **both** those pictures.
- **Both of** Paul's sisters are married.   또는   **Both** Paul's sisters are married.
그러나 **Neither of** Paul's sisters is married. (Neither Paul's sisters는 틀림)

나는 저 그림이 둘 다 좋아.

D

both of them / neither of us

| both either neither | of | them us you |

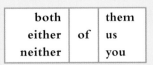

- Paul has got two sisters. **Both of them** are married.
- Sue and I didn't eat anything. **Neither of us** was hungry.
  수와 나는 아무것도 먹지 않았다. 우리 둘 다 배고프지 않았다.
- Who are those two people? I **don't** know **either of them**.

I can't either / neither can I → Unit 43

Exercises

83.1 *both/either/neither*를 써 넣으시오. 필요한 경우 *of*를 쓰시오.

1. Last year I went to Miami and Seattle. I liked ___*both*___ cities very much.
2. There were two pictures on the wall. I didn't like ___*either of*___ them.
3. It was a good football game. _____ teams played well.
4. It wasn't a good football game. _____ team played well.
5. "Is your friend Canadian or American?" "_____ . She's Australian."
6. We went away for two days, but the weather was bad. It rained _____ days.
7. *A:* I bought two newspapers. Which one do you want?
   B: _____ . It doesn't matter which one.
8. I invited Donna and Mike to the party, but _____ them came.
9. "Do you go to work by car or by bus?" "_____ . I always walk."
10. "Which jacket do you prefer, this one or that one?" "I don't like _____ them."
11. "Do you work, or are you a student?" "_____ . I work, and I'm a student, too."
12. Paula and I didn't know the time because _____ us had a watch.
13. Helen has two sisters and a brother. _____ sisters are married.
14. Helen has two sisters and a brother. I know her brother, but I haven't met
    _____ her sisters.

83.2 그림에 맞게 문장을 완성하시오. *Both ...* 또는 *Neither ...*를 사용하시오.

1. ___*Both cups are*___ _____ empty.
2. _____ are open.
3. _____ wearing a hat.
4. _____ beards.
5. _____ to the airport.
6. _____ right.

83.3 두 사람이 질문에 같은 대답을 했습니다. *Both/Neither of them ...*을 사용하여 문장을
쓰시오.

1. Are you married?	No	No →	1. ___Neither of them is married.___
2. How old are you?	21	21 →	2. ___Both of them are 21.___
3. Are you a student?	Yes	Yes →	3. _____ students.
4. Do you have a car?	No	No	4. _____ a car.
5. Where do you live?	Boston	Boston	5. _____
6. Do you like to cook?	Yes	Yes	6. _____
7. Can you play the piano?	No	No	7. _____
8. Do you read the newspaper?	Yes	Yes	8. _____
9. Are you interested in sports?	No	No	9. _____

a lot   much   many

A

| a lot of money | not much money | a lot of books | not many books |

much + 셀 수 없는 명사
(**much food / much money** 등):
- Did you buy **much food**?
- We don't have **much luggage**.
- How **much money** do you want?
- *A:* Do you have any **money**?
  돈 좀 있니?
- *B:* I have some, but **not much**.
  좀 있지만, 많지는 않아.

many + 복수 명사
(**many books / many people** 등):
- Did you buy **many books**?
- We don't know **many people**.
- How **many photos** did you take?
- *A:* Did you take any **photos**?
  사진 좀 찍었니?
- *B:* I took some, but **not many**.
  찍긴 찍었는데 많이 찍지는 않았어.

a lot of 다음에는 셀 수 있는 명사와 셀 수 없는 명사 모두 가능하다.
- We bought **a lot of food**.
- Paula doesn't have **a lot of** free **time**.

- We bought **a lot of books**.
- Did they ask **a lot of questions**?

동사의 수에 유의하자.
- There **is** a lot of **food/money/ water** … (단수 동사)

- There **are** a lot of **trees/shops/ people** … (복수 동사)
- A lot of **people speak** English.
  (A lot of people speaks는 틀림)

B

의문문과 부정문에서는 **much**를 사용한다.
- Do you drink **much coffee**?
- I don't drink **much coffee**.

하지만 긍정문에서는 일반적으로 **much**를 사용하지 않는다.
- I drink **a lot of coffee**. (I drink much coffee는 틀림)
- "Do you drink much coffee?" "Yes, **a lot**." (Yes, much는 틀림)

many와 **a lot of**는 모든 종류의 문장(긍정/부정/의문)에 사용한다.
- We have **many** friends / **a lot of** friends.
- We don't have **many** friends / **a lot of** friends.
- Do you have **many** friends / **a lot of** friends?

C

much와 **a lot**은 명사 없이 쓸 수 있다.
- Donna spoke to me, but she didn't say **much**. 다나는 내게 말을 걸었지만, 말을 많이 하지는 않았다.
- "Do you watch TV **much**?" "No, **not much**." (= not often)
- We like movies, so we go to the movies **a lot**. (go to the movies much는 틀림)
- I don't like him very **much**.

Exercises

84.1 *much* 또는 *many*를 써 넣으시오.

1. Did you buy __*much*__ food?
2. There aren't _____ hotels in this town.
3. We don't have _____ gas. We need to stop and get some.
4. Were there _____ people on the train?
5. Did _____ students fail the exam?
6. Paula doesn't have _____ money.
7. I wasn't hungry, so I didn't eat _____ .
8. I don't know where Gary lives these days. I haven't seen him for _____ years.

How much 또는 *How many*를 써 넣으시오.

9. _____ people are coming to the party?
10. _____ milk should I get at the store?
11. _____ bread did you buy?
12. _____ players are there on a football team?

84.2 *much/many* + 아래의 단어를 사용하여 문장을 완성하시오.

~~books~~   countries   luggage   people   time   times

1. I don't read very much. I don't have __*many books*__ .
2. Hurry up! We don't have _____ .
3. Do you travel a lot? Have you been to _____ ?
4. Tina hasn't lived here very long, so she doesn't know _____ .
5. "Do you have _____ ?"   "No, only this bag."
6. I know Tokyo very well. I've been there _____ .

84.3 *a lot of* + 아래의 단어를 사용하여 문장을 완성하시오.

accidents   ~~books~~   fun   interesting things   traffic

1. I like reading. I have __*a lot of books*__ .
2. We enjoyed our visit to the museum. We saw _____ .
3. This road is very dangerous. There are _____ .
4. We enjoyed our vacation. We had _____ .
5. It took me a long time to drive here. There was _____ .

84.4 다음 중에는 *much*의 쓰임이 자연스럽지 않은 문장이 있습니다. 자연스럽지 않은 문장은 고치고, 자연스러운 문장은 *OK*라고 쓰시오.

1. Do you drink <u>much coffee</u>?   __*OK*__
2. I drink <u>much tea</u>.   __*a lot of tea*__
3. It was a cold winter. We had <u>much snow</u>. _____
4. There wasn't <u>much snow</u> last winter.   _____
5. It costs <u>much money</u> to travel around the world. _____
6. This pen was cheap. It didn't cost <u>much</u>. _____
7. Do you know <u>much</u> about computers?   _____
8. "Do you have any luggage?"   "Yes, <u>much</u>." _____

84.5 *much*와 *a lot*을 사용하여 다음 사람들에 대한 문장을 쓰시오.

1. Jim loves movies. (go to the movies)   __*He goes to the movies a lot.*__
2. Nicole thinks TV is boring. (watch TV)   __*She doesn't watch TV much.*__
3. Tina is a good tennis player. (play tennis) She _____
4. Martin doesn't like to drive. (use his car) He _____
5. Paul spends most of the time at home. (go out) _____
6. Sue has been all over the world. (travel)   _____

(a) little (a) few

A

(a) little + 셀 수 없는 명사:

(a) little water
(a) little time
(a) little money
(a) little soup

a little water

(a) few + 복수 명사:

(a) few books
(a) few questions
(a) few people
(a) few days

a few books

B

a little = 약간 (some but not much)

- She didn't eat anything, but she drank **a little water**.
  그녀는 아무것도 먹지 않았지만 물은 조금 마셨다.
- I speak **a little Spanish**.
  (= some Spanish but not much)
- A: Can you speak Spanish?
  B: **A little**.

a few = 몇몇 (some but not many)

- Excuse me, I have to make **a few phone calls**.
  실례합니다만 전화를 몇 통 걸어야 해요.
- We're going away for **a few days**.
- I speak **a few words** of Spanish.
- A: Do you have any stamps?
  B: Yes, **a few**. Do you want one?

C

~~a~~ **little** (a 없이) = 거의 없는 (almost no / almost nothing)

- There was **little food** in the fridge. It was almost empty.

very little도 뜻이 비슷하다.

- Dan is very thin because he eats **very little**. (= almost nothing)
  댄은 거의 먹지를 않기 때문에 무척 말랐다.

~~a~~ **few** (a 없이) = 거의 없는 (almost no)

- There were **few people** in the theater. It was almost empty.

very few도 뜻이 비슷하다.

- Your English is very good. You make **very few mistakes**.
  영어를 매우 잘하시는군요. 실수를 거의 안 하시네요.

D

little과 **a little**

a little은 긍정적인 의미이다.
- They have **a little** money, so they're not poor. (= 돈이 좀 있음)

little(또는 **very little**)은 부정적인 의미이다.
- They have (**very**) **little** money. They are very poor. (= 돈이 거의 없음)

few와 **a few**

a few는 긍정적인 의미이다.
- I have **a few** friends, so I'm not lonely. (= 친구가 몇 명 있음)

few(또는 **very few**)는 부정적인 의미이다.
- I'm sad and I'm lonely. I have (**very**) **few** friends. (= 친구가 거의 없음)

I have **a little** money.

I have **little** money.

I have **a few** friends.

I have **few** friends.

Exercises

85.1 *a little* 또는 *a few*를 사용하여 질문에 답하시오.

1. "Do you have any money?" "Yes, _a little_ ."
2. "Do you have any envelopes?" "Yes, _____ ."
3. "Do you want sugar in your coffee?" "Yes, _____ , please."
4. "Did you take any pictures when you were on vacation?" "Yes, _____ ."
5. "Does your friend speak English?" "Yes, _____ ."
6. "Are there any good restaurants in this town?" "Yes, _____ ."

85.2 *a little / a few* + 아래의 단어를 써 넣으시오.

> chairs   days   fresh air   friends   milk   Russian   times   ~~years~~

1. Martin speaks Italian well. He lived in Italy for _a few years_ .
2. Can I have _____ in my coffee, please?
3. "When did Julia leave?" "_____ ago."
4. "Do you speak any foreign languages?" "I can speak _____ ."
5. "Are you going out alone?" "No, I'm going with _____ ."
6. "Have you ever been to Mexico?" "Yes, _____ ."
7. There wasn't much furniture in the room – just a table and _____ .
8. I'm going out for a walk. I need _____ .

85.3 *very little / very few* + 아래의 단어를 사용하여 문장을 완성하시오.

> coffee   hotels   ~~mistakes~~   people   rain   time   work

1. Your English is very good. You make _very few mistakes_ .
2. I drink _____ . I don't like it.
3. The weather here is very dry in summer. There is _____ .
4. It's difficult to find a place to stay in this town. There are _____ .
5. Hurry up. We've got _____ .
6. The town is very quiet at night. _____ go out.
7. Some people in the office are very lazy. They do _____ .

85.4 *little / a little* 또는 *few / a few*를 써 넣으시오.

1. There was _little_ food in the fridge. It was almost empty.
2. "When did Sarah go out?" "_____ minutes ago."
3. I can't decide now. I need _____ time to think about it.
4. There was _____ traffic, so we arrived earlier than we expected.
5. The bus service isn't very good at night – there are _____ buses after 9:00.
6. "Would you like some soup?" "Yes, _____ , please."
7. They sent us a map, so we had _____ trouble finding their house.

85.5 틀린 곳을 찾아 고치시오. 맞으면 *OK*라고 쓰시오.

1. We're going away (for few days) next week.   _for a few days_
2. Everybody needs little luck.   _____
3. I can't talk to you now – I've got few things to do.   _____
4. I eat very little meat – I don't like it very much.   _____
5. Excuse me, can I ask you few questions?   _____
6. There were little people on the bus – it was almost empty.   _____
7. Martin is a very private person. Few people know him well.   _____

old/nice/interesting 등 (형용사)

A

형용사 + 명사 (nice day / blue eyes 등)

형용사 + 명사	
It's a **nice**	**day** today.
Laura has **brown**	**eyes**.
There's a very **old**	**church** in this town.
Do you like **Italian**	**food**?
I don't speak any **foreign**	**languages**.
There are some **beautiful yellow**	**flowers** in the garden.

형용사는 명사 앞에 온다.

- They live in a **modern house**. (a house modern은 틀림)
- Have you met any **famous people**? (people famous는 틀림)

영어의 형용사는 어미 변화가 없다.

a **different** place   **different** places (differents는 틀림)

B

be (am/is/was 등) + 형용사

- The weather **is nice** today.
- These flowers **are** very **beautiful**.
- **Are** you **cold**? Should I close the window?
  추우세요? 창문을 닫아 줄까요?
- **I'm hungry**. Can I have something to eat?
- The movie **wasn't** very **good**. It was **boring**.
- Please **be quiet**. I'm reading.
  좀 조용히 해. 책 읽고 있단 말이야.

I'm hungry.

C

look/feel/smell/taste/sound + 형용사

You **look tired**.
Yes, I **feel tired**.

You **sound happy**.

It **smells good**.
It **tastes good**.

- "You **look tired**." "Yes, I **feel tired**."
- Gary told me about his new job. It **sounds** very **interesting**.
  게리가 자기 새 일에 대해 이야기해 줬다. 그 일은 무척 재미있어 보였다.
- I'm not going to eat this fish. It doesn't **smell good**.

비교:

He	is feels looks	tired.

They	are look sound	happy.

It	is smells tastes	good.

get + 형용사 (get hungry/tired 등) → Unit 57   something/anybody + 형용사 → Unit 80

Exercises

86.1 단어를 올바른 순서로 배열하시오.

1　(new / live in / house / they / a)　　　_They live in a new house._
2.　(like / jacket / I / that / green)　　　I _____
3.　(music / like / do / classical / you?)　　Do _____
4.　(had / wonderful / a / I / trip)　　　_____
5.　(went to / restaurant / a / Japanese / we)　_____

86.2 아래에서 형용사(*dark/foreign* 등)와 명사(*air/job* 등)를 하나씩 골라 문장을 완성하시오.

| air | dangerous | ~~foreign~~ | hot | knife | long | vacation |
| clouds | dark | fresh | job | ~~languages~~ | sharp | water |

1. Do you speak any _foreign languages_ ?
2. Look at those _____ . It's going to rain.
3. Sue works very hard, and she's very tired. She needs a _____ .
4. You need _____ to make tea.
5. Can you open the window? We need some _____ .
6. I need a _____ to cut these onions.
7. Firefighting is a _____ .

86.3 아래의 상자에서 단어를 하나씩 골라 그림에 맞는 문장을 쓰시오.

| feel(s) | look(s) | ~~sound(s)~~ | | ~~happy~~ | nice | surprised |
| look(s) | smell(s) | taste(s) | + | new | sick | terrible |

1. You _sound happy_ .
2. It _____ .
3. I _____ .
4. You _____ .
5. They _____ .
6. It _____ .

86.4 A와 B는 의견이 다릅니다. 주어진 단어를 사용하여 B의 말을 완성하시오.

	A		B	
1.	You look tired.	I do? I _don't feel tired_ .	(feel)
2.	This is a new coat.	It is? It doesn't _____ .	(look)
3.	I'm American.	You are? You _____ .	(sound)
4.	You look cold.	Really? I _____ .	(feel)
5.	These bags are heavy.	They are? They _____ .	(look)
6.	That soup looks good.	Maybe, but it _____ .	(taste)

quickly/badly/suddenly 등 (부사)

A

7:10   7:12   7:15

He ate his dinner very **quickly**.
그는 저녁을 매우 빨리 먹었다.

Suddenly, the shelf fell down.
갑자기 선반이 떨어졌다.

quickly와 **suddenly**는 부사이다.

형용사 + **-ly** → 부사:

형용사	quick	bad	sudden	careful	heavy	
부사	quickly	badly	suddenly	carefully	heavily	등

철자법은 부록 5 참조.   eas**y** → eas**ily**   heav**y** → heav**ily**

B

부사는 상황이나 동작을 설명해 준다. 즉, 어떤 것이 **어떻게** 발생하는지, 또는 누가 어떤 것을 **어떻게** 하는지를 설명한다.

- The train **stopped suddenly**.
  기차가 갑자기 멈췄다.
- I **opened** the door **slowly**.
- Please **listen carefully**.
  잘 들으세요.
- I **understand** you **perfectly**.

It's **raining heavily**. 비가 심하게 내리고 있다.

비교:

형용사	부사
■ Sue is very **quiet**. 수는 말이 별로 없다.	■ Sue **speaks** very **quietly**. (speaks very quiet는 틀림) 수는 무척 조용히 말한다.
■ **Be careful!**	■ **Listen carefully!** (listen careful은 틀림)
■ It was a **bad game**.	■ Our team **played badly**. (played bad는 틀림)
■ I **felt nervous**. 나는 초조했다. (= I was nervous)	■ I **waited nervously**. 나는 초조하게 기다렸다.

C

hard   fast   late   early

이 단어들은 형용사와 부사 모두로 쓰인다.

■ Sue's job **is** very **hard**. 수의 일은 매우 어렵다.	■ Sue **works** very **hard**. (very hardly는 틀림) 수는 매우 열심히 일한다.
■ Ben is **a fast runner**.	■ Ben can **run fast**.
■ The bus **was late/early**.	■ I **went** to bed **late/early**.

D

good (형용사) → **well** (부사)

■ Your English **is** very **good**.	■ You **speak** English very **well**. (very good은 틀림)
■ It was a **good game**. 훌륭한 경기였어.	■ Our team **played well**. 우리 팀은 선전했다.

well은 '건강한'이라는 뜻의 형용사로도 쓰인다(= not sick, in good health).

- "How are you?"   "**I'm** very **well**, thank you. And you?"

Exercises

87.1 그림을 보고 문장을 완성하시오. 아래의 부사를 사용하시오.

angrily   badly   dangerously   fast   ~~heavily~~   quietly

1. It's raining _heavily_ .
2. He sings very _____ .
3. They came in _____ .
4. She shouted at me _____ .
5. She can run very _____ .
6. He was driving _____ .

87.2 아래의 상자에서 단어를 하나씩 골라 문장을 완성하시오.

come	know	sleep	win	+	~~carefully~~	clearly	hard	well
explain	~~listen~~	think	work		carefully	easily	quickly	well

1. I'm going to tell you something very important, so please _listen carefully_ .
2. They _____ . At the end of the day they're always tired.
3. I'm tired this morning. I didn't _____ last night.
4. You play chess much better than me. When we play, you always _____ .
5. _____ before you answer the question.
6. I've met Alice a few times, but I don't _____ her very _____ .
7. Our teacher doesn't _____ things very _____ . We never understand him.
8. Helen! I need your help. _____ !

87.3 맞는 것을 고르시오.

1. Don't eat so ~~quick~~ / quickly. It's not good for you. (*quickly*가 맞음)
2. Why are you angry / angrily? I didn't do anything.
3. Can you speak slow / slowly, please?
4. Come on, Dave! Why are you always so slow / slowly?
5. Bill is a very careful / carefully driver.
6. Jane is studying hard / hardly for her exams.
7. "Where's Diane?" "She was here, but she left sudden / suddenly."
8. Please be quiet / quietly. I'm studying.
9. Some companies pay their workers very bad / badly.
10. Those oranges look nice / nicely. Can I have one?
11. I don't remember much about the accident. Everything happened quick / quickly.

87.4 *good* 또는 *well*을 써 넣으시오.

1. Your English is very _good_ . You speak it very _well_ .
2. Jackie did very _____ on the quiz today.
3. The party was very _____ . I enjoyed it a lot.
4. Martin has a difficult job, but he does it _____ .
5. How are your parents? Are they _____ ?
6. Did you have a _____ vacation? Was the weather _____ ?

old/older expensive / more expensive

A

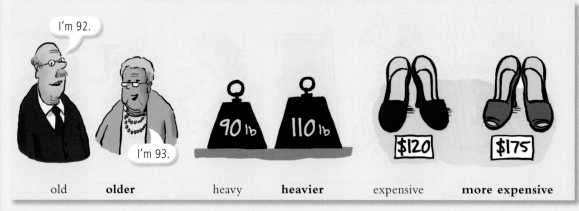

| old | **older** | heavy | **heavier** | expensive | **more expensive** |

older / **heavier** / **more expensive**는 비교급이다.

비교급의 형태는 **-er** (**older**) 또는 **more** … (**more expensive**)이다.

B

older/heavier 등

짧은 단어 (1음절) → **-er**:

| old → **older** | slow → **slower** | cheap → **cheaper** |
| nice → **nicer** | late → **later** | big → **bigger** |

철자법은 부록 5 참조.   big → bi**gg**er   hot → ho**tt**er   thin → thi**nn**er

-y로 끝나는 단어 → **-ier**:

| easy → **easier** | heavy → **heavier** | early → **earlier** |

- Rome is **old**, but Athens is **older**. (more old는 틀림)
- Is it **cheaper** to go by car or by train? (more cheap는 틀림)
  차로 가는 게 더 싸니, 기차로 가는 게 더 싸니?
- Helen wants a **bigger** car.
- This coat is OK, but I think the other one is **nicer**.
- Don't take the bus. It's **easier** to take a taxi. (more easy는 틀림)

far → farther:

- "How **far** is it to the station? A mile?" 역까지 거리가 얼마나 돼? 1마일?
  "No, it's **farther**. About two miles." 아니, 더 멀어. 2마일쯤.

C

more …

긴 단어 (2/3/4음절) → **more** …:

| careful → **more careful** | polite → **more polite** |
| expensive → **more expensive** | interesting → **more interesting** |

- You should be **more careful**.
- I don't like my job. I want to do something **more interesting**.
  나는 내 일을 좋아하지 않는다. 나는 더 재미있는 일을 하고 싶다.
- Is it **more expensive** to go by car or by train?

D

good/well → better   bad → worse

- The weather wasn't very **good** yesterday, but it's **better** today.
- "Do you feel **better** today?" "No, I feel **worse**."
- Which is **worse** – a headache or a toothache? 어느 쪽이 더 끔찍해 — 두통 아니면 치통?

Exercises

88.1 그림을 보고 비교급(*older* / *more interesting* 등)을 쓰시오.

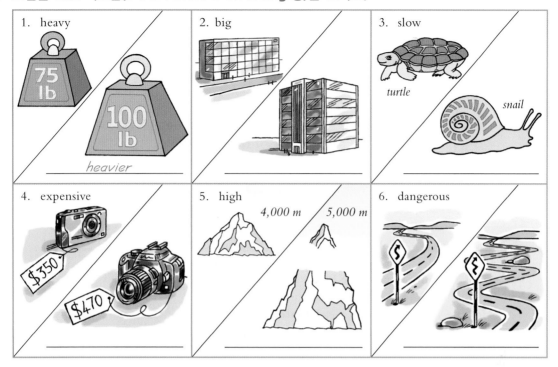

1. heavy — _heavier_
2. big — _____
3. slow turtle snail — _____
4. expensive $350 $470 — _____
5. high 4,000 m 5,000 m — _____
6. dangerous — _____

88.2 비교급을 쓰시오.

1. old _____older_____
2. strong _____
3. happy _____
4. modern _____
5. important _____
6. good _____
7. large _____
8. serious _____
9. pretty _____
10. crowded _____

88.3 반대말을 쓰시오.

1. younger _____older_____
2. colder _____
3. cheaper _____
4. better _____
5. nearer _____
6. easier _____

88.4 비교급을 사용하여 문장을 완성하시오.

1. Helen's car isn't very big. She wants a _bigger_ one.
2. My job isn't very interesting. I want to do something _more interesting_ .
3. You're not very tall. Your brother is _____ .
4. David doesn't work very hard. I work _____ .
5. My chair isn't very comfortable. Yours is _____ .
6. Your idea isn't very good. My idea is _____ .
7. These flowers aren't very nice. The blue ones are _____ .
8. My suitcase isn't very heavy. Your suitcase is _____ .
9. I'm not very interested in art. I'm _____ in history.
10. It isn't very warm today. It was _____ yesterday.
11. These tomatoes don't taste very good. The other ones tasted _____ .
12. Peru isn't very big. Brazil is _____ .
13. Los Angeles isn't very beautiful. San Francisco is _____ .
14. This knife isn't very sharp. Do you have a _____ one?
15. People today aren't very polite. In the past they were _____ .
16. The weather isn't too bad today. Often it is much _____ .

older than ... more expensive than ...

A

I'm **taller than** you.

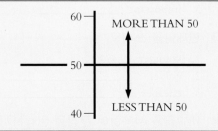

Hotel Prices
[per room per night]

Capitol Hotel	$350
Grand Hotel	$130
Western Hotel	$175

She's **taller than** him.
그녀는 그보다 키가 크다.

The Capitol Hotel is **more expensive than** the Grand Hotel.
캐피톨 호텔은 그랜드 호텔보다 더 비싸다.

비교급 뒤에는 **than**을 쓴다(**older than** ... / **more expensive than** ... 등).

- Athens is **older than** Rome.
- Are oranges **more expensive than** bananas?
- It's easier to take a taxi **than** to take the bus.
- "How are you today?" "Not bad. **Better than** yesterday."
- The restaurant is **more crowded than** usual. 그 식당은 평소보다 더 붐볐다.

B

보통 than 뒤에는 목적격을 쓴다: than **me** / than **him** / than **her** / than **us** / than **them**

다음 두 가지 형태를 모두 쓸 수 있다.

- I can run faster **than him**. 또는 I can run faster **than he can**.
- You are a better singer **than me**. 또는 You are a better singer **than I am**.
- I got up earlier **than her**. 또는 I got up earlier **than she did**.

C

more/less than ...

- *A:* How much did your shoes cost? Fifty dollars?
  B: No, **more than** that. (= **more than** $50)
- The movie was very short – **less than** an hour.
- They've got **more money than** they need.
- You go out **more than** me.

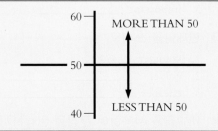

60 —

MORE THAN 50

50 —

40 —

LESS THAN 50

D

a little older / **much older** 등

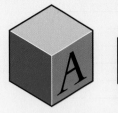

Box A is **a little bigger** than Box B.
A 상자는 B 상자보다 조금 더 크다.

Box C is **much bigger** than Box D.
C 상자는 D 상자보다 훨씬 더 크다.

a little (조금)	bigger older better	than ...
much (훨씬)	more difficult more expensive	

- Canada is **much bigger** than France.
- Sue is a **little older** than Gary – she's 25 and he's 24.
- The hotel was **much more expensive** than I expected. 그 호텔은 내가 예상한 것보다 훨씬 더 비쌌다.
- You go out **much more** than me.

old → older, expensive → more expensive → Unit 88   not as ... as → Unit 90

Exercises

89.1 *than*을 사용하여 **Liz**와 **Ben**에 대한 문장을 쓰시오.

 Liz   Ben

Liz	Ben
1. I'm 26.	1. I'm 24.
2. I'm not a very good swimmer.	2. I'm a very good swimmer.
3. I'm 5 feet 10 inches tall.	3. I'm 5 feet 8 inches tall.
4. I start work at 8:00.	4. I start work at 8:30.
5. I don't work very hard.	5. I work very hard.
6. I don't have much money.	6. I have a lot of money.
7. I'm a very good driver.	7. I'm not a very good driver.
8. I'm not very patient.	8. I'm very patient.
9. I'm not a very good dancer.	9. I'm a good dancer.
10. I'm very intelligent.	10. I'm not very intelligent.
11. I speak Spanish very well.	11. I don't speak Spanish very well.
12. I don't go to the movies very much.	12. I go to the movies a lot.

1. Liz *is older than Ben*   .
2. Ben *is a better swimmer than Liz*   .
3. Liz is _____ .
4. Liz starts _____ Ben.
5. Ben _____ .
6. Ben has _____ .

7. Liz is a _____ .
8. Ben _____ .
9. Ben _____ .
10. Liz _____ .
11. Liz _____ .
12. Ben _____ .

89.2 *than*을 사용하여 문장을 완성하시오.

1. He isn't very tall. You're *taller than him* 또는 *taller than he is*   .
2. She isn't very old. You're _____ .
3. I don't work very hard. You work _____ .
4. He doesn't watch TV very much. You _____ .
5. I'm not a very good cook. You _____ .
6. We don't know many people. You _____ .
7. They don't have much money. You _____ .
8. I can't run very fast. You can _____ .
9. She hasn't been here very long. You _____ .
10. They didn't get up very early. You _____ .
11. He wasn't very surprised. You _____ .

89.3 *a little* 또는 *much* + 비교급(*older/better* 등)을 사용하여 문장을 완성하시오.

1. Emma is 18 months old. Gary is 16 months old.
   Emma *is a little older than Gary*   .
2. Jack's mother is 52. His father is 69.
   Jack's mother _____ .
3. My camera cost $100. Yours cost $96.
   My camera _____ .
4. Yesterday I felt terrible. Today I feel OK.
   I feel _____ .
5. Today the temperature is 12 degrees Celsius. Yesterday it was 10 degrees Celsius.
   It's _____ .
6. Sarah is an excellent volleyball player. I'm not very good.
   Sarah _____ .

not as ... as

A

not as ... as

I'm 93.

I'm 96.

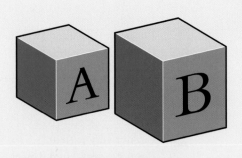

She's old, but she's **not as old as** he is.
그녀는 늙었지만, 그만큼 늙지는 않았다.

Box A is**n't as big as** Box B.
A 상자는 B 상자만큼 크지 않다.

- Rome is **not as old as** Athens. (= Athens is older)
- The Grand Hotel is**n't as expensive as** the Western. (= the Western is **more expensive**)
- I do**n't** play soccer **as often as** you. (= you play **more often**)
  나는 너만큼 축구를 자주 하지 않는다.
- The weather is better than it was yesterday. It is**n't as cold**. (= as cold **as it was yesterday**)

B

not as much as ... / not as many as ...: ···만큼 많지 않은

- I don't have **as much money as** you. (= you have **more money**)
- I don't know **as many people as** you. (= you know **more people**)
  나는 너만큼 사람들을 많이 알지 못한다.
- I don't go out **as much as** you. (= you go out **more**)

C

not as ... as와 than의 비교:

- Rome is **not as old as** Athens. 로마는 아테네만큼 오래되지 않았다.
  Athens is **older than** Rome. (older as Rome은 틀림)
- Tennis is**n't as popular as** soccer. 테니스는 축구만큼 인기있지 않다.
  Soccer is **more popular than** tennis. 축구가 테니스보다 더 인기있다.
- I do**n't** go out **as much as** you.
  You go out **more than** me.

D

보통 as **me** / as **him** / as **her** 등으로 쓴다.
다음 두 가지 형태를 모두 쓸 수 있다.

- She's not as old **as him**.   또는   She's not as old **as he is**.
- You don't work as hard **as me**.   또는   You don't work as hard **as I do**.

E

the same as ...: ···와 같은

- The weather today is **the same as** yesterday.
- My hair is **the same color as** yours. 내 머리는 네 머리와 같은 색깔이다.
- I arrived at **the same time as** Tim. 나는 팀과 같은 시간에 도착했다.

Exercises

90.1 그림을 보고 A, B, C에 대한 문장을 쓰시오.

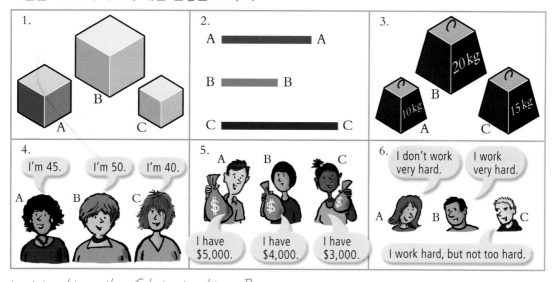

1. A is _bigger than C, but not as big as B_ .
2. A is _____ B, but not _____ C.
3. C is _____ A, but _____ .
4. A is _____ , but _____ .
5. B has _____ .
6. C works _____ .

90.2 as ... as ...를 사용하여 문장을 쓰시오.

1. Athens is older than Rome.   Rome _isn't as old as Athens_ _____ .
2. My room is bigger than yours.   Your room isn't _____ .
3. You got up earlier than me.   I didn't _____ .
4. We played better than them.   They _____ .
5. I've been here longer than you.   You _____ .
6. She's more nervous than him.   He _____ .

90.3 as 또는 than을 써 넣으시오.

1. Athens is older _than_ Rome.
2. I don't watch TV as much _____ you.
3. You eat more _____ me.
4. I'm more tired today _____ I was yesterday.
5. Joe isn't as intelligent _____ he thinks.
6. Belgium is smaller _____ Switzerland.
7. Brazil isn't as big _____ Canada.
8. I can't wait more _____ an hour.

90.4 Julia와 Andy, Laura에 대한 문장을 완성하시오. the same age / the same street 등의 표현을 사용하시오.

Julia
I'm 22.
I live on Hill Street.
I got up at 7:15.
I don't have a car.

Andy
I'm 24.
I live on Baker Street.
I got up at 7:15.
My car is dark blue.

Laura
I'm 24.
I live on Hill Street.
I got up at 7:45.
I have a car. It's dark blue.

1. (age)   _Andy is the same age as Laura_ _____ .
2. (street) Julia lives _____ .
3. (time)   Julia got up _____ .
4. (color) Andy's _____ .

the oldest   the most expensive

A

MOTEL PRICES IN
JAMESTOWN
[Per room per night]

Best West Motel	$135	Oak Tree Motel	$85
Sleep Inn	$105	Cozy Cabins	$60
Rainbow Motel	$95	Lake View Inn	$50

Box A is **bigger than** Box B.
A 상자는 B 상자보다 크다.
Box A is **bigger than** all the other boxes.
A 상자는 다른 모든 상자들보다 크다.
Box A is **the biggest** box.
A 상자가 가장 큰 상자이다.

The Best West Motel is **more expensive than** the Sleep Inn.
The Best West Motel is **more expensive than** all the other motels in town.
The Best West Motel is **the most expensive** motel in town.

bigger / older / more expensive 등은 비교급이다. (Unit 88 참조)

biggest / oldest / most expensive 등은 최상급이다.

B

최상급의 형태는 **-est** (**oldest**) 또는 **most** ... (**most expensive**)이다.

짧은 단어 (**old/cheap/nice** 등) → **the -est**:
　　　　old → **the oldest**　　　cheap → **the cheapest**　　　nice → **the nicest**
그러나　good → **the best**　　bad → **the worst**
철자법은 부록 5 참조.　　big → the biggest　　hot → the hottest

-y (**easy/heavy** 등)로 끝나는 단어 → **the -iest**:
　　　　easy → **the easiest**　　heavy → **the heaviest**　　pretty → **the prettiest**

긴 단어 (**careful/expensive/interesting** 등) → the **most** ...:
　　　　careful → **the most careful**　　　interesting → **the most interesting**

C

최상급 앞에는 **the**를 붙인다(**the** oldest ... / **the** most expensive ... 등).
- The church is very old. It's **the oldest** building in the town.
  (= it is **older than** all the other buildings)
- What is **the longest** river in the world?
- Money is important, but it isn't **the most important** thing in life.
  돈은 중요하지만, 인생에서 가장 중요한 것은 아니다.
- Excuse me, where is **the nearest** bank?

D

최상급은 명사 없이도 쓸 수 있다(**the oldest / the best / the most expensive** 등).
- Ken is a good player, but he isn't **the best** on the team. 켄은 좋은 선수지만, 팀에서 최고는 아니다.
  (**the best** = the best player)

E

최상급 + **I've ever** ... / **you've ever** ... 등: 이제껏 가장 …
- The movie was very bad. I think it's **the worst** movie **I've ever seen**.
- What is **the most unusual** thing **you've ever done**? 이제껏 해본 일 중 가장 특이한 일이 뭐니?

Exercises

91.1 비교급(*older* 등)과 최상급(*the oldest* 등)을 사용하여 문장을 쓰시오.

1.

big/small
(A/D) _A is bigger than D._
(A) _A is the biggest._
(B) _B is the smallest._

2.

A ———————— A
B ———— B
C —————————— C
D ——————————————— D

long/short
(C/A) C is _____ A.
(D) D is _____
(B) B is _____

3.

I'm 23.   I'm 19.   I'm 24.   I'm 21.

A   B   C   D

young/old
(D/C) D _____
(C) _____
(B) _____

4.

$25 $45 $50 $30
A   B   C   D

expensive/cheap
(D/A) _____
(C) _____
(A) _____

5.

RESTAURANT A *excellent*
RESTAURANT B *not bad*
RESTAURANT C *good but not wonderful*
RESTAURANT D *awful*

good/bad
(A/C) _____
(A) _____
(D) _____

91.2 최상급(*the oldest* 등)을 사용하여 문장을 완성하시오.

1. This building is very old. It's _the oldest building_ in town.
2. It was a very happy day. It was _____ of my life.
3. It's a very good movie. It's _____ I've ever seen.
4. She's a very popular singer. She's _____ in the country.
5. It was a very bad mistake. It was _____ I've ever made.
6. It's a very pretty city. It's _____ I've ever seen.
7. It was a very cold day. It was _____ of the year.
8. He's a very boring person. He's _____ I've ever met.

91.3 최상급(*the longest* 등)을 사용하여 문장을 쓰시오. 각각의 상자에서 한 단어씩 사용하시오.

~~Sydney~~	Alaska	high	~~city~~	river	Africa	South America
Everest	the Nile	large	country	state	~~Australia~~	the world
Brazil	Jupiter	long	mountain	planet	the United States	the solar system

1. _Sydney is the largest city in Australia._
2. Everest _____
3. _____
4. _____
5. _____
6. _____

enough

A

I only have two dollars – not **enough** for a taxi.

She isn't going to take a taxi.
She doesn't have **enough money**.
그녀는 택시를 타지 않을 것이다.
그녀는 충분한 돈을 가지고 있지 않다.

He can't reach the shelf.
He isn't **tall enough**.
그는 책장에 손이 닿지 않는다.
그는 키가 충분히 크지 않다.

B

enough + 명사 (**enough money** / **enough people** 등)

- "Is there **enough salt** in the soup?"   "Yes, it's fine."
- We wanted to play football, but we didn't have **enough players**.
- Why don't you buy a car? You've got **enough money**. (money enough는 틀림)

enough (명사 없이)

- I've got some money, but not **enough** to buy a car.
  (= I need more money to buy a car)
- "Would you like some more to eat?" 좀 더 드시겠어요?
  "No, thanks. I've had **enough**." 아뇨, 괜찮아요. 충분히 먹었어요.
- You're always at home. You don't go out **enough**.

C

형용사 + **enough** (**good enough** / **tall enough** 등)

- "Do you want to go swimming?" 수영하러 가고 싶니?
  "No, it isn't **warm enough**." 아니, 날씨가 충분히 따뜻하지 않아. (enough warm은 틀림)
- Can you hear the radio? Is it **loud enough** for you?
- Don't buy that coat. It's nice, but it isn't **long enough**. (= it's too short)

어순에 주의하자:

enough + 명사	형용사 + **enough**
enough money	tall **enough**
enough time	good **enough**
enough people	old **enough**

D

그 밖의 enough 표현

enough for somebody/something
…에게 충분한

enough to do something
…을 하기에 충분한

enough for somebody/something
  to do something
…가 …을 하기에 충분한

- This sweater isn't **big enough for me**.
- I don't have **enough money for a new car**.
- I don't have **enough money to buy** a new car. (for buy는 틀림)
- Is your English **good enough to have** a conversation? (for have는 틀림)
- There aren't **enough chairs for everybody to sit** down.
  모두가 앉을 수 있을 만큼 의자가 충분치 않다.

Exercises

92.1 그림을 보고 문장을 완성하시오. *enough* + 아래의 단어를 사용하시오.

chairs   ~~money~~   paint   wind

1. She doesn't have _enough money_ .
2. There aren't _____ .
3. She doesn't have _____ .
4. There isn't _____ .

92.2 그림을 보고 문장을 완성하시오. 아래의 형용사 + *enough*를 사용하시오.

big   long   strong   ~~tall~~

1. He _isn't tall enough_ .
2. The car _____ .
3. His legs aren't _____ .
4. He _____ .

92.3 *enough*를 아래의 단어와 함께 사용하여 문장을 완성하시오.

big   eat   ~~loud~~   old   practice   ~~salt~~   space   time   tired

1. "Is there _enough salt_ in the soup?"   "Yes, it's fine."
2. Can you hear the radio? Is it _loud enough_ for you?
3. He can quit school if he wants – he's _____ .
4. When I visited New York last year, I didn't have _____ to see all the things I wanted to see.
5. This house isn't _____ for a large family.
6. Tina is very thin. She doesn't _____ .
7. My office is very small. There isn't _____ .
8. It's late, but I don't want to go to bed now. I'm not _____ .
9. Lisa isn't a very good tennis player because she doesn't _____ .

92.4 *enough*와 괄호 안의 단어를 사용하여 문장을 완성하시오.

1. We don't have _enough money to buy_ a new car.   (money / buy)
2. This knife isn't _____ tomatoes.   (sharp / cut)
3. The water wasn't _____ swimming.   (warm / go)
4. Do we have _____ sandwiches?   (bread / make)
5. We played well, but not _____ the game.   (well / win)
6. I don't have _____ the newspaper.   (time / read)

too

A

Yuck!

The shoes are **too big** for him.
신발이 그에겐 너무 크다.

There is **too much** sugar in it.
거기엔 설탕이 너무 많이 들어가 있다.

B

too + 형용사/부사 (**too big** / **too hard** 등): 너무 …한

It's **too loud**.

- Can you turn the radio down?
  It's **too loud**. (= louder than I want)
- I can't work. I'm **too tired**.
- I think you work **too hard**.
  넌 너무 열심히 일하는 것 같아.

C

too much / too many: 지나치게 많은 (지나치게 많이)

- I don't like the weather here. There is **too much rain**. (= more rain than is good)
- Let's go to another restaurant. There are **too many people** here. 다른 식당에 가자. 여기는 사람이 너무 많아.
- Emily studies all the time. I think she studies **too much**.
- Traffic is a problem in this town. There are **too many cars**. 이 마을은 교통이 문제다. 차가 너무 많다.

D

too와 **not enough**의 비교:

too big

- The hat is **too big** for him.
- The radio is **too loud**. Can you turn it down, please?
  라디오 소리가 너무 커. 좀 줄여 줄래?
- There's **too much sugar** in my coffee.
  (= more sugar than I want)
- I don't feel very well. I ate **too much**.

not big enough

- The hat is**n't** big **enough** for him. (= it's **too small**)
- The radio is**n't** loud **enough**. Can you turn it up, please?
  라디오 소리가 너무 작아. 소리 좀 키워 줄래?
- There's **not enough sugar** in my coffee.
  (= I need more sugar)
- You're very thin. You do**n't** eat **enough**.

E

그 밖의 **too** 표현

too … for somebody/something
…에 너무 …한

too … to do something
…하기에는 너무 …한

too … for somebody **to do** something
누가 …하기에는 너무 …한

- These shoes are **too big for me**.
- It's a small house – **too small for a large family**.
  그 집은 작다. 대가족이 살기에는 너무 작다.

- I'm **too tired to go** out. (for go out은 틀림)
- It's **too cold to sit** outside. 야외에 앉기에는 너무 춥다.

- She speaks **too fast for me to understand**.

to …와 **for …** → Unit 55   **much/many** → Unit 84   **enough** → Unit 92

Exercises

93.1 그림을 보고 문장을 완성하시오. **too** + 아래의 단어를 사용하시오.

big   **crowded**   **fast**   **heavy**   ~~**loud**~~   **low**

1. The music is ___*too loud*___ .
2. The box is _____ .
3. The net is _____ .
4. She's driving _____ .
5. The ball is _____ .
6. The museum is _____ .

93.2 **too / too much / too many** 또는 **enough**를 써 넣으시오.

1. You're always at home. You don't go out ___*enough*___ .
2. I don't like the weather here. There's ___*too much*___ rain.
3. I can't wait for them. I don't have _____ time.
4. There was nowhere to sit on the beach. There were _____ people.
5. You're always tired. I think you work _____ hard.
6. "Did you have _____ to eat?"   "Yes, thank you."
7. You drink _____ coffee. It's not good for you.
8. You don't eat _____ vegetables. You should eat more of them.
9. I don't like the weather here. It's _____ cold.
10. Our team didn't play well. We made _____ mistakes.
11. "Would you like some ice in your tea?"   "Yes, but not _____ ."

93.3 **too/enough**와 주어진 단어를 사용하여 문장을 완성하시오.

1. I couldn't work. I ___*was too tired*___ . (tired)
2. Can you turn the radio up, please? It ___*isn't loud enough*___ . (loud)
3. I don't want to walk home. It's _____ . (far)
4. Don't buy anything in that store. It _____ . (expensive)
5. You can't put all your things in this bag. It _____ . (big)
6. I couldn't do the exercise. It _____ . (difficult)
7. Your work needs to be better. It _____ . (good)
8. I can't talk to you now. I _____ . (busy)
9. I thought the movie was boring. It _____ . (long)

93.4 **too** (+ 형용사) + **to** ...를 사용하여 문장을 완성하시오.

1. (I'm not going out / cold)   It's ___*too cold to go out*___ .
2. (I'm not going to bed / early)   It's _____ .
3. (they're not getting married / young)   They're _____ .
4. (nobody goes out at night / dangerous)
   It's _____ .
5. (don't call Sue now / late)
   It's _____ .
6. (I didn't say anything / surprised)
   I was _____ .

187

He **speaks English** very well.
(어순 1)

동사 + 목적어

Sue **reads** **a newspaper** every day.
주어 동사 목적어

동사(**reads**)와 목적어(**a newspaper**)는 보통 나란히
붙여 쓴다.

- Sue **reads a newspaper** every day.
  (Sue reads every day a newspaper는 틀림)

Sue (주어) *a newspaper* (목적어)

동사 + 목적어	
He **speaks**	**English** very well. (He speaks very well English는 틀림)
I **like**	**Italian food** very much. (I like very much …는 틀림)
Did you **watch**	**television** all night? (Did you watch all night …는 틀림)
Paul often **wears**	**a black hat**. (Paul wears often …은 틀림)
We **invited**	**a lot of people** to the party.
I **opened**	**the door** slowly.
Why do you always **make**	**the same mistake**? 넌 왜 항상 똑같은 실수를 하니?
I'm going to **borrow**	**some money** from the bank. 난 은행에서 돈을 좀 빌릴 거야.

장소와 시간

We went **to a party** **last night** .
장소(*where?*) 시간(*when?*)

장소 표현은 일반적으로 시간 표현 앞에 쓴다.

- We went **to a party last night**. (We went last night to a party는 틀림)

	장소 (어디서?)	+	시간 (언제? 얼마 동안? 얼마나 자주?)	
Lisa walks	**to work**		**every day**.	(… every day to work는 틀림)
Will you be	**at home**		**tonight**?	(… Tonight at home은 틀림)
I usually go	**to bed**		**early**.	(… early to bed는 틀림)
We arrived	**at the airport**		**at 7:00**.	
They've lived	**in the same house**		**for 20 years**.	
Joe's father has been	**in the hospital**		**since June**. 조의 아버지는 6월부터 입원해 계셨다.	

Exercises

94.1 틀린 문장을 고치시오. 맞는 문장에는 **OK**라고 쓰시오.

1. Did you watch (all night television)?   *Did you watch television all night?*
2. Sue reads a newspaper every day.   *OK*
3. I like very much this picture. _____
4. Tom started last week his new job. _____
5. I want to speak English fluently. _____
6. Jane bought for her friend a present. _____
7. I drink every day three cups of coffee. _____
8. Don't eat your dinner too quickly! _____
9. I borrowed from my brother 50 dollars. _____

94.2 단어를 올바른 순서로 배열하시오.

1. (the door / opened / I / slowly)   *I opened the door slowly.*
2. (a new computer / I / last week / bought)   I _____
3. (finished / Paul / quickly / his work) _____
4. (Emily / very well / French / doesn't speak) _____
5. (a lot of shopping / did / I / yesterday) _____
6. (New York / do you know / well?) _____
7. (we / enjoyed / very much / the party) _____
8. (the problem / carefully / I / explained) _____
9. (we / at the airport / some friends / met) _____
10. (did you buy / in Canada / that jacket?) _____
11. (every day / do / the same thing / we) _____
12. (football / don't like / very much / I) _____

94.3 단어를 올바른 순서로 배열하시오.

1. (to work / every day / walks / Lisa)   *Lisa walks to work every day.*
2. (at the hotel / I / early / arrived) I _____
3. (goes / every year / to Puerto Rico / Julia) Julia _____
4. (we / since 2002 / here / have lived) We _____
5. (in Florida / Sue / in 1984 / was born)
   Sue _____
6. (didn't go / yesterday / Paul / to work)
   Paul _____
7. (to a wedding / last weekend / went / Helen)
   Helen _____
8. (I / in bed / this morning / my breakfast / had)
   I _____
9. (in September / Barbara / to college / is going)
   Barbara _____
10. (I / a beautiful bird / this morning / in the garden / saw)
    I _____
11. (many times / have been / my parents / to Tokyo)
    My _____
12. (my umbrella / I / last night / left / in the restaurant)
    I _____
13. (to the movies / tomorrow night / are you going?)
    Are _____
14. (the children / I / took / this morning / to school)
    I _____

always/usually/often 등
(어순 2)

A

다음 단어들(always/never 등)은 문장 중간에 동사와 함께 쓴다.

always	often	ever	rarely	also	already	all
usually	sometimes	never	seldom	just	still	both

- My brother **never speaks** to me.
- She**'s always** late.
- Do you **often go** to restaurants?
- I **sometimes eat** too much. (또는 **Sometimes** I eat too much.)
- "Don't forget to call Laura." 로라에게 전화하는 것 잊지 마.
  "I**'ve already called** her." 벌써 전화했어.
- I've got three sisters. They**'re all** married. 난 누나가 셋 있다. 그들은 모두 결혼했다.

B

always/never 등은 동사 앞에 쓴다.

동사	
always	go
often	play
never	have
등	등

- I **always drink** coffee in the morning.
  (I drink always coffee는 틀림)
- Helen **often goes** to Chicago on business. (Helen goes often은 틀림)
  헬렌은 사업차 종종 시카고에 간다.
- You **sometimes look** unhappy.
- They **usually have** dinner at 7:00.
- We **rarely** (또는 **seldom**) **watch** television.
  우리는 거의 텔레비전을 보지 않는다.
- Richard is a good swimmer. He **also plays** tennis and volleyball.
  (He plays also tennis는 틀림)
- I've got three sisters. They **all live** in the same city.

하지만 am/is/are/was/were의 경우, always/never 등을 be동사 뒤에 쓴다.

am is are was were	always often never 등

- I **am always tired**. (I always am tired는 틀림)
- They **are never** at home during the day. 그들은 낮에는 절대 집에 없다.
- It **is usually** very cold here in the winter. 이곳은 겨울에는 보통 굉장히 춥다.
- When I was a child, I **was often** late for school.
- "Where's Laura?" "She**'s still** in bed."
- I've got two brothers. They**'re both** doctors.

C

동사가 2개인 경우, always/never 등을 두 동사 사이에 쓴다(have … been / can … find 등).

동사 1		동사 2
will can do 등	always often never 등	go find remember 등
have has		gone been 등

- I **will always remember** you.
- It **doesn't often rain** here.
- Do you **usually drive** to work?
  평상시 승용차로 출근하세요?
- I **can never find** my keys.
- Have you **ever been** to Egypt?
- **Did** the phone **just ring**? 전화가 방금 울렸니?
- The children **have all finished** their homework.

always/never + 단순현재 → Unit 5   just/already + 현재완료 → Unit 20   all → Units 81–82
both → Unit 83   still → Unit 96

Exercises

95.1 질문에 대한 Paul의 대답을 읽고, *often/never* 등을 사용하여 Paul에 대한 문장을 쓰시오.

  Paul

1.	Do you ever play tennis?	Yes, often.	_Paul often plays tennis._
2.	Do you get up early?	Yes, always.	He _____
3.	Are you ever late for work?	No, never.	He _____
4.	Do you ever get angry?	Sometimes.	_____
5.	Do you ever go swimming?	Rarely.	_____
6.	Are you at home in the evenings?	Yes, usually.	_____

95.2 다음 문장에 *never/always/usually* 등을 넣으시오.

1. My brother speaks to me. (never)   _My brother never speaks to me._
2. Susan is polite. (always)   Susan _____
3. I finish work at 5:00. (usually)   I _____
4. Sarah has started a new job. (just)   Sarah _____
5. I go to bed before midnight. (rarely)   _____
6. The bus isn't late. (usually)   _____
7. I don't eat fish. (often)   _____
8. I will forget what you said. (never)   _____
9. Have you lost your passport? (ever)   _____
10. Do you work in the same place? (still)   _____
11. They stay at the same hotel. (always)   _____
12. Jane doesn't work on Saturdays. (usually)   _____
13. Is Tina here? (already)   _____
14. What do you have for breakfast? (usually)   _____
15. I can remember his name. (never)   _____

95.3 *also*를 사용하여 질문에 답하시오.

1. Do you play football? (basketball)   _Yes, and I also play basketball._
2. Do you speak Italian? (French)   Yes, and I _____
3. Are you tired? (hungry)   Yes, and _____
4. Have you been to Mexico? (Guatemala)   Yes, _____
5. Did you buy any clothes? (some books)   _____

95.4 *both*와 *all*을 사용하여 문장을 쓰시오.

I live in Lima.
I play soccer.
I'm a student.
I have a car.

I live in Lima.
I play soccer.
I'm a student.
I have a car.

I'm married.
I was born in Venezuela.
I live in Miami.

1. _They both live in Lima._
    They _____ soccer.
    _____ students.
    _____ cars.

2. They _____ married.
    They _____ Venezuela.
    _____

still yet already

A

still

한 시간 전

An hour ago it was raining.
한 시간 전에는 비가 내리고 있었다.

The rain
hasn't stopped.

비는 그치지 않았다.

지금

It is **still** raining now.
비는 지금도 여전히 내리고 있다.

still = 여전히, 전과 다름 없이

■ I had a lot to eat, but I'm **still** hungry. (= 전에도 배가 고팠고 지금도 배가 고픔)
■ "Did you sell your car?" "No, I **still** have it."
■ "Do you **still** live in Los Angeles?" "No, I live in San Francisco now."

B

yet

20분 전

Bill will be here soon.

Twenty minutes ago they were
waiting for Bill.
20분 전 그들은 빌을 기다리고
있었다.

지금

Where's Bill? He's very late.

They are **still** waiting for Bill.
Bill **hasn't come yet**.
그들은 여전히 빌을 기다리고 있다.
빌은 아직 오지 않았다.

yet = 아직, 지금까지는 (until now)

yet은 부정문(He **hasn't** come yet.)과 의문문(**Has he** come yet?)에 쓴다.

yet은 주로 문장 끝에 온다.

■ A: Where's Emma?
 B: She **isn't** here **yet**. (= 여기 오겠지만 아직까지는 오지 않았음)
■ A: What are you doing tonight?
 B: I **don't** know **yet**. (= 나중에는 알겠지만 지금은 모름)
■ A: Are you ready to go **yet**?
 B: **Not yet**. In a minute. (= 준비가 되겠지만 지금은 준비되지 않았음)
■ A: Have you decided what to do **yet**?
 B: No, I'm still thinking about it.

yet과 **still**의 비교:

■ She hasn't left **yet**. = She's **still** here. (she is yet here는 틀림)
■ I haven't finished my homework **yet**. = I'm **still** doing it.

C

already = 벌써, 예상보다 일찍 (earlier than expected)

■ "What time is Joe coming?" "He's **already** here." (= 우리의 예상보다 일찍)
■ "I'm going to tell you what happened." 무슨 일이 있었는지 말해 줄게.
 "That's not necessary. I **already** know." 필요없어. 벌써 알고 있어.
■ Sarah isn't coming to the movies with us. She has **already** seen the film.

Exercises

96.1 당신은 2년 만에 Tina를 만났습니다. *still*을 사용하여 Tina에게 질문을 하시오.

2년 전의 Tina

1. I play the piano.
2. I have an old car.
3. I'm a student.
4. I'm studying Japanese.
5. I go to the movies a lot.
6. I want to be a teacher.

1. _Do you still play the piano?_
2. Do you _____
3. Are _____
4. _____
5. _____
6. _____

96.2 보기를 잘 보고, 각 상황에 대해 세 개의 문장을 쓰시오.

이전   지금

1.
(before) _They were waiting for the bus._
(still) _They are still waiting._
(yet) _The bus hasn't come yet._

2. I'm looking for a job.
(before) He was _____
(still) He _____
(yet) _____ yet.

3.
(before) She _____ asleep.
(still) _____
(yet) _____

4.
(before) They _____
(still) _____
(yet) _____
dinner   dinner

96.3 아래의 상황을 읽고 *yet*을 사용하여 질문을 쓰시오.

1. You and Sue are going out together. You are waiting for her to get ready. Maybe she is ready now. You ask her: _Are you ready yet?_
2. You are waiting for Helen to arrive. She wasn't here 10 minutes ago. Maybe she is here now. You ask somebody: _____ Helen _____
3. Anna had a blood test and is waiting for the results. Maybe she has gotten her results. You ask her: _____ you _____
4. A few days ago you spoke to Tom. He wasn't sure where to go for his vacation. Maybe he has decided. You ask him: _____

96.4 *already*를 사용하여 문장을 완성하시오.

1. What time is Joe coming?
2. Do you and Joe want to see the movie?
3. I have to see Julia before she leaves.
4. Do you need a pen?
5. Should I pay the bill?
6. Should I tell Paul about the meeting?

1. _He's already_ here.
2. No, we _'ve already seen_ it.
3. It's too late. She _____ .
4. No, thanks. I _____ one.
5. No, that's OK. I _____ .
6. No, he _____ . I told him.

Give me that book!   Give it to me!

A

give	lend	pass	send	show

이 동사들(**give/lend** 등)은 아래의 두 가지
구조가 가능하다:

give + 사물 + **to** 사람
- I gave **the keys to Sarah**.

give + 사람 + 사물
- I gave **Sarah the keys**.

Sarah

B

give + 사물 + **to** 사람

		사물	**to** 사람
That's my book.	**Give**	it	**to** me.
These are Sue's keys. Can you	**give**	them	**to** her?
Can you	**give**	these flowers	**to** your mother?
I	**lent**	my car	**to** a friend of mine.
Did you	**send**	a postcard	**to** Kate?
We've seen these pictures. You	**showed**	them	**to** us yesterday.

C

give + 사람 + 사물

		사람	사물
	Give	me	that book. It's mine.
Tom	**gave**	his mother	some flowers.
I	**lent**	Joe	some money.
How much money did you	**lend**	him?	
I	**sent**	you	an e-mail. Did you get it?
Nicole	**showed**	us	her vacation photos.
Can you	**pass**	me	the salt, please?

'**buy/get** + 사람 + 사물'도 많이 쓰인다.
- I **bought** my mother some flowers. (= I bought some flowers **for** my mother.)
- Can you **get** me a newspaper when you go out? (= get a newspaper **for** me)

D

다음 문장에서는 두 가지 구조가 가능하다.
- I **gave** the keys **to Sarah**.
  I **gave Sarah** the keys.
  (그러나 I gave to Sarah the keys는 틀림)

- That's my book. Can you **give** it **to me**?
  Can you **give me** that book?
  (그러나 Can you give to me that book?은 틀림)

하지만 목적어로 **it**이나 **them**이 올 때는 첫번째 구조(**give** + 사물 + **to** 사람)만 가능하다.
- I gave **it to her**. (I gave her it은 틀림)
- Here are the keys. Give **them to your father**. (Give your father them은 틀림)

Exercises

97.1 Mark는 필요없는 물건을 여러 사람에게 주었습니다.

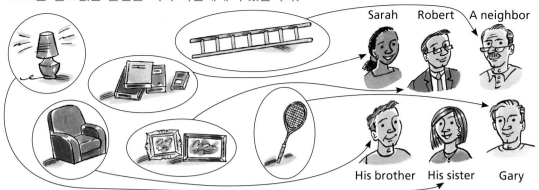

*He gave ...*로 시작하는 문장을 쓰시오.

1. What did Mark do with the armchair?   *He gave it to his brother.*
2. What did he do with the tennis racket?   He gave _____
3. What happened to the books?   He _____
4. What about the lamp?   _____
5. What did he do with the pictures?   _____
6. And the ladder?   _____

97.2 당신은 친구들에게 그림 속의 물건을 선물했습니다. 각각을 문장으로 쓰시오.

1. Paul	2. Joanna	3. Richard	4. Emma	5. Rachel	6. Kevin

1. *I gave Paul a book.* _____   4. _____
2. I gave _____   5. _____
3. I _____   6. _____

97.3 *Can you give me ... ?* / *Can you pass me ... ?* 등으로 시작하는 의문문을 쓰시오.

1. (you want the salt)   (pass)   *Can you pass me the salt?* _____
2. (you need an umbrella)   (lend)   Can you _____
3. (you want my address)   (give)   Can _____ your _____
4. (you need 20 dollars)   (lend)   _____
5. (you want some information)   (send)   _____
6. (you want to see the letter)   (show)   _____
7. (you want some stamps)   (get)   _____

97.4 맞는 것을 고르시오.

1. ~~I gave to Sarah the keys.~~ / I gave Sarah the keys. (*I gave Sarah the keys*가 맞음)
2. I'll lend to you some money if you want. / I'll <u>lend you some money</u> if you want.
3. Did you <u>send the letter me</u>? / Did you <u>send the letter to me</u>?
4. I want to <u>buy for you a present</u>. / I want to <u>buy you a present</u>.
5. Can you <u>pass to me the sugar</u>, please? / Can you <u>pass me the sugar</u>, please?
6. This is Lisa's bag. Can you <u>give it to her</u>? / Can you <u>give her it</u>?
7. I <u>showed to the police officer my driver's license</u>. /
   I <u>showed the police officer my driver's license</u>.

and but or so because

A

and   but   or   so   because

이 단어들(**접속사**)은 두 문장을 연결할 때 쓴다. 접속사는 두 개의 짧은 문장들을 연결하여 하나의 긴 문장을 만든다.

| 문장 A | The car stopped. | The driver got out. | 문장 B |

The car stopped, **and** the driver got out.

B

and/but/or

	문장 A		문장 B
	We stayed at home	**and**	(we)* watched television.
	My sister is married	**and**	(she)* lives in Houston.
	He doesn't like her,	**and**	she doesn't like him.
	I bought a newspaper,	**but**	I didn't read it.
	It's a nice house,	**but**	it doesn't have a garage.
	Do you want to go out,	**or**	are you too tired?

*"we"와 "she"는 반복할 필요가 없다.

여러 개를 나열할 때는 쉼표(,)를 사용한다. 마지막 항목 앞에는 **and**를 쓴다.

■ I got home, had something to eat, sat down in an armchair, **and** fell asleep.

나는 집에 와서, 뭔가를 먹고, 안락의자에 앉아, 잠이 들었다.

■ Karen is at work, Sue has gone shopping, **and** Chris is playing football.

C

so (결과를 나타낼 때 사용)

	문장 A		문장 B
	It was very hot,	**so**	I opened the window.
	Joe plays a lot of sports,	**so**	he's very fit.
	They don't like to travel,	**so**	they haven't been to many places.

D

because (이유를 나타낼 때 사용)

	문장 A		문장 B
	I opened the window	**because**	it was very hot.
	Joe can't come to the party	**because**	he's leaving town.
	Lisa is hungry	**because**	she didn't have breakfast.

because는 문장 앞에 올 수도 있다. 그 경우에는 쉼표를 찍는다.

■ **Because it was very hot**, I opened the window.

E

한 문장에 한 개 이상의 접속사가 들어갈 수도 있다.

■ It was late **and** I was tired, **so** I went to bed.
■ I love New York, **but** I wouldn't like to live there **because** it's too big.
나는 뉴욕을 좋아하지만, 너무 크기 때문에 거기서 살고 싶지는 않다.

Exercises

98.1 두 문장을 *and/but/or*를 사용하여 연결하시오.

I stayed at home.	I didn't have your number.
I bought a newspaper.	Should I wait here?
I went to the window.	I didn't read it.
I wanted to call you.	I took the bus this morning.
I jumped into the river.	I watched television.
I usually drive to work.	I swam to the other side.
Do you want me to come with you?	I looked out.

1. _I stayed at home and watched television._
2. _I bought a newspaper, but I didn't read it._
3. I _____
4. _____
5. _____
6. _____
7. _____

98.2 그림을 보고 문장을 완성하시오. *and/but/so/because*를 사용하시오.

1. It was very hot, _so he opened the window._
2. They couldn't play tennis _____
3. They went to the museum, _____
4. Bill wasn't hungry, _____
5. Helen was late _____
6. Sue said _____

98.3 어제 한 일을 문장으로 쓰시오. 괄호 안의 접속사를 사용하시오.

1. (and) _Last night I stayed at home and studied._
2. (because) _I went to bed very early because I was tired._
3. (but) _____
4. (and) _____
5. (so) _____
6. (because) _____

When ...

When I went out, it was raining.

이 문장은 두 부분으로 이루어져 있다.

<u>when I went out</u> + <u>it was raining</u>

다음 두 가지 구조로 쓸 수 있다.

- ■ **When I went out**, it was raining. 또는
  It was raining when I went out.

when ...이 문장의 맨 앞에 올 때는 쉼표(,)를 사용한다.

- ■ { **When** you're tired, don't drive.
  { Don't drive **when** you're tired.

- ■ { Helen was 25 **when** she got married.
  { **When** Helen got married, she was 25.

before/while/after도 같은 식으로 쓴다.

- ■ { Always look both ways **before** you cross the street. 길을 건너기 전에는 항상 양쪽을 살펴라.
  { **Before** you cross the street, always look both ways.

- ■ { **While** I was waiting for the bus, it began to rain. 버스를 기다리고 있을 때 비가 내리기 시작했다.
  { It began to rain **while** I was waiting for the bus.

- ■ { He never played football again **after** he broke his leg.
  { **After** he broke his leg, he never played football again.
  그는 다리를 다치고 나서는 다시는 축구를 하지 않았다.

When I am ... / When I go ... 등

Next week Sarah is going to New York.
She has a friend, Lisa, who lives in New York,
but Lisa is also going away – to Mexico.
So they won't see each other in New York.

Lisa **will be** in Mexico **when** Sarah **is** in
New York.

이 문장의 시간은 **미래**(다음주)이지만
"... **when** Sarah **is** in New York"에서처럼
현재를 사용한다.
(when Sarah will be in New York은 틀림)

I'll be in Mexico when you're here.

Sarah   Lisa

when 다음에는 현재(**I am** / **I go** 등)를 미래의 의미로 사용한다.

- ■ **When** I **get** home tonight, I'm going to take a shower. (When I will get home은 틀림)
- ■ I can't talk to you now. I'll talk to you later **when** I **have** more time.
  지금은 말할 수 없어. 나중에 시간이 더 있을 때 이야기할게.

before/while/after/until도 같은 식으로 사용한다.

- ■ Please close the window **before** you **go** out. (before you will go는 틀림)
  나가기 전에 창문을 닫아라.
- ■ Rachel is going to stay in our apartment **while** we **are** away. (while we will be는 틀림)
  우리가 집을 비우는 동안 레이첼은 우리 아파트에 머물 계획이다.
- ■ I'll wait here **until** you **come** back. (until you will come back은 틀림)

Exercises

99.1 아래의 상자에서 한 문장씩 골라 ***When***으로 시작하는 문장을 쓰시오.

When +	I went out I'm tired I called her I go on vacation the program ended I got to the hotel	+	I turned off the TV I always go to the same place there were no rooms it was raining there was no answer I like to watch TV

1. _When I went out, it was raining._
2. _____
3. _____
4. _____
5. _____
6. _____

99.2 아래의 구절을 사용하여 문장을 완성하시오.

somebody broke into the house	before they came here	when they heard the news
before they crossed the street	while they were away	they didn't believe me
they went to live in France		

1. They looked both ways _before they crossed the street._
2. They were very surprised _____
3. After they got married, _____
4. Their house was damaged in a storm _____
5. Where did they live _____ ?
6. While we were asleep, _____
7. When I told them what happened, _____

99.3 맞는 것을 고르시오.

1. I stay / I'll stay here until you come / you'll come back. (*I'll stay*와 *you come*이 맞음)
2. I'm going to bed when I finish / I'll finish my work.
3. We must do something before it's / it will be too late.
4. Helen is moving away soon. I'm / I'll be very sad when she leaves / she'll leave.
5. Don't go out yet. Wait until the rain stops / will stop.
6. We come / We'll come and visit you when we're / we'll be in Toronto again.
7. When I come / I'll come to see you tomorrow, I bring / I'll bring your DVDs.
8. I'm going to Quebec next week. I hope to see some friends of mine while I'm / I'll be there.
9. "I need your address." "OK, I give / I'll give it to you before I go / I'll go."
10. I'm not ready yet. I tell / I'll tell you when I'm / I'll be ready.

99.4 자신의 생각대로 문장을 완성하시오.

1. Can you close the window before _you go out_ ?
2. What are you going to do when _____ ?
3. When I have enough money, _____ .
4. I'll wait for you while _____ .
5. When I start my new job, _____ .
6. Will you be here when _____ ?

If we go ... If you see ... 등

if는 문장의 맨 앞이나 중간에 쓸 수 있다:

if를 맨 앞에 쓸 경우

If we take the bus,	it will be cheaper.
If you don't hurry,	you'll miss the train.
If you're hungry,	have something to eat.
If the phone rings,	can you answer it, please?

if를 중간에 쓸 경우

It will be cheaper	**if** we take the bus.
You'll miss the train	**if** you don't hurry.
I'm going to the concert	**if** I can get a ticket.
Is it OK	**if** I use your phone?

대화에서는 **if** ... 부분만 단독으로 쓰기도 한다.
- "Are you going to the concert?" 콘서트에 갈 거니?
  "Yes, **if I can get a ticket**." 응, 표를 구할 수 있으면.

If you see Ann tomorrow ... 등

if 뒤에는 현재시제를 쓴다. 즉, **if** you will see가 아니라 if you **see**라고 해야 한다.
- **If** you **see** Ann tomorrow, can you ask her to call me?
- **If I'm** late tonight, don't wait for me. (if I will be는 틀림)
- What should we do **if** it **rains**? (if it will rain은 틀림)
- **If** I **don't feel** well tomorrow, I'll stay home. 내일 몸이 좋지 않으면 난 집에 있을래.

if와 **when**

if I go out = 외출할 수도 있지만 확실치 않은 상황에서 사용
- *A:* Are you going out later? 나중에 나갈 거니?
  B: Maybe. **If I go out**, I'll close the windows. 어쩌면. 나간다면 창문을 닫을게.

when I go out = 외출을 반드시 하는 상황에서 사용
- *A:* Are you going out later? 나중에 나갈 거니?
  B: Yes, I am. **When I go out**, I'll close the windows. 응. 나갈 때 창문을 닫을게.

when과 **if**의 비교:
- **When** I get home tonight, I'm going to take a shower.
- **If** I'm late tonight, don't wait for me. (When I'm late는 틀림)
- We're going to play basketball **if** it doesn't rain. (when it doesn't rain은 틀림)

Exercises

100.1 아래의 상자에서 한 문장씩 골라 *If*로 시작하는 문장을 쓰시오.

If +		**+**	
	~~you don't hurry~~		we can have lunch now
	you pass the driving test		you can have them
	you fail the driving test		I can lend you some
	you don't want this magazine		you'll get your license
	you want those pictures		~~you'll be late~~
	you're busy now		I'll throw it away
	you're hungry		we can talk later
	you need money		you can take it again

1. _If you don't hurry, you'll be late._
2. If you pass _____
3. If _____
4. _____
5. _____
6. _____
7. _____
8. _____

100.2 맞는 것을 고르시오.

1. If I'm / ~~I'll be~~ late tonight, don't wait for me. (*I'm*이 맞음)
2. Will you call me if I give / I'll give you my phone number?
3. If there is / will be a fire, the alarm will ring.
4. If I don't see you tomorrow morning, I call / I'll call you in the afternoon.
5. I'm / I'll be surprised if Martin and Jane get / will get married.
6. Do you go / Will you go to the party if they invite / they'll invite you?

100.3 자신의 생각대로 문장을 완성하시오.

1. I'm going to the concert if _I can get a ticket._
2. If you don't hurry, _you'll miss the train._
3. I don't want to disturb you if _____
4. If you go to bed early tonight, _____
5. Turn the television off if _____
6. Tina won't pass her driving test if _____
7. If I have time tomorrow, _____
8. We can go to the beach tomorrow if _____
9. I'll be surprised if _____

100.4 *if* 또는 *when*을 써 넣으시오.

1. _If_ I'm late tonight, don't wait for me.
2. I'm going shopping now. _____ I come back, we can have lunch.
3. I'm thinking of going to see Tim. _____ I go, will you come with me?
4. _____ you don't want to go out tonight, we can stay at home.
5. Is it OK _____ I close the window?
6. John is still in high school. _____ he finishes, he wants to go to college.
7. Do you want to go on a picnic tomorrow _____ the weather is good?
8. We're going to Mexico City next week. We're going to look for a hotel _____ we get there. I don't know what we'll do _____ we don't find a room.

If I had ...   If we went ... 등

A

Dan은 빠른 차를 좋아하지만 그는 차가 없다.
그에게는 차 살 돈이 없다.

If he **had** the money, he **would buy** a fast car.
(돈이 있다면 그는 빠른 차를 살 것이다.)

had는 과거이지만, 이 문장에서 **had**는 과거를
의미하지 않는다. **If** he **had** the money = if he
had the money *now* (but he doesn't have it).

If I **had** the money, . . .

| If | I
you
it
they 등 | **had/knew/lived/went** (등) ... ,
didn't have / didn't know (등) ... ,
were ... ,
could ... , | I
you
it
they 등 | **would(n't)**

could(n't) | buy ...
be ...
have ...
go ... 등 |

다음 두 구조로 쓸 수 있다.

- **If** he **had** the money, he would buy a car.
또는   He would buy a car **if** he **had** the money.

I'd / she'd / they'd 등 = I **would** / she **would** / they **would** 등

- I don't know the answer. **If** I **knew** the answer, **I'd tell** you.
  난 답을 몰라. 답을 알면 너한테 말해 줄 거야.
- It's raining, so we're not going out. **We'd get** wet **if** we **went** out.
- Jane lives in a city. She likes cities. She **wouldn't be** happy **if** she **lived** in the country.
- **If** you **didn't have** a job, what **would** you **do**? (but you *have* a job – 하지만 직업이 있음)
- I'm sorry I can't help you. **I'd help** you **if** I **could**. (but I *can't* – 하지만 도와줄 수 없음)
- **If** we **had** a car, we **could travel** more. (but we *don't* have a car, so we *can't* travel much
  – 하지만 차가 없어서 여행을 많이 할 수 없음)

B

If (I) **was/were** ...

if I/he/she/it **was**와 **if** I/he/she/it **were** 모두 쓸 수 있다.

- It's not a very nice place. I wouldn't go there **if I
  were you**. (또는 ... **if I was** you)
- It would be nice **if the weather was** better.
  (또는 ... **if the weather were** better)
- What would Tom do **if he were** here?
  (또는 ... **if he was** here)

I wouldn't go out **if** I **were** you.

C

비교:

if I have / if it is 등	**if I had / if it was** 등
■ I want to go and see Helen. **If** I **have** time, I **will go** today. (= 어쩌면 시간이 있을 수도 있고, 그래서 갈지도 모름)	■ I want to go and see Helen. **If** I **had** time, I **would go** today. (= 오늘은 시간이 없어서 가지 않을 것임)
■ I like that jacket. **I'll buy** it **if** it **isn't** too expensive. (= 어쩌면 무척 안 비쌀 수도 있음)	■ I like that jacket, but it's very expensive. **I'd buy** it **if** it **wasn't** so expensive. (= 비싸서 사지 않을 것임)
■ **I'll help** you **if** I **can**. (= 어쩌면 내가 도와줄 수도 있음)	■ **I'd help** you **if** I **could**, but I can't. (= 도와줄 수 없음)

if we go / if I have / if I can 등 → Unit 100

Exercises

101.1 문장을 완성하시오.

1. I don't know the answer. If I __*knew*__ the answer, I'd tell you.
2. I have a car. I couldn't travel very much if I __*didn't have*__ a car.
3. I don't want to go out. If I _____ to go out, I'd go.
4. We don't have a key. If we _____ a key, we could get into the house.
5. I'm not hungry. I would have something to eat if I _____ hungry.
6. Sue enjoys her work. She wouldn't do it if she _____ it.
7. He can't speak any foreign languages. If he _____ speak a foreign language, maybe he would get a better job.
8. You don't try hard enough. If you _____ harder, you would have more success.
9. I have a lot to do today. If I _____ so much to do, we could go out.

101.2 동사를 올바른 형태로 써 넣으시오.

1. If __*he had*__ the money, he would buy a fast car. (he / have)
2. Jane likes living in a city. __*She wouldn't be*__ happy if she lived in the country. (she / not / be)
3. If I wanted to learn Italian, _____ to Italy. (I / go)
4. I haven't told Helen what happened. She'd be angry if _____ . (she / know)
5. If _____ a map, I could show you where I live. (we / have)
6. What would you do if _____ a lot of money? (you / win)
7. It's not a very good hotel. _____ there if I were you. (I / not / stay)
8. If _____ closer to Miami, we would go there more often. (we / live)
9. I'm sorry you have to go now. _____ nice if you had more time. (it / be)
10. I'm not going to take the job. I'd take it if _____ better. (the salary / be)
11. I don't know anything about cars. If my car broke down, _____ what to do. (I / not / know)
12. If you could change one thing in the world, what _____ ? (you / change)

101.3 문장을 완성하시오. 아래의 구문에서 동사를 알맞은 형태로 고쳐 사용하시오.

we (have) a bigger house	~~it (be) a little cheaper~~	I (watch) it
we (buy) a bigger house	every day (be) the same	I (be) bored
we (have) some pictures on the wall	the air (be) cleaner	

1. I'd buy that jacket if __*it was a little cheaper*_____ .
2. If there was a good movie on TV tonight, _____ .
3. This room would be nicer if _____ .
4. If there wasn't so much traffic, _____ .
5. Life would be boring if _____ .
6. If I had nothing to do, _____ .
7. We could invite all our friends to stay if _____ .
8. If we had more money, _____ .

101.4 자신의 생각대로 문장을 완성하시오.

1. I'd be happier if __*I had less work*__
2. If I could go anywhere in the world, _____ .
3. I wouldn't be very happy if _____ .
4. I'd buy _____ if _____ .
5. If I saw an accident in the street, _____ .
6. The world would be a better place if _____ .

a person **who** ... a thing **that/which** ...
(관계사절 1)

A

I can speak six languages.

I met a woman. **She** can speak six languages.	1

두 문장

she → who

한 문장   2
I met **a woman who** can speak six languages.

1. 나는 한 여자를 만났다. 그녀는 6개국어를 할 수 있다.
2. 나는 6개국어를 할 수 있는 여자를 만났다.

Jack

Jack was wearing a hat. **It** was too big for him.	1

두 문장

it → that 또는 which

한 문장   2
Jack was wearing **a hat that** was too big for him.
또는
Jack was wearing **a hat which** was too big for him.

1. 잭은 모자를 쓰고 있었다. 그것은 그에게 너무 컸다.
2. 잭은 자기에게 너무 큰 모자를 쓰고 있었다.

B

who: 사람 (사물에는 쓰지 않음)

A thief is **a person**	**who** steals things.	
Do you know **anybody**	**who** can play the piano?	
The man	**who** called	didn't give his name.
The people	**who** work in the office	are very friendly.

C

that: 사물 또는 사람

An airplane is **a machine**	**that** flies.	
Emma lives in **a house**	**that** is 100 years old.	
The people	**that** work in the office	are very friendly.

사람에 대해 **that**을 쓸 수도 있지만 **who**를 쓰는 것이 더 일반적이다.

D

which: 사물 (사람에는 쓰지 않음)

An airplane is **a machine**	**which** flies. (a machine who ...는 틀림)
Emma lives in **a house**	**which** is 100 years old.

which는 사람에 대해 쓰지 않는다.

■ Do you remember **the woman who** played the piano at the party?
  (the woman which ...는 틀림)

의문문에서의 who와 which → Units 46, 48   the people we met (관계사절 2) → Unit 103

Exercises

102.1 아래의 어구를 사용하여 **A ... is a person who ...** 구조로 문장을 쓰시오. 필요하면 사전을 찾아보시오.

~~a thief~~	a dentist	doesn't tell the truth	is sick in the hospital
a butcher	a fool	takes care of your teeth	~~steals things~~
a musician	a genius	is very intelligent	does stupid things
a patient	a liar	plays a musical instrument	sells meat

1. _A thief is a person who steals things._
2. A butcher is a person _____
3. A musician _____
4. _____
5. _____
6. _____
7. _____
8. _____

102.2 두 문장을 하나로 만드시오.

1. (A man called. He didn't give his name.)
   The man who called didn't give his name.
2. (A woman opened the door. She was wearing a yellow dress.)
   The woman _____ a yellow dress.
3. (Some students took the test. Most of them passed.)
   Most of the students _____
4. (A police officer stopped our car. He wasn't very friendly.)
   The _____

102.3 **who** 또는 **which**를 써 넣으시오.

1. I met a woman __who__ can speak six languages.
2. What's the name of the man _____ just started working in your office?
3. What's the name of the river _____ flows through the town?
4. Where is the picture _____ was hanging on the wall?
5. Do you know anybody _____ wants to buy a car?
6. You always ask questions _____ are difficult to answer.
7. I have a friend _____ is very good at fixing cars.
8. I think everybody _____ went to the party really enjoyed it.
9. Why does he always wear clothes _____ are too small for him?

102.4 틀린 문장이 있으면 고쳐 쓰시오. 맞는 문장에는 **OK**라고 쓰시오.

1. A thief is a person which steals things. _a person who steals_
2. An airplane is a machine that flies. _OK_
3. A coffee maker is a machine who makes coffee. _____
4. Have you seen the money that was on the table? _____
5. I don't like people which never stop talking. _____
6. I know somebody that can help you. _____
7. I know somebody who works in that store. _____
8. Correct the sentences who are wrong. _____
9. My neighbor bought a car who cost $60,000. _____

the people **we met**
the hotel **you stayed at** (관계사절 2)

A

Kate

	두 문장	1
The man is carrying a bag. It's very heavy.		

		2
The bag (that) he is carrying is very heavy.		
└─────── 한 문장 ───────┘		

1. 남자는 가방을 들고 있다. 그것은 매우 무겁다.
2. 그가 들고 있는 가방은 매우 무겁다.

	두 문장	3
Kate won some money. What is she going to do with it?		

		4
What is Kate going to do with **the money** **(that) she won**?		
└─────── 한 문장 ───────┘		

3. 케이트는 돈을 좀 땄다. 그녀는 그 돈으로 무엇을 할까?
4. 케이트는 딴 돈으로 무엇을 할까?

that은 쓸 수도 있고 생략할 수도 있다.
- The bag **that** he is carrying ...   또는   The bag he is carrying ...
- ... the money **that** Kate won?   또는   ... the money Kate won?

목적어일 경우 **that/who/which**는 생략이 가능하다.

주어	동사	목적어	
The man	was carrying	a bag	→ **the bag** (that) **the man was carrying**
Kate	won	some money	→ **the money** (that) **Kate won**
You	wanted	some books	→ **the books** (that) **you wanted**
We	met	some people	→ **the people** (who) **we met**

- Did you find **the books you wanted**? (또는 ... the books **that** you wanted?)
- **The people we met** were very friendly. (또는 The people **who** we met ...)
- **Everything I said** was true. (또는 Everything **that** I said ...)

목적어를 반복하지 않도록 주의하자.
- The movie **we saw** was very good. (The movie we saw it was ...는 틀림)

B

이따금 동사 뒤에 전치사(**to/in/at** 등)가 오기도 한다.

Eve **is talking to** a man.	→	Do you know **the man Eve is talking to**?
We **stayed at** a hotel.	→	**The hotel we stayed at** was near the station.
I **told** you **about** some books.	→	These are **the books I told you about**.

전치사 뒤에 목적어를 반복하지 않도록 주의하자.
- ... the books **I told you about**. (the books I told you about them은 틀림)

장소 뒤에는 **where**를 쓸 수 있다.
- **The hotel where** we stayed was near the station. (= The hotel we stayed at ...)

C

주어일 경우에는 **who/that/which**를 써야 한다. (Unit 102 참조)
- I met a woman **who can speak** six languages. (**who**가 주어)
- Jack was wearing a hat **that was** too big for him. (**that**이 주어)

a person who ... , a thing that/which ... (관계사절 1) → **Unit 102**

Exercises

103.1 두 문장을 하나로 만드시오.

1. (Helen took some pictures. Have you seen them?)
   Have you seen the pictures Helen took?
2. (You gave me a pen. I've lost it.)
   I've lost the _____
3. (Sue is wearing a jacket. I like it.)
   I like the _____
4. (I gave you some flowers. Where are they?)
   Where are the _____ ?
5. (He told us a story. I didn't believe it.)
   I _____
6. (You bought some oranges. How much were they?)
   How _____ ?

103.2 두 문장을 하나로 만드시오.

1. (I was carrying a bag. It was very heavy.)
   The bag I was carrying was very heavy.
2. (You cooked a meal. It was excellent.)
   The _____
3. (I'm wearing shoes. They aren't very comfortable.)
   The shoes _____
4. (We invited some people to dinner. They didn't come.)
   The _____

103.3 당신은 친구에게 질문을 하고 있습니다. 아래의 문장을 완성하시오.

1. Your friend stayed at a hotel. You ask:
   What's the name of _the hotel you stayed at?_
2. Your friend was talking to some people. You ask:
   Who are the people _____ ?
3. Your friend was looking for some keys. You ask:
   Did you find the _____ ?
4. Your friend is going to a party. You ask:
   Where is the _____ ?
5. Your friend was talking about a movie. You ask:
   What's the name of _____ ?
6. Your friend is listening to some music. You ask:
   What's that _____ ?
7. Your friend was waiting for an e-mail. You ask:
   Did you get _____ ?

103.4 *where*를 사용하여 문장을 완성하시오.

1. John stayed at a hotel. You ask him:
   Did you like _the hotel where you stayed_ ?
2. Sue had dinner in a restaurant. You ask her:
   What's the name of the restaurant _____ ?
3. Sarah lives in a town. You ask her:
   How big is the _____ ?
4. Richard works in a factory. You ask him:
   Where exactly is _____ ?

at 8:00   on Monday   in April

A   at (시간 등)

at	8:00 10:30 midnight 등
	night the end of ...

- I start work **at 8:00** in the morning.
- The banks close **at 5:00**.

- I can't sleep **at night**.
- I'm taking a trip **at the end of** October.

B   on (날짜, 요일, 휴일 등)

MONDAY
JUNE
6

(on)	Sunday(s) / Monday(s) 등
	April 25 / June 6 등
	Monday morning / Tuesday afternoon / Friday night 등
	New Year's Day 등

on은 생략할 수도 있다.

- Bye! See you **on Friday**.   또는   See you **Friday**.
- Do you work **on Sundays**?   또는   Do you work **Sundays**?
- The concert is **on November 20**.   또는   The concert is **November 20**.
- I'm leaving **on Friday night**.   또는   I'm leaving **Friday night**.

on the weekend / **on weekends**는 on을 생략하지 않는다.

- They like to eat out **on the weekend** / **on weekends**.

C   in (달, 해, 계절, 오전, 오후 등)

in	April/June 등 2009/1968 등
	the spring/summer/fall/winter the morning/afternoon/evening

- I'm taking a trip **in October**.
- Amy was born **in 1988**.
- The park is beautiful **in the fall**.
- Do you often go out **in the evening**?

D

아래의 표현 앞에는 **at/on/in**을 쓰지 않는다.

| **this ...** (this morning / this week 등) |
| **every ...** (every day / every week 등) |
| **last ...** (last August / last week 등) |
| **next ...** (next Monday / next week 등) |

- What are you doing **this weekend**?
- We go on vacation **every summer**. **Last summer** we went to Europe.
- I'm leaving **next Monday**. (on next Monday는 틀림)

E

in five minutes / **in a few days** / **in six weeks** / **in two years** 등

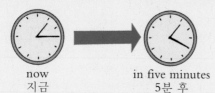

now
지금

in five minutes
5분 후

- Hurry! The train leaves **in five minutes**.
  서둘러! 기차가 5분 후에 떠나.
- Bye! I'll see you **in a few days**.
  안녕! 며칠 있다가 보자.

Exercises

104.1 *at* 또는 *in*을 써 넣으시오.

1. Amy was born __in__ 1988.
2. I got up _____ 8:00 this morning.
3. I like to get up early _____ the morning.
4. I like to look at the stars _____ night.
5. My brother got married _____ May.
6. We often go to the beach _____ the summer.
7. Let's meet _____ 7:30 tomorrow night.
8. The company started _____ 1989.
9. I'll send you the money _____ the end of the month.
10. The café is open _____ the evening. It closes _____ midnight.

104.2 *at/on/in*을 써 넣으시오.

1. __on__ June 6
2. __in__ the evening
3. _____ half past two
4. _____ Wednesday
5. _____ 1997
6. _____ September
7. _____ September 24
8. _____ Thursday
9. _____ 11:45
10. _____ New Year's Eve
11. _____ noon
12. _____ the morning
13. _____ Friday morning
14. _____ Saturday night
15. _____ night
16. _____ the end of the day
17. _____ the weekend
18. _____ the winter

104.3 맞는 문장을 고르시오. 둘 다 맞으면 *both*라고 쓰시오.

A	B	
1. I'm taking a trip in October.	I'm taking a trip on October.	_A_
2. Do you work Sundays?	Do you work on Sundays?	_both_
3. I always feel tired at the evening.	I always feel tired in the evening.	_____
4. I'm leaving next Saturday.	I'm leaving on next Saturday.	_____
5. Tim started his new job on May 18.	Tim started his new job May 18.	_____
6. Laura finished high school in 2002.	Laura finished high school 2002.	_____
7. We meet on every Tuesday.	We meet every Tuesday.	_____
8. We don't often go out in night.	We don't often go out at night.	_____
9. I can't meet you Thursday.	I can't meet you on Thursday.	_____
10. Lisa saw Sam Monday night.	Lisa saw Sam on Monday night.	_____
11. I'm leaving in the end of this month.	I'm leaving at the end of this month.	_____
12. Tim goes to the gym on Fridays.	Tim goes to the gym Fridays.	_____

104.4 *in* ...을 넣어 문장을 쓰시오.

1. It's 8:25 now. The train leaves at 8:30.   _The train leaves in five minutes._
2. It's Monday today. I'll call you on Thursday.   I'll _____ days.
3. Today is June 14. My exam is on June 28.   My _____
4. It's 3:00 now. Tom will be here at 3:30.   Tom _____

104.5 필요한 경우 *at/on/in*을 써 넣으시오. 전치사가 필요없는 문장은 '—' 표시를 하시오.

1. They like to eat out __on__ weekends.
2. I'm going __—__ next Friday. (전치사 필요없음)
3. I always feel tired _____ the evening.
4. Will you be at home _____ this evening?
5. We went to France _____ last summer.
6. Laura was born _____ 1994.
7. What are you doing _____ the weekend?
8. I call Robert _____ every Sunday.
9. Should we play tennis _____ next Sunday?
10. I couldn't go to the party _____ last weekend.
11. I'm going out. I'll be back _____ an hour.
12. I don't often go out _____ night.

from ... to   until   since   for

A

from ... to ...: ···부터 ···까지

- We lived in Japan **from** 1996 **to** 2005.
- I work **from** Monday **to** Friday.

from ... until ... 도 같은 뜻이다.

- We lived in Japan **from** 1996 **until** 2005.

from Monday to Friday

Monday — Friday

B

until ...: ···까지

until	Friday December 3:00 I come back

- They're leaving town tomorrow.
  They'll be away **until Friday**.
- I went to bed early, but I wasn't tired.
  I read a book **until 3:00 a.m.**
- Wait here **until I come back**.

until Friday

Friday

till 도 같은 뜻이다.

- Wait here **till** I come back.

비교:

- "**How long** will you be away?" 얼마 동안 가 있을 거야?   "**Until** Monday." 월요일까지.
- "**When** are you coming back?" 언제 돌아오니?   "**On** Monday." 월요일에.

C

since + 과거의 한 때: ···이래로

since 는 현재완료(**have been / have done** 등)와 함께 쓴다.

since	Monday 2002 2:30 I arrived

- Joe is in the hospital. He has been
  in the hospital **since Monday**.
  (= 월요일부터 지금까지)
- Sue and Dave have been
  married **since 2002**.
  (= 2002년부터 지금까지)
- It has been raining **since I arrived**.
  내가 도착한 이후 계속 비가 오고 있다.

since Monday

Monday — now

비교:

- We lived in Japan **from** 1996 **to** 2005.
  We lived in Japan **until** 2005.
- Now we live in Denver. We came to Denver **in** 2005.
  We have lived in Denver **since** 2005. (= 2005년부터 지금까지)

for 다음에는 기간(**three days / 10 years** 등)이 나온다.

- Joe has been in the hospital **for three days**. (since three days는 틀림)

D

for + 기간: ···동안

for	three days 10 years five minutes a long time

- Gary stayed with us **for
  three days**.
  게리는 우리 집에 3일 동안 머물렀다.
- I'm going away **for
  a few weeks**.
- I'm going away **for the weekend**.
- They've been married **for 10 years**.

for three days

Sunday   Monday   Tuesday

현재완료 + for/since → Units 17–18   현재완료 (I have lived)와 단순과거 (I lived) → Unit 21

Exercises

105.1 정보를 읽고 문장을 완성하시오. *from ... to / until / since*를 사용하시오.

Alex

Jin Sook

Beth

Adam

I live in Japan now.
I lived in Canada before.
I came to Japan in 2003.

I live in Australia now.
I lived in South Korea before.
I came to Australia in 2007.

I work in a restaurant now.
I worked in a hotel before.
I started work in the restaurant in 2005.

I'm a journalist now.
I was a teacher before.
I started work as a journalist in 2002.

1. (Alex / Canada / 1995 → 2003)   Alex lived ___*in Canada from 1995 to 2003*___ .
2. (Alex / Canada / → 2003)   Alex lived in Canada _____ 2003.
3. (Alex / Japan / 2003 →)   Alex has lived in Japan _____ .
4. (Jin Sook / South Korea → 2007)   Jin Sook lived in _____ .
5. (Jin Sook / Australia / 2007 →)   Jin Sook has lived in _____ .
6. (Beth / a hotel / 2002–2005)   Beth worked _____ 2002 _____ .
7. (Beth / a restaurant / 2005 →)   Beth has worked _____ .
8. (Adam / a teacher / 1996–2002)   Adam was a _____ .
9. (Adam / a journalist / 2002 →)   Adam has been _____ .

이번에는 *for*를 사용하여 문장을 쓰시오.

10. (Alex / Canada)   ___*Alex lived in Canada for eight years*___
11. (Alex / Japan)   Alex has lived in Japan _____ .
12. (Jin Sook / Australia)   Jin Sook has _____ .
13. (Beth / a hotel)   Beth worked _____ .
14. (Beth / restaurant)   Beth _____ .
15. (Adam / a teacher)   Adam _____ .
16. (Adam / a journalist)   Adam _____ .

105.2 *until/since/for*를 써 넣으시오.

1. Sue and Dave have been married ___*since*___ 2002.
2. I was tired this morning. I stayed in bed _____ 10:00.
3. We waited for Sue _____ half an hour, but she didn't come.
4. "Did you just get here?"   "No, I've been here _____ 7:30."
5. "How long did you stay at the party last night?"   "_____ midnight."
6. Dan and I are good friends. We have known each other _____ 10 years.
7. I'm tired. I'm going to lie down _____ a few minutes.
8. (착륙하는 비행기 안에서) Please stay in your seats _____ the airplane reaches the gate.
9. This is my house. I've lived here _____ I was seven years old.
10. Jack is out of town. He'll be away _____ Wednesday.
11. Next week I'm going to Chicago _____ three days.
12. I usually finish work at 5:30, but sometimes I work _____ 6:00.
13. "How long have you known Anna?"   "_____ we were in high school."
14. Where have you been? I've been waiting for you _____ 20 minutes.

before after during while

A

before, during, after

before the movie
영화상영 전에

during the movie
영화상영 중에

after the movie
영화상영 후에

- Everybody feels nervous **before a test**. 시험 전에는 누구나 긴장한다.
- I fell asleep **during the movie**.
- We were tired **after our visit** to the museum.

B

before, while, after

before we played
경기를 하기 전에

while we were playing
경기를 하던 중에

after we played
경기를 한 후에

- Don't forget to close the window **before you go out**.
- I often fall asleep **while I'm reading**.
- They watched TV **after they did the dishes**. 그들은 설거지를 하고 나서 텔레비전을 봤다.

C

during, while, for

during 다음에는 **명사**가 오고(during **the movie**), **while** 다음에는 '주어 + 동사'가 온다(while **I'm reading**).

- We didn't speak **during the meal**. 우리는 식사중에 이야기하지 않았다.

그러나 We didn't speak **while we were eating**. (during we were eating은 틀림)

for 다음에는 **기간**(three days / two hours / a year 등)이 온다.

- We played basketball **for two hours**. (during two hours는 틀림)
- I lived in Florida **for a year**. (during a year는 틀림)

D

before/after 다음에는 **-ing**가 올 수 있다(**before going** / **after eating** 등).

- I always have breakfast **before going** to work. (= before I go to work)
- **After doing** the dishes, they watched TV. (= after they did)

주의: **before/after** 뒤에는 to ...를 쓰지 않는다.

- **Before eating** the apple, I washed it carefully. (before to eat는 틀림)
- I started work **after reading** the newspaper. (after to read는 틀림)

과거진행 (I was -ing) → Units 13–14   before/after/while/when → Unit 99
for → Unit 105   전치사 + -ing → Unit 113

Exercises

106.1 아래의 단어를 사용하여 문장을 완성하시오.

after during	+	lunch the end they went to Mexico
before while		the concert ~~the test~~ you're waiting
		the course the night

1. Everybody was nervous _before the test_ .
2. I usually work four hours in the morning and another three hours _____ .
3. The movie was really boring. We left _____ .
4. Anna went to night school to learn German. She learned a lot _____ .
5. My aunt and uncle lived in Chicago _____ .
6. *A:* Somebody broke a window _____ . Did you hear anything?
   B: No, I was asleep all the time.
7. Would you like to sit down _____ ?
8. "Are you going home _____ ?"   "Yes, I have to get up early tomorrow."

106.2 *during/while/for*를 써 넣으시오.

1. We didn't speak _while_ we were eating.
2. We didn't speak _during_ the meal.
3. Gary called _____ you were out.
4. I stayed in Rome _____ five days.
5. Sally didn't read any newspapers _____ she was on vacation.
6. The students looked very bored _____ the class.
7. I fell out of bed _____ I was asleep.
8. Last night I watched TV _____ three hours.
9. I don't usually watch TV _____ the day.
10. Do you ever watch TV _____ you are having dinner?

106.3 *-ing (doing, having* 등)를 사용하여 문장을 완성하시오.

1. After _doing_ the dishes, they watched TV.
2. I felt sick after _____ too much chocolate.
3. I'm going to ask you a question. Think carefully before _____ it.
4. I felt awful when I got up this morning. I felt better after _____ a shower.
5. After _____ my work, I left the office and went home.
6. Before _____ to a foreign country, you should try and learn a little of
   the language.

106.4 *before/after + -ing*를 사용하여 문장을 쓰시오.

1. They did the dishes. Then they watched TV.
   After _doing the dishes, they watched TV._
2. John finished high school. Then he worked in a bookstore for two years.
   John worked _____
3. I read for a few minutes. Then I went to sleep.
   Before _____
4. We walked for three hours. We were very tired.
   After _____
5. Let's have a cup of coffee. Then we'll go out.
   Let's _____

in at on (장소 1)

A in

in a store
in a room
in a car
in the water

in a garden
in a town
in a park
in Brazil

- "Where's David?"   "In the kitchen. / In the garden. / In Seoul."
- What's in that box / in that bag / in that closet?
- Rachel works in a store / in a bank / in a factory.
- I went for a swim in the river / in the pool / in the ocean.
- Milan is in the north of Italy. Naples is in the south.
- I live in a big city, but I'd like to live in the country.

B at

at the bus stop   at the door   at the traffic light   at her desk

- There's somebody at the bus stop / at the door.
- The car is waiting at the traffic light. 차가 교통신호를 기다리고 있다.
- Jane is working at her desk.

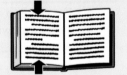

at the top (of the page)

at the top / at the bottom / at the end (of ...): (…의) 위에/바닥에/끝에

- Write your name at the top of the page. 페이지 위쪽에 이름을 쓰시오.
- My house is at the end of the street.

at the bottom (of the page)

C on

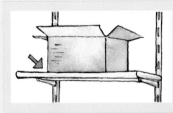

on a shelf
on a plate
on a balcony
on the floor
등

on a wall
on the ceiling
on a door
등

- There are some books on the shelf and some pictures on the wall.
- There are a lot of apples on those trees.
- Don't sit on the grass. It's wet.
- There is a stamp on the envelope. 봉투에 우표가 붙어 있다.

on a horse / on a bicycle / on a motorcycle:

- Who is that man on the motorcycle?
  오토바이에 타고 있는 저 남자는 누구냐?

stamp

John Smith
5 Maple Street
Northport, NY
11768

envelope

Exercises

107.1 그림을 보고 질문에 답하시오. *in/at/on*을 사용하시오.

1. (the kitchen)
2. (the box)
3. (the box)
4. (the wall)
5. (the bus stop)
6. (the field)
7. (the balcony)
8. (the pool)
9. (the window)
10. (the ceiling)
11. (the table)
12. (the table)

1. Where is he? *In the kitchen.*
2. Where are the shoes? _____
3. Where is the pen? _____
4. Where is the clock? _____
5. Where is the bus? _____
6. Where are the horses? _____
7. Where are they standing? _____
8. Where is she swimming? _____
9. Where is he standing? _____
10. Where is the spider? _____
11. Where is he sitting? _____
12. Where is she sitting? _____

107.2 *in/at/on*을 써 넣으시오.

1. Don't sit __*on*__ the grass. It's wet.
2. What do you have _____ your bag?
3. Look! There's a man _____ the roof. What's he doing?
4. There are a lot of fish _____ this river.
5. Our house is number 45 – the number is _____ the door.
6. "Is the post office near here?"   "Yes, turn left _____ the traffic light."
7. I have a small vegetable garden _____ the backyard.
8. My sister lives _____ Daegu.
9. There's a small park _____ the top of the hill.
10. I think I heard the doorbell. There's somebody _____ the door.
11. Munich is a large city _____ the south of Germany.
12. There's a gas station _____ the end of the block.
13. It's difficult to carry a lot of things _____ a bicycle.
14. I looked at the list of names. My name was _____ the bottom.
15. There is a mirror _____ the wall _____ the living room.

in   at   on (장소 2)

A

in

in bed
in the hospital
in the sky
in the world
in a newspaper / **in** a book
in a photograph / **in** a picture
in a car / **in** a taxi
in the middle (of …)

- "Where's Kate?"   "She's **in bed**."
- David's father is sick. He's **in the hospital**.
- I like to look at the stars **in the sky** at night.
- What's the largest city **in the world**?
- I read about the accident **in the newspaper**.
- You look sad **in this photograph**. 이 사진에서 당신은 슬퍼 보입니다.
- Did you come here **in your car**? 여기는 당신 차로 오셨나요?
- There's a big tree **in the middle** of the yard.

B

at

at work / **at** school
at the station / **at** the airport
at the post office / **at** the supermarket
at Jane's (house) / **at** my sister's (house) / **at** the doctor's / **at** the hairdresser's 등
at a concert / **at** a party / **at** a football game 등

- "Where's Kate?"   "She's **at work**."
- Do you want me to meet you **at the station**?
- I saw your brother **at the post office** today.
- *A:* Where were you yesterday? 어제 어디 있었니?
  B: **At my sister's**. 언니 집에.
- I saw Tom **at the doctor's**.
- There weren't many people **at the party**.

home은 **at**과 함께 쓸 수도 있고 생략할 수도 있다(**be/stay home** 또는 **be/stay at home**).
- Is Tom **at home**?   또는   Is Tom **home**?

보통 건물(호텔, 레스토랑 등) 앞에는 **at**이나 **in**을 모두 쓸 수 있다.
- We stayed **at** a nice hotel.   또는   We stayed **in** a nice hotel.

C

at school과 **in school** 모두 가능하나, 두 표현 간에는 의미상의 차이가 있다.

She's **at** school = 지금 학교에 있음
- "Where's your sister? Is she home?"   "No, she's **at school**."

She's **in** school = 지금 학생임 (She's a student in high school / college / medical school 등)
- "Does your sister have a job?"   "No, she's still **in school**."

D

on

on a bus

on the second floor

on the way from A to B

on a bus / **on** a train / **on** a plane / **on** a ship
on the first floor (또는 ground floor), **on** the second floor 등
on the way (to …) / **on** the way home
on a street

- Did you come here **on the bus**?
- The office is **on the second floor**. (in the second floor는 틀림)
- I met Ann **on the way** to work / **on the way** home.
- My brother lives **on** a nice street.

Exercises

108.1 그림을 보고 질문에 답하시오. *in/at/on*을 사용하시오.

1. (the hospital)	2. (the airport)	3. (bed)	4. (a ship)
5. (the sky)	6. (a party)	7. (the doctor's) Steve	8. (the second floor) RESTAURANT 2nd FLOOR
9. (work)	10. (a plane)	11. (a taxi)	12. (a wedding)

1. Where is she? *In the hospital.*
2. Where are they? _____
3. Where is he? _____
4. Where are they? _____
5. Where are the stars? _____
6. Where are they? _____

7. Where is Steve? _____
8. Where is the restaurant? _____
9. Where is she? _____
10. Where are they? _____
11. Where are they? _____
12. Where are they? _____

108.2 *in/at/on*을 써 넣으시오.

1. "Where's your sister? Is she home?" "No, she's ___at___ school."
2. There was a big table _____ the middle of the room.
3. What is the longest river _____ the world?
4. Were there many people _____ the concert last night?
5. Will you be _____ home tomorrow afternoon?
6. Who is the man _____ this picture? Do you know him?
7. "Is your son going to get married soon?" "No, he's still _____ college."
8. Gary is coming by bus. I'm going to meet him _____ the station.
9. Charlie is _____ the hospital. He had an operation yesterday.
10. How many pages are there _____ this book?
11. "Are you hungry after your trip?" "Yes, there was nothing to eat _____ the plane."
12. I'm sorry I'm late. My car broke down _____ the way here.
13. "Is Tom here?" "No, he's _____ his brother's."
14. Don't believe everything you read _____ the newspaper!
15. I walked to work, but I came home _____ the bus.
16. *A:* (전화상에서) Can I speak to Anne, please?
    B: No, sorry. She'll be _____ the university until 5:00 today.

to in at (장소 3)

A

to

go/come/return/walk (등) to ...

-to New York City→

- We're **going to New York** on Sunday.
- I want to **go to Mexico** next year.
- We **walked** from my house **to the mall**.
- What time do you **go to bed**?

- The bus is **going to the airport**.
- Karen didn't **go to work** yesterday.
  캐런은 어제 직장에 가지 않았다.
- I **went to a party** last night.
- We'd like you to **come to our house**.

in/at (→ Units 106–107)

be/stay/do something (등) in ...

in New York City

- The Statue of Liberty **is in New York**.
- My brother **lives in Mexico**.
- The best stores **are in the mall**.
- I like **to read in bed**.

be/stay/do something (등) at ...

DEPARTURES

- The bus **is at the airport**.
- Sarah **wasn't at work** yesterday.
- I **met a lot of people at the party**.
- Helen **stayed at her brother's house**.
  헬렌은 오빠 집에 머물렀다.

B

home

go/come/walk (등) **home** (to를 쓰지 않음)

- I'm tired. I'm **going home**.
  (to home은 틀림)
- Did you **walk home**?

be/stay (at) **home** (at을 써도 되고 안 써도 됨)

- I'm **staying home** tonight.
  (또는 I'm **staying at home**.)

그러나 do something (**work, watch TV** 등)
at home

- Dan doesn't go to an office. He **works
  at home**.

C

arrive와 **get**

arrive in + 나라/도시 (**arrive in Mexico / arrive in Tokyo** 등):

- They **arrived in Brazil** last week. (arrived to Brazil은 틀림)

arrive at + 그 외의 장소 (**arrive at the station / arrive at work** 등):

- What time did you **arrive at the hotel**? (arrive to the hotel은 틀림)

get to (장소):

- What time did you **get to the hotel**?
- What time did you **get to Tokyo**?

get home / arrive home (전치사를 쓰지 않음):

- I was tired when I **got home**.   또는   I was tired when I **arrived home**.

Exercises

109.1 *to* 또는 *in*을 써 넣으시오.

1. I like reading __*in*__ bed.
2. We're going _____ Italy next month.
3. Sue is on vacation _____ Mexico right now.
4. I have to go _____ the bank today.
5. I was tired, so I stayed _____ bed.
6. What time do you usually go _____ bed?
7. Does this bus go _____ the airport?
8. Would you like to live _____ another country?

109.2 필요할 경우 *to* 또는 *at*을 써 넣으시오. 전치사가 필요없는 문장은 '—' 표시를 하시오.

1. Paula didn't go __*to*__ work yesterday.
2. I'm tired. I'm going __*–*__ home. (전치사 필요없음)
3. Tina is sick. She went _____ the doctor.
4. Would you like to come _____ a party on Saturday?
5. "Is Liz _____ home?" "No, she went _____ work."
6. There were 20,000 people _____ the football game.
7. Why did you go _____ home early last night?
8. A boy jumped into the river and swam _____ the other side.
9. There were a lot of people waiting _____ the bus stop.
10. We had dinner _____ a restaurant, and then we went back _____ the hotel.

109.3 필요할 경우 *to/at/in*을 써 넣으시오. 전치사가 필요없는 문장은 '—' 표시를 하시오.

1. Joe is coming tomorrow. I'm meeting him __*at*__ the airport.
2. We're going _____ a concert tomorrow night.
3. I went _____ Chile last year.
4. How long did you stay _____ Chile?
5. Next year we hope to go _____ Japan to visit some friends.
6. Do you want to go _____ the movies tonight?
7. Did you park your car _____ the station?
8. After the accident, three people were taken _____ the hospital.
9. How often do you go _____ the dentist?
10. "Is Sarah here?" "No, she's _____ Helen's."
11. My house is _____ the end of the block on the left.
12. I went _____ Maria's house, but she wasn't _____ home.
13. There were no taxis, so we had to walk _____ home.
14. "Who did you meet _____ the party?" "I didn't go _____ the party."

109.4 필요할 경우 *to/at/in*을 써 넣으시오. 전치사가 필요없는 문장은 '—' 표시를 하시오.

1. What time do you usually get _____ work?
2. What time do you usually get _____ home?
3. What time did you arrive _____ the party?
4. When did you arrive _____ Dallas?
5. What time does the plane get _____ Paris?
6. We arrived _____ home very late.

109.5 자신에 대한 문장을 완성하시오. *to/at/in*을 사용하시오.

1. At 3:00 this morning I was __*in bed*_____.
2. Yesterday I went _____.
3. At 11:00 yesterday morning I was _____.
4. One day I'd like to go _____.
5. I don't like going _____.
6. At 9:00 last night I was _____.

UNIT 110

next to, between, under 등

A

next to / between / in front of / in back of: 옆에 / 사이에 / 앞에 / 뒤에

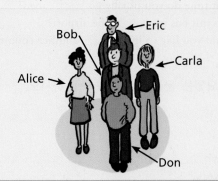

Alice is **next to** Bob.   또는   Alice is **beside** Bob.
Bob is **between** Alice and Carla.
Don is **in front of** Bob.
Eric is **in back of** Bob.

또한
Alice is **on the left**. 앨리스는 왼쪽에 있다.
Carla is **on the right**.
Bob is **in the middle** (of the group).

B

across from / in front of: 건너편에 / 앞에

Anne is sitting **in front of** Bruce.
Anne is sitting **across from** Chris.
Chris is sitting **across from** Anne.
크리스는 앤의 건너편에 앉아 있다.

C

by (= next to): 옆에

by the window

- Who is that man standing **by the window**?
  창문 옆에 서 있는 남자는 누구입니까?
- Our house is **by the ocean**. (= next to the ocean)
- If you feel cold, why don't you sit **by the fire**?
  추우면 난로 옆에 앉지 그래?

D

under: 아래에

under the table   **under** a tree

- The cat is **under the table**.
- The girl is standing **under a tree**.
- I'm wearing a jacket **under my coat**.
  나는 코트 속에 재킷을 입고 있다.

E

above / below: 위에 / 밑에

A is **above the line**.
A는 선 위에 있다.
(= higher than the line)

B is **below the line**.
(= lower than the line)

The pictures are
above the shelves.

The shelves are
below the pictures.
책장은 그림 밑에 있다.

Exercises

110.1 그림 속의 사람들은 어디에 있습니까? 문장을 완성하시오.

Alan   Barbara   Kevin

Donna   Emily   Fred

1. Kevin is standing __*in back of*__ Fred.
2. Fred is sitting _____ Emily.
3. Emily is sitting _____ Barbara.
4. Emily is sitting _____ Donna and Fred.
5. Donna is sitting _____ Emily.
6. Fred is sitting _____ Kevin.
7. Alan is standing _____ Donna.
8. Alan is standing _____ left.
9. Barbara is standing _____ middle.

110.2 그림을 보고 문장을 완성하시오.

Anna   Paul

1. The cat is __*under*__ the table.
2. There is a big tree _____ the house.
3. The plane is flying _____ the clouds.
4. She is standing _____ the piano.
5. The movie theater is _____ the right.
6. She's sitting _____ the phone.
7. The calendar is _____ the clock.
8. The cabinet is _____ the sink.
9. There are some shoes _____ the bed.
10. The plant is _____ the piano.
11. Paul is sitting _____ Anna.
12. In Japan people drive _____ the left.

110.3 그림을 보고 화살표로 표시된 곳의 위치를 설명하시오.

Paul's office

supermarket   theater

bookstore

fountain

bank

1. (next to) __*The bank is next to the*__
   __*bookstore.*__
2. (in front of) The _____ in front of
   _____
3. (across from) _____
   _____
4. (next to) _____
   _____
5. (above) _____
   _____
6. (between) _____

up, over, through 등

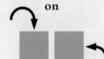

- Jane is going **to** France next week.
- We walked **from** the hotel **to** the station.
- A lot of English words come **from** Latin.
  많은 영어 단어들은 라틴어에서 유래한다.

from

into (in)

- We jumped **into** the water.
- A man came **out of** the house and got **into** a car.
- Why are you looking **out of** the window?
- I took the old batteries **out of** the radio.
  나는 오래된 건전지를 라디오에서 꺼냈다.

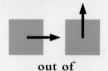
out of

put something **in**이라고 한다(into는 잘 쓰지 않음).

- I **put** new batteries **in** the radio.

on

- Don't put your feet **on** the table.
- Please take your feet **off** the table.
- I'm going to hang some pictures **on** the wall.
- Be careful! Don't fall **off** your bicycle.
- We got **on** the bus downtown.

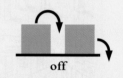
off

up

- We walked **up** the hill to the house.
  우리는 언덕을 걸어올라 집으로 갔다.
- Be careful! Don't fall **down** the stairs.
  조심해. 계단에서 떨어지지 마.

down

over

- The plane flew **over** the mountains.
- I jumped **over** the wall into the garden.
- Some people say it is unlucky to walk **under** a ladder.

under

through

- A bird flew into the room **through** a window.
  새가 창문을 통해 방 안으로 들어왔다.
- The old highway goes **through** the town.
- The new road goes **around** the town.
- The bus stop is just **around** the corner.
  버스 정류장은 모퉁이를 돌면 바로 있다.
- I walked **around** the town and took some pictures.

around

around the town

along

- I was walking **along** the road with my dog.
- Let's go for a walk **along** the river.
- The dog swam **across** the river.

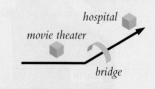
across

past

- They walked **past** me without speaking.
  그들은 말 없이 나를 지나쳐 걸어갔다.
- A: Excuse me, how do I get to the hospital?
- B: Go along this street, **past** the movie theater, under the bridge, and the hospital is on the left.

hospital
movie theater
bridge

get in/on 등 → Unit 57   **in/on** → Units 107–108   **to** → Unit 109   **fall off / run away** 등 → Unit 115

Exercises

111.1 당신은 행인에게 길을 가르쳐 주고 있습니다.
그림을 보고 **Go ...**로 시작하는 문장을 쓰시오.

1. Go past the church.
2. Go _____ the bridge.
3. _____ the hill.
4. _____ the steps.
5. _____ this street.
6. _____
7. _____
8. _____
9. _____
10. _____

111.2 그림을 보고 문장을 완성하시오.

1. The dog swam _across_ the river.
2. A book fell _____ the shelf.
3. A plane flew _____ the town.
4. A woman got _____ the car.
5. A girl ran _____ the street.
6. Suddenly a car came _____ the corner.
7. They drove _____ the town.
8. They got _____ the train.
9. The moon travels _____ the earth.
10. They got _____ the house _____ a window.

111.3 *over/from/to* 등을 사용하여 문장을 완성하시오.

1. I looked _____ the window and watched the people in the street.
2. My house is near here. It's just _____ the corner.
3. "Where's my phone?" "You put it _____ your bag."
4. How far is it _____ here _____ the airport?
5. We walked _____ the museum for an hour and saw a lot of interesting things.
6. You can put your coat _____ the back of the chair.
7. In tennis, you have to hit the ball _____ the net.
8. Silvia took a key _____ her bag and opened the door.

223

A | on

on vacation on television on the radio on the phone on fire on time (= 늦지 않게)

- Jane isn't at work this week. She's **on vacation**.
- We watched the news **on television**.
- We listened to the news **on the radio**.
- I spoke to Rachel **on the phone** last night.
- The house is **on fire**! Call the fire department.
  집이 불타고 있어! 소방서에 전화해.
- "Was the train late?" 기차가 늦었니?
  "No, it was **on time**." 아니. 정시에 도착했어.

B | at

at (the age of) 21 / **at 50 kilometers an hour** / **at 100 degrees** 등:

- Lisa got married **at 21**. (또는 ... **at the age of 21**.)
- A car uses more gas **at 70 miles an hour** than **at 55**.
  차는 시속 55마일보다 70마일로 달릴 때 연료를 더 많이 쓴다.
- Water boils at **100 degrees Celsius**.

C | by

by bus

by car / **by bus** / **by plane** / **by bike** 등:

- Do you like traveling **by train**?
- Jane usually goes to work **by bike**.

그러나 **on foot**:

- You can't get there **by car**. You have to go **on foot**. (= you have to walk)

on foot

a book **by** ... / a painting **by** ... / a piece of music **by** ... 등:

- Have you read any books **by Charles Dickens**?
- **Who** is that painting **by**? Picasso?
  저 그림은 누구 작품이지? 피카소?

수동태 뒤의 **by** (→ Unit 22):

- I was bitten **by a dog**. 나는 개에게 물렸다.

the title (제목)
by
the writer (작가)

D | with/without

- Did you stay at a hotel or **with friends**?
  호텔에 머물렀니, 친구 집에 있었니?
- Wait for me. Please don't go **without me**.
- Do you like your coffee **with** or **without milk**?
- I cut the paper **with a pair of scissors**.

a man **with** a beard / a woman **with** glasses 등:

- Do you know that man **with the beard**?
- I'd like to have a house **with a big yard**.

a man **with a** beard   a woman **with** glasses
수염 난 남자   안경 쓴 여자

E | about

talk/speak/think/hear/know about ...:

- Some people **talk about their work** all the time.
- I don't **know** much **about cars**.

a book / a question / a program / information (등) **about** ...:

- There was **a program about** volcanoes on TV last night. Did you see it?
  어젯밤에 TV에서 화산에 관한 프로그램을 했어. 봤니?

Exercises

112.1 *on* + 아래의 단어를 사용하여 문장을 완성하시오.

the phone   ~~the radio~~   television   time   vacation

1. We heard the news __*on the radio*__ .
2. Please don't be late. Try to get here _____ .
3. I won't be here next week. I'm going _____ .
4. "Did you see Linda?"   "No, but I talked to her _____ ."
5. "What's _____ tonight?"   "Nothing that I want to watch."

112.2 그림을 보고 *at/by/with* 등을 사용하여 문장을 완성하시오.

1. I cut the paper __*with*__ a pair of scissors.
2. Last year they took a trip around the world _____ boat.
3. Who is the woman _____ short hair?
4. They are talking _____ the weather.
5. The car is _____ fire.
6. She's listening to some music _____ Mozart.
7. The plane is flying _____ 600 miles an hour.
8. They're _____ vacation.
9. Do you know the man _____ sunglasses?
10. He's reading a book _____ grammar _____ Vera P. Bull.

112.3 *at/by/with* 등을 사용하여 문장을 완성하시오.

1. In tennis, you hit the ball _____ a racket.
2. It's cold today. Don't go out _____ a coat.
3. *Hamlet*, *Othello*, and *Macbeth* are plays _____ William Shakespeare.
4. Do you know anything _____ computers?
5. My grandmother died _____ the age of 98.
6. How long does it take to go from New York to Los Angeles _____ plane?
7. I didn't go to the football game, but I watched it _____ television.
8. My house is the one _____ the red door on the right.
9. These trains are very fast. They can travel _____ very high speeds.
10. You can't get there _____ car. There's no road.
11. Can you give me some information _____ hotels in this town?
12. I was arrested _____ two police officers and taken to the police station.
13. The buses here are very good. They're almost always _____ time.
14. What would you like to drink _____ your meal?
15. We traveled from Los Angeles to Seattle _____ train.
16. The museum has some paintings _____ Frida Kahlo.

afraid of ... , good at ... 등
of/at/for 등 (전치사) + -ing

A

afraid of ... / good at ... 등 (형용사 + 전치사)

Help!

He's afraid of me.

I'm not very good at math.

I'm fed up with my job.

afraid of ...: ···를 두려워하는	■ Are you **afraid of** dogs?
angry/mad at somebody: ···에게 화난	■ Why are you **mad at** me? What did I do?
angry/mad about something: ···로 화난	■ Are you **angry about** last night? 어젯밤 일로 화났니?
different from ...: ···와 다른	■ Lisa is very **different from** her sister.
fed up with ...: ···에 싫증난	■ I'm **fed up with** my job. I want to do something different. (= I've had enough of my job) 난 내 일이 신물 나. 뭔가 다른 일을 하고 싶어.
full of ...: ···로 가득 찬	■ The room was **full of people**.
good at ...: ···를 잘하는	■ Are you **good at** math?
bad at ...: ···를 못하는	■ Tina is very **bad at** tennis.
interested in ...: ···에 흥미 있는	■ I'm not **interested in** sports.
married to ...: ···와 결혼한	■ Sue is **married to** a dentist. (= her husband is a dentist)
nice/kind of somebody to ...: ···가 친절하게도 ···해주다	■ It was **kind of** you to help us. Thank you very much. 도와주시다니 정말 친절하시군요. 정말 감사합니다.
be **nice/kind to** somebody: ···에게 친절하다	■ David is very friendly. He's always very **nice to** me.
sorry about a situation: ···에 대해 유감스러운	■ I'm afraid I can't help you. I'm **sorry about** that.
sorry for/about doing something: ···에 대해 미안한	■ I'm **sorry for/about** not calling you yesterday. (또는 I'm sorry I didn't call you) 어제 전화 안 해서 미안하
be/feel **sorry for** somebody: ···가 안됐다고 생각하다	■ I feel **sorry for** them. They are in a very difficult situation. 그 사람들이 안됐어요. 그들은 무척 어려운 사정에 처해 있어

B

of/at/for (등) + **-ing**

전치사(**of/at/for** 등) 뒤의 동사는 **-ing** 형태로 쓴다.

I'm not very good **at**	**telling**	stories.
Are you fed up **with**	**doing**	the same thing every day?
I'm sorry **for**	not **calling**	you yesterday.
Thank you **for**	**helping**	me.
Mark is thinking **of**	**buying**	a new car.
Tom left **without**	**saying**	goodbye. (= he didn't say goodbye)
After	**doing**	the housework, they went shopping.

before/after -ing → Unit 106   **think about/of** → Unit 114

Exercises

113.1 그림을 보고 *of/with/in* 등을 사용하여 문장을 완성하시오.

1. He's afraid __of__ dogs.
2. She's interested _____ science.
3. She's married _____ a soccer player.
4. She's very good _____ languages.
5. He's fed up _____ the weather.
6. *A:* Can I help you?
   B: Thanks, that's very kind _____ you.

113.2 *in/of/with* 등을 사용하여 문장을 완성하시오.

1. I'm not interested __in__ sports.
2. I'm not very good _____ sports.
3. I like Sarah. She's always very nice _____ me.
4. I'm sorry _____ your broken window. It was an accident.
5. He's very brave. He isn't afraid _____ anything.
6. It was very nice _____ Jane to let us stay in her apartment.
7. Life today is very different _____ life 50 years ago.
8. Are you interested _____ politics?
9. I feel sorry _____ her, but I can't help her.
10. Chris was angry _____ what happened.
11. These boxes are very heavy. They are full _____ books.
12. What's wrong? Are you mad _____ me?

113.3 괄호 안의 단어를 사용하여 문장을 완성하시오.

1. I'm not very __good at telling__ stories. (good / tell)
2. I wanted to go to the movies, but Paula wasn't _____ . (interested / go)
3. Sue isn't very _____ up in the morning. (good / get)
4. Let's go! I'm _____ . (fed up / wait)
5. I'm _____ you up in the middle of the night. (sorry / wake)
6. Sorry I'm late! _____ . (thank you / wait)

113.4 *without -ing*를 사용하여 문장을 완성하시오.

1. (Tom left / he didn't say goodbye) __Tom left without saying goodbye.__
2. (Sue walked past me / she didn't speak)
   Sue walked _____
3. (don't do anything / ask me first)
   Don't _____
4. (I went out / I didn't lock the door)
   I _____

113.5 괄호 안의 단어를 사용하여 자신에 대한 문장을 쓰시오.

1. (interested) __I'm interested in sports.__
2. (afraid) I'm _____
3. (not very good) I'm not _____
4. (not interested) _____
5. (fed up) _____

UNIT 114

listen to ... , look at ... 등
(동사 + 전치사)

A

ask (somebody) **for** ...: ···에게 ···를 청하다

- A man stopped me and **asked** me **for** money.
  한 남자가 나를 멈춰 세우더니 돈을 달라고 했다.

belong to ...: ···에 속하다

- Does this book **belong to** you? (= Is this your book?)

happen to ...: ···에게 일어나다

- I can't find my pen. What's **happened to** it?
  펜을 찾을 수가 없어. 어떻게 된 거야?

listen to ...: ···를 듣다

- **Listen to** this music. It's great.

look at ...: ···를 보다

- He's **looking at** his watch.
- **Look at** these flowers!
  They're beautiful.
- Why are you **looking at** me like that?

look for ...: ···를 찾다

- She's lost her key.
  She's **looking for** it.
- I'm **looking for** Sarah.
  Have you seen her?

speak/talk to somebody
about something: ···에게
···에 대해 말하다

- Did you **talk to** Paul **about** the problem?
  폴에게 그 문제에 대해 말했니?
- (전화상에서) Can I **speak to** Chris, please?

take care of ...: ···를 돌보다

- When Pat is at work, a friend of hers **takes care** of her children.
- Don't lose this book. **Take care of** it.

thank somebody **for** ...:
···에 대해 ···에게 감사하다

- **Thank** you very much **for** your help.

think about ... 또는 **think of** ...:
···에 대해 생각하다

- He never **thinks about** (또는 **of**) other people.
  그는 다른 사람들 생각은 전혀 안 한다.
- Mark is **thinking of** (또는 **about**) buying a new computer.

wait for ...: ···를 기다리다

- **Wait for** me. I'm almost ready.

write (**to**) ...: ···에게 편지 쓰다

- I tried calling the company, but they didn't answer, so I **wrote to** them. (또는 I **wrote** them)

B

call, e-mail, text

call somebody, **e-mail** somebody, **text** somebody (전치사 없음): ···에게 전화/이메일/문자하다

- I have to **call** my parents tonight. (call to ...는 틀림)
- A: Could you use your cell phone when you were in Europe?
  B: No. My friends and family **e-mailed** me instead of calling.
- Let Sam know where to meet us. **E-mail** or **text** him before he leaves work.
  샘한테 우리와 어디서 만나는지 알려줘요. 샘이 회사에서 출발하기 전에 이메일이나 문자를 보내요.

C

depend

depend on ...: ···에 달려 있다, ···에 따라 다르다

- A: Do you like eating in restaurants?
  B: Sometimes. It **depends on** the restaurant. (it depends of는 틀림)

it depends 뒤에 **what/where/how** 등이 올 때는 **on**을 써도 되고 생략해도 된다.

- A: Do you want to come out with us? 우리랑 같이 갈래?
  B: It **depends where** you're going.   또는   It **depends on where** you're going.
  그건 너희가 어딜 가느냐에 달렸지.

 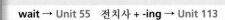 **wait** → Unit 55   전치사 + -ing → Unit 113

Exercises

114.1 그림을 보고 *to/for/at* 등을 사용하여 문장을 완성하시오.

1. She's looking ___at___ her watch.
2. He's listening _____ the radio.
3. They're waiting _____ a taxi.
4. Paul is talking _____ Jane.
5. They're looking _____ a picture.
6. Sue is looking _____ Tom.

114.2 필요한 경우 전치사(*to/for/about* 등)를 넣어 문장을 완성하시오.

1. Thank you very much ___for___ your help.
2. This isn't my umbrella. It belongs _____ a friend of mine.
3. Who's going to take care _____ your dog while you're out of town?
4. (전화상에서) Can I speak _____ Steven Davis, please?
5. (전화상에서) Thank you _____ calling. Goodbye.
6. Excuse me, I'm looking _____ Hill Street. Can you tell me where it is?
7. We're thinking _____ going to Australia next year.
8. We asked the waiter _____ tea, but he brought us coffee.
9. "Do you like to read books?" "It depends _____ the book."
10. John was talking, but nobody was listening _____ what he was saying.
11. I want to take your picture. Please look _____ the camera and smile.
12. We waited _____ Karen until 2:00, but she didn't come.
13. What happened _____ Ella last night? Why didn't she come to the party?
14. Don't forget to call _____ your mother tonight.
15. He's alone all day. He never talks _____ anybody.
16. "How much does it cost to stay at this hotel?" "It depends _____ the room."
17. It will be faster if you e-mail _____ me, but you can also write _____ me at this address.
18. Catherine is thinking _____ changing jobs.
19. I looked _____ the newspaper, but I didn't read it carefully.
20. When you're sick, you need somebody to take care _____ you.
21. Barry is looking _____ a job. He wants to work in a hotel.
22. I don't want everyone to hear my conversation with Jane. I'll text _____ her.

114.3 *It depends* ...를 사용하여 질문에 답하시오.

1. Do you want to go out with us?   _It depends where you're going._
2. Do you like to eat in restaurants?   _It depends on the restaurant._
3. Do you enjoy watching TV?   It depends _____
4. Can you do something for me?   It _____
5. Are you leaving town this weekend?   _____
6. Can you lend me some money?   _____

go in, fall off, run away 등
(동사구 1)

동사구: 동사 (**go/look/be** 등) + **in/out/up/down** 등

in

get in

- ■ Kate opened the door of the car and **got in**. (= **into** the car)
- ■ I waited outside the store. I didn't **go in**.

out

look out

- ■ I went to the window and **looked out**.
- ■ A car stopped, and a woman **got out**. (= **out of** the car)

on

get on

- ■ The bus came, and I **got on**.

off

fall off

- ■ Be careful! Don't **fall off**.

up

stand up

- ■ She **stood up** and left the room.
- ■ I usually **get up** early. (= get out of bed)
- ■ We **looked up** at the stars in the sky.

down

fall down

- ■ The picture **fell down**.
- ■ Would you like to **sit down**?
- ■ **Lie down** on the floor.

away 또는 off

run away

- ■ The thief **ran away**. (또는 ... **ran off**)
- ■ Emma got into the car and **drove away**.
  엠마는 차에 타고 가버렸다.

be/go away (= in/to another place)
- ■ Tim has **gone away** for a few days.

back

go

come back

- ■ Go away and don't **come back**!
- ■ We went out for dinner and then **went back** to our hotel.

be back
- ■ Tim is away. He'll **be back** on Monday.

over

move over   *pull over*

- ■ There was an empty seat, so he **moved over**. 빈자리가 있어서 그는 자리를 옮겼다.
- ■ I was tired of driving and **pulled over**. 나는 운전하는 데 지쳐서 길가에 차를 세웠다.

around

John!

turn around

- ■ Somebody shouted my name, so I **turned around**. 누가 내 이름을 큰소리로 불러서 나는 뒤를 돌아봤다.
- ■ We went for a long walk. After an hour we **turned around** and went back.

Exercises

115.1 그림을 보고 문장을 완성하시오. 아래의 동사 + *in/out/up* 등을 사용하시오.

> got   got   ~~looked~~   looked   rode   sat   turned   went

1. I went to the window and _*looked out*_ .
2. The door was open, so we _____ .
3. He heard a plane, so he _____ .
4. She got on her bike and _____ .
5. I said hello, and he _____ .
6. The bus stopped, and she _____ .
7. There was a free seat, so she _____ .
8. A car stopped, and two men _____ .

115.2 *out/away/back* 등을 사용하여 문장을 완성하시오.

1. "What happened to the picture on the wall?" "It fell _*down*_ ."
2. Please don't walk _____ . I have something to tell you.
3. Lisa heard a noise in back of her, so she turned _____ to see what it was.
4. I'm going _____ now to do some shopping. I'll be _____ at 5:00.
5. I'm really tired. I'm going to lie _____ on the sofa.
6. I can't see the movie screen. Would you please move _____ ?
7. Mark is from Utah. He lives in Boston now, but he wants to go _____ to Utah.
8. We don't have a key to the house, so we can't get _____ .
9. I was very tired this morning. I couldn't get _____ .
10. *A:* When are you going _____ ?
    B: On the fifth. And I'm coming _____ on the twenty-fourth.

115.3 다음 문제를 풀기 전에 **242쪽(부록 6)**을 공부하시오. 아래의 동사 + *on/off/up* 등을 사용하여 문장을 완성하시오. 필요한 경우, 동사를 알맞은 형태로 고치시오.

> break   get   go   slow   take   work
> fall   give   hold   speak   ~~wake~~   + along/on/off/up/down/over/out

1. I went to sleep at 10:00 and _*woke up*_ at 8:00 the next morning.
2. "It's time to go." "_____ a minute. I'm not ready yet."
3. The train _____ and finally stopped.
4. I like flying, but I'm always nervous when the plane _____ .
5. Tony doesn't see his sister much. They don't _____ very well.
6. It's difficult to hear you. Can you _____ a little?
7. This car isn't very good. It has _____ many times.
8. When babies try to walk, they sometimes _____ .
9. Ben isn't in good shape because he doesn't _____ at the gym anymore.
10. I tried to find a job, but I _____ . It was impossible.
11. The fire alarm _____ , and everyone had to leave the building.

put on your shoes   put your shoes on
(동사구 2)

A

동사구(**put on** / **take off** 등)가 **목적어**를 가질 수도 있다. 예를 들어,

동사	목적어		동사	목적어
put on	your coat		**take off**	your shoes

다음 두 가지 구조로 쓸 수 있다.

> **put on** your coat
> 또는 **put** your coat **on**

다음 두 가지 구조로 쓸 수 있다.

> **take off** your shoes
> 또는 **take** your shoes **off**

그러나 목적어가 **it/them** (**대명사**)일 경우에는 항상 **on/off** 앞에 온다.

> put **it** on (put on it은 틀림)

> take **them** off (take off them은 틀림)

- It was cold, so I **put on** my coat.
  (또는 I **put** my coat **on**)
- Here's your coat. **Put it on**.

- I'm going to **take off** my shoes.
  (또는 **take** my shoes **off**)
- Your shoes are dirty. **Take them off**.

B

'동사구 + 목적어'의 예:

---

turn on / **turn off** (lights, machines, faucets 등):
(불, 기계, 수도꼭지 등을) 켜다/끄다, 틀다/잠그다

- It was dark, so I **turned on** the light.
  (또는 I **turned** the light **on**)
- I don't want to watch this program.
  You can **turn it off**.

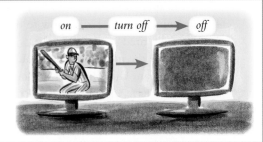

---

pick up / **put down**: 들어올리다/내려놓다

- Those are my keys on the floor. Can you
  pick them up for me?
- I stopped reading and **put** my book **down**.
  (또는 **put down** my book)
  나는 읽기를 멈추고 책을 내려놓았다.

---

bring back / **take back** / **give back** / **put back**:
다시 가져오다 / 다시 가져가다 / 돌려주다 / 다시 넣다

- You can take my umbrella, but please **bring
  it back**. 내 우산을 가져가도 좋지만, 꼭 돌려줘.
- I **took** my new sweater **back** to
  the store. It was too small for me.
- I have Rachel's keys. I have to
  give them back to her.
- I read the letter and then **put it
  back** in the envelope.

Exercises

116.1 그림을 보고 이 사람들이 무엇을 했는지 쓰시오.

1. He _turned on the light_ .
2. She _____ .
3. He _____ .
4. She _____ .
5. He _____ .
6. She _____ .

116.2 다음 문장들은 세 가지 형태로 쓸 수 있습니다. 아래의 표를 완성하시오.

1.	I turned on the radio.	_I turned the radio on._	_I turned it on._
2.	He put on his jacket.	He _____	He _____
3.	She _____	She took her glasses off.	_____
4.	I picked up the phone.	_____	_____
5.	They gave back the key.	_____	_____
6.	_____	We turned the lights off.	_____

116.3 아래의 동사구와 *it/them*을 사용하여 문장을 완성하시오.

bring back	**pick up**	**take back**	**turn off**	~~**turn on**~~

1. I wanted to watch something on television, so I _turned it on_ .
2. My new lamp doesn't work. I'm going to _____ to the store.
3. There were some gloves on the floor, so I _____ and put them on the table.
4. When I finished working on the computer, I _____ .
5. Thank you for lending me these books. I won't forget to _____ .

116.4 다음 문제를 풀기 전에 **243쪽(부록 7)**을 공부하시오. 아래의 동사구를 사용하여 문장을 완성하시오. 필요한 경우, *it/them/me*를 넣으시오.

fill out	**knock over**	**put out**	~~**tear down**~~	**try on**
give up	**look up**	**show around**	**throw away**	~~**turn down**~~

1. They _tore_ a lot of houses _down_ when they built the new road.
2. That music is very loud. Can you _turn it down_ ?
3. I _____ a glass and broke it.
4. "What does this word mean?" "Here's a dictionary. You can _____ ."
5. I want to keep these magazines. Please don't _____ .
6. I _____ a pair of shoes at the store, but I didn't buy them.
7. I visited a school last week. One of the teachers _____ .
8. "Do you play the piano?" "No, I started to learn, but I _____ after a month."
9. Somebody gave me a form and told me to _____ .
10. Smoking isn't allowed here. Please _____ your cigarette _____ .

능동태와 수동태

1.1 현재와 과거

	능동태	수동태
단순현재	■ We **make** butter from milk. ■ Somebody **cleans** these rooms every day. ■ People never **invite** me to parties. ■ How **do** they **make** butter?	■ Butter **is made** from milk. ■ These rooms **are cleaned** every day. ■ I **am** never **invited** to parties. ■ How **is** butter **made**?
단순과거	■ Somebody **stole** my car last week. ■ Somebody **stole** my keys yesterday. ■ They **didn't invite** me to the party. ■ When **did** they **build** these houses?	■ My car **was stolen** last week. ■ My keys **were stolen** yesterday. ■ I **wasn't invited** to the party. ■ When **were** these houses **built**?
현재진행	■ They **are building** a new airport at this time. (= 아직 끝나지 않았음) ■ They **are building** some new houses near the river.	■ A new airport **is being built** at this time. ■ Some new houses **are being built** near the river.
과거진행	■ When I was here a few years ago, they **were building** a new airport. (= 그 당시 아직 끝나지 않았음)	■ When I was here a few years ago, a new airport **was being built**.
현재완료	■ Look! They **have painted** the door. ■ These shirts are clean. Somebody **has washed** them. ■ Somebody **has stolen** my car.	■ Look! The door **has been painted**. ■ These shirts are clean. They **have been washed**. ■ My car **has been stolen**.
과거완료	■ Tina said that somebody **had stolen** her car.	■ Tina said that her car **had been stolen**.

1.2 *will / can / must / have to* 등

능동태	수동태
■ Somebody **will clean** the office tomorrow. ■ Somebody **must clean** the office at night. ■ I think they**'ll invite** you to the party. ■ They **can't repair** my watch. ■ You **should wash** this sweater by hand. ■ They **are going to build** a new airport. ■ Somebody **has to wash** these clothes. ■ They **had to take** the injured man to the hospital.	■ The office **will be cleaned** tomorrow. ■ The office **must be cleaned** at night. ■ I think you**'ll be invited** to the party. ■ My watch **can't be repaired**. ■ This sweater **should be washed** by hand. ■ A new airport **is going to be built**. ■ These clothes **have to be washed**. ■ The injured man **had to be taken** to the hospital.

불규칙동사 (Unit 25 참조)

원형	과거형	과거분사형
be	was/were	been
beat	beat	beaten
become	became	become
begin	began	begun
bite	bit	bitten
blow	blew	blown
break	broke	broken
bring	brought	brought
build	built	built
buy	bought	bought
catch	caught	caught
choose	chose	chosen
come	came	come
cost	cost	cost
cut	cut	cut
do	did	done
draw	drew	drawn
drink	drank	drunk
drive	drove	driven
eat	ate	eaten
fall	fell	fallen
feel	felt	felt
fight	fought	fought
find	found	found
fly	flew	flown
forget	forgot	forgotten
get	got	gotten
give	gave	given
go	went	gone
grow	grew	grown
hang	hung	hung
have	had	had
hear	heard	heard
hide	hid	hidden
hit	hit	hit
hold	held	held
hurt	hurt	hurt
keep	kept	kept
know	knew	known
leave	left	left
lend	lent	lent
let	let	let

원형	과거형	과거분사형
lie	lay	lain
light	lit	lit
lose	lost	lost
make	made	made
mean	meant (ment)*	meant (ment)*
meet	met	met
pay	paid	paid
put	put	put
quit	quit	quit
read (reed)*	read (red)*	read (red)*
ride	rode	ridden
ring	rang	rung
rise	rose	risen
run	ran	run
say	said (sed)*	said (sed)*
see	saw	seen
sell	sold	sold
send	sent	sent
shine	shone	shone
shoot	shot	shot
show	showed	shown
shut	shut	shut
sing	sang	sung
sit	sat	sat
sleep	slept	slept
speak	spoke	spoken
spend	spent	spent
stand	stood	stood
steal	stole	stolen
swim	swam	swum
take	took	taken
teach	taught	taught
tear	tore	torn
tell	told	told
think	thought	thought
throw	threw	thrown
understand	understood	understood
wake	woke	woken
wear	wore	worn
win	won	won
write	wrote	written

* 발음 주의

유형별 불규칙동사

과거형과 과거완료형이 같은 경우:

1.
cost	→ cost	let	→ let
cut	→ cut	put	→ put
hit	→ hit	quit	→ quit
hurt	→ hurt	shut	→ shut

2.
lend	→ lent	lose	→ lost
send	→ sent	shoot	→ shot
spend	→ spent	light	→ lit
build	→ built	sit	→ sat

keep	→ kept
sleep	→ slept

feel	→ felt
leave	→ left
meet	→ met
mean	→ meant (ment)*

3.
bring	→ brought
buy	→ bought
fight	→ fought
think	→ thought
catch	→ caught
teach	→ taught

4.
sell	→ sold
tell	→ told

find	→ found
have	→ had
hear	→ heard (herd)*
hold	→ held
read	→ read (red)*
say	→ said (sed)*

pay	→ paid
make	→ made

stand	→ stood
understand	→ understood

* 발음 주의

과거형과 과거완료형이 다른 경우:

1.
break	→ broke	→ broken
choose	→ chose	→ chosen
speak	→ spoke	→ spoken
steal	→ stole	→ stolen
wake	→ woke	→ woken

2.
drive	→ drove	→ driven
ride	→ rode	→ ridden
rise	→ rose	→ risen
write	→ wrote	→ written

beat	→ beat	→ beaten
bite	→ bit	→ bitten
hide	→ hid	→ hidden

3.
eat	→ ate	→ eaten
fall	→ fell	→ fallen
forget	→ forgot	→ forgotten
get	→ got	→ gotten
give	→ gave	→ given
see	→ saw	→ seen
take	→ took	→ taken

4.
blow	→ blew	→ blown
grow	→ grew	→ grown
know	→ knew	→ known
throw	→ threw	→ thrown
fly	→ flew	→ flown
draw	→ drew	→ drawn
show	→ showed	→ shown

5.
begin	→ began	→ begun
drink	→ drank	→ drunk
swim	→ swam	→ swum
ring	→ rang	→ rung
sing	→ sang	→ sung
run	→ ran	→ run

6.
come	→ came	→ come
become	→ became	→ become

축약형 (he's / I'd / don't 등)

4.1 말할 때 *I am*은 보통 한 단어처럼 발음된다. 축약형(*I'm*)은 이러한 것을 표기하는 방식이다.

I am → **I'm**	■ **I'm** feeling tired this morning.
it is → **it's**	■ "Do you like this jacket?" "Yes, **it's** nice."
they have → **they've** 등	■ "Where are your friends?" "**They've** gone home."

축약형을 쓸 때는 생략부호(')를 사용한다.
I ̸am→ **I'm**   he ̸is→ **he's**   you ̸have→ **you've**   she ̸will → **she'll**

4.2 대명사 *I/he/she* 등은 다음과 같은 축약형을 사용한다.

		I'm	he's	she's	it's			
am → 'm	**I'm**							
is → 's			**he's**	**she's**	**it's**			
are → 're						**we're**	**you're**	**they're**
have → 've	**I've**					**we've**	**you've**	**they've**
has → 's			**he's**	**she's**	**it's**			
had → 'd	**I'd**		**he'd**	**she'd**		**we'd**	**you'd**	**they'd**
will → 'll	**I'll**		**he'll**	**she'll**		**we'll**	**you'll**	**they'll**
would → 'd	**I'd**		**he'd**	**she'd**		**we'd**	**you'd**	**they'd**

■ **I've** got some new shoes.
■ **We'll** probably go out tonight.
■ **It's** 10:00. **You're** late again.

's = is 또는 has:
■ **She's** going out tonight. (she's going = she **is** going)
■ **She's** gone out. (she's gone = she **has** gone)

'd = would 또는 had:
■ *A:* What would you like to eat?
  B: **I'd** like a salad, please. (I'd like = I **would** like)
■ I told the police that **I'd** lost my passport. (I'd lost = I **had** lost)

문장 끝에는 **'m/'s/'d** 등의 축약형을 사용하지 않는다(Unit 41 참조).
■ "Are you tired?" "Yes, **I am**." (Yes, I'm은 틀림)
■ She isn't tired, but he **is**. (... but he's는 틀림)

4.3 *I/you/he/she* 등과 같은 대명사뿐만 아니라 그밖의 다른 단어들도 축약형(특히 **'s**)으로 쓸 수 있다.
■ **Who's** your favorite singer? (= who **is**)
■ **What's** the time? (= what **is**)
■ **There's** a big tree in the yard. (= there **is**)
■ **My sister's** working in London. (= my sister **is** working)
■ **Paul's** gone out. (= Paul **has** gone out)
■ **What color's** your car? (= What color **is** your car?)

축약형 (he's / I'd / don't 등)

4.4 부정어의 축약형 (Unit 44 참조):

isn't	(= is not)	**don't**	(= do not)	**can't**	(= cannot)
aren't	(= are not)	**doesn't**	(= does not)	**couldn't**	(= could not)
wasn't	(= was not)	**didn't**	(= did not)	**won't**	(= will not)
weren't	(= were not)			**wouldn't**	(= would not)
hasn't	(= has not)			**shouldn't**	(= should not)
haven't	(= have not)			**mustn't**	(= must not)
hadn't	(= had not)				

- We went to her house, but she **wasn't** at home.
- "Where's David?"　"I **don't** know. I **haven't** seen him."
- You work all the time. You **shouldn't** work so hard.
- I **won't** be here tomorrow.　(= I will not)

4.5 **'s** (생략부호 + **s**)

's는 다음과 같이 여러 의미로 쓰인다.

(1) **'s** = **is** 또는 **has** (부록 4.2 참조)

(2) **let's** = let **us** (Unit 37 참조)
- It's a beautiful day. **Let's** go outside.　(= **Let us** go outside.)

(3) Kate**'s** camera = her camera
　my brother**'s** car = his car
　the manager**'s** office = his/her office 등
　(Unit 65 참조)

비교:
- **Kate's** camera was very expensive.　(**Kate's** camera = **her** camera)
- **Kate's** a very good photographer.　(**Kate's** = Kate **is**)
- **Kate's** got a new camera.　(Kate**'s** got = Kate **has** got)

철자

5.1 단어 + -s / -es (birds/watches 등)

명사 + **s** (복수) (Unit 67 참조)

bird → bird**s**   mistake → mistake**s**   hotel → hotel**s**

동사 + **s** (he/she/it -**s**) (Unit 5 참조)

think → think**s**   live → live**s**   remember → remember**s**

그러나

-s / **-sh** / **-ch** / **-x**로 끝나는 단어 뒤에는 + **es**

bus → bus**es**   pass → pass**es**   address → address**es**

dish → dish**es**   wash → wash**es**   finish → finish**es**

wat**ch** → wat**ches**   tea**ch** → tea**ches**   sandwi**ch** → sandwi**ches**

box → box**es**

또한

potato → potato**es**   tomato → tomato**es**

do → do**es**   go → go**es**

-f / **-fe** → **-ves**

shel**f** → shel**ves**   kni**fe** → kni**ves**   그러나   roo**f** → roo**fs**

5.2 -y로 끝나는 단어 (baby → babies / study → studied 등)

-y → **-ies**

study → stud**ies** (studys는 틀림)   family → famil**ies** (familys는 틀림)

story → stor**ies**   city → cit**ies**   baby → bab**ies**

try → tr**ies**   marry → marr**ies**   fly → fl**ies**

-y → **-ied** (Unit 11 참조)

study → stud**ied** (studyed는 틀림)

try → tr**ied**   marry → marr**ied**   copy → cop**ied**

-y → **-ier** / **-iest** (Units 88, 91 참조)

easy → eas**ier**/eas**iest** (easyer/easyest는 틀림)

happy → happ**ier**/happ**iest**   lucky → luck**ier**/luck**iest**

heavy → heav**ier**/heav**iest**   funny → funn**ier**/funn**iest**

-y → **-ily** (Unit 87 참조)

easy → eas**ily** (easyly는 틀림)

happy → happ**ily**   heavy → heav**ily**   lucky → luck**ily**

-ay / **-ey** / **-oy** / **-uy**로 끝나는 단어는 **y**가 **i**로 바뀌지 않는다.

holiday → holiday**s** (holidaies는 틀림)

enjoy → enjoy**s**/enjoy**ed**   stay → stay**s**/stay**ed**   buy → buy**s**   key → key**s**

그러나

say → **said**   pay → **paid**   (불규칙동사)

5.3 *-ing*

-e로 끝나는 동사 (mak**e**/writ**e**/driv**e** 등) → ~~e~~**ing**

make → mak**ing**   write → writ**ing**   come → com**ing**   dance → danc**ing**

-ie로 끝나는 동사 → **-ying**:

lie → l**ying**   die → d**ying**   tie → t**ying**

5.4 stop → stop**ped**, big → big**g**er 등

모음과 자음:

모음: a e i o u

자음: b c d f g k l m n p r s t w y

한 개의 모음 + 한 개의 자음으로 끝나는 단어(예를 들어, s**top**, b**ig**, g**et** 등)의 뒤에 **-ing/-ed/-er/-est**를 붙일 경우에는 자음을 중복시킨다(**pp/gg/tt** 등).

예:

	V + C				
stop	ST **O** **P**	p → **pp**	stop**p**ing	stop**p**ed
run	R **U** **N**	n → **nn**	run**n**ing	
get	G **E** **T**	t → **tt**	get**t**ing	
swim	SW **I** **M**	m → **mm**	swim**m**ing	
big	B **I** **G**	g → **gg**	big**g**er	big**g**est
hot	H **O** **T**	t → **tt**	hot**t**er	hot**t**est
thin	TH **I** **N**	n → **nn**	thin**n**er	thin**n**est

V = 모음 (*vowel*)
C = 자음 (*consonant*)

자음을 중복하지 않는 경우:

(1) 단어가 두 개의 자음으로 끝날 때 (C + C):

	C + C		
help	HE **L** **P**	help**ing**	help**ed**
work	WO **R** **K**	work**ing**	work**ed**
fast	FA **S** **T**	fast**er**	fast**est**

(2) 단어가 두 개의 모음 + 자음으로 끝날 때 (V + V + C):

	V + V + C		
need	N **E** **E** **D**	need**ing**	need**ed**
wait	W **A** **I** **T**	wait**ing**	wait**ed**
cheap	CH **E** **A** **P**	cheap**er**	cheap**est**

(3) 2음절 이상의 긴 단어에서 마지막 음절에 강세가 없을 때:

	강세		
happen	**HAP**-pen	→	happen**ing**/happen**ed** (happe**nn**ed는 틀림)
visit	**VIS**-it	→	visit**ing**/visit**ed**
remember	re-**MEM**-ber	→	remember**ing**/remember**ed**

그러나

prefer	pre-**FER**	(마지막 음절에 강세)	→ prefer**r**ing/prefer**r**ed
begin	be-**GIN**	(마지막 음절에 강세)	→ begin**n**ing

(4) 단어가 **-y** 또는 **-w**로 끝날 때 (단어 끝에 오는 **y**와 **w**는 자음이 아님):

enjoy → enjoy**ing**/enjoy**ed**   snow → snow**ing**/snow**ed**   few → few**er**/few**est**

동사구 (take off / give up 등)

다음은 중요한 동사구들의 예이다(Unit 115 참조).

out	**look out** / **watch out** = 조심하다

■ **Look out!** There's a car coming.

work out = 운동하다

■ Sarah **works out** at the gym two or three times a week.

work out

on	**come on** = 서두르다

■ **Come on!** Everybody is waiting for you.

go on = 계속하다, 지속되다

■ I'm sorry I interrupted. **Go on**.
(= continue what you were saying)

■ How long will this hot weather **go on**?

keep on = (이야기 등을) 계속하다

■ I asked them to be quiet, but they **kept on** talking.

hold on = 기다리다

■ Can you **hold on** a minute? (= can you wait?)

Hold on a minute.

off	**take off** = (비행기가) 이륙하다

take off

■ The plane **took off** 20 minutes late but arrived on time.

go off = (폭탄이) 폭발하다, (경보, 시계알람 등이) 울리다

■ A bomb **went off** and caused a lot of damage.

■ A car alarm **goes off** if somebody tries to break into the car.

go off

up	**clean up** = 청소하다, 정리하다

■ After the party, it took two hours to **clean up**.

give up = 포기하다

■ I know it's difficult, but don't **give up**. (= don't stop trying)

grow up = 어른이 되다

■ What does your son want to do when he **grows up**?

grow up

hurry up = 서두르다

■ **Hurry up!** We don't have much time.

speak up = 더 크게 말하다

■ I can't hear you. Can you **speak up**, please?

wake up = 잠에서 깨다

■ I often **wake up** in the middle of the night.

wake up

down	**slow down** = 속도를 줄이다

■ You're driving too fast. **Slow down**!

break down = (차, 기계 등이) 고장나다

■ Sue was very late because her car **broke down**.

break down

along	**get along** = 문제 없이 잘 지내다

■ Sam doesn't visit his parents often. He doesn't **get along** with his father.

over	**fall over** = 넘어지다, 중심을 잃다

■ I **fell over** because my shoes were too big for me.

fall over

부록 7 동사구 + 목적어 (put out a fire / try on clothes 등)

다음은 자주 쓰이는 동사구 + 목적어의 예이다(Unit 116 참조).

out

fill out (a form) = (서류를) 작성하다
- Can you **fill out this form**, please?

put out (a fire, a cigarette 등) = (불, 담뱃불 등을) 끄다
- The fire department arrived and **put the fire out**.

cross out (a mistake, a word 등) = (실수, 틀린 단어 등을) 지우다
- If you make a mistake, **cross it out**.

fill out

put out　　*cross out*

on

try on (clothes) = (옷이 맞는지) 입어보다
- (가게에서) Where can I **try these pants on**?

up

give up (something) = 포기하다
- Sue **gave up her job** when her baby was born. (= she stopped working)
- Tom's doctor told him he had to **give up smoking**.

look up (a word in a dictionary) = (사전에서 단어를) 찾아보다
- I didn't know the meaning of the word, so I **looked it up** in a dictionary.

turn up (the TV, radio, music, heat 등) = (TV, 라디오, 음악 소리, 난방 등을) 높이다
- Can you **turn the radio up**? I can't hear it.

wake up (somebody who is sleeping) = (자는 사람을) 깨우다
- I have to get up early tomorrow. Can you **wake me up** at 6:30?

down

tear down (a building) = (건물을) 부수다
- They are going to **tear down** the school and build a new one.

tear down

turn down (the TV, radio, music, heat 등) = (TV, 라디오, 음악 소리, 난방 등을) 낮추다
- The music is too loud. Can you **turn it down**?

over

knock over (a cup, a glass, a person 등) = (컵, 잔, 사람 등을) 엎지르다/넘어뜨리다
- Be careful. Don't **knock your cup over**.

knock over

away

throw away (garbage, things you don't want) = (쓰레기, 원치 않는 물건 등을) 버리다
- These apples are bad. Should I **throw them away**?
- Don't **throw away that picture**. I want it.

throw away

put (something) **away** = 치우다/정리정돈하다
- After they finished playing, the children **put their toys away**.

back

pay (somebody) **back** = (누구에서) 빌린 돈을 갚다
- Thank you for lending me the money. I'll **pay you back** next week.

around

show (somebody) **around** = (누구를) 구경시켜 주다
- We visited a factory last week. The manager **showed us around**.

추가연습문제

---

am/is/are   Units 1–2

1 아래의 단어와 *is/isn't/are/aren't*를 사용하여 그림에 맞는 문장을 쓰시오.

~~The windows~~	**on the table**
~~Lisa~~	hungry
Kate	asleep
The children	~~open~~
Gary	full
The books	near the station
The hotel	a doctor
The bus	~~happy~~

1. *The windows are open.*
2. *Lisa isn't happy.*
3. Kate _____
4. _____
5. _____
6. _____
7. _____
8. _____

2 문장을 완성하시오.

1. "Are you hungry?"　"No, but _____I'm_____ thirsty."
2. "___How are___ your parents?"　"They're fine."
3. "Is Anna at home?"　"No, _____ at work."
4. "_____ my keys?"　"On your desk."
5. Where is Paul from? _____ American or Canadian?
6. _____ very hot today. The temperature is 38 degrees Celsius.
7. "Are you a teacher?"　"No, _____ a student."
8. "_____ your umbrella?"　"Green."
9. Where's your car? _____ in the parking lot?
10. "_____ tired?"　"No, I'm fine."
11. "These shoes are nice. How _____ ?"　"Seventy-five dollars."

현재진행 (*I'm working / are you working* 등)　　Units 3–4

3 괄호 안의 단어를 사용하여 문장을 쓰시오.

1. *A:* Where are your parents?
   B: ___They're watching TV.___ (they / watch / TV)
2. *A:* Paula is going out.
   B: ___Where's she going?___ (where / she / go?)
3. *A:* Where's David?
   B: _____ (he / take / a shower)
4. *A:* _____ (the children / play?)
   B: No, they're asleep.
5. *A:* _____ (it / rain?)
   B: No, not any more.
6. *A:* Where are Sue and Steve?
   B: _____ (they / come / now)
7. *A:* _____ (why / you / stand / here?)
   B: _____ (I / wait / for somebody)

단순현재 (*I work / she doesn't work / do you work* 등)　　Units 5–7

4 단순현재를 사용하여 문장을 완성하시오.

1. ___Sue always gets___ to work early. (Sue / always / get)
2. ___We don't watch___ TV very often. (we / not / watch)
3. How often ___do you wash___ your hair? (you / wash)
4. I want to go to the movies, but _____ to go. (Sam / not / want)
5. _____ to go out tonight? (you / want)
6. _____ near here? (Helen / live)
7. _____ a lot of people. (Sarah / know)
8. I enjoy traveling, but _____ very much. (I / not / travel)
9. What time _____ in the morning? (you / usually / get up)
10. My parents are usually at home at night.
    _____ very often. (they / not / go out)
11. _____ work at 5:00. (Tom / always / leave)
12. *A:* What _____ ? (Julia / do)
    B: _____ in a hotel. (she / work)

5 질문과 이에 대한 Claire의 대답을 읽고 Claire에 대해 쓰시오.

			Claire	
1.	Are you married?	No.		1. ___She isn't married.___
2.	Do you live in Houston?	Yes.		2. ___She lives in Houston.___
3.	Are you a student?	Yes.		3. _____
4.	Do you have a car?	No.		4. _____
5.	Do you go out a lot?	Yes.		5. _____
6.	Do you have a lot of friends?	Yes.		6. _____
7.	Do you like Houston?	No.		7. _____
8.	Do you like to dance?	Yes.		8. _____
9.	Are you interested in sports?	No.		9. _____

6 문장을 완성하시오.

1.
   ___What's your name___ ?
   _____ married?
   Where _____ ?
   _____ any children?
   How _____ ?

   Brian.
   Yes, I am.
   On State Street.
   Yes, a daughter.
   She's three.

2.
   _____ ?
   _____ ?
   _____ your job?
   _____ a car?
   _____ to work by car?

   I'm 29.
   I work in a supermarket.
   No, I hate it.
   Yes, I do.
   No, I usually go by bus.

3.
   ___Who is this man___ ?
   _____ ?
   _____ ?
   _____ in New York?

   That's my brother.
   Michael.
   He's a travel agent.
   No, in Los Angeles.

7 주어진 단어를 사용하여 문장을 쓰시오. 모든 문장은 현재시제입니다.

1. (Sarah often / tennis)   ___Sarah often plays tennis.___
2. (my parents / a new car)   ___My parents have a new car.___ 또는
                                 ___My parents have got a new car.___
3. (my shoes / dirty)   ___My shoes are dirty.___
4. (Sonia / 32 years old)   Sonia _____
5. (I / two sisters)   _____
6. (we often / TV at night)   _____
7. (Jane never / a hat)   _____
8. (my car / a flat tire)   _____
9. (these flowers / beautiful)   _____
10. (Mary / German very well)   _____

8 문장을 완성하시오.

1. Please be quiet. *I'm working* (I/work).

2. *Do you go* (you/go) to the movies a lot?

3. What _____ _____ (you/cook)?

4. Jack _____ (play) the piano very well.

5. _____ (I/leave) now. Goodbye!

6. _____ (it/rain). Can I take this umbrella?

7. _____ (I/not/watch) TV very much.

8. Excuse me, _____ _____ (we/look) for the museum.

9. What's this word? How _____ (you/pronounce) it?

9 맞는 것을 고르시오.

1. "~~Are you speaking~~ / Do you speak English?"　"Yes, a little." (*Do you speak*가 맞음)
2. Sometimes we're going / we go away on weekends.
3. It's a nice day today. The sun is shining / shines.
4. *(You meet Kate in the street.)* Hello, Kate. Where are you going / do you go?
5. How often are you taking / do you take a vacation?
6. Emily is a writer. She's writing / She writes children's books.
7. I'm never reading / I never read newspapers.
8. "Where are Michael and Jane?"　"They're watching / They watch TV in the living room."
9. Helen is in her office. She's talking / She talks to somebody.
10. What time are you usually having / do you usually have dinner?
11. John isn't at home right now. He's visiting / He visits some friends.
12. "Would you like some coffee?"　"No, thanks. I'm not drinking / I don't drink coffee."

10   한 단어를 써 넣어 문장을 완성하시오.

1. I got up early and ___*took*___ a shower.
2. Tom was tired last night, so he _____ to bed early.
3. I _____ this pen on the floor. Is it yours?
4. Kate got married when she _____ 23.
5. Helen is learning to drive. She _____ her first lesson yesterday.
6. "I've got a new job."   "Yes, I know. David _____ me."
7. "Where did you buy that book?"   "It was a present. Jane _____ it to me."
8. We _____ hungry, so we had something to eat.
9. "Did you enjoy the movie?"   "Yes, I _____ it was very good."
10. "Did Andy come to your party?"   "No, we _____ him, but he didn't come."

11   질문과 그에 대한 Kevin의 대답을 읽고 어린 시절의 Kevin에 대해 쓰시오.

Kevin

When you were a child …		
Were you tall?	No.	1. _He wasn't tall._
Did you like school?	Yes.	2. _He liked school._
Were you good at sports?	Yes.	3. He _____
Did you play soccer?	Yes.	4. _____
Did you work hard at school?	No.	5. _____
Did you have a lot of friends?	Yes.	6. _____
Did you have a bicycle?	No.	7. _____
Were you a quiet child?	No.	8. _____

12   질문을 완성하시오.

1. _Did you have_ _____ a nice vacation?   Yes, it was great, thanks.
2. _Where did you go_ _____ ?   To the Bahamas.
3. _____ there?   Five days.
4. _____ the Bahamas?   Yes, very much.
5. _____ ?   I have friends there, so I stayed with them.
6. _____ good?   Yes, it was warm and sunny.
7. _____ back?   Yesterday.

13   괄호 안의 동사를 알맞은 형태(긍정, 부정 또는 의문문)로 써 넣으시오.

1. It was a good party. ___*I enjoyed*___ it. (I / enjoy)
2. "___*Did you do*___ the dishes?" (you / do)   "No, ___*I didn't have*___ time." (I / have)
3. "Did you call Adam?"   "No, I'm sorry, _____." (I / forget)
4. I like your new watch. Where _____ it? (you / get)
5. I saw Lucy at the party, but _____ to her. (I / speak)
6. *A:* _____ a nice weekend? (you / have)
   B: Yes, I visited some friends of mine.
7. Paul wasn't well yesterday, so _____ to work. (he / go)
8. "Is Mary here?"   "Yes, _____ five minutes ago." (she / arrive)
9. Where _____ before he moved here? (Robert / live)
10. The restaurant wasn't expensive. _____ very much. (the meal / cost)

14 단순과거 또는 과거진행을 사용하여 문장을 완성하시오.

1. It __*was raining*__ (rain) when we __*went*__ (go) out.

2. When I arrived at the office, Jane and Paul _____ (work) at their desks.

3. I _____ (open) the window because it was hot.

4. The phone _____ (ring) when Sue _____ (cook) dinner.

5. I _____ (hear) a noise outside, so I _____ (look) out of the window.

6. Tom _____ (look) out of the window when the accident _____ (happen).

7. Richard had a book in his hand, but he _____ (not/read) it. He _____ (watch) TV.

8. Erin bought a magazine, but she _____ (not/read) it. She didn't have time.

9. I _____ (finish) lunch, _____ (pay) the bill, and _____ (leave) the restaurant.

10. I _____ (see) Kate this morning. I _____ (walk) along the street and she _____ (wait) for the bus.

15 다음 시제 중 하나를 택해 문장을 완성하시오.

> 단순현재 (**I work/drive** 등)   현재진행 (**I am working/driving** 등)
>
> 단순과거 (**I worked/drove** 등)   과거진행 (**I was working/driving** 등)

1. You can turn off the TV. I *'m not watching* (not / watch) it.
2. Last night Jenny ___*fell*___ (fall) asleep while she ___*was reading*___ (read).
3. Listen! Somebody _____ (play) the piano.
4. "Do you have my key?"   "No, I _____ (give) it back to you."
5. David is very lazy. He _____ (not / like) to work hard.
6. Where _____ (your parents / go) on vacation last year?
7. I _____ (see) Diane yesterday. She _____ (drive) her new car.
8. *A:* _____ (you / watch) TV very much?
   B: No, I don't have a TV.
9. *A:* What _____ (you / do) at 6:00 last Sunday morning?
   B: I was in bed asleep.
10. Andy isn't at home very much. He _____ (go) out a lot.
11. I _____ (try) to find a job right now. It's very hard.
12. I'm tired this morning. I _____ (not / sleep) very well last night.

현재완료 (*I have done / she has been* 등)   **Units 16–21**

16 그림을 보고 문장을 완성하시오. 현재완료를 사용하시오.

5. _____ to Chile?

Yes, I went there a few years ago.

6. How long _____ here?

Since 2005.

7. Do you know Alan?

Alan

Yes, we _____ each other for years.

8. The weather is terrible today. It _____ all day.

17 빈칸에 **1–3개**의 단어를 넣어 문장을 완성하시오.

1. Mark and Liz are married. They __*have been*__ married for five years.
2. David has been watching TV __*since*__ 5:00.
3. Martin is at work. He _____ at work since 8:30.
4. "Did you just arrive in Miami?"   "No, I've been here _____ five days."
5. I've known Helen _____ we were in high school.
6. "My brother lives in Los Angeles."   "Really? How long _____ there?"
7. George has had the same job _____ 20 years.
8. Some friends of ours are staying with us. They _____ here since Monday.

18 문장을 완성하시오. 자신에 대해 사실대로 쓰시오.

1. I've never __*ridden a horse.*__
2. I've __*been to Montreal*__ many times.
3. I've just _____
4. I've _____
   (once / twice / a few times / many times)
5. I haven't _____ yet.
6. I've never _____
7. I've _____ since _____
8. I've _____ for _____

19 현재완료 또는 단순과거를 사용하여 문장을 완성하시오. 긍정 또는 부정형으로 써 넣으시오.

1. *A:* Do you like London?
   B: I don't know. I _haven't been_ there.

2. *A:* Have you seen Kate?
   B: Yes, I _saw_ her five minutes ago.

3. *A:* That's a nice sweater. Is it new?
   B: Yes, I _____ it last week.

4. *A:* Are you tired this morning?
   B: Yes, I _____ to bed late last night.

5. *A:* Is the new French movie good?
   B: Yes, really good. I _____ it three times.

6. *A:* Do you like your new job?
   B: I _____ . My first day is next Monday.

7. *A:* The weather isn't very nice today, is it?
   B: No, but it _____ nice yesterday.

8. *A:* Was Helen at the party on Saturday?
   B: I don't think so. I _____ her there.

9. *A:* Is your son still in school?
   B: No, he _____ college two years ago.

10. *A:* Is Silvia married?
    B: Yes, she _____ married for five years.

11. *A:* Have you heard of George Washington?
    B: Of course. He _____ the first president of the United States.

12. *A:* How long does it take to make a pizza?
    B: I don't know. I _____ a pizza.

20 현재완료 또는 단순과거를 사용하여 문장을 쓰시오.

1. *A:* Have you been to Thailand?
   B: Yes, _I went there last year._ (I / go / there / last year)

2. *A:* Do you like London?
   B: I don't know. _I've never been there._ (I / never / there)

3. *A:* Where is Paul these days?
   B: He's living in Chicago. He _____ (live / there / since last May)

4. *A:* Has Catherine gone home?
   B: Yes, _____ (she / leave / at 4:00)

5. *A:* New York is my favorite city.
   B: It is? _____ ? (how many times / you / there?)

6. *A:* You look tired.
   B: Yes, _____ (I / tired / all day)

7. *A:* I can't find my address book. Have you seen it?
   B: _____ (it / on the table / last night)

8. *A:* Do you know the Japanese restaurant on First Street?
   B: Yes, _____ (I / eat / there a few times)

9. *A:* Paula and Sue are here.
   B: Are they? _____ ? (what time / they / get / here?)

21 현재완료 또는 단순과거를 사용하여 문장을 완성하시오.

1. *A:* <u>*Have you been*</u> to France?
   B: Yes, many times.
   A: When _____ the last time?
   B: Two years ago.

2. *A:* Is this your car?
   B: Yes, it is.
   A: How long _____ it?
   B: It's new. I _____ it yesterday.

   Is this your car?

3. *A:* Where do you live?
   B: On Maple Street.
   A: How long _____ there?
   B: Five years. Before that _____
       on Mill Road.
   A: How long _____ on
       Mill Road?
   B: About three years.

   Where do you live?

4. *A:* What do you do?
   B: I work in a store.
   A: How long _____ there?
   B: Nearly two years.
   A: What _____ before that?
   B: I _____ a taxi driver.

   What do you do?

22 자신에 대한 문장을 쓰시오.

1. (yesterday morning)   <u>*I was late for work yesterday morning.*</u>
2. (last night)   _____
3. (yesterday afternoon) _____
4. (… days ago)   _____
5. (last week)   _____
6. (last year)   _____

23　맞는 것을 고르시오.

1. "___*Is Sue working? (C)*___"　"No, she's on vacation."

　　A Does Sue work?　　**B** Is working Sue?　　**C** Is Sue working?　　**D** Does work Sue?

2. "Where _____?"　"In Dallas."

　　A lives your uncle　　**B** does your uncle live　　**C** your uncle lives　　**D** does live your uncle

3. I speak Italian, but _____ French.

　　A I no speak　　**B** I'm not speaking　　**C** I doesn't speak　　**D** I don't speak

4. "Where's Tom?"　"_____ a shower at the moment."

　　A He's taking　　**B** He take　　**C** He takes　　**D** He has taken

5. Why _____ angry with me yesterday?

　　A were you　　**B** was you　　**C** you were　　**D** have you been

6. My favorite movie is *Cleo's Dream*. _____ it four times.

　　A I'm seeing　　**B** I see　　**C** I was seeing　　**D** I've seen

7. I _____ out last night. I was too tired.

　　A don't go　　**B** didn't went　　**C** didn't go　　**D** haven't gone

8. Liz is from Chicago. She _____ there all her life.

　　A is living　　**B** has lived　　**C** lives　　**D** lived

9. My friend _____ for me when I arrived.

　　A waited　　**B** has waited　　**C** was waiting　　**D** has been waiting

10. "How long _____ English?"　"Six months."

　　A do you learn　　**B** are you learning　　**C** you are learning　　**D** have you been learning

11. Joel is Canadian, but he lives in Peru. He has been there _____.

　　A for three years　　**B** since three years　　**C** three years ago　　**D** during three years

12. "What time _____?"　"About an hour ago."

　　A has Lisa called　　**B** Lisa has called　　**C** did Lisa call　　**D** is Lisa calling

13. What _____ when you saw her?

　　A did Sue wear　　**B** was Sue wearing　　**C** has Sue worn　　**D** was wearing Sue

14. "Can you drive?"　"No, _____ a car, but I want to learn."

　　A I never drive　　**B** I'm never driving　　**C** I've never driven　　**D** I was never driving

15. I saw Helen at the station when I was going to work this morning, but she

　　_____ me.

　　A didn't see　　**B** don't see　　**C** hasn't seen　　**D** didn't saw

24 문장을 완성하시오.

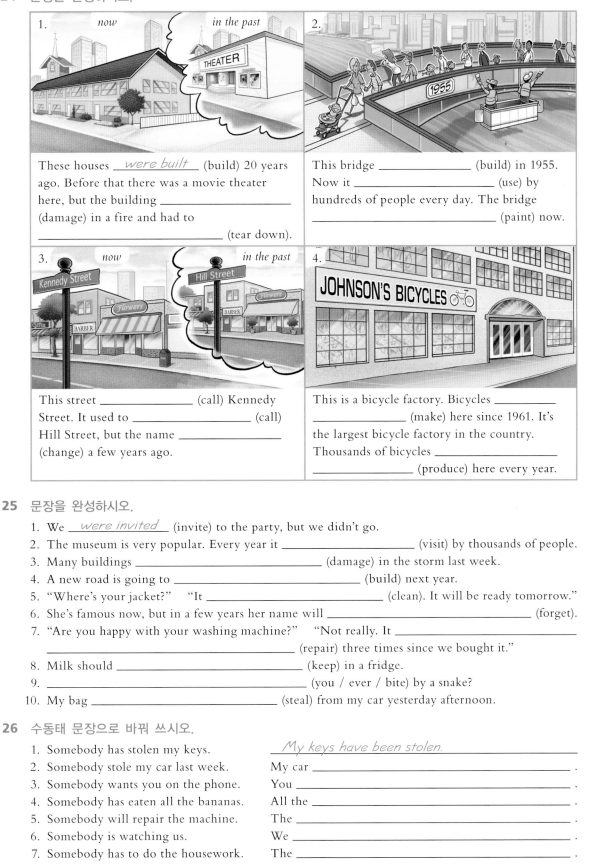

1. *now*   *in the past*

These houses _*were built*_ (build) 20 years ago. Before that there was a movie theater here, but the building _____ (damage) in a fire and had to _____ (tear down).

2.

This bridge _____ (build) in 1955. Now it _____ (use) by hundreds of people every day. The bridge _____ (paint) now.

3. *now*   *in the past*

This street _____ (call) Kennedy Street. It used to _____ (call) Hill Street, but the name _____ (change) a few years ago.

4.

This is a bicycle factory. Bicycles _____ _____ (make) here since 1961. It's the largest bicycle factory in the country. Thousands of bicycles _____ _____ (produce) here every year.

25 문장을 완성하시오.

1. We _*were invited*_ (invite) to the party, but we didn't go.
2. The museum is very popular. Every year it _____ (visit) by thousands of people.
3. Many buildings _____ (damage) in the storm last week.
4. A new road is going to _____ (build) next year.
5. "Where's your jacket?"   "It _____ (clean). It will be ready tomorrow."
6. She's famous now, but in a few years her name will _____ (forget).
7. "Are you happy with your washing machine?"   "Not really. It _____ _____ (repair) three times since we bought it."
8. Milk should _____ (keep) in a fridge.
9. _____ (you / ever / bite) by a snake?
10. My bag _____ (steal) from my car yesterday afternoon.

26 수동태 문장으로 바꿔 쓰시오.

1. Somebody has stolen my keys.   _*My keys have been stolen.*_
2. Somebody stole my car last week.   My car _____ .
3. Somebody wants you on the phone.   You _____ .
4. Somebody has eaten all the bananas.   All the _____ .
5. Somebody will repair the machine.   The _____ .
6. Somebody is watching us.   We _____ .
7. Somebody has to do the housework.   The _____ .

27 주어진 동사를 능동태 또는 수동태로 써 넣어 문장을 완성하시오.

1. They _are building_ (build) a new airport now.
2. These shirts are clean now. They _have been washed_ 또는 _were washed_ (wash).
3. "How did you fall?" "Somebody _____ (push) me."
4. "How did you fall?" "I _____ (push)."
5. I can't find my bag. Somebody _____ (take) it!
6. My watch is broken. It _____ (repair) at the moment.
7. Who _____ (invent) the camera?
8. When _____ (the camera / invent)?
9. These shirts are clean now. They _____ (wash).
10. These shirts are clean now. I _____ (wash) them.
11. The letter was for me, so why _____ (they / send) it to you?
12. The information will _____ (send) to you as soon as possible.

미래 **Units 26–29**

28 맞는 것을 고르시오.

1. _We're having (B)_ a party next Sunday. I hope you can come.
   A We have **B** We're having **C** We'll have

2. Do you know about Karen? _____ her job. She told me last week.
   A She quits **B** She's going to quit **C** She'll quit

3. There's a program on TV that I want to watch. _____ in five minutes.
   A It starts **B** It's starting **C** It will start

4. The weather is nice now, but I think _____ later.
   A it rains **B** it's raining **C** it will rain

5. "What _____ next weekend?" "Nothing. I have no plans."
   A do you do **B** are you doing **C** will you do

6. "When you see Tina, can you ask her to call me?" "OK, _____ her."
   A I ask **B** I'm going to ask **C** I'll ask

7. "What would you like to drink, tea or coffee?" "_____ tea, please."
   A I have **B** I'm going to have **C** I'll have

8. Don't take that newspaper away. _____ it.
   A I read **B** I'm going to read **C** I'll read

9. Rachel is sick, so _____ to the party tomorrow night.
   A she doesn't come **B** she isn't coming **C** she won't come

10. I want to meet Sarah at the station. What time _____ ?
    A does her train arrive **B** is her train going to arrive **C** is her train arriving

11. "Will you be at home tomorrow night?" "No, _____ ."
    A I go out **B** I'm going out **C** I'll go out

12. "_____ you tomorrow?" "Yes, fine."
    A Do I call **B** Am I going to call **C** Shall I call

29 문장을 완성하시오.

1. *A:* _Did you go_ (you / go) out last night?
   B: No, _____ (I / stay) home.
   A: What _____ (you / do)?
   B: _____ (I / watch) TV.
   A: _____ (you / go) out tomorrow night?
   B: Yes, _____ (I / go) to the movies.
   A: What movie _____ (you / see)?
   B: _____ (I / not / know). _____ (I / not / decide) yet.

2. *A:* Are you visiting here?
   B: Yes, we are.
   A: How long _____ (you / be) here?
   B: _____ (we / arrive) yesterday.
   A: And how long _____ (you / stay)?
   B: Until the end of next week.
   A: And _____ (you / like) it here?
   B: Yes, _____ (we / have) a wonderful time.

3. *A:* Oh, _____ (I / just / remember) – _____ (Karen / call) while you were out.
   B: _____ (she / always / call) when I'm not here.
      _____ (she / leave) a message?
   A: No, but _____ (she / want) you to call her back as soon as possible.
   B: OK, _____ (I / call) her now.
      _____ (you / know) her number?
   A: It's in my address book. _____ (I / get) it for you.

4. *A:* _____ (I / go) out with Chris and Steve tonight.
      _____ (you / want) to come with us?
   B: Yes, where _____ (you / go)?
   A: To the Italian restaurant on North Avenue. _____ (you / ever / eat) there?
   B: Yes, _____ (I / be) there two or three times. In fact I
      _____ (go) there last night, but I'd love to go again!

5. *A:* _____ (I / lose) my glasses again.
      _____ (you / see) them?
   B: _____ (you / wear) them
      when _____ (I / come) in.
   A: Well, _____ (I / not / wear)
      them now, so where are they?
   B: _____ (you / look) in the kitchen?
   A: No, _____ (I / go) and look now.

30   Rachel이 친구 Carolyn에 대하여 말하고 있습니다. 동사를 알맞은 형태로 써 넣어 문장을 완성하시오.

> Carolyn is my best friend. I remember very well the first time
> (1) _____ (we / meet). It was our first day at high
> school, and (2) _____ (we / sit) next to each other in
> the first class. (3) _____ (we / not / know) any other
> students in our class, and so (4) _____ (we / become)
> friends. We found that (5) _____ (we / like) the
> same things, especially music and sports, and so
> (6) _____ (we / spend) a lot of time together.
> (7) _____ (we / finish) school five years ago, but
> (8) _____ (we / meet) as often as we can. For the last
> six months Carolyn (9) _____ (be) in Mexico – right
> now (10) _____ (she / work) in a school as a teaching
> assistant. (11) _____ (she / come) back to the States
> next month, and when (12) _____ (she / come) back,
> (13) _____ (we / have) lots of things to talk about.
> (14) _____ (it / be) really nice to see her again.

Rachel

31   Nick은 친구 Jon과 함께 세계여행을 하고 있습니다. Nick과 부모님 사이에 오간 이메일을 읽고 동사를 알맞은 형태로 써 넣어 문장을 완성하시오.

Nick

> Dear Mom and Dad,
>
> We're in Los Angeles, the first stop on our round-the-world
> trip! (1) _*We arrived*_ (we / arrive) here yesterday, and now
> (2) _____ (we / stay) at a hotel near the
> airport. The flight was twelve hours, but
> (3) _____ (we / enjoy) it.
> (4) _____ (we / watch) some movies and
> (5) _____ (sleep) for a few hours, which
> is unusual for me – usually (6) _____
> (I / not / sleep) well on planes.
>
> Today is a rest day for us and (7) _____
> (we / not / do) anything special, but tomorrow
> (8) _____ (we / go) to Hollywood
> (9) _____ (see) the movie studios.
> (10) _____ (we / not / decide) yet what
> to do after Los Angeles. Jon (11) _____
> (want) to drive up the coast to San Francisco, but I'd prefer
> (12) _____ (go) south to San Diego.
>
> I hope all is well with you – (13) _____
> (I / send) you another e-mail next week.
>
> Love,
>
> Nick

Dear Nick,

Thanks for your e-mail. It's good to hear that (14) _____
(you / have) a good time. We're fine – Ellie and Jo (15) _____
(study) hard for their exams next month. Dad has been busy at work, and last week
(16) _____ (he / have) a lot of important meetings. He's a little
tired – I think (17) _____ (he / need) a good rest.

Keep in touch!
Love,
Mom

한 달 후…

Hi Mom and Dad,

(18) _____ (we / be) in California for a month now.
(19) _____ (we / get) back to Los Angeles yesterday after
(20) _____ (see) many wonderful places. I think the place
(21) _____ (I / like) most was Yosemite National Park – it's
beautiful there and (22) _____ (we / go) biking a lot. The day
before (23) _____ (we / leave), Jon
(24) _____ (have) an accident on his bike. Luckily
(25) _____ (he / not / injure), but the bike
(26) _____ (damage).

(27) _____ (we / change) our travel plans since my last
message: now (28) _____ (we / leave) for Hawaii on Monday
(not Tuesday). (29) _____ (we / stay) there for a week before
(30) _____ (fly) to New Zealand.
(31) _____ (that / be) different, I'm sure!

All the best to Ellie and Jo for their exams.
Love,
Nick

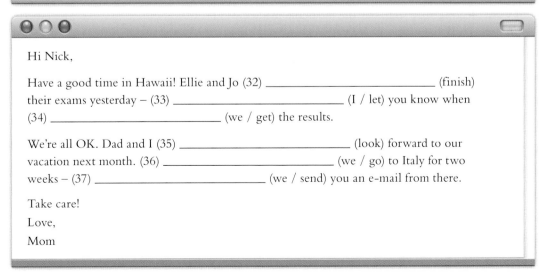

Hi Nick,

Have a good time in Hawaii! Ellie and Jo (32) _____ (finish)
their exams yesterday – (33) _____ (I / let) you know when
(34) _____ (we / get) the results.

We're all OK. Dad and I (35) _____ (look) forward to our
vacation next month. (36) _____ (we / go) to Italy for two
weeks – (37) _____ (we / send) you an e-mail from there.

Take care!
Love,
Mom

32　맞는 것을 고르시오.

1. Don't forget __to turn (B)__ off the light before you go out.
   A turn　　**B** to turn　　**C** turning

2. It's late. I should _____ now.
   A go　　**B** to go　　**C** going

3. I'm sorry, but I don't have time _____ to you now.
   A for talking　　**B** to talk　　**C** talking

4. Gary is always in the kitchen. He enjoys _____ .
   A cook　　**B** to cook　　**C** cooking

5. We've decided _____ away for a few days.
   A go　　**B** to go　　**C** going

6. You're making too much noise. Can you please stop _____ ?
   A shout　　**B** to shout　　**C** shouting

7. Would you like _____ to dinner on Sunday?
   A come　　**B** to come　　**C** coming

8. That bag is too heavy for you. Let me _____ you.
   A help　　**B** to help　　**C** helping

9. There's a swimming pool near my house. I go _____ every day.
   A to swim　　**B** to swimming　　**C** swimming

10. Did you use a dictionary _____ the letter?
    A to translate　　**B** for translating　　**C** for translate

11. I'd love _____ a car like yours.
    A have　　**B** to have　　**C** having

12. Could you _____ me with this bag, please?
    A help　　**B** to help　　**C** helping

13. I don't mind _____ here, but I'd prefer to sit by the window.
    A sit　　**B** to sit　　**C** sitting

14. Do you want _____ you?
    A that I help　　**B** me to help　　**C** me helping

15. I usually read the newspaper before _____ work.
    A start　　**B** to start　　**C** starting

16. I wasn't feeling very well, but the medicine made me _____ better.
    A feel　　**B** to feel　　**C** feeling

17. Shall I call the restaurant _____ a table?
    A for reserve　　**B** for reserving　　**C** to reserve

18. Tom looked at me without _____ anything.
    A say　　**B** saying　　**C** to say

1. Can you pass _the sugar_, please?

2. Do you have _____?
No, I can't drive.

3. Do we have any milk?
Yes, there's some in _____.

4. What do you do?
I'm _____.

5. I don't feel very well. I don't want to go to _____.

6. What did you do last night?
I went to _____.

7. Shall we walk home?
No, let's take _____.

8. Can you play _____?
Yes, but not very well.

9. I'm interested in _____.

10. What's the difference between those cars?
Nothing, they're _____.

34 필요한 곳에 **a/an** 또는 **the**를 써 넣으시오. 필요없는 곳에는 '**—**' 표시를 하시오.

1. Who is ___*the*___ best player on your team?
2. I don't watch ___-___ TV very often.
3. "Is there ___*a*___ bank near here?"   "Yes, at ___*the*___ end of this block."
4. I can't ride _____ horse.
5. _____ sky is very clear tonight.
6. Do you live here, or are you _____ tourist?
7. What did you have for _____ lunch?
8. Who was _____ first president of _____ United States?
9. "What time is it?"   "I don't know. I don't have _____ watch."
10. I'm sorry, but I've forgotten your name. I can never remember _____ names.
11. What time is _____ next train to Boston?
12. Kate never sends _____ e-mails. She prefers to call people.
13. "Where's Sue?"   "She's in _____ backyard."
14. Excuse me, I'm looking for _____ Majestic Hotel. Is it near here?
15. Gary was sick _____ last week, so he didn't go to _____ work.
16. Everest is _____ highest mountain in _____ world.
17. I usually listen to _____ radio while I'm having _____ breakfast.
18. I like _____ sports. My favorite sport is _____ basketball.
19. Julia is _____ doctor. Her husband is _____ art teacher.
20. My apartment is on _____ second floor. Turn left at _____ top of _____ stairs, and it's on _____ right.
21. After _____ dinner, we watched _____ TV.
22. I've been to _____ northern Mexico but not to _____ south.

전치사

Units 104–109, 112

35 전치사(**in/for/by** 등)를 써 넣으시오.

1. Helen is studying math ___*in*___ college.
2. What is the longest river _____ Europe?
3. Is there anything _____ TV tonight?
4. We arrived _____ the hotel after midnight.
5. "Where's Mike?"   "He's _____ vacation."
6. Tom hasn't gotten up yet. He's still _____ bed.
7. Lisa is away. She's been away _____ Monday.
8. The next meeting is _____ April 15.
9. We traveled across Canada _____ train.
10. There's too much sugar _____ my coffee.
11. Kevin lived in Las Vegas _____ six months. He didn't like it very much.
12. Were there a lot of people _____ the party?
13. I don't know any of the people _____ this photo.
14. The train was very slow. It stopped _____ every station.
15. I like this room. I like the pictures _____ the walls.
16. "Did you paint that picture?"   "No, it was given to me _____ a friend of mine."
17. I'm going away _____ a few days. I'll be back _____ Thursday.
18. Silvia has gone _____ Italy. She's _____ Milan right now.
19. Emma quit school _____ sixteen and got a job _____ a bookstore.

학습가이드

어느 단원을 공부해야 할지 잘 모를 경우에는, 이 학습가이드를 활용하십시오.

문제를 읽고 보기 중에서 맞는 답을 고르십시오. 정답이 하나 이상인 문제들도 있습니다.

답을 모르거나 확신이 서지 않는 경우에는 오른쪽에 적힌 단원을 학습하십시오. 해당 단원에 올바른 문장이 들어 있습니다.

학습가이드 정답은 **306쪽**에 있습니다.

정답을 모를 때는 다음 단원을 학습하십시오.

학습
단원

현재

1.1 _____ . Can you close the window, please?　　**1**
   A I cold　　**B** I'm cold　　**C** I have cold　　**D** It has cold

1.2 Tom _____ in politics.　　**1**
   A isn't interested　　**B** not interested　　**C** doesn't interested
   D doesn't interest

1.3 "_____ ?"　"No, she's out."　　**2**
   A Is at home your mother　　**B** Does your mother at home
   C Is your mother at home　　**D** Are your mother at home

1.4 These postcards are nice. _____　　**2**
   A How much are they?　　**B** How many are they?
   C How much they are?　　**D** How much is they?

1.5 Look, there's Sarah. _____ a brown coat.　　**3, 24**
   A She wearing　　**B** She has wearing　　**C** She is wearing
   D She's wearing

1.6 You can turn off the television. _____ it.　　**3, 24**
   A I'm not watch　　**B** I'm not watching　　**C** I not watching
   D I don't watching

1.7 "_____ today?"　"Yes, he is."　　**4, 24**
   A Is working Paul　　**B** Is work Paul　　**C** Is Paul work
   D Is Paul working

1.8 Look, there's Emily! _____　　**4, 24**
   A Where she is going?　　**B** Where she go?　　**C** Where's she going?
   D Where she going?

1.9 The earth _____ around the sun.　　**5, 24**
   A going　　**B** go　　**C** goes　　**D** does go　　**E** is go

1.10 We _____ late on weekends.　　**5, 24, 95**
   A often sleep　　**B** sleep often　　**C** often sleeping　　**D** are often sleep

1.11 We _____ television very often.　　**6, 24**
   A not watch　　**B** doesn't watch　　**C** don't watch　　**D** don't watching
   E watch not

1.12 "_____ on Sundays?"   "No, not usually."

    A Do you work   **B** Are you work   **C** Does you work

    D Do you working   **E** Work you

1.13 I don't understand this sentence. What _____ ?

    A mean this word   **B** means this word   **C** does mean this word

    D does this word mean   **E** this word means

1.14 Please be quiet. _____

    A I working.   **B** I work.   **C** I'm working.   **D** I'm work.

1.15 Tom _____ a shower every morning.

    A takes   **B** taking   **C** is taking   **D** take

1.16 What _____ on weekends?

    A do you usually   **B** are you usually doing   **C** are you usually do

    D do you usually do   **E** you do usually

1.17 Sarah isn't feeling well. _____ a headache.

    A She have   **B** She have got   **C** She has   **D** She's got

1.18 Mr. and Mrs. Harris _____ any children.

    A don't have   **B** doesn't have   **C** no have   **D** haven't got

    E hasn't got

과거

2.1 The weather _____ last week.

    A is nice   **B** was nice   **C** were nice   **D** nice   **E** had nice

2.2 Why _____ late this morning?

    A you was   **B** did you   **C** was you   **D** you were   **E** were you

2.3 Terry _____ in a bank from 2001 to 2008.

    A work   **B** working   **C** works   **D** worked   **E** was work

2.4 Caroline _____ to the movies three times last week.

    A go   **B** went   **C** goes   **D** got   **E** was

2.5 I _____ television yesterday.

    A didn't watch   **B** didn't watched   **C** wasn't watched

    D don't watch   **E** didn't watching

2.6 "How _____ ?"   "I don't know. I didn't see it."

    A happened the accident   **B** did happen the accident

    C does the accident happen   **D** did the accident happen

    E the accident happened

2.7 What _____ at 11:30 yesterday?

    A were you doing   **B** was you doing   **C** you were doing

    D were you do   **E** you was doing

2.8 Jack was reading a book when the phone _____ .

    A ringing   **B** ring   **C** rang   **D** was ringing   **E** was ring

2.9 I saw Lucy and Steve this morning. They _____ at the bus stop.

    A waiting   **B** waited   **C** were waiting   **D** was waiting

    E were waited

2.10 Dave _____ in a factory. Now he works in a supermarket.

    A working   **B** works   **C** work   **D** use to work

    E used to work

현재완료

3.1 "Where's Rebecca?" "_____ to bed."

    A She is gone   **B** She has gone   **C** She goes   **D** She have gone

    E She's gone

3.2 "Are Diane and Paul here?" "No, they _____ ."

    A don't arrive yet   **B** have already arrived   **C** haven't already arrived

    D haven't arrived yet

3.3 My sister _____ by plane.

    A has never travel   **B** has never traveled   **C** is never traveled

    D has never been traveled   **E** have never traveled

3.4 _____ that woman before, but I can't remember where.

    A I see   **B** I seen   **C** I've saw   **D** I've seen   **E** I've seeing

3.5 "How long _____ married?" "Since 1998."

    A you are   **B** you have been   **C** has you been   **D** are you

    E have you been

3.6 "Do you know Lisa?" "Yes, _____ her for a long time."

    A I knew   **B** I've known   **C** I know   **D** I am knowing

3.7 Richard has been in Canada _____ .

    A for six months   **B** since six months   **C** six months ago

    D in six months

3.8 "When did Tom leave?" "_____ ."

    A For ten minutes   **B** Since ten minutes   **C** Ten minutes ago

    D In ten minutes

3.9 We _____ a vacation last year.

    A don't take   **B** haven't taken   **C** hasn't taken   **D** didn't take

    E didn't took

3.10 Where _____ on Sunday afternoon? I couldn't find you.

    A you were   **B** you have been   **C** was you   **D** have you been

    E were you

수동태

4.1 This house _____ 100 years ago.

    A is built   **B** is building   **C** was building   **D** was built   **E** built

22, 24

4.2 We _____ to the party last week.

    A didn't invite   **B** didn't invited   **C** weren't invited

    D wasn't invited   **E** haven't been invited

22, 24

4.3 "Where _____ born?" "In Cairo."

    A you are   **B** you were   **C** was you   **D** are you   **E** were you

22

4.4 My car is at the garage. It _____ .

    A is being repaired   **B** is repairing   **C** have been repaired

    D repaired   **E** repairs

23

4.5 I can't find my keys. I think _____ .

    A they've been stolen   **B** they are stolen   **C** they've stolen

    D they're being stolen

23

동사 형태

5.1 It _____ , so we didn't need an umbrella.

    A wasn't rained   **B** wasn't rain   **C** didn't raining   **D** wasn't raining

24

5.2 Somebody _____ this window.

    A has broke   **B** has broken   **C** has breaked   **D** has break

25

미래

6.1 Andrew _____ tennis tomorrow.

    A is playing   **B** play   **C** plays   **D** is play

26

6.2 _____ out tonight?

    A Are you going   **B** Are you go   **C** Do you go   **D** Go you

    E Do you going

26

6.3 "What time is the concert tonight?" "It _____ at 7:30."

    A is start   **B** is starting   **C** starts   **D** start   **E** starting

26

6.4 What _____ to the wedding next week?

    A are you wearing   **B** are you going to wear   **C** do you wear

    D you are going to wear

27

6.5 I think Kelly _____ her driver's test.

    A passes   **B** will pass   **C** will be pass   **D** will passing

28

6.6 _____ to the movies on Saturday. Do you want to come with us?

    A We go   **B** We'll go   **C** We're going   **D** We will going

26, 28

6.7 "_____ you tomorrow, OK?" "OK, bye."

    A I call   **B** I calling   **C** I'm calling   **D** I'll call

29

6.8 There's a good program on TV tonight. _____ it.

    A I watch   **B** I'll watch   **C** I'm going to watch   **D** I'll watching

27, 29

6.9 It's a nice day. _____ for a walk?

    A Do we go   **B** Shall we go   **C** Should we go   **D** We go

    E Go we

29

조동사, 명령문 등

7.1 _____ to the movies tonight, but I'm not sure.

A I'll go **B** I'm going **C** I may go **D** I might go

7.2 "_____ here?" "Sure."

A Can I sit **B** Do I sit **C** May I sit **D** Can I to sit

7.3 I'm having a party next week, but Paul and Rachel _____ .

A can't come **B** can't to come **C** can't coming **D** couldn't come

7.4 Before Maria came to the United States, she _____ understand much English.

A can **B** can't **C** not **D** couldn't **E** doesn't

7.5 We _____ walk home last night. There were no buses.

A have to **B** had to **C** must **D** must to **E** must have

7.6 You worked 10 hours today. You _____ tired.

A must **B** can **C** must be **D** can be **E** must to be

7.7 It's a good movie. You _____ go and see it.

A should to **B** ought to **C** ought **D** should **E** have

7.8 What time _____ go to the dentist tomorrow?

A you must **B** you have to **C** have you to **D** do you have to

7.9 We _____ wait very long for the bus – it came in a few minutes.

A don't have to **B** hadn't to **C** didn't have to **D** didn't had to
E mustn't

7.10 "_____ some coffee?" "No, thank you."

A Are you liking **B** You like **C** Would you like **D** Do you like

7.11 I don't really want to go out. _____ home.

A I rather stay **B** I'd rather stay **C** I'd rather to stay
D I'd prefer to stay

7.12 Please _____ . Stay here with me.

A don't go **B** you no go **C** go not **D** you don't go

7.13 It's a nice day. _____ out.

A Let's to go **B** Let's go **C** Let's going **D** We go

there와 *it*

8.1 Excuse me, _____ a hotel near here?

A has there **B** is there **C** there is **D** is it

8.2 _____ a lot of accidents on this road. It's very dangerous.

A Have **B** It has **C** There have **D** They are **E** There are

8.3 I was hungry when I got home, but _____ anything to eat.

A there wasn't **B** there weren't **C** it wasn't **D** there hasn't been

8.4 _____ two miles from our house to downtown.

A It's **B** It has **C** There is **D** There are

8.5 _____ true that you're moving to Dallas?

A Is there **B** Is it **C** Is **D** Are you

조동사

9.1 I haven't seen the movie, but my sister _____ .
    A does   **B** is   **C** has seen   **D** has   **E** hasn't

9.2 I don't like hot weather, but Sue _____ .
    A does   **B** doesn't   **C** do   **D** does like   **E** likes

9.3 "Nicole got married last week." "_____ ? Really?"
    A Got she   **B** She got   **C** She did   **D** She has

9.4 You haven't met my mother, _____ ?
    A haven't you   **B** have you   **C** did you   **D** you have
    E you haven't

9.5 Bill doesn't watch TV. He doesn't read newspapers, _____ .
    A too   **B** either   **C** neither   **D** never

9.6 "I'd like to go to Australia." "_____ ."
    A So do I   **B** So am I   **C** So would I   **D** Neither do I
    E So I would

9.7 Sue _____ much on weekends.
    A don't   **B** doesn't   **C** don't do   **D** doesn't do

의문문

10.1 "When _____ ?" "I'm not sure. More than 100 years ago."
    A did the telephone invent   **B** has the telephone invented
    C was invented the telephone   **D** was the telephone invented
    E the telephone was invented

10.2 "I broke my finger last week." "How _____ that?"
    A did you   **B** you did   **C** you did do   **D** did you do

10.3 Why _____ me last night? I was waiting for you to call.
    A didn't you call   **B** you not call   **C** you don't call   **D** you didn't call

10.4 "Who _____ in this house?" "I don't know."
    A lives   **B** does live   **C** does lives   **D** living

10.5 What _____ when you told him the story?
    A said Paul   **B** did Paul say   **C** Paul said   **D** did Paul said

10.6 "Tom's father is in the hospital." "_____ "
    A In which hospital he is?   **B** In which hospital he is in?
    C Which hospital he is in?   **D** Which hospital is he in?

10.7 Did you have a good vacation? _____
    A How was the weather like?   **B** What was the weather like?
    C What the weather was like?   **D** Was the weather like?

10.8 _____ taller – Joe or Gary?
    A Who is   **B** What is   **C** Which is   **D** Who has

10.9 There are four umbrellas here. _____ is yours?
    A What   **B** Who   **C** Which   **D** How   **E** Which one

10.10   How long _____ to cross the Atlantic by ship?   **49**
      A   is it   **B**   does it need   **C**   does it take   **D**   does it want

10.11   I don't remember what _____ at the party.   **50**
      A   Jenny was wearing   **B**   was wearing Jenny   **C**   was Jenny wearing

10.12   "Do you know _____ ?"   "Yes, I think so."   **50**
      A   if Jack is at home   **B**   is Jack at home   **C**   whether Jack is at home
      D   that Jack is at home

간접화법

11.1   I saw Steve a week ago. He said that _____ me, but he didn't.   **51**
      A   he call   **B**   he calls   **C**   he'll call   **D**   he's going to call
      E   he would call

11.2   "Why did Tim go to bed so early?"   "He _____ ."   **51**
      A   said he was tired   **B**   said that he was tired   **C**   said me he was tired
      D   told me he was tired   **E**   told that he was tired

-*ing*와 *to* …

12.1   You shouldn't _____ so hard.   **52**
      A   working   **B**   work   **C**   to work   **D**   worked

12.2   It's late. I _____ now.   **52**
      A   must to go   **B**   have go   **C**   have to going   **D**   have to go

12.3   Tina has decided _____ her car.   **53**
      A   sell   **B**   to sell   **C**   selling   **D**   to selling

12.4   I don't mind _____ early.   **53**
      A   get up   **B**   to get up   **C**   getting up   **D**   to getting up

12.5   Do you like _____ early?   **53**
      A   get up   **B**   to get up   **C**   getting up   **D**   to getting up

12.6   Do you want _____ you some money?   **54**
      A   me lend   **B**   me lending   **C**   me to lend   **D**   that I lend

12.7   He's very funny. He makes _____ .   **54**
      A   me laugh   **B**   me laughing   **C**   me to laugh   **D**   that I laugh

12.8   Paula went to the store _____ some fruit.   **55**
      A   for get   **B**   for to get   **C**   for getting   **D**   to get   **E**   get

go, get, do, make, have

13.1   The water looks nice. I'm going _____ .   **56**
      A   for a swim   **B**   on a swim   **C**   to swimming   **D**   swimming

13.2   I'm sorry your mother is sick. I hope she _____ better soon.   **57**
      A   has   **B**   makes   **C**   gets   **D**   goes

13.3   Kate _____ the car and drove away.   **57**
      A   went into   **B**   went in   **C**   got in   **D**   got into

13.4   "Shall I open the window?"   "No, it's OK. I'll _____ it."   **58**
      A   do   **B**   make   **C**   get   **D**   open

13.5 I'm sorry, I _____ a mistake.
    A did   **B** made   **C** got   **D** had

13.6 _____ enough time to do everything you wanted?
    A Have you   **B** Had you   **C** Do you have   **D** Did you have

대명사와 소유격

14.1 I don't want this book. You can have _____ .
    A it   **B** them   **C** her   **D** him

14.2 Sue and Kevin are going to the movies. Do you want to go with _____ ?
    A her   **B** they   **C** them   **D** him

14.3 I know Donna, but I don't know _____ husband.
    A their   **B** his   **C** she   **D** her

14.4 Hawaii is famous for _____ beaches.
    A his   **B** its   **C** it's   **D** their

14.5 I didn't have an umbrella, so Helen gave me _____ .
    A her   **B** hers   **C** her umbrella   **D** she's

14.6 I went to the movies with a friend of _____ .
    A mine   **B** my   **C** me   **D** I   **E** myself

14.7 We had a good vacation. We enjoyed _____ .
    A us   **B** our   **C** ours   **D** ourself   **E** ourselves

14.8 Kate and Helen are good friends. They know _____ well.
    A each other   **B** them   **C** themselves   **D** theirselves

14.9 Have you met _____ ?
    A the wife of Mr. Black   **B** Mr. Black wife   **C** the wife Mr. Black
    D Mr. Black's wife   **E** the Mr. Black's wife

14.10 Have you seen _____ ?
    A the car of my parents   **B** my parent's car   **C** my parents' car
    D my parents car

*a*와 *the*

15.1 I'm going to buy _____ .
    A hat and umbrella   **B** a hat and a umbrella
    C a hat and an umbrella   **D** an hat and an umbrella

15.2 "What do you do?" "_____ ."
    A I dentist   **B** I'm a dentist   **C** I'm dentist   **D** I do dentist

15.3 I'm going shopping. I need _____ .
    A some new jeans   **B** a new jeans   **C** a new pair of jeans
    D a new pair jeans

15.4 I like the people here. _____ very friendly.
    A She is   **B** They are   **C** They is   **D** It is   **E** He is

15.5 We can't get into the house without _____ .
    A some key   **B** a key   **C** key

15.6 I'd like _____ about hotels in Mexico City.

A some information   **B** some informations   **C** an information

69

15.7 We enjoyed our vacation. _____ was very nice.

A Hotel   **B** A hotel   **C** An hotel   **D** The hotel

70, 71

15.8 The table is in _____ .

A middle of room   **B** middle of the room
C the middle of the room   **D** the middle of room

71

15.9 What did you have for _____ ?

A the breakfast   **B** breakfast   **C** a breakfast

71

15.10 I finish _____ at 5:00 every day.

A the work   **B** work   **C** a work

72

15.11 I'm tired. I'm going _____ .

A in bed   **B** in the bed   **C** to a bed   **D** to the bed   **E** to bed

72

15.12 We don't eat _____ very often.

A the meat   **B** some meat   **C** a meat   **D** meat

73

15.13 _____ is in New York.

A The Times Square   **B** Times Square

74

15.14 My friends are staying at _____ .

A the Regent Hotel   **B** Regent Hotel

74

한정사와 대명사

16.1 "I'm going on vacation next week." "Oh, _____ nice."

A it's   **B** this is   **C** that's

75

16.2 "Is there a bank near here?" "Yes, there's _____ on the corner."

A some   **B** it   **C** one   **D** a one

76

16.3 This cup is dirty. Can I have _____ ?

A clean one   **B** a clean one   **C** clean   **D** a clean

76

16.4 I'm going shopping. I'm going to buy _____ clothes.

A any   **B** some

77

16.5 "Where's your luggage?" "I don't have _____ ."

A one   **B** some   **C** any

77

16.6 Tracey and Jeff _____ .

A have no children   **B** don't have no children
C don't have any children   **D** have any children

78, 79

16.7 "How much money do you have?" "_____ ."

A No   **B** No one   **C** Any   **D** None

78

16.8 There is _____ in the room. It's empty.

A anybody   **B** nobody   **C** anyone   **D** no one

79, 80

16.9 "What did you say?" "_____ ."

A Nothing   **B** Nobody   **C** Anything   **D** Anybody

79, 80

16.10 I'm hungry. I want _____ .
  A something for eat **B** something to eat **C** something for eating

80

16.11 It rained _____ last week.
  A all day **B** all days **C** every days **D** every day

81

16.12 _____ friends.
  A Everybody need **B** Everybody needs **C** Everyone need
  D Everyone needs

81

16.13 _____ children like to play.
  A Most **B** The most **C** Most of **D** The most of

82

16.14 I like _____ those pictures.
  A both **B** both of **C** either **D** either of

83

16.15 I haven't read _____ these books.
  A neither **B** neither of **C** either **D** either of

83

16.16 Do you have _____ friends?
  A a lot of **B** much **C** many **D** much of **E** many of

84

16.17 We like movies, so we go to the movies _____ .
  A a lot of **B** much **C** many **D** a lot

84

16.18 There were _____ people in the theater. It was almost empty.
  A a little **B** few **C** little **D** a few of

85

16.19 They have _____ money, so they're not poor.
  A a little **B** a few **C** few **D** little **E** little of

85

형용사와 부사

17.1 I don't speak any _____ .
  A foreign languages **B** languages foreign **C** languages foreigns

86

17.2 He ate his dinner very _____ .
  A quick **B** quicker **C** quickly

87

17.3 You speak English very _____ .
  A good **B** fluent **C** well **D** slow

87

17.4 Helen wants _____ .
  A a more big car **B** a car more big **C** a car bigger **D** a bigger car

88

17.5 "Do you feel better today?" "No, I feel _____ ."
  A good **B** worse **C** more bad **D** more worse

88

17.6 Athens is older _____ Rome.
  A as **B** than **C** that **D** of

89

17.7 I can run faster _____ .
  A than him **B** that he can **C** than he can **D** as he can **E** as he

89

17.8 Tennis isn't _____ soccer.
  A popular as **B** popular than **C** as popular than
  D so popular that **E** as popular as

90

17.9 The weather today is the same _____ yesterday.

A as   **B** that   **C** than   **D** like

17.10 The Best West Motel is _____ in town.

A the more expensive motel   **B** the most expensive motel
C the motel most expensive   **D** the motel the more expensive
E the motel more expensive

17.11 The movie was very bad. I think it's the _____ movie I've ever seen.

A worse   **B** baddest   **C** most bad   **D** worst   **E** more worse

17.12 Why don't you buy a car? You've got _____ .

A enough money   **B** money enough   **C** enough of money

17.13 Is your English _____ a conversation?

A enough good to have   **B** good enough for have   **C** enough good for
D good enough to have

17.14 I'm _____ out.

A too tired for go   **B** too much tired for going   **C** too tired to go
D too much tired to go

어순

18.1 Sue is interested in the news. She _____ .

A reads every day a newspaper   **B** reads a newspaper every day
C every day reads a newspaper

18.2 _____ coffee in the morning.

A I drink always   **B** Always I drink   **C** I always drink

18.3 _____ during the day.

A They are at home never   **B** They are never at home
C They never are at home   **D** Never they are at home

18.4 "Where's Emma?" "She _____ ."

A isn't here yet   **B** isn't here already   **C** isn't here still

18.5 I locked the door, and I gave _____ .

A Sarah the keys   **B** to Sarah the keys   **C** the keys Sarah
D the keys to Sarah

접속사와 관계대명사

19.1 I can't talk to you now. I'll talk to you later when _____ more time.

A I'll have   **B** I had   **C** I have   **D** I'm going to have

19.2 _____ late tonight, don't wait for me.

A If I'm   **B** If I'll be   **C** When I'm   **D** When I'll be

19.3 I don't know the answer. If I _____ the answer, I'd tell you.

A know   **B** would know   **C** have known   **D** knew

19.4 I like that jacket. _____ it if it wasn't so expensive.

A I buy   **B** I'll buy   **C** I bought   **D** I'd bought   **E** I'd buy

19.5   Emma lives in a house _____ is 100 years old.

     A who   **B** that   **C** which   **D** it   **E** what

19.6   The people _____ work in the office are very friendly.

     A who   **B** that   **C** they   **D** which   **E** what

19.7   Did you find the books _____ ?

     A who you wanted   **B** that you wanted   **C** what you wanted

     D you wanted   **E** you wanted it

19.8   I met _____ can speak six languages.

     A a woman who   **B** a woman which   **C** a woman   **D** a woman she

전치사

20.1   Bye! See you _____ .

     A Friday   **B** at Friday   **C** in Friday   **D** on Friday

20.2   Hurry! The train leaves _____ five minutes.

     A at   **B** on   **C** from   **D** after   **E** in

20.3   "How long will you be away?"   "_____ Monday."

     A On   **B** To   **C** Until   **D** Till   **E** Since

20.4   We played basketball yesterday. We played _____ two hours.

     A in   **B** for   **C** since   **D** during

20.5   I always have breakfast before _____ to work.

     A I go   **B** go   **C** to go   **D** going

20.6   Write your name _____ the top of the page.

     A at   **B** on   **C** in   **D** to

20.7   There are a lot of apples _____ those trees.

     A at   **B** on   **C** in   **D** to

20.8   What's the largest city _____ the world?

     A at   **B** on   **C** in   **D** of

20.9   The office is _____ the second floor.

     A at   **B** on   **C** in   **D** to

20.10   I met a lot of people _____ the party.

     A on   **B** to   **C** in   **D** at

20.11   I want to go _____ Mexico next year.

     A at   **B** on   **C** in   **D** to

20.12   What time did you arrive _____ the hotel?

     A at   **B** on   **C** in   **D** to

20.13   "Where is Don in this picture?"   "Don is _____ Bob."

     A at front of   **B** in the front of   **C** in front of   **D** in front from

20.14   I jumped _____ the wall into the garden.

     A on   **B** through   **C** across   **D** over   **E** above

20.15   Jane isn't at work this week. She's _____ vacation.

     A on   **B** in   **C** for   **D** to   **E** at

20.16 Do you like traveling _____ ?
    A with train   **B** with the train   **C** in train   **D** on train
    E by train

112

20.17 I'm not very good _____ telling stories.
    A on   **B** with   **C** at   **D** in   **E** for

113

20.18 Tom left without _____ goodbye.
    A say   **B** saying   **C** to say   **D** that he said

113

20.19 I have to call _____ tonight.
    A with my parents   **B** to my parents   **C** at my parents   **D** my parents

114

20.20 "Do you like eating in restaurants?"   "Sometimes. It depends
    _____ the restaurant."
    A in   **B** at   **C** of   **D** on   **E** over

114

동사구

21.1 A car stopped and a woman got _____ .
    A off   **B** down   **C** out   **D** out of

115

21.2 It was cold, so I _____ .
    A put on my coat   **B** put my coat on   **C** put the coat on me
    D put me the coat on

116

21.3 I have Rachel's keys. I have to _____ to her.
    A give back   **B** give them back   **C** give back them   **D** give it back

116

해답 (Exercises)

UNIT 1

1.1
2. they're
3. it isn't / it's not
4. that's
5. I'm not
6. you aren't / you're not

1.2
2. 'm/am
3. is
4. are
5. 's/is
6. are
7. is . . . are
8. 'm/am . . . is

1.3
2. I'm / I am
3. He's / He is
4. they're / they are
5. It's / It is
6. You're / You are
7. She's / She is
8. Here's / Here is

1.4
모범답안:
1. My name is Sumi.
2. I'm from Seoul.
3. I'm 25.
4. I'm a cook.
5. My favorite colors are black and white.
6. I'm interested in plants.

1.5
2. 're/are cold.
3. 's/is hot.
4. He's / He is afraid.
5. They're / They are hungry.
6. She's / She is angry.

1.6
2. 's/is windy today.
   또는   isn't / 's not windy today.
3. hands are cold.   또는   hands aren't / are not cold.
4. Brazil is a very big country.
5. Diamonds aren't / are not cheap.
6. Toronto isn't / is not in the United States.
8. I'm / I am hungry.   또는   I'm not / I am not hungry.

9. I'm / I am a good swimmer.
   또는   I'm not / I am not a good swimmer.
10. I'm / I am interested in politics.   또는   I'm not / I am not interested in politics.

UNIT 2

2.1
2. f
3. h
4. c
5. a
6. e
7. b
8. i
9. d

2.2
3. Is your job interesting?
4. Are the stores open today?
5. Where are you from?
6. Are you interested in sports?
7. Is the post office near here?
8. Are your children at school?
9. Why are you late?

2.3
2. Where's / Where is
3. How old are
4. How much are
5. What's / What is
6. Who's / Who is
7. What color are

2.4
2. Are you Australian?
3. How old are you?
4. Are you a teacher?
5. Are you married?
6. Is your wife a lawyer?
7. Where's / Where is she from?
8. What's / What is her name?
9. How old is she?

2.5
2. Yes, I am.   또는   No, I'm not.
3. Yes, it is.   또는   No, it isn't. / No, it's not.
4. Yes, they are.   또는   No, they aren't. / No, they're not.
5. Yes, it is.   또는   No, it isn't. / No, it's not.
6. Yes, I am.   또는   No, I'm not.

UNIT 3

3.1
2. 's/is waiting
3. 're/are playing

4. He's / He is lying
5. They're / They are having
6. She's / She is sitting

3.2
2. 's/is cooking
3. 're/are standing
4. 's/is swimming
5. 're/are staying
6. 's/is taking
7. 're/are building
8. 'm/am leaving

3.3
3. 's/is sitting on the floor.
4. She isn't / She's not reading a book.
5. She isn't / She's not playing the piano.
6. She's / She is laughing.
7. She's / She is wearing a hat.
8. She isn't / She's not writing a letter.

3.4
3. I'm sitting on a chair.   또는   I'm not sitting on a chair.
4. I'm eating.   또는   I'm not eating.
5. It's raining.   또는   It isn't raining. / It's not raining.
6. I'm studying English.
7. I'm listening to music.   또는   I'm not listening to music.
8. The sun is shining.   또는   The sun isn't shining.
9. I'm wearing shoes.   또는   I'm not wearing shoes.
10. I'm not reading a newspaper.

UNIT 4

4.1
2. Are you leaving now?
3. Is it raining?
4. Are you enjoying the movie?
5. Is that clock working?
6. Are you waiting for a bus?

4.2
2. is . . . going?
3. are you eating?
4. are you crying?
5. are they looking at?
6. is he laughing?

4.3

3. Are you listening to me?
4. Where are your friends going?
5. Are your parents watching television?
6. What is Jessica cooking?
7. Why are you looking at me?
8. Is the bus coming?

4.4

2. Yes, I am.   또는   No, I'm not.
3. Yes, I am.   또는   No, I'm not.
4. Yes, it is.   또는   No, it isn't. / No, it's not.
5. Yes, I am.   또는   No, I'm not.
6. Yes, I am.   또는   No, I'm not.

UNIT 5

5.1

2. thinks   5. has
3. flies   6. finishes
4. dances

5.2

2. live   5. They go
3. She eats   6. He sleeps
4. He plays

5.3

2. open   7. costs
3. closes   8. cost
4. teaches   9. boils
5. meet   10. like . . . likes
6. washes

5.4

2. I never go to the movies.
3. Martina always works hard.
4. Children usually like chocolate.
5. Julia always enjoys parties.
6. I often forget people's names.
7. Tim never watches television.
8. We usually have dinner at 6:30.
9. Jenny always wears nice clothes.

5.5

모범답안:
2. I sometimes read in bed.
3. I often get up before 7:00.
4. I never go to work by bus.
5. I always drink coffee in the morning.

UNIT 6

6.1

2. doesn't play the piano very well.
3. don't know my phone number.
4. We don't work very hard.
5. Mike doesn't have a car.
6. You don't do the same thing every day.

6.2

1. doesn't like classical music. like (또는 I don't like)
2. don't like boxing. likes boxing. like (또는 I don't like) boxing.
3. Bill and Rose like horror movies. Carol doesn't like horror movies. I like (또는 I don't like) horror movies.

6.3

모범답안:
2. I never go to the theater.
3. I don't ride a bicycle very often.
4. I never eat in restaurants.
5. I travel by train a lot.

6.4

2. doesn't use
3. don't go
4. doesn't wear
5. don't know
6. doesn't cost
7. don't see

6.5

3. don't know
4. doesn't talk
5. drinks
6. don't believe
7. like
8. doesn't eat

UNIT 7

7.1

2. Do . . . play tennis?
3. Does . . . live near here?
4. Do Tom's friends play tennis? / Do they play tennis?
5. Does your brother speak English? / Does he speak English?
6. Do you do yoga every morning?
7. Does Paul often travel on business? / Does he often travel on business?
8. Do you want to be famous?
9. Does Anna work hard? / Does she work hard?

7.2

3. How often do you watch TV?
4. What do you want for dinner?
5. Do you like football?
6. Does your brother like football?
7. What do you do in your free time?
8. Where does your sister work?
9. Do you ever go to the movies?
10. What does this word mean?
11. Does it often snow here?
12. What time do you usually go to bed?
13. How much does it cost to call Mexico?
14. What do you usually have for breakfast?

7.3

2. Do you enjoy / Do you like
3. do you start
4. Do you work
5. do you get
6. does he do
7. does he teach
8. Does he enjoy / Does he like

7.4

2. Yes, I do.   또는   No, I don't.
3. Yes, I do.   또는   No, I don't.
4. Yes, it does.   또는   No, it doesn't.
5. Yes, I do.   또는   No, I don't.

UNIT 8

8.1

2. No, she isn't. Yes, she does. She's playing the piano.
3. Yes, he does. Yes, he is. He's washing a window.
4. No, they aren't. Yes, they do. They teach.

8.2

2. don't   6. do
3. are   7. does
4. does   8. doesn't
5. 's/is . . . don't

8.3

4. 's/is singing
5. She wants
6. do you read
7. you're / you are sitting
8. I don't / I do not understand
9. I'm / I am going . . . Are you coming
10. does your father finish
11. I'm not / I am not listening
12. He's / He is cooking
13. doesn't usually drive . . . usually walks
14. doesn't like . . . She prefers

UNIT 9

9.1

2. he's got
3. they've got
4. she hasn't got
5. it's got
6. I haven't got

9.2

2. 's got a computer. 또는 has a computer.
3. He hasn't got a dog. 또는 He doesn't have a dog.
4. He hasn't got a cell phone. 또는 He doesn't have a cell phone.
5. He's got a watch. 또는 He has a watch.
6. He's got two brothers and a sister. 또는 He has two brothers and a sister.
7. I've got a computer. / I have a computer. 또는 I haven't got a computer. / I don't have a computer.
8. I've got a dog. / I have a dog. 또는 I haven't got a dog. / I don't have a dog.
9. I've got a bike. / I have a bike. 또는 I haven't got a bike. / I don't have a bike.
10. (모범답안) I've got a brother and a sister.

9.3

3. He has a new job.
4. They don't have much money.
5. Do you have an umbrella?
6. We have a lot of work to do.
7. I don't have your phone number.
8. Does your father have a car?
9. How much money do we have?

9.4

3. has
4. don't
5. got
6. have
7. doesn't

9.5

3. have four wheels.
4. has a lot of friends.
5. don't have a key.
6. has six legs.
7. don't have much time.

UNIT 10

10.1

2. were at the movies.
3. was at the station.
4. Mr. and Mrs. Hall were in/at a restaurant.
5. Ben was at the beach.
6. (모범답안) I was at work.

10.2

2. is . . . was
3. 'm/am
4. was
5. were
6. 're/are
7. Was
8. was
9. are . . . were

10.3

2. wasn't . . . was
3. was . . . were
4. Were . . . was . . . wasn't. 또는 wasn't. . . was.
5. were
6. weren't . . . were

10.4

2. Was your exam difficult?
3. Where were Sue and Chris last week?
4. How much was your new camera?
5. Why were you angry yesterday?
6. Was the weather nice last week?

UNIT 11

11.1

2. opened
3. started . . . ended
4. wanted
5. happened

6. rained
7. enjoyed . . . stayed
8. died

11.2

2. saw
3. played
4. paid
5. visited
6. bought
7. went
8. thought
9. copied
10. knew
11. put
12. spoke

11.3

2. got
3. had
4. left
5. drove
6. got
7. parked
8. walked
9. checked
10. had
11. waited
12. departed
13. arrived
14. took

11.4

2. lost her keys
3. met her friends
4. bought two newspapers.
5. went to the movies.
6. ate an orange.
7. took a shower.
8. came (to see us)

11.5

모범답안:
2. I got up late yesterday.
3. I met some friends at lunchtime.
4. I went to the supermarket.
5. I called a lot of people.
6. I lost my keys.

UNIT 12

12.1

2. didn't work
3. didn't go
4. didn't have
5. didn't do

12.2

2. Did you enjoy the party?
3. Did you have a nice vacation?
4. Did you finish work early?
5. Did you sleep well last night?

12.3

2. got up before 7:00. 또는 didn't get up before 7:00.
3. I took a shower. 또는 I didn't take a shower.
4. I bought a magazine. 또는 I didn't buy a magazine.

5. I ate meat. 또는
   I didn't eat meat.

6. I went to bed before 10:30.
   또는   I didn't go to bed before
   10:30.

12.4

2. did you get to work
3. Did you win
4. did you go
5. did it cost
6. Did you go to bed late
7. Did you have a nice time
8. did it happen / did that happen

12.5

2. bought	6. didn't have
3. Did it rain	7. did you do
4. didn't stay	8. didn't know
5. opened	

UNIT 13

13.1

2. were at the supermarket.
   were buying food.

3. was in his car. He was driving.

4. Tracey was at the station. She
   was waiting for a train.

5. Mr. and Mrs. Hall were in the
   park. They were walking.

6. (모범답안) I was at a café. I
   was having coffee with some
   friends.

13.2

2. was playing tennis.

3. she was reading a/the
   newspaper.

4. she was cooking (lunch).

5. she was having/eating breakfast.

6. she was cleaning the kitchen.

13.3

2. What were you doing
3. Was it raining
4. Why was Sue driving
5. Was Tim wearing

13.4

2. He was carrying a bag.

3. He wasn't going to the dentist.

4. He was eating an ice cream
   cone.

5. He wasn't carrying an
   umbrella.

6. He wasn't going home.

7. He was wearing a hat.

8. He wasn't riding a bicycle.

UNIT 14

14.1

1. happened . . . was painting
   . . . fell

2. arrived . . . got . . . were
   waiting

3. was walking . . . met . . .
   was going . . . was carrying
   . . . stopped

14.2

2. was studying

3. did the mail arrive . . .
   came . . . was having

4. didn't go

5. were you driving . . .
   stopped . . . wasn't driving

6. Did your team win . . .
   didn't play

7. did you break . . . were playing
   . . . hit . . . broke

8. Did you see . . . was wearing

9. were you doing

10. lost . . . did you get . . . climbed

UNIT 15

15.1

2. used to play
3. She used to be
4. They used to live
5. He used to wear glasses.
6. used to be a hotel.

15.2

2. used to play

3.–6.

   She used to go out three or four
   nights a week. / She used to go
   out a lot.

   She used to play a musical
   instrument. / She used to play
   the guitar.

   She used to read a lot. / She
   used to like to read.

   She used to take two or three
   trips a year. / She used to travel
   a lot.

15.3

3. used to have
4. used to be
5. go/commute
6. used to eat
7. watches
8. used to live
9. get
10. did . . . use to play

UNIT 16

16.1

3. you ever been to South Korea?

4. Have you ever lost your
   passport?

5. Have you ever flown in a
   helicopter?

6. Have you ever won a race?

7. Have you ever been to Peru?

8. Have you ever driven a bus?

9. Have you ever broken your leg?

16.2

Helen:

2. 's/has been to South Korea
   once.

3. She's / She has never won a
   race.

4. She's / She has flown in a
   helicopter a few times.

모범답안:

5. 've/have never been to New
   York.

6. I've / I have played tennis
   many times.

7. I've / I have never driven a
   truck.

8. I've / I have been late for work
   a few times.

16.3

2–6.

   's/has done a lot of interesting
   things.

   She's / She has traveled all over
   the world.   또는
   She's / She has been all over
   the world.

   She's / She has been married
   three times.

   She's / She has written 10
   books.

   She's / She has met a lot of
   interesting people.

16.4

3. Have you ever written

4. She's / She has never met

5. they've / they have read

6. I've / I have never been . . .
   my brother has been

7. She's / She has seen . . . I've /
   I have never seen

8. I've / I have traveled

UNIT 17

17.1
3. 've/have been
4. 's/has been
5. 've/have lived 또는 've/have been living
6. 's/has worked 또는 's/has been working
7. 's/has had
8. 've/have been studying

17.2
2. have they been there / in Brazil?
3. have . . . known her/Amy?
4. How long has she been studying Italian?
5. How long has he lived / been living in Seattle?
6. How long have you been a teacher?
7. How long has it been raining?

17.3
2. has lived in South Korea all her life.
3. have been on vacation since Sunday.
4. has been shining all day.
5. has been waiting for 10 minutes.
6. has had a beard since he was 20.

17.4
2. I know
3. I've known
4. have you been waiting
5. works
6. She has been reading
7. have you lived
8. I've had
9. is . . . He has been

UNIT 18

18.1
3. for   6. for
4. since   7. for
5. since   8. for . . . since

18.2
모범답안:
2. A year ago.
3. A few weeks ago.
4. Two hours ago.
5. Six months ago.

18.3
3. for 20 years.
4. 20 years ago.
5. an hour ago.
6. a few days ago.
7. for six months.
8. for a long time

18.4
2. been here since Tuesday.
3. raining for an hour.
4. known Sue since 2002.
5. been married for six months.
6. been studying medicine (at the university) for three years.
7. played / been playing the piano since he was seven years old.

18.5
모범답안:
2. I've been to New York three times.
3. I've been studying English for six months.
4. I've known Chris for a long time.
5. I've had a headache since I got up this morning.

UNIT 19

19.1
2. 's/has closed the door
3. 've/have gone to bed
4. 's/has stopped raining
5. 's/has taken a shower
6. picture has fallen down

19.2
2. I've / I have written them a letter.
3. She's / She has broken her arm.
4. They've / They have moved to Seattle.
5. I've / I have made a big mistake.
6. I've / I have lost my wallet. Have you seen it anywhere?
7. Have you heard? Mark has gotten married.
8. Brian took my bike again without asking.
9. Did you tell your friends the good news?
10. We didn't / did not pay the electric bill.

UNIT 20

20.1
2. 's/has just gotten up.
3. 've/have just bought a car.
4. has just started.

20.2
2. 've/have already seen
3. 've/have already called him/ Tom.
4. 's/has already left/gone to work.
5. 've/have already read it.
6. 's/has already started (it).

20.3
2. Have you told your father about the accident yet?
3. I've / I have just eaten a big dinner, so I'm not hungry.
4. Jenny can watch TV because she's / she has already done her homework.
5. You can't go to bed – you haven't brushed your teeth yet.
6. You can't talk to Pete because he's / he has just gone home.
7. Nicole has just gotten out of the hospital, so she can't go to work.
9. The mail carrier didn't come yet.
10. I just spoke to your sister.
11. Did Mario buy a new computer yet?
12. Ted and Alice didn't tell anyone they're getting married yet.
13. We already did our packing for our trip.
14. I just swam a mile.

20.4
2. Have . . . met your new neighbors yet?
3. Have you paid your phone bill yet?
4. Has Tom/he sold his car yet?

UNIT 21

21.1
2. started (it)
3. arrived
4. she went out
5. I wore it

21.2
3. I finished
4. *OK*

5. did you finish
6. *OK*
7. died
8. were you / did you go

21.3
3. played
4. did you go
5. Have you ever met
6. wasn't / was not
7. 's/has visited
8. turned
9. lived
10. haven't / have not been

21.4
1. Did you have
   was
2. 's/has won
   Have you seen
   saw
3. 's/has had . . . was . . .
   worked . . . didn't enjoy
4. 've/have seen . . . 've/have
   never spoken . . . Have you
   ever spoken
   met

UNIT 22

22.1
3. is made from sand.
4. Stamps are sold in a post office.
5. This word isn't / is not used
   very often.
6. Are we allowed to park here?
7. How is this word pronounced?
9. was painted last month.
10. My phone was stolen a few days
    ago.
11. Three people were injured in
    the accident.
12. When was this bridge built?
13. I wasn't / was not woken up by
    the noise.
14. How were these windows
    broken?
15. Were you invited to Jon's party
    last week?

22.2
2. Soccer is played in most . . .
3. Why was the letter sent to . . . ?
4. . . . where cars are repaired.
5. Where were you born?
6. How many languages are
   spoken . . . ?
7. . . . but nothing was stolen.
8. When was the bicycle invented?

22.3
3. is made
4. were damaged
5. was given
6. are shown
7. were invited
8. was made
9. was stolen . . . was found

22.4
2. was born in São Paulo.
3. parents were born in Rio de
   Janeiro.
4. was born in . . .
5. My mother was born in . . .

UNIT 23

23.1
2. is being built.
3. are being cleaned/washed.
4. is being cut.

23.2
3. has been broken.
4. is being repaired.
5. The car has been damaged.
6. The houses are being
   torn down.
7. The trees have been cut down.
8. They have been invited to
   a party.

23.3
3. has been repaired / was
   repaired
4. was repaired
5. are made
6. were they built
7. Is the computer being used
   (또는 Is anybody using the
   computer)
8. are they called
9. were stolen
10. was damaged . . . hasn't / has
    not been repaired

UNIT 24

24.1
3. are   7. do
4. Does   8. Is
5. Do   9. does
6. Is   10. Are

24.2
2. don't
3. 'm/am not
4. isn't
5. don't

6. doesn't
7. 'm/am not
8. 're not / aren't

24.3
2. Did   7. were
3. were   8. Has
4. was   9. did
5. Has   10. have
6. did

24.4
2. was   6. 've/have
3. Have   7. is
4. are   8. was
5. were   9. has

24.5
3. eaten   8. understand
4. enjoying   9. listening
5. damaged   10. pronounced
6. use   11. open
7. gone

UNIT 25

25.1
3. said   10. happened
4. brought   11. heard
5. paid   12. put
6. enjoyed   13. caught
7. bought   14. watched
8. sat   15. understood
9. left

25.2
2. began   begun
3. ate   eaten
4. drank   drunk
5. drove   driven
6. spoke   spoken
7. wrote   written
8. came   come
9. knew   known
10. took   taken
11. went   gone
12. gave   given
13. threw   thrown
14. got   gotten

25.3
3. slept   10. built
4. saw   11. learned
5. rained   12. ridden
6. lost . . . seen 13. known
7. stolen   14. fell . . . hurt
8. went   15. ran . . . run
9. finished

25.4

2. told
3. won
4. met
5. woken up
6. swam
7. thought
8. spoken
9. cost
10. driven
11. sold
12. flew

UNIT 26

26.1

2. is going
3. is meeting Dave.
4. Karen is having
5. Tom and Sue are going to a party.

26.2

2. Are you working next week?
3. What are you doing tomorrow night?
4. What time are your friends coming?
5. When is Liz going on vacation?

26.3

모범답안:

3. I'm going away this weekend.
4. I'm playing basketball tomorrow.
5. I'm meeting a friend tonight.
6. I'm going to the movies on Thursday night.

26.4

3. Karen is getting
4. are going . . . are they going
5. ends
6. I'm not going
7. I'm going . . . We're meeting
8. are you getting . . . leaves
9. does the movie begin
10. are you doing . . . I'm working

UNIT 27

27.1

2. 'm going to take a bath.
3. 'm going to buy a car.
4. 're going to play soccer.

27.2

3. 'm/am going to walk
4. 's/is going to stay
5. 'm/am going to eat
6. 're/are going to give
7. 's/is going to lie down
8. Are . . . going to watch
9. is . . . going to do

27.3

2. is going to fall (down).
3. is going to turn (left).
4. 's/is going to kick the ball.

27.4

모범답안:

1. I'm going to call Maria tonight.
2. I'm going to get up early tomorrow.
3. I'm going to buy some shoes tomorrow.

UNIT 28

28.1

2. she'll be
3. she was
4. she'll be
5. she's
6. she was
7. she'll be

28.2

모범답안:

2. I'll be at home.
3. I'll probably be in bed.
4. I'll be at work.
5. I don't know where I'll be.

28.3

2. 'll/will
3. won't
4. won't
5. 'll/will
6. 'll/will
7. won't

28.4

3. think we'll win the game.
4. I don't think I'll be here tomorrow.
5. I think Sue will like her present.
6. I don't think they'll get married.
7. I don't think you'll like the movie.

28.5

2. are you doing
3. They're leaving
4. will lend
5. I'm going
6. will call
7. He's working
8. won't take
9. are coming

UNIT 29

29.1

2. I'll send
3. I'll eat
4. I'll sit
5. I'll do
6. I'll stay
7. I'll show

29.2

2. think I'll have
3. I don't think I'll play
4. I think I'll buy
5. I don't think I'll buy

29.3

2. I'll do
3. I watch
4. I'll go
5. is going to buy
6. I'll give
7. Are you doing . . . I'm going
8. I'm working
9. I'll buy

29.4

2. g
3. b
4. e
5. i
6. a
7. h
8. c
9. f

UNIT 30

30.1

2. might see you tomorrow.
3. Sarah might forget to call.
4. It might snow today.
5. I might be late tonight.
6. Mark might not be here next week.
7. I might not have time to go out.

30.2

2. might take a trip.
3. I might see her on Monday.
4. I might have fish.
5. I might take a taxi.
6. I might buy/get a new car.

30.3

3. might get up early.
4. He isn't / He's not working tomorrow.
5. He might be at home tomorrow morning.
6. He might watch television.
7. He's going out in the afternoon.
8. He might go shopping.

30.4

모범답안:

1. I might read a newspaper.
2. I might go out with some friends at night.
3. I might have an egg for breakfast.

UNIT 31

31.1
2. Can you ski?
3. Can you play chess?
4. Can you run 10 kilometers?
5. Can you drive (a car)?
6. Can you ride (a horse)?

모범답안:
7. I can/can't swim.
8. I can/can't ski.
9. I can/can't play chess.
10. I can/can't run 10 kilometers.
11. I can/can't drive (a car).
12. I can/can't ride (a horse).

31.2
2. can see
3. can't hear
4. can't find
5. can speak

31.3
2. couldn't eat
3. can't decide
4. couldn't find
5. can't go
6. couldn't go

31.4
2. Can/Could you pass the salt (please)?
3. Can/Could you turn down the radio (please)?
4. Can/Could I have your phone number (please)?
5. Can/Could I look at your newspaper (please)? 또는 Can/Could I have a look at your newspaper (please)?
6. Can/Could I use your pen (please)?

UNIT 32

32.1
2. must be hungry
3. must be good
4. must be very happy
5. must be for you
6. must be in the kitchen

32.2
2. must like
3. must have
4. must drink
5. must work

32.3
3. must not
4. must
5. must not
6. must not
7. must

32.4
2. must know
3. must wear
4. must get
5. must take
6. must be

32.5
3. must
4. had to
5. mustn't
6. must
7. mustn't
8. had to

UNIT 33

33.1
2. You should go
3. You should eat
4. you should visit
5. you should wear
6. You should read

33.2
2. shouldn't eat so much.
3. She shouldn't work so
4. He shouldn't drive so fast.

33.3
2. I should learn (to drive)?
3. Do you think I should get another job?
4. Do you think I should invite Gary (to the party)?

33.4
3. I think you should sell it.
4. I think she should take a trip.
5. I don't think they should get married.
6. I don't think you should go to work.
7. I think he should go to the doctor.
8. I don't think we should stay there.

33.5
모범답안:
2. I think everybody should have enough food.
3. I think people should drive more carefully.

4. I don't think the police should carry guns.
5. I think I should get more exercise.

UNIT 34

34.1
2. have to take
3. has to read
4. have to speak
5. has to travel
6. have to hit

34.2
2. have to go
3. had to buy
4. have to change
5. had to answer
6. have to wake
7. have to take

34.3
2. did he have to wait
3. does she have to go
4. did you have to pay
5. do you have to do
6. did they have to leave early
7. does he have to go to Moscow

34.4
2. doesn't have to wait.
3. didn't have to get up early.
4. doesn't have to work (so) hard.
5. don't have to leave now.
6. didn't have to tell me something I already know

34.5
모범답안:
2. I have to go to work every day.
3. I had to go to the dentist yesterday.
4. I have to go shopping tomorrow.
5. I had to take the bus to work last week.
6. I had to go to bed at 9:00 when I was younger.

UNIT 35

35.1
2. Would you like an apple?
3. Would you like some coffee? / a cup of coffee?
4. Would you like some cheese? / a piece of cheese?
5. Would you like a sandwich?
6. Would you like some cake? / a piece of cake?

35.2

2. Would you like to play tennis tomorrow?
3. Would you like to come to a concert next week?
4. Would you like to borrow my umbrella?

35.3

2. Do you like
3. Would you like
4. would you like
5. Would you like
6. I like
7. would you like
8. Would you like
9. Do you like
10. I'd like
11. I'd like
12. do you like

UNIT 36

36.1

2. 'd rather read
3. I'd rather have
4. I'd rather wait

36.2

2. would you rather have/eat dinner
3. would you rather have/drink
4. would you rather watch
5. would you rather call him

36.3

2. take
3. to go
4. get/have/find
5. carry/do
6. see / call / talk to / speak to . . . to send / to write

36.4

2. I'd rather be a journalist / a school teacher.
3. I'd rather live in a big city / in a small town.
4. I'd rather have a small house / a big house.
5. I'd rather study electronics/ philosophy.
6. I'd rather watch a soccer game / a movie.

UNIT 37

37.1

3. Don't buy
4. Smile

5. Don't sit
6. Have
7. Don't forget
8. Sleep
9. Be . . . Don't drop

37.2

2. let's take the bus
3. let's watch TV
4. let's go to a restaurant
5. let's wait a little

37.3

3. No, let's not go out.
4. No, don't close the window.
5. No, don't call me (tonight).
6. No, let's not wait for Andy.
7. No, don't turn on the light.
8. No, let's not take a taxi.

UNIT 38

38.1

3. There's / There is a hospital.
4. There isn't a swimming pool.
5. There are two movie theaters.
6. There isn't a university.
7. There aren't any big hotels.

38.2

모범답안:

3. There is a university in . . .
4. There are a lot of big shops.
5. There isn't an airport.
6. There aren't many factories.

38.3

2. There's / There is
3. is there
4. There are
5. are there
6. There isn't
7. Is there
8. Are there
9. There's / There is . . . There aren't

38.4

2.–6.

There are eight planets in the solar system.
There are five players on a basketball team.
There are twenty-six letters in the English alphabet.
There are thirty days in September.
There are fifty states in the United States.

38.5

2. It's
3. There's
4. There's . . . Is it
5. Is there . . . there's
6. It's
7. Is there

UNIT 39

39.1

2. There was a carpet
3. There were three pictures
4. There was a small table
5. There were some flowers
6. There were some books
7. There was an armchair
8. There was a sofa

39.2

3. There was
4. Was there
5. there weren't
6. There wasn't
7. Were there
8. There wasn't
9. There was
10. there weren't

39.3

2. There are
3. There was
4. There's / There is
5. There's been / There has been 또는 There was
6. there was
7. there will be
8. there were . . . there are
9. There have been
10. there will be 또는 there are

UNIT 40

40.1

2. It's cold.
3. It's windy.
4. It's sunny/clear. 또는 It's a nice day.
5. It's snowing.
6. It's cloudy.

40.2

2. It's / It is
3. Is it
4. is it . . . it's / it is
5. It's / It is
6. Is it
7. is it

8. It's / It is

9. It's / It is

40.3

2. far is it from the hotel to the beach?

3. How far is it from New York to Washington?

4. How far is it from your house to the airport?

40.4

3. It

4. It . . . It

5. There

6. it

7. It . . . there

8. It

40.5

2. It's nice to see you again

3. It's impossible to work in this office

4. It's easy to make friends

5. It's interesting to visit different places

6. It's dangerous to go out alone

UNIT 41

41.1

2. is   5. will

3. can   6. was

4. has

41.2

2. 'm not   5. isn't

3. weren't   6. hasn't

4. haven't

41.3

3. doesn't   6. does

4. do   7. don't

5. did   8. didn't

41.4

모범답안:

2. I like sports, but my sister doesn't.

3. I don't eat meat, but Jenny does.

4. I'm American, but my husband isn't.

5. I haven't been to Japan, but Jenny has.

41.5

2. wasn't   7. has

3. is   8. do

4. does   9. hasn't

5. can't   10. will

6. did   11. might

41.6

2. Yes, I do.   또는   No, I don't.

3. Yes, I do.   또는   No, I don't.

4. Yes, it is.   또는   No, it isn't.

5. Yes, I am.   또는   No, I'm not.

6. Yes, I do.   또는   No, I don't.

7. Yes, I will.   또는   No, I won't.

8. Yes, I have.   또는   No, I haven't.

9. Yes, I did.   또는   No, I didn't.

10. Yes, I was.   또는   No, I wasn't.

UNIT 42

42.1

2. You do?   5. I do?

3. You didn't?   6. She did?

4. She doesn't?

42.2

3. You have?   8. You aren't?

4. She can't?   9. You did?

5. You were?   10. She does?

6. You didn't?   11. You won't?

7. There is?   12. It isn't?

42.3

2. aren't they   5. don't you

3. wasn't she   6. doesn't he

4. haven't you   7. won't you

42.4

2. are you   6. didn't she

3. isn't she   7. was it

4. can't you   8. doesn't she

5. do you   9. will you

UNIT 43

43.1

2. either   5. either

3. too   6. either

4. too   7. too

43.2

2. So am I.

3. So have I.

4. So do I.

5. So will I.

6. So was I.

7. Neither can I.

8. Neither did I.

9. Neither have I.

10. Neither am I.

11. Neither do I.

43.3

1. So am I.

2. So can I.   또는   I can't.

3. Neither am I.   또는   I am.

4. So do I.   또는   I don't.

5. Neither do I.   또는   I do.

6. So did I.   또는   I didn't.

7. Neither have I. 또는   I have.

8. Neither do I.   또는   I do.

9. So am I.   또는   I'm not.

10. Neither was I. 또는   I was.

11. Neither did I. 또는   I did.

12. So do I.   또는   I don't.

UNIT 44

44.1

2. They aren't / They're not married.

3. I haven't had dinner.

4. It isn't cold today.

5. We won't be late.

6. You shouldn't go.

44.2

2. I don't like cheese.

3. They didn't understand.

4. He doesn't live here.

5. Don't go away!

6. I didn't do the dishes.

44.3

2. They haven't arrived.

3. I didn't go to the bank.

4. He doesn't speak Japanese.

5. We weren't angry.

6. He won't be happy.

7. Don't call me tonight.

8. It didn't rain yesterday.

9. I couldn't hear them.

10. I don't believe you.

44.4

2. 'm not / am not

3. can't

4. doesn't

5. isn't / 's not

6. don't . . . haven't

7. Don't

8. didn't

9. haven't

10. won't

11. didn't

12. weren't

13. hasn't

14. shouldn't

44.5

3. He wasn't born in Los Angeles.

4. He doesn't like Los Angeles.

5. He'd like to live someplace else.

6. He can drive.
7. He hasn't traveled abroad.
8. He doesn't read the newspaper.
9. He isn't interested in politics.
10. He usually watches TV at night.
11. He didn't watch TV last night.
12. He went out last night.

UNIT 45

45.1
3. Were you late this morning?
4. Has Kate seen that movie?
5. Will you be here tomorrow?
6. Is Paul going out tonight?
7. Do you like your job?
8. Does Nicole live near here?
9. Did you enjoy the movie?
10. Did you have a good vacation?

45.2
2. Do you use . . . a lot?
3. Did you use it yesterday?
4. Do you enjoy driving?
5. Are you a good driver?
6. Have you ever had an accident?

45.3
3. What are the children doing?
4. How is cheese made?
5. Is your sister coming to the party?
6. Why don't you tell the truth?
7. Have your guests arrived yet?
8. What time does your plane leave?
9. Why didn't Jenny go to work?
10. Was your car damaged in the accident?

45.4
3. are you reading?
4. did she go to bed?
5. are they going (on vacation)?
6. did you see him?
7. can't you come (to the party)?
8. has she moved?
9. (money) do you need?
10. doesn't she like you?
11. does it rain?
12. did you do it? / the shopping?

UNIT 46

46.1
2. fell off the shelf?
3. Who wants to see

4. Who took your umbrella? / Who took it?
5. What made you sick?
6. Who's / Who is coming?

46.2
3. Who did you call?
4. What happened last night?
5. Who knows the answer?
6. Who did the dishes?
7. What did Jane/she do?
8. What woke you up?
9. Who saw the accident?
10. Who did you see?
11. Who has your pen / it?
12. What does this word / it mean?

46.3
2. called you?
   did she want?
3. Who did you ask? What did he say?
4. Who got married? Who told you?
5. Who did you meet? What did she tell you?
6. Who won? What did you do (after the game)?
7. Who gave you the book? What did Catherine give you?

UNIT 47

47.1
2. are . . . looking for?
3. Who did you go to the movies with?
4. What/Who was the movie about?
5. Who did you give the money to?
6. Who was the book written by?

47.2
2. are they looking at?
3. is he going to?
4. are they talking about?
5. is she listening to?
6. are they waiting for?

47.3
2. Which hotel did . . . stay at?
3. Which team does he belong to / play for?
4. Which school did you go to?

47.4
2. What is the food like?
3. What are the people like?
4. What is the weather like?

47.5
2. What was the movie like?
3. What were the classes like?
4. What was the hotel like?

UNIT 48

48.1
3. color is it?
4. What time did you
5. What type of music do you like?
6. What kind of car do you want (to buy)?

48.2
2. Which coat
3. Which movie/film
4. Which bus

48.3
3. Which   7. Which
4. What   8. Who
5. What   9. What
6. Which   10. Which

48.4
2. How far
3. How old
4. How often
5. How deep
6. How long

48.5
2. How heavy is this box?
3. How old are you?
4. How much did you spend?
5. How often do you watch TV?
6. How far is it from New York to Los Angeles?

UNIT 49

49.1
2. How long does it take to get from Houston to Mexico City by car?
3. How long does it take to get from Tokyo to Kyoto by train?
4. How long does it take to get from JFK Airport to Manhattan by bus?

49.2

모범답안:

2. It takes . . . hours to fly from . . . to Australia.
3. It takes . . . years to become a doctor in Korea.
4. It takes . . . to walk from my home to the nearest supermarket.
5. It takes . . . to get from my house to the nearest airport.

49.3

2. How long did it take you to walk to the station?
3. How long did it take him/Tom to paint the bathroom?
4. How long did it take you to learn to ski?
5. How long did it take them to repair the computer?

49.4

2. It took us 20 minutes to walk/get home.
3. It took me six months to learn to drive.
4. It took Mark/him three hours to drive/get to Houston.
5. It took Lisa/her a long time to find/get a job.
6. It took me . . . to . . .

UNIT 50

50.1

2. where she/Sue is.
3. I don't know how old it is.
4. I don't know when he'll / Paul will be here.
5. I don't know why he was angry.
6. I don't know how long she/Donna has lived here.

50.2

2. where she/Susan works
3. what he/Peter said
4. why he went home early
5. what time the meeting begins
6. how the accident happened

50.3

2. are you
3. they are
4. the museum is
5. do you want
6. elephants eat
7. it is

50.4

2. if/whether they are married?
3. Do you know if/whether Sue knows Bill?
4. Do you know if/whether Gary will be here tomorrow?
5. Do you know if/whether he passed his exam?

50.5

2. you know where Paula is?
3. Do you know if/whether she is / she's working today?
4. Do you know what time she starts work?
5. Do you know if/whether the banks are open tomorrow?
6. Do you know where Sarah and Tim live?
7. Do you know if/whether they went to Jane's party?

50.6

모범답안:

2. Do you know what time the bus leaves?
3. Excuse me, can you tell me where the station is?
4. I don't know what I'm going to do tonight.
5. Do you know if there's a restaurant near here?
6. Do you know how much it costs to rent a car?

UNIT 51

51.1

2. She said (that) she was very busy.
3. She said (that) she couldn't go to the party.
4. He said (that) he had to go out.
5. He said (that) he was learning Russian.
6. She said (that) she didn't feel very well.
7. They said (that) they'd / they would be home late.
8. She said (that) she'd / she had just gotten back from vacation.
9. She said (that) she was going to buy a new computer.
10. They said (that) they didn't have a key.

51.2

2. (that) she wasn't hungry
3. (that) he needed it

4. (that) she didn't want to go
5. (that) I could have it
6. (that) he'd / he would send me a postcard
7. (that) he'd / he had gone home
8. (that) he wanted to watch TV
9. (that) she was going to the movies

51.3

3.	said	7.	said
4.	told	8.	told
5.	tell	9.	tell
6.	say	10.	say

UNIT 52

52.1

3. call
4. call Paul
5. to call Paul
6. to call Paul
7. call Paul
8. to call Paul
9. call Paul
10. call Paul

52.2

3. get
4. going
5. watch
6. flying
7. listening
8. eat
9. waiting
10. wear
11. doing . . . staying

52.3

4. to go
5. rain
6. to leave
7. help
8. studying
9. to go
10. wearing
11. to stay
12. taking
13. to have
14. hear
15. go
16. listening
17. to make
18. to be . . . take
19. use

UNIT 53

53.1
3. to see
4. to swim
5. cleaning
6. to ask
7. visiting
8. going
9. to be
10. waiting
11. to do
12. to speak
13. to go
14. crying / to cry
15. to work . . . talking

53.2
2. to help
3. to see
4. reading
5. to lose
6. to send
7. raining
8. to go
9. watching / to watch
10. to wait

53.3
2. going / to go to museums
3. to go
4. writing / to write e-mails
5. to go (there)
6. traveling by train
7. walking

53.4
모범답안:
1. I enjoy cooking.
2. I don't like driving / to drive.
3. If it's a nice day tomorrow, I'd like to have a picnic by the lake.
4. When I'm on vacation, I like to do / doing very little.
5. I don't mind traveling alone, but I prefer to travel with somebody.
6. I wouldn't like to live in a big city.

UNIT 54

54.1
2. you to listen carefully.
3. want you to be angry.
4. want me to wait for you?
5. I don't want you to call me tonight.
6. I want you to meet Sarah.

54.2
2. me to turn left after the bridge.
3. him to go to the doctor.
4. me to help her.
5. him to come back in 10 minutes.
6. me use his phone.
7. her not to call before 8:00.
8. her to play the piano.

54.3
2. to repeat
3. wait
4. to arrive
5. to get
6. go
7. borrow
8. to tell
9. to make/get
10. think

UNIT 55

55.1
2.–4.
   to a coffee shop to meet a friend.
   I went to the drugstore to get some medicine.
   I went to the supermarket to buy some food.

55.2
2. to read the newspaper
3. to open this door
4. to get some fresh air
5. to wake him up
6. to see who it was

55.3
모범답안:
2. I don't have time to talk to you now.
3. I called Ann to tell her about the party.
4. I'm going out to do some shopping.
5. I borrowed some money to buy a car.

55.4
2. to	7. to
3. to	8. to
4. for	9. for
5. to	10. for
6. for	11. to . . . for

55.5
2. for the movie to begin
3. for it to arrive
4. for you to tell me

UNIT 56

56.1
3. to
4. to
5. – (전치사 필요없음)
6. for
7. to
8. on . . . to
9. for
10. on
11. to
12. – (전치사 필요없음)
13. on
14. for
15. on

56.2
2. went fishing
3. goes swimming
4. going skiing
5. go shopping
6. went jogging/running

56.3
2. to college
3. shopping
4. to bed
5. home
6. skiing
7. riding
8. for a walk
9. on vacation . . . to Hawaii

UNIT 57

57.1
2. get your jacket
3. get a doctor
4. get another one
5. gets the job
6. get some milk
7. get a ticket
8. gets a good salary
9. get a lot of rain
10. get a new computer

57.2
2. getting dark
3. getting married
4. getting ready
5. getting late

57.3

2. get wet
3. got married
4. gets angry
5. got lost
6. get old
7. got better

57.4

2. got to New York at 12:00.
3. I left the party at 11:15 and got home at midnight.
4. (모범답안) I left home at 8:30 and got to the airport at 10:00.

57.5

2. got off
3. got out of
4. got on

UNIT 58

58.1

2.	do	7.	done
3.	make	8.	make
4.	made	9.	making
5.	did	10.	do
6.	do	11.	doing

58.2

2. 're/are doing (their) homework.
3. 's/is doing the shopping   또는 's/is shopping.
4. They're / They are doing (their) laundry.
5. She's / She is making a phone call.
6. He's / He is making the/his bed.
7. She's / She is doing/washing the dishes.
8. He's / He is making a (shopping) list.
9. They're / They are making a movie.
10. He's / He is taking a picture/ photograph.

58.3

2.	make	8.	make
3.	do	9.	do
4.	done	10.	making
5.	made	11.	made
6.	did	12.	make . . . do
7.	do		

UNIT 59

59.1

3. He doesn't have / hasn't got
4. Gary had
5. Do you have / Have you got
6. we didn't have
7. She doesn't have / hasn't got
8. Did you have

59.2

2. 's/is having a cup of tea.
3. 's/is having breakfast.
4. 're/are having fun.
5. They're / They are having dinner.
6. They're / They are having an argument.

59.3

3. Have a good/great trip!
4. Did you have a nice/good weekend?
5. Did you have a nice/good vacation?
6. Have a great/good time!   또는 Have fun!
7. Are you going to have a (birthday) party?

59.4

2. have something to eat
3. had a glass of water
4. had a bad dream
5. had an accident
6. have a baby

UNIT 60

60.1

2.	him	5.	him
3.	them	6.	them
4.	her	7.	her

60.2

2. I . . . them
3. he . . . her
4. they . . . us
5. we . . . him
6. she . . . them
7. they . . . me
8. she . . . you

60.3

2. him
3. like it
4. you like it
5. don't like her
6. Do you like them

60.4

2.	him	8.	them
3.	them	9.	me
4.	they	10.	her
5.	us	11.	them
6.	it	12.	he . . . it
7.	She		

60.5

2. it to him
3. give them to her
4. give it to me
5. give it to them
6. give them to us

UNIT 61

61.1

2. her
3. our hands
4. his hands
5. their hands
6. your hands

61.2

2. their
3. our
4. with her
5. live with my
6. lives with his parents.
7. with your parents
8. live with their parents.

61.3

2.	their	6.	their
3.	his	7.	her
4.	his	8.	their
5.	her		

61.4

2.	his	8.	her
3.	Their	9.	their
4.	our	10.	my
5.	her	11.	Its
6.	my	12.	His . . . his
7.	your		

61.5

2. my key
3. Her husband
4. your coat
5. their homework
6. his name
7. Our house

UNIT 62

62.1
2. mine
3. ours
4. hers
5. theirs
6. yours
7. mine
8. his

62.2
2. yours
3. my . . . Mine
4. Yours . . . mine
5. her
6. My . . . hers
7. their
8. Ours

62.3
3. friend of hers
4. friends of ours
5. friend of mine
6. friend of his
7. friends of yours

62.4
2. Whose camera
   hers.
3. Whose gloves are
   're/are mine.
4. Whose hat is this?
   It's his.
5. Whose money is this?
   It's yours.
6. Whose books are these?
   They're / They are ours.

UNIT 63

63.1
2. her . . . her name.
3. know them . . . can't remember
   their
4. know you . . . I can't remember
   your name.

63.2
2. him
3. them at their
4. with me at my
5. with her at her
6. to stay with you at your

63.3
2. hers
3. him mine
4. our . . . us theirs
5. her . . . her his
6. your . . . you ours
7. their . . . them yours

63.4
2. them
3. him
4. our
5. yours
6. us
7. her
8. their
9. mine

UNIT 64

64.1
2. myself
3. herself
4. themselves
5. myself
6. himself
7. yourself
8. yourselves

64.2
2. was by himself.
3. go out by yourself.
4. went to the movies by myself.
5. lives by herself.
6. live by themselves.

64.3
2. see each other.
3. call each other a lot.
4. They don't know each other.
5. They're / They are sitting next
   to each other.
6. They gave each other presents /
   a present.

64.4
3. each other
4. yourselves
5. us
6. ourselves
7. each other
8. each other
9. them
10. themselves

UNIT 65

65.1
3. Pedro's
4. brother
5. Daniel's
6. Paul's
7. grandmother
8. sister
9. Julia's
10. father.
11. Alberto's

65.2
2. Andy's
3. Dave's
4. Jane's
5. Diane's
6. Alice's

65.3
3. OK
4. Simon's phone number
5. My brother's job
6. OK
7. OK
8. Paula's favorite color
9. your mother's birthday
10. My parents' house
11. OK
12. OK
13. Sylvia's party
14. OK

UNIT 66

66.1
2. a
3. a
4. an
5. a
6. an
7. a
8. an
9. an

66.2
2. a vegetable
3. a game
4. a tool
5. a mountain
6. a planet
7. a fruit
8. a river
9. a flower
10. a musical instrument

66.3
2. a sales clerk.
3. an architect.
4. He's a taxi driver.
5. He's an electrician.
6. She's a photographer.
7. She's a nurse.
8. a/an . . .

66.4
2.–8.
   Tom never wears a hat.
   I can't ride a bicycle.
   My brother is an artist.
   Rebecca works in an office.
   Jane wants to learn a
     foreign language.
   Mike lives in an old house.
   Tonight I'm going to a party.

UNIT 67

67.1
2. boats
3. women
4. cities

5. umbrellas
6. addresses
7. knives
8. sandwiches
9. families
10. feet
11. holidays
12. potatoes

67.2
2. teeth
3. people
4. children
5. fish
6. leaves

67.3
3. . . . with a lot of beautiful **trees**.
4. . . . with two **men**.
5. *OK*
6. . . . three **children**.
7. Most of my **friends** are **students**.
8. He put on his **pajamas** . . .
9. *OK*
10. Do you know many **people** . . .
11. I like your **pants**. Where did you get **them**?
12. . . . full of **tourists**.
13. *OK*
14. **These scissors aren't** . . .

67.4
2. are   7. Do
3. don't   8. are
4. watch   9. them
5. were   10. some
6. live

UNIT 68

68.1
3. a pitcher
4. water
5. toothpaste
6. a toothbrush
7. an egg
8. money
9. a wallet
10. sand
11. a bucket
12. an envelope

68.2
3. . . . **a** hat.
4. . . . **a** job?

5. *OK*
6. . . . **an** apple . . .
7. . . . **a** party . . .
8. . . . **a** wonderful thing.
9. . . . **an** island.
10. . . . **a** key.
11. *OK*
12. . . . **a** good idea.
13. . . . **a** car?
14. . . . **a** cup of coffee?
15. *OK*
16. . . . **a** coat.

68.3
2. a piece of wood
3. a glass of water
4. a bar of soap
5. a cup of tea
6. a piece of paper
7. a bowl of soup
8. a loaf of bread
9. a jar of honey

UNIT 69

69.1
2. a newspaper/paper, some flowers / a bunch of flowers, and a pen.
3. I bought some stamps, some postcards, and some bread / a loaf of bread.
4. I bought some toothpaste / a tube of toothpaste, some soap / a bar of soap, and a comb.

69.2
2. Would you like some coffee / a cup of coffee?
3. Would you like some cookies / a cookie?
4. Would you like some bread? (또는 . . . a piece of bread? / a slice of bread?)
5. Would you like a sandwich?
6. Would you like some cake / a piece / slice of cake

69.3
2. some . . . some
3. some
4. a . . . some
5. an . . . some
6. a . . . a . . . some
7. some
8. some
9. some . . . a

69.4
2. eyes
3. hair
4. information
5. chairs
6. furniture
7. job
8. wonderful weather

UNIT 70

70.1
3. a
4. the
5. an
6. the . . . the
7. a . . . a
8. a . . . a
9. . . . **a** student . . . **a** journalist . . . **an** apartment near **the** college . . . **The** apartment is . . .
10. . . . two children, **a** boy and **a** girl. **The** boy is seven years old, and **the** girl is three . . . in **a** factory . . . doesn't have **a** job . . .

70.2
2. **the** airport
3. **a** cup
4. **a** nice picture
5. **the** dictionary
6. **the** floor

70.3
2. . . . send me **a** postcard.
3. What is **the** name of . . .
4. . . . **a** very big country.
5. What is **the** largest . . .
6. . . . **the** color of **the** carpet.
7. . . . **a** headache.
8. . . . **an** old house near **the** station.
9. . . . **the** name of **the** director of **the** movie . . .

UNIT 71

71.1
3. . . . **the** second floor.
4. . . . **the** moon?
5. . . . **the** best hotel in this town?
6. *OK*
7. . . . **the** football stadium?
8. . . . **the** end of May.
9. *OK*
10. . . . **the** first time I met her.

11. *OK*

12. **The** Internet is a good place to get information.

13. *OK*

14. . . . on **the** top shelf on **the** right.

15. . . . in **the** country about 10 miles from **the** nearest town.

71.2

2. the same time
3. the same age
4. the same color
5. the same problem

71.3

2. **the** guitar
3. breakfast
4. television/TV
5. **the** ocean
6. **the** bottom

71.4

2. **the** name
3. **The** sky
4. television
5. **The** police
6. **the** capital
7. lunch
8. **the** middle

UNIT 72

72.1

2. **the** movies
3. **the** hospital
4. **the** airport
5. home
6. jail/prison

72.2

3. school
4. **the** station
5. home
6. bed
7. **the** post office

72.3

2. **the** movies
3. go to bed
4. go to jail/prison
5. go to **the** dentist
6. go to college
7. go to **the** hospital / are taken to **the** hospital

72.4

3. **the** doctor
4. *OK*
5. *OK*
6. *OK*
7. **the** bank
8. *OK*
9. *OK*
10. *OK*
11. **the** station
12. *OK*
13. **the** hospital
14. *OK*
15. **the** theater

UNIT 73

73.1

모범답안:

2. I don't like dogs.
3. I hate museums.
4. I love big cities.
5. Tennis is all right.
6. I love chocolate.
7. I don't like computer games.
8. I hate parties.

73.2

모범답안:

2. I'm not interested in politics.
3. I know a lot about sports.
4. I don't know much about art.
5. I don't know anything about astronomy.
6. I know a little about economics.

73.3

3. friends
4. parties
5. **The** stores
6. **the** milk
7. milk
8. basketball
9. computers
10. **The** water
11. cold water
12. **the** salt
13. **the** people
14. Vegetables
15. **The** houses
16. **the** words
17. pictures
18. **the** pictures
19. English . . . international business
20. Money . . . happiness

UNIT 74

74.1

3. Sweden
4. **The** Amazon
5. Asia
6. **The** Pacific
7. **The** Rhine
8. Kenya
9. **The** United States
10. **The** Andes
11. Bangkok
12. **The** Alps
13. **The** Red Sea
14. Jamaica
15. **The** Bahamas

74.2

3. *OK*
4. **the** Philippines
5. **the** south of France
6. **the** Washington Monument
7. *OK*
8. **the** Museum of Art
9. *OK*
10. Belgium is smaller than **the** Netherlands.
11. **the** Mississippi . . . **the** Nile
12. **the** National Gallery
13. **the** Park Hotel near Central Park
14. *OK*
15. **The** Rocky Mountains are in North America.
16. *OK*
17. **the** United Kingdom
18. **the** west of Ireland
19. **the** University of Michigan
20. **The** Panama Canal joins **the** Atlantic Ocean and **the** Pacific Ocean.

UNIT 75

75.1

2. that house
3. these postcards
4. those birds
5. this seat
6. These dishes

75.2

2. Is that your umbrella?
3. Is this your book?
4. Are those your books?
5. Is that your bicycle/bike?
6. Are these your keys?
7. Are those your keys?

8. Is this your watch?
9. Are those your glasses?
10. Are these your gloves?

75.3
2. that's
3. This is
4. That's
5. that
6. this is
7. That's
8. that's

UNIT 76

76.1
2. need one
3. I'm going to get one
4. I don't have one
5. I just had one
6. there's one on First Avenue

76.2
2. a new one
3. a better one
4. an old one
5. a big one
6. a different one

76.3
2. ones?
   green ones.
3. Which one?
   The one . . . a/the red door.
4. Which ones?
   The ones on the top shelf.
5. Which one?
   The black one.
6. Which one?
   The one on the wall.
7. Which one?
   The tall one with long hair.
8. Which ones?
   The yellow ones.
9. Which one?
   The one . . . a/the mustache
   and glasses.
10. Which ones?
    The ones I took at the party
    last week.

UNIT 77

77.1
2. some
3. any
4. any
5. any
6. some
7. any

8. some
9. some
10. any . . . any
11. some . . . any
12. some

77.2
2. some questions
3. any pictures
4. any . . . languages
5. some friends
6. some milk
7. any batteries
8. some . . . air
9. some fruit
10. any help

77.3
3. I have some
4. I don't have any
5. I didn't buy any
6. I bought some
7. I didn't make any

77.4
2. something
3. anything
4. anything
5. Somebody/Someone
6. anything
7. anybody/anyone
8. something
9. anything
10. anybody/anyone

UNIT 78

78.1
2. no stores near here.
3. Carla has no free time.
4. There is no light in this room.
6. There isn't any milk in the
   fridge.
7. There aren't any buses today.
8. Tom doesn't have any brothers
   or sisters.

78.2
2. any		8. no	
3. any		9. any	
4. no		10. no	
5. any		11. None	
6. no		12. any	
7. any			

78.3
2. no money
3. any questions
4. no friends

5. no difference
6. any furniture
7. no answer
8. any air conditioning
9. no line

78.4
모범답안:
2. Three.
3. Two cups.
4. None.
5. None.

UNIT 79

79.1
2. nobody in the office.
3. have nothing to do.
4. There's nothing on TV.
5. There was no one at home.
6. We found nothing.

79.2
2. anybody on the bus.
3. I don't have anything to read.
4. I don't have anyone to
   help me.
5. She didn't hear anything.
6. We don't have anything
   for dinner.

79.3
3a. Nothing.
4a. Nobody. / No one.
5a. Nobody. / No one.
6a. Nothing.
7a. Nothing.
8a. Nobody. / No one.
3b. want anything.
4b. didn't meet anybody/
    anyone. 또는 met nobody /
    no one.
5b. Nobody / No one knows
6b. I didn't buy anything.
    또는 I bought nothing.
7b. Nothing happened.
8b. Nobody / No one was late.

79.4
3. anything
4. Nobody / No one
5. Nothing
6. anything
7. anybody/anyone
8. nothing
9. anything
10. anything
11. nobody / no one

12. anything
13. Nothing
14. Nobody / No one . . .
    anybody/anyone

UNIT 80

80.1
2. something
3. somewhere
4. somebody/someone

80.2
2a. Nowhere.
3a. Nothing.
4a. Nobody. / No one.
2b. going anywhere.
3b. I don't want anything.
4b. I'm not looking for anybody/
    anyone.

80.3
3. anything
4. anything
5. somebody/someone
6. something
7. anybody/anyone . . . nobody /
   no one
8. anything
9. Nobody / No one
10. anybody/anyone
11. Nothing
12. anywhere
13. somewhere
14. anything
15. anybody/anyone

80.4
2. anything to eat
3. nothing to do
4. anywhere to sit
5. something to drink
6. nowhere to park
7. something to read
8. somewhere to stay

UNIT 81

81.1
2. Every day
3. every time
4. Every room
5. every word

81.2
2. every day
3. all day
4. every day

5. all day
6. all day
7. every day

81.3
2. every
3. all
4. all
5. Every
6. all
7. every
8. all
9. every

81.4
2. everything
3. Everybody/Everyone
4. everything
5. everywhere
6. Everybody/Everyone
7. everywhere
8. Everything

81.5
2. is
3. has
4. likes
5. has 또는 is
6. was
7. makes
8. Is . . . Does

UNIT 82

82.1
3. Some
4. Most of
5. most
6. any of
7. all 또는 all of
8. None of
9. any of
10. Most
11. most of
12. Some
13. All 또는 All of
14. some of
15. most of

82.2
2. All of them.
3. Some of them.
4. None of them.
5. Most of them.
6. None of it.

82.3
3. Some people . . .
4. Some of **the** questions . . .
   또는 Some questions . . .
5. *OK*
6. All insects . . .

7. *OK* (또는 . . . all **of** these
   books)
8. Most of **the** students . . . 또는
   Most students . . .
9. *OK*
10. . . . most of **the** night

UNIT 83

83.1
3. Both
4. Neither
5. Neither
6. both
7. Either
8. neither of
9. Neither
10. either of
11. Both
12. neither of
13. Both
14. either of

83.2
2. Both windows
3. Neither man is 또는 Neither
   of them is . . .
4. Both men have (got) 또는
   Both of them have . . .
5. Both buses / Both of the buses
   go 또는 . . . are going
6. Neither answer / Neither of the
   answers is

83.3
3. Both of them are
4. Neither of them has
5. Both of them live in Boston.
6. Both of them like to cook.
7. Neither of them can play
   the piano.
8. Both of them read the
   newspaper.
9. Neither of them is interested
   in sports.

UNIT 84

84.1
2. many
3. much
4. many
5. many
6. much
7. much
8. many
9. How many
10. How much
11. How much
12. How many

84.2
2. much time
3. many countries
4. many people
5. much luggage
6. many times

84.3

2. a lot of interesting things
3. a lot of accidents
4. a lot of fun
5. a lot of traffic

84.4

3. a lot of snow
4. *OK*
5. a lot of money
6. *OK*
7. *OK*
8. a lot

84.5

3. plays tennis a lot.
4. doesn't use his car much.
   (또는 . . . a lot.)
5. He doesn't go out much.
   (또는 . . . a lot.)
6. She travels a lot.

UNIT 85

85.1

2. a few
3. a little
4. a few
5. a little
6. a few

85.2

2. a little milk
3. A few days
4. a little Russian
5. a few friends
6. a few times
7. a few chairs
8. a little fresh air

85.3

2. very little coffee
3. very little rain
4. very few hotels
5. very little time
6. Very few people
7. very little work

85.4

2. A few   5. few
3. a little   6. a little
4. little   7. little

85.5

2. . . . **a** little luck
3. . . . **a** few things
4. *OK*
5. . . . **a** few questions
6. . . . **few** people
7. *OK*

UNIT 86

86.1

2. like that green jacket.
3. you like classical music?
4. I had a wonderful trip.
5. We went to a Japanese
   restaurant.

86.2

2. dark clouds
3. long vacation
4. hot water
5. fresh air
6. sharp knife
7. dangerous job

86.3

2. looks new.
3. feel sick.
4. look surprised.
5. smell nice.
6. tastes terrible.

86.4

2. look new.
3. don't sound American.
4. don't feel cold.
5. don't look heavy.
6. doesn't taste good.

UNIT 87

87.1

2. badly   5. fast
3. quietly   6. dangerously
4. angrily

87.2

2. work hard
3. sleep well
4. win easily
5. Think carefully
6. know her very well
7. explain things clearly/well
8. Come quickly

87.3

2. angry   8. quiet
3. slowly   9. badly
4. slow   10. nice (Unit
5. careful   86C 참고)
6. hard   11. quickly
7. suddenly

87.4

2. well   5. well
3. good   6. good . . . good
4. well

UNIT 88

88.1

2. bigger
3. slower
4. more expensive
5. higher
6. more dangerous

88.2

2. stronger
3. happier
4. more modern
5. more important
6. better
7. larger
8. more serious
9. prettier
10. more crowded

88.3

2. hotter/warmer
3. more expensive
4. worse
5. farther
6. more difficult 또는 harder

88.4

3. taller
4. harder
5. more comfortable
6. better
7. nicer
8. heavier
9. more interested
10. warmer
11. better
12. bigger
13. more beautiful
14. sharper
15. more polite
16. worse

UNIT 89

89.1

3. taller than Ben.
4. work earlier than
5. works harder than Liz.
6. more money than Liz.
7. better driver than Ben.
8. is more patient than Liz.
9. is a better dancer than Liz. /
   dances better than Liz.
10. is more intelligent than Ben.

11. speaks Spanish better than Ben. / speaks better Spanish than Ben. / 's Spanish is better than Ben's.
12. goes to the movies more than Liz. / more often than Liz.

89.2
2. older than her. / than she is.
3. harder than me. / than I do.
4. watch TV more than him. / than he does.
5. 're/are a better cook than me. / than I am. 또는 cook better than me. / than I do.
6. know more people than us. / than we do.
7. have more money than them. / than they do.
8. run faster than me. / than I can.
9. 've/have been here longer than her. / than she has.
10. got up earlier than them. / than they did.
11. were more surprised than him. / than he was.

89.3
2. is much younger than his father.
3. cost a little more than yours. / than your camera. 또는 was a little more expensive than . . .
4. much better today than yesterday. / than I did yesterday. / than I felt yesterday.
5. a little warmer today than yesterday. / than it was yesterday.
6. is a much better volleyball player than me. / than I am. 또는 is much better at volleyball than me. / than I am. 또는 plays volleyball much better than me. / than I do.

UNIT 90

90.1
2. longer than . . . as long as
3. heavier than . . . not as heavy as B.
4. older than C . . . not as old as B.

5. more money than C but not as much as A. 또는 . . . but less (money) than A.
6. harder than A but not as hard as B.

90.2
2. as big as mine. / as my room.
3. get up as early as you. / as you did.
4. didn't play as well as us. / as we did.
5. haven't been here as long as me. / as I have.
6. isn't as nervous as her. / as she is.

90.3
2. as   6. than
3. than   7. as
4. than   8. than
5. as

90.4
2. on the same street as Laura.
3. at the same time as Andy.
4. car is the same color as Laura's.

UNIT 91

91.1
2. longer than
   the longest.
   the shortest.
3. is younger than C.
   C is the oldest.
   B is the youngest.
4. D is more expensive than A.
   C is the most expensive.
   A is the cheapest.
5. A is better than C.
   A is the best.
   D is the worst.

91.2
2. the happiest day
3. the best movie
4. the most popular singer
5. the worst mistake
6. the prettiest city
7. the coldest day
8. the most boring person

91.3
2. is the highest mountain in the world.
3.–6.
   Brazil is the largest country in South America.

Alaska is the largest state in the United States.
The Nile is the longest river in Africa. / in the world.
Jupiter is the largest planet in the solar system.

UNIT 92

92.1
2. enough chairs
3. enough paint
4. enough wind

92.2
2. isn't big enough.
3. long enough.
4. isn't strong enough.

92.3
3. old enough
4. enough time
5. big enough
6. eat enough
7. enough space
8. tired enough
9. practice enough

92.4
2. sharp enough to cut
3. warm enough to go
4. enough bread to make
5. well enough to win
6. enough time to read

UNIT 93

93.1
2. too heavy
3. too low
4. too fast
5. too big
6. too crowded

93.2
3. enough
4. too many
5. too
6. enough
7. too much
8. enough
9. too
10. too many
11. too much

93.3
3. too far.
4. 's/is too expensive.
5. 's not / isn't big enough.
6. was too difficult.

7. 's not / isn't good enough.

8. 'm/am too busy.

9. was too long.

93.4

2. too early to go to bed.

3. too young to get married.

4. too dangerous to go out at night.

5. too late to call Sue (now).

6. too surprised to say anything.

UNIT 94

94.1

3. I like this picture very much.

4. Tom started his new job last week.

5. *OK*

6. Jane bought a present for her friend. 또는 Jane bought her friend a present.

7. I drink three cups of coffee every day.

8. *OK*

9. I borrowed 50 dollars from my brother.

94.2

2. bought a new computer last week.

3. Paul finished his work quickly.

4. Emily doesn't speak French very well.

5. I did a lot of shopping yesterday.

6. Do you know New York well?

7. We enjoyed the party very much.

8. I explained the problem carefully.

9. We met some friends at the airport.

10. Did you buy that jacket in Canada?

11. We do the same thing every day.

12. I don't like football very much.

94.3

2. arrived at the hotel early.

3. goes to Puerto Rico every year.

4. have lived here since 2002.

5. was born in Florida in 1984.

6. didn't go to work yesterday.

7. went to a wedding last weekend.

8. had my breakfast in bed this morning.

9. is going to college in September.

10. saw a beautiful bird in the garden this morning.

11. parents have been to Tokyo many times.

12. left my umbrella in the restaurant last night.

13. you going to the movies tomorrow night?

14. took the children to school this morning.

UNIT 95

95.1

2. always gets up early.

3. 's/is never late for work.

4. He sometimes gets angry.

5. He rarely goes swimming.

6. He's / He is usually at home in the evenings.

95.2

2. is always polite.

3. usually finish work at 5:00.

4. has just started a new job.

5. I rarely go to bed before midnight.

6. The bus isn't usually late.

7. I don't often eat fish.

8. I will never forget what you said.

9. Have you ever lost your passport?

10. Do you still work in the same place?

11. They always stay at the same hotel.

12. Jane doesn't usually work on Saturdays.

13. Is Tina already here?

14. What do you usually have for breakfast?

15. I can never remember his name.

95.3

2. also speak French.

3. I'm also hungry.

4. and I've also been to Guatemala.

5. Yes, and I also bought some books.

95.4

1. both play
They're / They are both
They've both got / They both have

2. 're/are all
were all born in
They all live in Miami.

UNIT 96

96.1

2. still have an old car?

3. you still a student?

4. Are you still studying Japanese?

5. Do you still go to the movies a lot?

6. Do you still want to be a teacher?

96.2

2. looking for a job.
's/is still looking
(for a job).
He hasn't found a job

3. was
She's / She is still asleep.
She hasn't woken up yet. /
She isn't awake yet. 또는
She hasn't gotten up yet. /
She isn't up yet.

4. were having dinner. / were eating (dinner).
They're / They are still having dinner. / . . . still eating (dinner).
They haven't finished (dinner) yet. / They haven't finished eating (dinner) yet.

96.3

2. Is . . . here yet? 또는 Has . . . arrived/come yet?

3. Have . . . gotten the results of your blood test yet? /
Have . . . received the . . . / Do . . . have the . . .

4. Have you decided where to go (for vacation) yet? / Do you know where you're going (for vacation) yet?

96.4

3. 's/has already gone/left.

4. already have one. 또는 've/have already got one.

5. 've/have already paid it. 또는 already paid it.

6. already knows.

UNIT 97

97.1

2. it to Gary.

3. gave them to Sarah.

4. He gave it to his sister.

5. He gave them to Robert.

6. He gave it to a neighbor.

97.2

2. Joanna a plant.

3. gave Richard a tie.

4. I gave Emma some chocolates / a box of chocolates.

5. I gave Rachel some flowers / a bouquet of flowers.

6. I gave Kevin a pen.

97.3

2. lend me an umbrella?

3. you give me . . . address?

4. Can you lend me 20 dollars?

5. Can you send me some information?

6. Can you show me the letter?

7. Can you get me some stamps?

97.4

2. lend you some money

3. send the letter to me

4. buy you a present

5. pass me the sugar

6. give it to her

7. showed the police officer my driver's license

UNIT 98

98.1

3.–7.
went to the window and (I) looked out.

I wanted to call you, but I didn't have your number.

I jumped into the river and (I) swam to the other side.

I usually drive to work, but I took the bus this morning.

Do you want me to come with you, or should I wait here?

98.2

모범답안:

2. because it was raining. / because the weather was bad.

3. but it was closed.

4. so he didn't eat anything. / so he didn't want anything to eat.

5. because there was a lot of traffic. / because the traffic was bad.

6. goodbye, got into her car, and drove off/away.

98.3

모범답안:

3. I went to the movies, but the movie wasn't very good.

4. I went to a coffee shop and met some friends of mine.

5. There was a movie on television, so I watched it.

6. I got up in the middle of the night because I couldn't sleep.

UNIT 99

99.1

2. When I'm tired, I like to watch TV.

3. When I called her, there was no answer.

4. When I go on vacation, I always go to the same place.

5. When the program ended, I turned off the TV.

6. When I got to the hotel, there were no rooms.

99.2

2. when they heard the news.

3. they went to live in France.

4. while they were away.

5. before they came here.

6. somebody broke into the house.

7. they didn't believe me.

99.3

2. I finish

3. it's

4. I'll be . . . she leaves

5. stops

6. We'll come . . . we're

7. I come . . . I'll bring

8. I'm

9. I'll give . . . I go

10. I'll tell . . . I'm

99.4

모범답안:

2. you finish your work

3. I'm going to buy a motorcycle

4. you get ready

5. I won't have much free time

6. I come back

UNIT 100

100.1

2. the driving test, you'll get your license.

3. you fail the driving test, you can take it again.

4. If you don't want this magazine, I'll throw it away.

5. If you want those pictures, you can have them.

6. If you're busy now, we can talk later.

7. If you're hungry, we can have lunch now.

8. If you need money, I can lend you some.

100.2

2. I give

3. is

4. I'll call

5. I'll be . . . get

6. Will you go . . . they invite

100.3

모범답안:

3. you're busy.

4. you'll feel better in the morning.

5. you're not watching it.

6. she doesn't practice.

7. I'll go and see Chris.

8. the weather is good.

9. it rains today.

100.4

2. When

3. If

4. If

5. if

6. When

7. if

8. when . . . if

UNIT 101

101.1

3. wanted

4. had

5. were/was

6. didn't enjoy

7. could

8. tried

9. didn't have

101.2

3. I'd go / I would go

4. she knew

5. we had

6. you won

7. I wouldn't / would not stay

8. we lived

9. It would be

10. the salary was/were

11. I wouldn't / would not know

12. would you change

101.3

2. I'd watch it / I would watch it

3. we had some pictures on the wall

4. the air would be cleaner

5. every day was/were the same

6. I'd be bored / I would be bored

7. we had a bigger house / we bought a bigger house

8. we would/could buy a bigger house

101.4

모범답안:

2. If I could go anywhere in the world, I'd go to Antarctica.

3. I wouldn't be very happy if I didn't have any friends.

4. I'd buy a house if I had enough money.

5. If I saw an accident in the street, I'd try and help.

6. The world would be a better place if there were no guns.

UNIT 102

102.1

2. who sells meat.

3. is a person who plays a musical instrument.

4. A patient is a person who is sick in the hospital.

5. A dentist is a person who takes care of your teeth.

6. A fool is a person who does stupid things.

7. A genius is a person who is very intelligent.

8. A liar is a person who doesn't tell the truth.

102.2

2. who opened the door was wearing

3. who took the test passed (it).

4. police officer who stopped our car wasn't very friendly.

102.3

2. who

3. which

4. which

5. who

6. which

7. who

8. who

9. which

모든 문장에 **that**도 가능.

102.4

3. . . . a machine that/which makes coffee.

4. OK (which도 맞음)

5. . . . people who/that never stop talking.

6. OK (who도 맞음)

7. OK (that도 맞음)

8. . . . the sentences that/which are wrong.

9. . . . a car that/which cost $60,000.

UNIT 103

103.1

2. pen you gave me.

3. jacket Sue is wearing.

4. flowers I gave you?

5. didn't believe the story he told us.

6. much were the oranges you bought?

103.2

2. meal you cooked was excellent.

3. I'm wearing aren't very comfortable.

4. people we invited to dinner didn't come.

103.3

2. you were talking to?

3. the keys you were looking for?

4. party you're going to?

5. the movie you were talking about?

6. music you're listening to?

7. the e-mail you were waiting for?

103.4

2. where you had dinner?

3. town where you live?

4. the factory where you work?

UNIT 104

104.1

2. at   7. at

3. in   8. in

4. at   9. at

5. in   10. in . . . at

6. in

104.2

3. at   11. at

4. on   12. in

5. in   13. on

6. in   14. on

7. on   15. at

8. on   16. at

9. at   17. on

10. on   18. in

104.3

3. B   8. B

4. A   9. both

5. both   10. both

6. A   11. B

7. B   12. both

104.4

2. call you in three

3. exam is in two weeks. / . . . in 14 days.

4. will be here in half an hour. / . . . in 30 minutes.

104.5

3. in

4. – (전치사 필요없음)

5. – (전치사 필요없음)

6. in

7. on

8. – (전치사 필요없음)

9. – (전치사 필요없음)

10. – (전치사 필요없음)

11. in

12. at

UNIT 105

105.1

2. until 2003.

3. since 2003.

4. South Korea until 2007.

5. Australia since 2007.

6. in a hotel from . . . to 2005.

7. in a restaurant since 2005.

8. from 1996 to 2002.

9. a journalist since 2002.

11. for ____ years.

12. lived in Australia for _____
    years.
13. in a hotel for three years.
14. has worked in a restaurant for
    _____ years.
15. was a teacher for six years.
16. has been a journalist for _____
    years.

105.2
2. until   9. since
3. for   10. until
4. since   11. for
5. Until   12. until
6. for   13. Since
7. for   14. for
8. until

UNIT 106

106.1
2. after lunch
3. before the end
4. during the course
5. before they went to Mexico
6. during the night
7. while you're waiting
8. after the concert

106.2
3. while
4. for
5. while
6. during
7. while
8. for
9. during
10. while

106.3
2. eating
3. answering
4. taking
5. finishing/doing
6. going/traveling

106.4
2. in a bookstore for two years
   after finishing high school.
3. going to sleep, I read for a few
   minutes.
4. walking for three hours, we
   were very tired.
5. have a cup of coffee before
   going out.

UNIT 107

107.1
2. In the box.
3. On the box.
4. On the wall.
5. At the bus stop.
6. In the field.
7. On the balcony.
8. In the pool.
9. At the window.
10. On the ceiling.
11. On the table.
12. At the table.

107.2
2. in
3. on
4. in
5. on
6. at
7. in
8. in
9. at
10. at
11. in
12. at
13. on
14. at
15. on the wall in the living room

UNIT 108

108.1
2. At the airport.
3. In bed.
4. On a ship.
5. In the sky.
6. At a party.
7. At the doctor's.
8. On the second floor.
9. At work.
10. On a plane.
11. In a taxi.
12. At a wedding.

108.2
2. in   10. in
3. in   11. on
4. at   12. on
5. at   13. at
6. in   14. in
7. in   15. on
8. at   16. at
9. in

UNIT 109

109.1
2. to   6. to
3. in   7. to
4. to   8. in
5. in

109.2
3. to
4. to
5. (at) home . . . to work
6. at
7. – (전치사 필요없음)
8. to
9. at
10. at a restaurant . . . to the hotel

109.3
2. to
3. to
4. in
5. to
6. to
7. at
8. to
9. to
10. at
11. at
12. to Maria's house . . . (at) home
13. – (전치사 필요없음)
14. meet at the party . . . go to the
    party

109.4
1. to
2. – (전치사 필요없음)
3. at
4. in
5. to
6. – (전치사 필요없음)

109.5
모범답안:
2. Yesterday I went to work.
3. At 11:00 yesterday morning I
   was at work.
4. One day I'd like to go to
   Alaska.
5. I don't like going to parties.
6. At 9:00 last night I was at a
   friend's house.

UNIT 110

110.1
2. next to / by
3. in front of
4. between

5. next to / by
6. in front of
7. behind
8. on the
9. in the

110.2
2. behind
3. above
4. in front of
5. on
6. by / next to
7. below/under
8. above
9. under
10. by / next to
11. across from
12. on

110.3
2. fountain is . . . the theater.
3. The bank/bookstore is across from the theater. 또는 Paul's office is across from the theater. 또는 The theater is across from . . .
4. The bank/supermarket is next to the bookstore. 또는 The bookstore is next to the . . .
5. Paul's office is above the bookstore.
6. The bookstore is between the bank and the supermarket.

UNIT 111

111.1
2. under
3. Go up
4. Go down
5. Go along
6. Go into the hotel.
7. Go past the hotel.
8. Go out of the hotel.
9. Go over the bridge.
10. Go through the park.

111.2
2. off
3. over
4. out of
5. across
6. around
7. through
8. on
9. around
10. into . . . through

111.3
1. out of
2. around
3. in
4. from . . . to
5. around
6. on/over
7. over
8. out of

UNIT 112

112.1
2. on time
3. on vacation
4. on the phone
5. on television

112.2
2. by
3. with
4. about
5. on
6. by
7. at
8. on
9. with
10. about . . . by

112.3
1. with
2. without
3. by
4. about
5. at
6. by
7. on
8. with
9. at
10. by
11. about
12. by
13. on
14. with
15. by
16. by

UNIT 113

113.1
2. in
3. to
4. at
5. with
6. of

113.2
2. at
3. to
4. about
5. of
6. of
7. from
8. in
9. for
10. about
11. of
12. at

113.3
2. interested in going
3. good at getting
4. fed up with waiting
5. sorry for/about waking
6. Thank you for waiting.

113.4
2. past me without speaking.
3. do anything without asking me first.
4. went out without locking the door.

113.5
모범답안:
2. afraid of the dark.
3. very good at drawing.
4. I'm not interested in cars.
5. I'm fed up with living here.

UNIT 114

114.1
2. to
3. for
4. to
5. at
6. for

114.2
2. to
3. of
4. to
5. for
6. for
7. of/about
8. for
9. on
10. to
11. at
12. for

13. to
14. – (전치사 필요없음)
15. to
16. on
17. – (전치사 필요없음) . . . (to)
18. of/about
19. at
20. of
21. for
22. – (전치사 필요없음)

114.3
모범답안:
3. on the program.
4. depends (on) what it is.
5. It depends on the weather.
6. It depends (on) how much you want.

UNIT 115

115.1
2. went in
3. looked up
4. rode off/away
5. turned around
6. got off
7. sat down
8. got out

115.2
2. away
3. around

4. out . . . back
5. down
6. over
7. back
8. in
9. up
10. away . . . back

115.3
2. Hold on
3. slowed down
4. takes off
5. get along
6. speak up
7. broken down
8. fall over / fall down
9. work out
10. gave up
11. went off

UNIT 116

116.1
2. took off her hat. 또는 took her hat off.
3. put down his bag. 또는 put his bag down.
4. picked up the magazine. 또는 picked the magazine up.
5. put on his sunglasses. 또는 put his sunglasses on.
6. turned off the faucet. 또는 turned the faucet off.

116.2
2. put his jacket on.
   put it on.
3. took off her glasses.
   She took them off.
4. I picked the phone up.
   I picked it up.
5. They gave the key back.
   They gave it back.
6. We turned off the lights.
   We turned them off.

116.3
2. take it back
3. picked them up
4. turned it off
5. bring them back

116.4
3. knocked over
4. look it up
5. throw them away
6. tried on
7. showed me around
8. gave it up 또는 gave up
9. fill it out
10. put your cigarette out

해답 (추가연습문제)
(244쪽을 참고)

1
3. is a doctor.
4. The children are asleep.
5. Gary isn't hungry.
6. The books aren't on the table.
7. The hotel is near the station.
8. The bus isn't full.

2
3. she's / she is
4. Where are
5. Is he
6. It's / It is
7. I'm / I am   또는   No, I'm not. I'm
8. What color is
9. Is it
10. Are you
11. How much are they?

3
3. He's / He is taking a shower.
4. Are the children playing?
5. Is it raining?
6. They're / They are coming now.
7. Why are you standing here? I'm / I am waiting for somebody.

4
4. Sam doesn't want
5. Do you want
6. Does Helen live
7. Sarah knows
8. I don't travel
9. do you usually get up
10. They don't go out
11. Tom always leaves
12. does Julia do . . . She works

5
3. She's / She is a student.
4. She doesn't have a car.
5. She goes out a lot.
6. She has / She's got a lot of friends.
7. She doesn't like Houston.
8. She likes to dance.
9. She isn't / She's not interested in sports.

6
1. Are you
   do you live
   Do you have
   old is she
2. How old are you
   What do you do / Where do you work / What's your job
   Do you like/enjoy
   Do you have
   Do you (usually) go
3. What's his name
   What does he do / What's his job
   Does he live/work in

7
4. is 32 years old.
5. I have / I've got two sisters.
6. We often watch TV at night.
7. Jane never wears a hat.
8. My car has a flat tire.   또는
   My car's got / has got a flat tire.
9. These flowers are beautiful.
10. Mary speaks German very well.

8
3. are you cooking
4. plays
5. I'm leaving
6. It's raining
7. I don't watch
8. we're looking
9. do you pronounce

9
2. we go
3. shining
4. are you going
5. do you take
6. She writes
7. I never read
8. They're watching
9. She's talking
10. do you usually have
11. He's visiting
12. I don't drink

10
2. went
3. found
4. was
5. had/took
6. told
7. gave
8. were
9. thought
10. invited/asked

11
3. was good at sports.
4. He played soccer.
5. He didn't work hard at school.
6. He had a lot of friends.
7. He didn't have a bicycle.
8. He wasn't a quiet child.

12
3. How long were you / How long did you stay
4. Did you like/enjoy
5. Where did you stay?
6. Was the weather
7. When did you get/come

13
3. I forgot
4. did you get
5. I didn't speak
6. Did you have
7. he didn't go
8. she arrived
9. did Robert live
10. The meal didn't cost

14
2. were working
3. opened
4. rang . . . was cooking
5. heard . . . looked
6. was looking . . . happened
7. wasn't reading . . . was watching
8. didn't read
9. finished . . . paid . . . left
10. saw . . . was walking . . . was waiting

15

3. is playing
4. gave
5. doesn't like
6. did your parents go
7. saw . . . was driving
8. Do you watch
9. were you doing
10. goes
11. 'm/am trying
12. didn't sleep

16

2. haven't read / 've never read
3. Have you seen
4. 've/have had
5. Have you (ever) been
6. have you lived / have you been living / have you been
7. 've/have known
8. 's/has been raining   또는 has rained   또는   has been horrible/bad

17

3. 's/has been
4. for
5. since
6. has he lived / has he been
7. for
8. 've/have been

18

모범답안:
3. I've just started this exercise.
4. I've met Julia a few times.
5. I haven't had dinner yet.
6. I've never been to Australia.
7. I've lived here since I was born.
8. I've lived here for three years.

19

3. bought/got
4. went
5. 've/have seen   또는   saw
6. haven't started (it) (yet)
7. was
8. didn't see
9. finished   또는   graduated from
10. 's/has been
11. was
12. 've/have never made

20

3. 's/has lived there since last May.   또는   's been living . . .
4. she left at 4:00.
5. How many times have you been there?
6. I've / I have been tired all day.
7. It was on the table last night.
8. I've eaten there a few times.
9. What time did they get here?

21

1. was / did you go (there) / were you there
2. have you had bought/got
3. have you lived / have you been living / have you been we lived / we were did you live / were you
4. have you worked / have you been working did you do was / worked as

22

모범답안:
2. I didn't go out last night.
3. I was at work yesterday afternoon.
4. I went to a party a few days ago.
5. It was my birthday last week.
6. I went to South America last year.

23

2. B   9. C
3. D   10. D
4. A   11. A
5. A   12. C
6. D   13. B
7. C   14. C
8. B   15. A

24

1. was damaged . . . be torn down
2. was built . . . is used . . . is being painted
3. is called . . . be called . . . was changed
4. have been made . . . are produced

25

2. is visited
3. were damaged
4. be built
5. is being cleaned
6. be forgotten
7. has been repaired
8. be kept
9. Have you ever been bitten
10. was stolen

26

2. was stolen last week.
3. 're/are wanted on the phone.
4. bananas have been eaten.
5. machine will be repaired.
6. 're/are being watched.
7. housework has to be done.

27

3. pushed
4. was pushed
5. has taken   또는   took
6. is being repaired
7. invented
8. was the camera invented
9. 've/have been washed   또는   were washed
10. 've/have washed them.   또는   washed them.
11. did they send
12. be sent

28

2. B   8. B
3. A   9. B
4. C   10. A
5. B   11. B
6. C   12. C
7. C

29

1. B: I stayed
   A: did you do
   B: I watched
   A: Are you going
   B: I'm going
   A: are you going to see
   B: I don't know. I haven't decided

2. *A:* have you been
   B: We arrived
   A: are you staying / are you going to stay
   A: do you like
   B: we're having
3. *A:* I've just remembered / I just remembered – Karen called
   B: She always calls 또는 She's always calling . . . Did she leave
   A: she wants
   B: I'll call . . . Do you know
   A: I'll get
4. *A:* I'm going . . . Do you want
   B: are you going
   A: Have you ever eaten
   B: I've been . . . I went
5. *A:* I've lost / I lost . . . Have you seen
   B: You were wearing . . . I came
   A: I'm not wearing
   B: Have you looked / Did you look
   A: I'll go

30

1. we met
2. we sat / we were sitting
3. We didn't know
4. we became
5. we liked
6. we spent
7. We finished
8. we meet
9. has been
10. she's working
11. She's coming
12. she comes
13. we'll have / we're going to have
14. It will be

31

2. we're staying
3. we enjoyed
4. We watched
5. slept
6. I don't sleep
7. we're not doing / we're not going to do
8. we're going
9. to see

10. We haven't decided
11. wants
12. to go
13. I'll send
14. you're having
15. are studying / have been studying
16. he had
17. he needs
18. We've been
19. We got
20. seeing
21. I liked
22. we went
23. we left
24. had
25. he wasn't injured
26. was damaged
27. We've changed / We changed
28. we're leaving
29. We're staying / We're going to stay / We'll stay
30. flying
31. That will be / That's going to be
32. finished
33. I'll let
34. we get
35. are looking
36. We're going
37. we'll send

32

2.	A	11.	B
3.	B	12.	A
4.	C	13.	C
5.	B	14.	B
6.	C	15.	C
7.	B	16.	A
8.	A	17.	C
9.	C	18.	B
10	A		

33

2. a car
3. the fridge / the refrigerator
4. a teacher
5. school
6. the movies
7. a taxi
8. the piano
9. computers
10. the same

34

4. a horse
5. The sky
6. a tourist
7. for lunch (–)
8. the . . . the
9. a watch
10. remember names (–)
11. the next train
12. sends e-mails (–)
13. the backyard
14. the Majestic Hotel
15. sick last week (–) . . . to work (–)
16. the . . . the
17. to the radio . . . having breakfast (–)
18. like sports (–) . . . is basketball (–)
19. a . . . an
20. the . . . the . . . the . . . the
21. After dinner (–) . . . watched TV (–)
22. northern Mexico (–) . . . the south

35

2.	in	11.	for
3.	on	12.	at
4.	at	13.	in
5.	on	14.	at
6.	in	15.	on
7.	since	16.	by
8.	on	17.	for . . . on
9.	by	18.	to . . . in
10.	in	19.	at . . . in

해답 (학습가이드)

(263쪽 참조)

현재

1.1	B
1.2	A
1.3	C
1.4	A
1.5	C, D
1.6	B
1.7	D
1.8	C
1.9	C
1.10	A
1.11	C
1.12	A
1.13	D
1.14	C
1.15	A
1.16	D
1.17	C, D
1.18	A, D

과거

2.1	B
2.2	E
2.3	D
2.4	B
2.5	A
2.6	D
2.7	A
2.8	C
2.9	C
2.10	E

현재완료

3.1	B, E
3.2	D
3.3	B
3.4	D
3.5	E
3.6	B
3.7	A
3.8	C
3.9	D
3.10	E

수동태

4.1	D
4.2	C
4.3	E
4.4	A
4.5	A

동사 형태

5.1	D
5.2	B

미래

6.1	A
6.2	A
6.3	C
6.4	A, B
6.5	B
6.6	C
6.7	D
6.8	C
6.9	B, C

조동사, 명령문 등

7.1	C, D
7.2	A, C
7.3	A
7.4	D
7.5	B
7.6	C
7.7	B, D
7.8	C
7.9	C
7.10	C
7.11	B, D
7.12	A
7.13	B

there와 it

8.1	B
8.2	E
8.3	A
8.4	A
8.5	B

조동사

9.1	D
9.2	A
9.3	C
9.4	B
9.5	B
9.6	C
9.7	D

의문문

10.1	D
10.2	D
10.3	A
10.4	A
10.5	B
10.6	D
10.7	B
10.8	A
10.9	C, E
10.10	C
10.11	A
10.12	A, C

간접화법

11.1	E
11.2	A, B, D

-ing와 to …

12.1	B
12.2	D
12.3	B
12.4	C
12.5	B, C
12.6	C
12.7	A
12.8	D

go, get, do, make, have

13.1	A, D
13.2	C
13.3	C, D
13.4	A, D
13.5	B
13.6	D

대명사와 소유격

14.1	A
14.2	C
14.3	D
14.4	B
14.5	B, C
14.6	A
14.7	E
14.8	A
14.9	D
14.10	C

a와 the

15.1	C
15.2	B
15.3	A, C
15.4	B
15.5	B
15.6	A
15.7	D
15.8	C

15.9 B
15.10 B
15.11 E
15.12 D
15.13 B
15.14 A

한정사와 대명사

16.1 C
16.2 C
16.3 B
16.4 B
16.5 C
16.6 A, C
16.7 D
16.8 B, D
16.9 A
16.10 B
16.11 D
16.12 B, D
16.13 A
16.14 A, B
16.15 D
16.16 A, C
16.17 D
16.18 B
16.19 A

형용사와 부사

17.1 A
17.2 C
17.3 C
17.4 D
17.5 B
17.6 B
17.7 A, C
17.8 E
17.9 A
17.10 B
17.11 D
17.12 A
17.13 D
17.14 C

어순

18.1 B
18.2 C
18.3 B
18.4 A
18.5 A, D

접속사와 관계대명사

19.1 C
19.2 A
19.3 D
19.4 E
19.5 B, C
19.6 A, B
19.7 B, D
19.8 A

전치사

20.1 A, D
20.2 E
20.3 C, D
20.4 B
20.5 A, D
20.6 A
20.7 B
20.8 C
20.9 B
20.10 D
20.11 D
20.12 A
20.13 C
20.14 D
20.15 A
20.16 E
20.17 C
20.18 B
20.19 D
20.20 D

동사구

21.1 C
21.2 A, B
21.3 B

영문 색인

단어 옆의 숫자는 쪽수가 아니라 해당 단원 번호임.